DEMOCRACY FROM SCRATCH

DEMOCRACY
FROM SCRATCH

OPPOSITION AND REGIME IN THE
NEW RUSSIAN REVOLUTION

M. Steven Fish

PRINCETON UNIVERSITY PRESS   PRINCETON, NEW JERSEY

Copyright © 1995 by Princeton University Press
Published by Princeton University Press, 41 William Street,
Princeton, New Jersey 08540
In the United Kingdom: Princeton University Press,
Chichester, West Sussex
All Rights Reserved

Library of Congress Cataloging-in-Publication Data

Fish, M. Steven, 1962–
Democracy from scratch : opposition and regime in
the new Russian revolution / M. Steven Fish.
p.   cm.
Includes bibliographical references and index.
ISBN 0-691-03703-5 (cl. : acid-free paper)
1. Political parties—Soviet Union.   2. Soviet Union—
Politics and government—1985–1991.   3. Democracy—
Russia (Federation)   4. Political parties—Russia (Federation)
5. Russia (Federation)—Politics and government—1991–
I. Title.
JN6598.A1F57   1994
320.947′09′049—dc20   94-21026   CIP

This book has been composed in Palatino

Princeton University Press books are printed
on acid-free paper and meet the guidelines
for permanence and durability of the Committee
on Production Guidelines for Book Longevity
of the Council on Library Resources

Printed in the United States of America

10 9 8 7 6 5 4 3 2

For Alyona ————————————————————————————————

AND MANY OTHER RUSSIAN DEMOCRATS

Contents

Acknowledgments _____

I HAVE incurred more debts in the course of writing this book than I can possibly acknowledge here. Alexander Dallin provided sage guidance throughout the entirety of the project. Philippe Schmitter furnished an invaluable comparative perspective and a great deal of intellectual inspiration. George Breslauer offered much incisive advice and criticism. Valerie Bunce, David Holloway, Gail Lapidus, Rose McDermott, Kelly Smith, and Michael Urban provided invaluable comments on all or parts of the manuscript. Gabriella Montinola furnished a critical eye, all manner of support, and much inspiration. I have also benefited greatly from contacts with many other friends, colleagues, and mentors, among them Daniel Abbasi, Larry Diamond, Alexander George, Mikhail Kamalov, Boris Kapustin, Terry Karl, Ol'ga Makarova, Elena Mal'teva, Sergei Markov, Michael McFaul, Kenneth Roberts, Evgenii Romanovskii, Sergei Vvedinskii, and Nikolai Zlobin.

I owe an enormous debt of gratitude to my parents, Michael Fish and Cherrie Robinson. It is due to their support and sacrifice over the course of a lifetime that our family, for better or worse, includes a professional scholar.

The field research on which this book is based was made possible by the generosity, hospitality, and companionship of countless friends and associates in Russia, many of whom come from the ranks of the courageous and energetic men and women who have made—and continue to make—Russia's democratic revolution. I would like to offer special thanks to Natalia Bondareva, Valentin and Liudmila Gubarev, Andrei Indrikov, Igor' Lukashev, Viktor and Svetlana Pestov, Aleksandr and Galina Romash, Vitalii Sekrieru, Sergei Shvets, and Evgenii Sukhovskii. These people took me into their homes during my travels. They plied me with tea, vodka, *pirozhki*, and above all delicious and interminable—that is to say, typically Russian—conversation. They gave generously of their time and wonderful humanity for no good reason at all, and for this I am deeply grateful.

I would also like to thank the Berkeley-Stanford Program in Soviet and Post-Soviet Studies, the Institute of International Education Edgar Bronfman Program, and the International Research and Exchanges Board for financial support for my field research.

A part of chapter 3 was reprinted by permission of the *Journal of Communist Studies* 7, 3 (September 1991), published by Frank Cass & Co., London.

I owe my most profound debt to Alyona Gaberland. Alyona is an artist, not a social scientist. But she taught me nearly all of what little I know about Russia. It is to her, with deepest gratitude, that I dedicate this work.

Abbreviations

CPSU	Communist Party of the Soviet Union
DDV	Movement for Democratic Choice
DPR	Democratic Party of Russia
DU	Democratic Union
KD/PNS	Constitutional Democrats/Party of Popular Freedom
KhDS	Christian Democratic Union
LDP	Liberal Democratic Party
MDG	Interregional Deputies Group
MOI	Moscow Union of Voters
OFT	United Workers' Front
ONF	Orel Popular Front
PKD	Party of Constitutional Democrats
RKhDD	Russian Christian Democratic Movement
RKhDP	Russian Christian Democratic Party
RPR	Republican Party of Russia
RSFSR	Russian Soviet Federated Socialist Republic
SDA	Social Democratic Association
SDPR	Social Democratic Party of Russia

DEMOCRACY FROM SCRATCH

I

Western Scholarship and the New Russian Revolution

FROM 1985 to 1991, one of the great political dramas of the twentieth century unfolded in Russia. Although it began as an effort at reform from above, the process of transformation was snatched from its initiators and became a revolution. Unlike the revolution of three-quarters of a century past, the new Russian revolution featured no vanguard party and no armed insurgency, and was not made in the name of a class or a single identifiable program or principle. Unlike many other revolutions, it was not fought to craft nationhood or to recapture lost national sovereignty. It was a popular, democratic revolution, but it differed from cases of "redemocratization" experienced in many other countries in recent decades. It was a revolution of a different type, waged by unlikely revolutionaries. The rebellion of most of its heroes did not predate the onset of the revolution itself.

This book is not about *"perestroika," "glasnost',"* or "reform," though these phenomena did provide crucial openings for the emergence of the organizations and movements that will be the subjects of examination. Nor is it about Mikhail Gorbachev, though it does focus mainly on the period of his rule. Rather, it investigates the organized, independent revolutionary opposition in Russia. It will be demonstrated that the old regime, though decaying, is not, or at least until the abortive coup attempt of August 1991 was not, in ruins; that the independent revolutionary forces of a new order, though not mature and firmly established, had by August 1991 already transformed Russian political society; and that the main dynamic in Russian politics during the Gorbachev period was not to be found in a division between "reformers" and "conservatives" within the official political leadership nor in a "search for a new order" under general conditions of powerlessness and disintegration. It was to be found, instead, in a tumultuous, chaotic, and sometimes violent struggle between a pact of domination that proved to be fundamentally, structurally unreformable and an energetic, dynamic, yet disorganized and poorly integrated insurgent political society whose form, character, and development were determined above all by its struggle with state institutions. It will be demonstrated that the new independent forces created a political society of a different type, one that resembles neither the subjugated, "totalized" society of the pre-1985 period nor the "civil" societies evident in the industrialized West and in many developing countries. Although the new political society was born and continues to develop under conditions of deep and rapid change, many of its institutional forms were already established by the time of the August 1991 putsch. The patterns of independent institutional organization and development established during 1985–91 have already begun, and will continue, to exert a powerful influence over the course of regime change in post-Soviet Russia.

Review and Critique of the Sovietological Literature

This chapter investigates how issues of state and society have been treated in writings on Russia and Soviet-type systems. It organizes and examines the major currents in scholarly thinking and provides a basis for comparison between them. It makes explicit some of the often unspoken theoretical assumptions and conceptual distinctions that have informed the evolution of thinking on politics in Russia. Finally, the review positions the approach taken in this book within a particular school of thought.

The literature is divided into four categories in a 2×2 matrix, illustrated in table 1. In some cases, several "schools of thought" are lumped together in a single category, and several scholars appear in more than one category. The categories are not entirely mutually exclusive; some works do not fit neatly into a single box. Many important ideas and their authors are not included in the scheme. The review is illustrative rather than exhaustive. It focuses on general patterns of reasoning and analytical approaches rather than on particular authors and their contributions.

The horizontal axis of the diagram divides the literature into two areas of focus: elite politics and state-society relations. Few important works focus *exclusively* on one area or the other. Yet most works concentrate mainly on one area, and distinct patterns of analysis have evolved within each of the two major approaches. The vertical axis distinguishes between traditional and revisionist thinking within the "sovietological tradition," including not only analyses of the Soviet Union, but also some works on Soviet-style socialism and Leninism in general. The terms "traditional" and "revisionist" are unpopular in sovietology. Yet, as in many other fields, they do capture a salient cleavage in world views and analytical approaches that developed at a time of intellectual ferment and endured as the field matured. In the case of

TABLE 1
Western Scholarship on Russia

		Area of Focus	
		Elite Politics	*State-Society Relations*
Sovietological Tradition	*Traditional*	*pre-1985* classical totalitarianism; "patterns of autocracy" (Friedrich and Brzezinski; Arendt) Neo-Weberian analyses, "neotraditionalism" (Moore, Jowitt) *post-1985* neototalitarian and continuity theses; ideology and political culture (Scanlan; Migranian; Vajda; Malia) **I**	*pre-1985* "dictatorship over needs"; predatory state; "system of domination" (Fehér, Heller, and Markus; Konrad and Szelenyi; Kolakowski) *post-1985* "movement society"; state-society conflict; structural-institutional approach (Fish) **IV**
	Revisionist	**II** *pre-1985* "interest groups" in the state; "bureaucratic pluralism"; "institutional pluralism" (Skilling and Griffiths; Hough; Solomon; Hill); dichotomous tradition of Leninism; "friends and foes of reform" (Cohen) *post-1985* Gorbachev/leadership-led democratization; Gorbachev as modernizer; "revolution from above" (Breslauer; White; Bialer)	**III** *pre-1985* contract theories; "welfare state authoritarianism"; "organized consensus" (Breslauer; Zaslavsky); macrosociological studies of social groups (Inkeles; Lapidus; Lane and O'Dell) *post-1985* new contract approach (Hauslohner); modernization approaches; "new middle class"; "civil society" (Starr; Lewin; Lapidus; Ruble)

scholarship on the Soviet Union and Soviet-style socialism, the cleavage developed in the mid-1960s, as many scholars sought explanations for change in the post-Stalin era. Each of the four boxes is subdivided into categories of pre-1985 and post-1985 writings. Examination of literature from the pre-1985 period illuminates how older assumptions and habits of analysis have influenced scholars' approaches to recent transformations.

Category I: Traditional State-Centric Approaches

The earlier literature in this category includes well-known classical writings on totalitarianism. This work was widely criticized for ignoring questions of change in Communist systems. Yet analysts such as Carl Friedrich and Zbigniew Brzezinski, who were pioneers in this area, did not presume to explain the origins of totalitarianism or to locate sources of change within such regimes; rather, they focused primarily on defining and classifying what they regarded as a regime of a new type. To the extent that they did discuss the origins of totalitarian dictatorship in the Soviet Union, they concentrated on the influence of the legacy of prerevolutionary autocracy on Russian political culture.[1] Other scholars did develop theoretical explanations for the origins of, and change within, totalitarian systems. Hannah Arendt explained the origins of both nazism and communism in terms of Durkheimian categories of anomie and societal breakdown.[2] Barrington Moore, applying a Weberian set of categories and assumptions, located an inherent tension, and consequent instability, in the Soviet regime deriving from the conflict between traditional and rational-technical imperatives.[3] Similarly working within a Weberian framework, and focusing explicitly on political modernization, Kenneth Jowitt identified what he regarded as a uniquely Leninist path of political development. At later stages, this path involved the inclusion of some societal groups in the larger political community, if not in the formal structure of power. In later works, Jowitt grappled with how decadent Leninist regimes struggle to identify "social combat tasks" to maintain the integrity of the party and justify its monopoly on power and authority. He argued that the rational and technical orientations associated with "modernity" cannot be fully realized by a party that holds a heroic and charismatic conception of itself as the exclusive repository of historical understanding. In an advanced stage of corruption, the regime assumes a "neotraditional" character in which the requirements of modernity are subordinated to the elite's desire for privilege and status.[4]

Despite their differences, these works are bound together by certain common orientations and habits of analysis. First, they focus on state institutions and primarily on the Leninist party, which is analyzed in terms of its own internal institutional features, particularly its ideology and organization. Its goals—nation building, rapid industrialization, realization of utopia, and external expansion—are regarded as internally generated and determinative of state behavior. Conflict and cleavage are conceptualized less as struggle among various state actors than as conflicting imperatives, generated within and experienced by the party-state as a whole. Indeed, the central cleavage identified by this literature lies not within the state or between state and society, but between the Leninist regime and regimes of other types.

If the analytic orientation found in this literature cannot be labeled anti-Marxist, it certainly may be regarded as "un-Marxist." In contrast with traditional Marxist thinking, ideology and beliefs are not regarded as justificationist and superstructural, but rather as deeply rooted institutions that preserve the state's organizational integrity and shape its policy. The state is not conceptualized in terms of class nor regarded as representative of the interests of a particular group in broader society. "Society" is not entirely excluded from these analyses, and an obvious cleavage between state and society is assumed, particularly during phases of open repression. Yet society is regarded more as an *object*—of coercion, atomization, indoctrination, mobilization, or "inclusion"—than as a prime mover. Finally, political culture, though conceptualized in various ways, figures prominently in these works. Brzezinski emphasizes the autocratic, authoritarian history of imperial Russia, while Moore and Jowitt focus on the significance of more immediate, particularly Leninist political culture and traditions.

Some of these assumptions found continued expression in a small but significant body of work on post-1985 Russia. The clearest example of what may be regarded as a "neototalitarian" or "continuity" thesis was outlined by James Scanlan. He too emphasized the dominance of a strong state and the weakness of society in Russia. First, he noted the underdevelopment of autonomous groups and networks among groups in prerevolutionary Russia and their subsequent extermination under bolshevism. He then asserted that given the underdevelopment and atomization of society, the state itself must create civil society by drastically reducing its control and by permitting free association. Having placed the burden of action on the state, Scanlan was skeptical that perestroika could create and guarantee the conditions necessary for the development of civil society. Pointing to the instrumentality of Marxist-Leninist views of the nature of rights, he asked: "How far can one realistically expect *perestroika* to go toward creating a society in which individual rights and social organizations restrain the actions of government?" Structural impediments imposed by the single-party-dominant system of rule also created difficulties. If individuals and groups lack genuine alternative political representation of their interests, "it is uncertain how 'institutionalized' their power will be, or remain if established. It is not clear that civil society can operate effectively on the organs of the state if it cannot threaten to withdraw its political support from the group administering those organs."[5]

Like Scanlan, other analysts have emphasized the weakness of society, the persistence of Marxist-Leninist beliefs, and the structural limitations imposed by the dominance of a single party. For instance, Andranik Migranian has argued that Russian society was so weak that the burden of "society-building" must fall on the state. To the extent that society was capable of self-organization, moreover, its potential was more destructive than creative. The specter of mass participation in the absence of well-established institutions to regulate political competition led Migranian to advocate a transitional "collective dictatorship," with the Communist Party serving as the only institution capable of preventing chaos and dangerous erosion of central authority. Migranian regarded the party as capable of carrying through *some type* of transition and devolution of power, though initially the process was likely to necessitate dictatorial methods.[6] In an even more pessimistic view of Russian society, Mihaly Vajda asserted that seven decades of Communist power had destroyed even the *potential* for independent organized action. As late as 1988, he argued that Russia possessed "no disposition for the self-regulation of society."[7] Martin Malia, in his celebrated "Z" article of 1990, emphasized the significance of both Russian and Soviet political culture and adduced what he regarded as illuminating examples of how official indoctrination had penetrated and continued to influence public consciousness.[8]

Having exposed the assumptions of these authors by placing their work in an older tradition of thought, and enjoying the luxury of retrospection, one can see that this group is highly vulnerable to criticism. First, adherents of these views overestimated the significance of political culture and ideology as barriers to organized, radical action from below. In addition to misjudging the potential strength and energy of society, they failed to distinguish between *official* and *societal* attitudes and beliefs. The older, pre-1985 writings reviewed above treated Leninist political culture and ideology as defining features of Leninist regimes and prime movers in their development and policies. But ideology and political culture were judged according to their influence within the framework of the party-state itself. The extent to which Leninist thought permeated popular consciousness was not regarded as particularly significant, since analysis focused on the state and society was regarded mainly as an object or tool of state policy. Yet the more recent analyses retained the emphasis on official ideology and political culture and *attributed them to society as a whole*. Thus, Scanlan referred to Marxist-Leninist ideas on rights, interests, and association as "Soviet attitudes and beliefs." He neglected the possibility that such ideas, pervasive as they may have been in official thinking, may never have sunk deep roots in society as a whole, and therefore may not constrain independent social actors.

Recent developments in Russia also revealed shortcomings in these scholars' conceptions of *the state*. Scanlan may well have been correct in his assertion that one-party rule and the emergence of civil society are incompatible. But the growth of independent opposition exposed the state's weakness—or at least lack of will—in the face of challenge; and the deepening of fissures in the Communist Party's ranks betrayed a lack of cohesiveness. Although he correctly perceived that the state would be unwilling or unable to empower society, he overestimated the state's capacity or will to thwart the emergence of organized social actors intent upon empowering themselves. Whether or not the state, even while decaying, was able to distort and disrupt the advent of independent politics is, of course, another question, which will be investigated at length in subsequent chapters. If Scanlan misjudged the party's strength and cohesiveness, Migranian grossly exaggerated its flexibility, inventiveness, and legitimacy. His contention that the party could smoothly devolve power to other groups and control the pace of transition was wildly optimistic. His belief that only the state could create a new political society, and that any transition must originate and be directed "from above," reflected both overestimation of the party and underestimation of the potential of independent societal forces.

In sum, habits of state-centric analysis, along with misuse of concepts of political culture inherited from earlier scholarly approaches, limit the utility of the works reviewed here for effective analysis of recent changes in Russian politics and state-society relations.

Category II: Revisionist State-Centric Approaches

Like the literature in category I, the works in the second category focus on state institutions. Yet, beginning in the mid-1960s, a number of scholars broke with the approaches reviewed above. They sought to escape from what they regarded as mistaken political-cultural notions and Cold War stereotypes, to account for transformations in the post-

Stalin state, and to integrate the study of the Soviet Union into the broader field of comparative politics.[9]

Within this literature, two trends predominated. The first may be labeled institutional-bureaucratic; the second, historical-ideological. Scholars whose analyses fell into the first group attempted to identify cleavages within and between state institutions and emphasized the significance of struggles over resources, influence on top state leaders, and access to privileges. In their search for a more differentiated analysis of elite politics, they imported theories of pluralism and interest groups and applied them to state actors. These theorists generated models of "bureaucratic pluralism" and "institutional pluralism" to describe a state that they believed had transformed itself from the autocratic, personalistic, totalitarian dictatorship of the Stalin period into an oligarchical bureaucratic apparatus, riven by internal divisions. Scholars working within this approach did not ignore entirely the tension between utopian, ideological impulses and the goals of rational-technical management. But in contrast to some proponents of the "traditional" approach reviewed above, revisionist scholars assumed that by the late 1960s, the latter imperative had triumphed in the calculations and policy decisions of the Soviet political elite. Charisma, ideology, and messianism had been decisively subordinated to the requirements of technological and economic development and regime stability. As in many other political systems, "interests" rather than ideas served as the major sources of division among elite actors.[10]

The second major approach in the revisionist literature on elite politics did not deemphasize the significance of ideas, but stressed what its exponents regarded as the duality of the Leninist tradition of political thought. While admitting that Stalinism had triumphed and continued to influence Soviet political institutions, sovietologists such as Stephen Cohen located a second, less authoritarian strand of thinking among the earlier Bolsheviks, best represented by the writings and political career of Nikolai Bukharin. There had always been an alternative to Stalinism, and the key to the prospects for change in the post-Stalin period could be found in the ability of Soviet "reformers" to revive the tradition of Bukharinist thought and policy extinguished in the 1930s. In his observations on the politics of the 1970s and early 1980s, Cohen conceptualized fissures within the elite less in terms of bureaucratic politics than as struggle between the "friends and foes" of reform. Ideas, as well as interests, continued to shape elite politics. The best hope for change lay with the possible ascendance of less dogmatic policymakers within the party-state apparat.[11]

In sum, the bureaucratic-institutional and historical-ideological tendencies within the older revisionist literature on elite politics differed somewhat in their explanations of change in the post-Stalin Soviet Union. Yet both focused mainly on high politics and official sources of change and were committed to exposing divisions within the ruling elite. Some scholars, however, objected to applying concepts such as "pluralism"—which traditionally had been used to describe competition among independent societal actors—to conflict within and among state institutions. Critics accused proponents of an interest group approach of "concept stretching" and argued that bureaucracies could not be described as "pluralist."[12]

Putting aside the question of terminology, other assumptions of the revisionist scholarship created the basis for more serious misconceptions. Some of these deeper problems and their consequences often went unnoticed by critics, many of whom themselves focused primarily on elite politics. First, revisionist scholars often disregarded the possibility that the deepest cleavage in Soviet politics lay not between "competing" interests within the state, but between the "ruling strata," however defined, and "everyone else"—that is, between state and society. Surely the KGB and the Ministry of Defense on occasion differed on questions of policy, and regional party secretaries vied for access to scarce resources. Similarly, Stalin and Bukharin undoubtedly differed over the pace of industrialization and the collectivization of agriculture. But, given state agencies' and officials' common and profound lack of accountability to broader society, how significant were these divisions within the context of the country as a whole?

A second and related consequence of revisionist thinking regarded the *functions* supposedly performed by state institutions in broader society. If the Soviet state by the 1970s had assumed institutional-structural characteristics more similar to those found in nonsocialist countries, including collective leadership and rational bureaucracy, then surely these structures must have operated in ways not wholly dissimilar to their counterparts in the West. Thus, many writers concluded that the Communist Party of the Soviet Union had become a genuine political party, and they attributed to it functions associated with parties in competitive systems. Ronald Hill and Peter Frank argued that the CPSU "aggregates interests" in broader society in much the same way that parties do in the West. A refusal to accept the CPSU as a genuine political party would lead only to "intellectual bankruptcy"; instead, by treating it as a normal party, "the concept of party itself is enriched" and the integration of sovietology into broader comparative politics is advanced.[13] Similarly, the soviets were sometimes assumed to operate somewhat like normal legislatures. Although the Communist Party appointed members of the USSR Supreme Soviet and soviets at all lower levels, and although not a single dissenting vote was re-

corded in a soviet session between the time of Stalin and the onset of
the Gorbachev period, Peter Vanneman referred to the soviets as one
of several "increasingly competitive sources of legitimacy" and suggested that they even functioned as "barometers of public opinion."[14]
In his examination of Soviet elections, Stephen White admitted that
participation in voting was required by law and that all ballots contained the name of only a single candidate, selected by the party apparat. Yet he argued that elections served as "evidence of the regime's
increasing ability to mobilize the population and to integrate them into
the political system."[15] To support their conclusions, such scholars
often adduced claims made in official Soviet sources, including Leonid
Brezhnev's public speeches.

While such analyses did pay needed attention to changes in the
post-Stalin state, they greatly exaggerated the extent to which these
changes produced convergence with systems of governance in the
West. The strong emphasis on elite politics, moreover, created a tendency to downplay division and conflict between state and society. Yet
habits of thought and analysis found in these earlier works have continued to find expression in much of the more recent scholarship on
the post-1985 period.

First, the tendencies to focus almost exclusively on elite politics, and
to frame political struggle in terms of debate between the "friends and
foes of reform" within the leadership, have blinded many analysts to
nonstate sources of ideas and pressure for change. In many scholarly
works on the Gorbachev period, proposals and programs were taken
seriously only if articulated by state leaders. The ideas generated by
and the persons associated with independent groups usually went unnoticed (at least until the abortive coup of August 1991), while great
effort was invested in analysis of speeches delivered at the latest Communist Party conference. In accordance with older habits of analysis,
the verb "to mobilize" was used transitively instead of intransitively—
that is, it was understood primarily in terms of state officials' strategic
use of popular sectors (e.g., "Gorbachev's plans to mobilize" this or
that "class" or sector of public opinion), rather than as autonomously
created, spontaneous, and self-sustaining action.[16] The continuing importance of close observation of elite politics, of course, should not be
underestimated. But the accompanying tendency to downplay society
became an especially serious hindrance to effective analysis during the
second half of the Gorbachev period, when autonomous political
forces radicalized and seized the initiative in formulating alternatives—usually *in opposition* to the policies of even "reformers" such as
Gorbachev.

In addition to underestimating societal forces, many observers also failed to draw a crucial analytical distinction between state and societal actors, a shortcoming also found in the traditional state-centric approaches reviewed in category I. This failing often resulted in miscalculation of the "readiness" of Russia for democracy and pluralism and of the likely speed of change. White, for example, asserted in 1990 that the development of even a "Soviet-style socialist pluralism" would likely require "many years of experiment and habituation."[17] In response, one might ask: "Habituation" by whom? If the writer had in mind state officials who stood to lose by democratization, one indeed might have expected the process of habituation to have taken a very long time. But how long does it take ordinary citizens to "learn democracy"—to tolerate differences of opinion, to participate responsibly in elections and in independent political action? In Russia, as elsewhere, the answer seems clear: far less time than many state officials would like to believe, and than many political scientists assume. White can be faulted neither for taking a skeptical view of the prospects for rapid democratization in general nor for failing to predict the rapidity with which old structures of domination would lose their authority. But his tendency, shared by many other scholars, to neglect basic analytical distinctions between state and societal actors led him to overlook deeper, institutional obstacles to democratization, located in structures of the state and the economy, in favor of attitudinal, political-cultural barriers, presumably shared by the population as a whole.

Indeed, to the extent that new revisionist state-centric analyses have addressed state-society relations at all, they often have fallen back on dubious political-cultural assumptions that figured less prominently in the older revisionist writings. "Russian society" was regarded as reflexively resistant to democracy and the market. It was also viewed as a repository of dangerous, unpredictable impulses; "populism" and "resurgent Russian nationalism" were seen as everywhere on the rise.[18] Radical democratic intellectuals were portrayed as irresponsible, quarrelsome malcontents who did not appreciate the necessity of gradualism and restraint.[19]

Such assumptions have gravely impaired scholars' analyses of post-1985 changes in state-society relations. Popular discontent with Gorbachev was viewed with incomprehension or attributed wholly to declining living standards and popular impatience. The popularity of Boris El'tsin, who broke with the Communist Party leadership in 1987, quit the party in 1990, and went on to win the presidency of the Russian Federation in 1991, has been similarly misunderstood. The possibility that El'tsin's relative popularity has been the product not of demagoguery but rather of public perceptions that he is a genuine democrat, committed to revolutionary regime change, and Gorbachev was not—an assumption taken for granted in assessing the differential in popularity between Lech Walesa and Wojciech Jaruzelski in Poland during the 1980s—was widely ignored or dismissed, at least until the abortive coup of August 1991.

Excessive attention to elite political actors, combined with facile political-cultural notions, has not only prejudiced observations of changes in state-society relations. Paradoxically, it may have also impaired scholars' understanding of *the state*. Specifically, such biases have led to undifferentiated evaluations of the possible motivations underlying official policies. Most Western observers have assumed that the main impetus for Gorbachev's reforms was a desire to modernize the country's economy and technological base, to stimulate development of its infrastructure, and to integrate the country into the global economy and polity.[20] Such a view is, of course, neither illogical nor entirely inconsistent with observable policy. Yet, in their focus on elite politics and in their assumptions regarding the global nature of the state's objectives, many scholars neglected the possibility that the impetus for reform grew not out of broad transformative aims, but primarily out of a defensive strategy for rejuvenating the party-state's hegemonic position over society as a whole. The political destruction of the party's most conservative and despised elements, by means of purge and subjection to limited competition through elections, was entirely consistent with this goal. That this strategy proved ineffective cannot be denied; but neither can the possibility that the consequences that followed from liberalization were entirely unintended. Rulers may well have seen pursuit of global objectives and protection of the basic structure of authority relations in society as fully compatible.

Discounting the possible predominance of the latter objective narrowed observers' understanding of official behavior. Gorbachev's crackdown on independent opposition, reversal of press liberalization, and appointment of hard-line officials to high positions beginning in the fall of 1990 thus were widely regarded in the West as temporary tactical maneuvers. Such an interpretation was not surprising, since these moves were highly inconsistent with Gorbachev's presumed goals of economic and political liberalization. Many Soviet citizens, however, regarded these actions as entirely consonant with what they perceived as the leadership's principal overriding objective: safeguarding the established, if decaying, system of authority relations in the country.

The revisionist elite politics approaches examined here exhibit striking limitations for generating concepts and ideas useful for understanding change in state-society relations in Russia. The following section examines scholarship within the revisionist tradition that has afforded closer attention to the roles of nonstate actors in politics.

Category III: Revisionist State-Society Approaches

Like the older elite politics approaches discussed above, writings classified in the third category include efforts to account for change in the Soviet system and to transcend the concepts of totalitarianism, political culture, tradition, and charisma that figured prominently in the writings found in category I. But this third group also sought to avoid the pitfalls of state-centric analysis and explicitly addressed problems of society and state-society relations. These analyses may be divided roughly into two types: social contract theories of state-society relations, and macrosociological studies of social groups.

Scholars employing the contract approach did not assume a monolithic state. But they did focus less on cleavages between various state actors than on the basic division between state and society. Rather than emphasizing structural divisions between state and society and factors such as repression, indoctrination, and mass mobilization, however, these scholars examined how state actors sought constituencies and built support among various societal groups. They acknowledged that only one side—the state—held a meaningful measure of decision-making power in the formulation of the "contract," and therefore they did not claim that the Soviet "social contract" corresponded to Rousseau's theory. But they did accept Rousseau's basic assumption that power must to some extent be rationally justifiable, or else it would create antinomies between rulers and ruled that would destabilize the social order. And in their observations of the Soviet Union during the 1970s and early 1980s, analysts were struck by signs of stability: low incidence of social upheaval, and ostensibly satisfactory economic growth and steady rises in living standards. If state-centric revisionist analyses attempted to locate and explain the presence of conflict and struggle—real politics—at the elite level, contract approaches tried to explain the apparent absence, or at least extreme stability, of real politics in state-society relations. Scholars working within the contract approach formulated such concepts as "welfare-state authoritarianism" and "organized consensus" to describe state strategies for building legitimacy and support among the broader population.[21]

The second major body of work comprised macrosociological studies of social groups. It included detailed studies on women, nationalities, occupational and professional groups, and the family, as well as Soviet or Russian society as a whole. Some of these works presented sophisticated treatments of demographic and social change among various groups. They did, of course, often reflect the obvious methodological difficulties created by paucity of reliable data on mass political life and interaction between citizens and the state. Consequently, most such works were stronger as sociology than as political science.[22]

For the purposes of analysis of society and state-society relations, the contract and macrosociological approaches represented an improvement over much of the state-centric revisionist scholarship. Society was not objectified to the same extent as in the latter literature, and some of the most egregious interpretive errors found there were avoided. In contrast to White's and Vanneman's extremely dubious interpretations of the functions of elections and legislatures, for example, Victor Zaslavsky and Robert Brym generated skeptical and insightful conclusions on the nature and consequences of such political participation.[23] In his analysis of how the state "organizes consensus" in society, moreover, Zaslavsky did not fail to account for the role of officially created structural barriers to the expression of discontent.[24]

In retrospect, however, it does seem that these works underestimated the roles of repression and fear in maintaining the apparent stability of society during the pre-1985 period. They also created an image of profound popular passivity, based on the assumption that the vast majority of Russians were content to exchange all political and civic aspirations for slow but steady improvements in material living standards. These works often manifested a certain justificationist empiricism (we observe neither social discontent nor terror and mass repression, therefore peace must exist between the regime and the population). Yet the temptations of such reasoning must have been great, given the obvious methodological limitations imposed by the lack of opportunities for direct observation and collection of data.

Both contract and macrosociological approaches have continued to find expression in post-1985 scholarship. Responding to the explosive growth in independent political activity and new opportunities for first-hand observation, scholars have elaborated on and reconceptualized these older approaches. Yet the persistence of outworn assumptions is starkly evident in much of even the best new work on state-society relations.

The new contract approach is best represented by Peter Hauslohner's 1987 article on Gorbachev's strategy for "rebuilding state legitimacy." Most significant for the purposes of this review are the writer's assumptions regarding the effectiveness of the social contract throughout the post-Stalin period, and the predictions he deduced from these assumptions. First, he posited the belief, also expressed in the older contract literature, that popular contentment, not coercion and the structure of economic production and distribution, best explained the quiescence of the Soviet population. The state's coercive apparatus, after all, became "less harsh and less visible over the past three decades." Further, he argued that "despite being given virtually no power over key political and economic decisions, most citizens have been allowed *considerable personal freedom as workers and consumers*" (emphasis added). Given the actual system of authority relations in the workplace, difficulties imposed by the *trudovaia kniga* (a permanent lifelong work history), which prevented a worker dismissed for "political reasons" from obtaining new employment elsewhere, the *propiska* system, which restricted individuals' rights to change residence, and a supply situation that forced consumers to seek basic goods on the black market, one may ask: Considerable freedom compared to whom? What is most significant about Hauslohner's analysis, however, are his conclusions regarding the compatibility of radical reform and the preservation of the Communist Party's monopoly on power and authority. He argued that "there is no obvious or logical reason why Party hegemony must inevitably be threatened by a partial reduction in the Party's day-to-day control over the economy and by transfer of the control given up to more democratic institutions."[25]

Herein lies a remarkable conclusion: that newly empowered democratic institutions and loci of independent economic power resulting from liberalization, be they soviets, trade unions, or cooperative associations, should *not* have been expected fundamentally to challenge the system of political domination. So satisfied were Soviet producers and consumers, so effective was the social contract between state and society, that the party could reduce its political control over the economy and transfer some power and responsibility to "more democratic institutions" without jeopardizing its hegemony. Hauslohner's article was published before mass labor unrest, more freely elected soviets, and radical democratic movements began to reshape Russian politics. It appeared, moreover, at a time when opportunities for first-hand observation of political life and of industrial-labor relations were only beginning to present themselves to Western scholars. Yet it may be argued that failure to anticipate the revolutionary consequences of even a limited measure of liberalization, and overestimation of the state's capacity for controlled devolution of power, resulted directly from the faulty assumptions of official flexibility, popular satisfaction, and regime legitimacy on which the contract approach was based.

Scholars working within the framework of macrosociology have generated somewhat different analyses. After 1985 they moved beyond the portraits of social groups found in the older sociological literature and attempted to identify the deep underlying forces pressing for political change. Some argued that forces of modernization, including economic development, urbanization, and improved educational attainment during recent decades had already produced a "civil society" in Russia even before the onset of the Gorbachev period, or at least paved the way for one. Socioeconomic change gave rise to a "new middle class" of white-collar workers and skilled professionals who were far more capable of independent thought and action. Economic development, combined with the command economy's sluggishness, engendered a working class that had a stake in an economy more responsive to its consumer demands. Improvements in communications enhanced citizens' ability to circumvent official restrictions on associational rights. Modernization not only produced a more differentiated, articulate, and reform-minded citizenry; it also engendered a state less secure in its monopoly on power and authority, and far more aware of its need to establish contact with its population. The consequent liberalization was a sign of rational state-led reform to accommodate mature social forces.[26] Thus, some scholars working within this approach held highly optimistic images of the present and future shape of Russian political society. Frederick Starr, for example, contended in 1990 that the Soviet Union would soon achieve a "civil society . . . and a democratic and relatively open system based on law rather than force and fully compatible with those prevailing from the Atlantic Ocean to Anatolia and from Lapland to Sicily."[27]

Analysts who employ modernization theory have avoided some of the pitfalls of state-centric interpretations and have stimulated productive debate on the role of societal actors in political change. Some of their general conclusions, moreover, appear consistent with the evidence. Russian society certainly proved to be sufficiently "modern" to generate an abundance of social movements under conditions of even limited liberalization. Yet if one is concerned with the institutional forms that such movements assumed and the social bases on which they were built, as well as with the extent to which new institutions created the foundation for democratic transition, some of the assumptions underlying the modernization approach require closer examination. Can it safely be assumed, for example, that industrialization exerted the same effects in Russia that it did in the West and many developing countries?

Although they do not always acknowledge it explicitly, scholars who employ a modernization framework rely extensively on Durkheim's concepts of division of labor and socioeconomic change. According to Durkheim, a central dynamic of history is found in the growing complexity of the division of labor, resulting from technical progress and innovation. Social change, in turn, is understood largely in terms of the effects of these processes on social structure. As Andrew Janos points out, in Durkheim's theory the transformation of society is understood not only as differentiation, but also as transformation in the systems of solidarity and integration. Durkheim understood "integration" largely in cultural terms, as a process by which individuals generate new forms of solidarity to replace older, mechanical forms based on ritual. Durkheim's pessimism derived largely from his fear that change in the consciousness of the individual could not be expected to keep pace with the rate of social change. This lag would lead to individual anomie and disorientation, creating conditions for the formation of destructive, radical political and religious movements. The process of healthy reintegration, therefore, stands out as the central challenge faced by industrial societies.[28]

Like Durkheim, students of Russian society who use modernization theory conceive of "modernity" largely in terms of technical progress, growing complexity in the division of labor, and consequent socioeconomic change. They view the rise of a "new middle class" in Russia during recent decades as a leading force in society-led reform. In some writings this class is seen as highly differentiated and not dissimilar from middle classes found in the West, consisting of a "working middle class," a stratum of upwardly mobile "yuppies," and so on.[29]

But it is questionable that the indicators cited in these writings—occupational stratification and differentiation in educational levels, income, and patterns of consumption—really demonstrate the existence of a new middle *class*, much less a highly differentiated one. In the West, the rise of a middle class was tied closely to the emergence of an independent (or partially independent) business class and to the separation of economic and political power. The middle class, through its organizations and its control over resources, counterbalanced state power and furnished the social basis for the growth of notions of reciprocity and citizenship.[30] But in Soviet Russia, where near-total étatization of property and fusion of political and economic power prevented the emergence of an independent business class, one may question whether a middle class of the Western type could have emerged, and whether industrialization could have produced patterns of societal differentiation similar to those found in the West.

In addition to confusing the *process* of industrialization with its *effects* on differentiation of social structure, analysts who use modernization theory neglect the problem of societal "reintegration," which figured prominently in Durkheim's work. In the West, the middle class realized its reintegrative potential through its political parties, cooperative and producers' associations, clubs, guilds, and "friendly societies." In addition to exerting class power in political life, these associations created the institutional framework for an independent civil society. The reintegrative potential of urbanization, moreover, was found precisely in how urbanization increased the *density and intensity of association* among individuals and groups.[31] In Russia, where free and independent association for any purposes deemed "political" was until recently banned, where even "nonpolitical" associations and the professions were closely regulated, and where the state controlled all mass communications and information, urbanization cannot possibly have carried the same potential for "reintegration" that it did in more open societies. In sum, it is injudicious to assume that industrialization in Russia produced patterns of social differentiation not dissimilar to those found in Western countries, and that societal "reintegration" simply followed automatically from the processes of differentiation.

Interestingly, older classics of modernization theory may contain clues to overcoming some of these problems. In his study of the industrial revolution in Britain, Neil Smelser elaborated on Durkheim's framework, arguing that the "transitional" phase between the "equilibrium" of traditional society and the "equilibrium of modernity" exhibits a distinct set of features, and indeed must be regarded as a separate stage. According to Smelser, the societal "differentiation" set in motion by industrialization can proceed normally, and produce socioeconomic modernization, only if the "disturbances" it creates are "brought into line by specific integrative measures." These "integrative measures" include the establishment of free trade unions, friendly societies, and professional organizations, as well as legal safeguards such as labor legislation. The logic of Smelser's argument suggests that without a measure of free association allowing for the creation of autonomous societal institutions, and without popular representation making possible certain legal protections, society can hardly be expected to overcome the disequilibrium of the transitional phase.[32] Drawing on Smelser's argument, one might ask: Might not a state apparatus, unaccountable to public opinion and committed to the étatization of associational life, have been able to block, or at least distort, the processes of societal differentiation and reintegration? If so, one might expect that the sudden, simultaneous birth of previously repressed, latent integrative institutions, after decades of industrialization, would create a society whose movements, institutional features, and organizational forms differ substantially from those found in societies in which differentiation and reintegration occurred gradually and incrementally.

Category IV: Traditional State-Society Approaches

Scholarship grouped in the fourth category diverges somewhat from approaches common in American sovietology. Though this literature has generated a great store of theoretical insights on state-society relations, it has been neglected by most Western students of Russia and the Soviet Union, for reasons that will be discussed below.

Perhaps the most complete expression of the ideas reviewed in this category is found in Ferenc Fehér, Agnes Heller, and György Markus's book, *Dictatorship over Needs*.[33] Writing in the late 1970s, the authors emphasized the enduring totalitarian nature of Soviet-style socialism. But they offered an analysis that differed considerably from that found in works reviewed in category I. The writings in the first category consisted largely of classical, state-centric models of totalitarianism and Weberian analyses that conceptualized the state in terms of elite beliefs and ideology, charisma, and the organizational structure of the Leninist party. Fehér, Heller, and Markus focused more explicitly on relations between state and society. Though they are associated with Marxist philosophical and sociological traditions, and particularly with the thinking of György Lukacs, they constructed the most thoroughgoing and devastating critique of Soviet-style socialism of any of the writers included in this review.

According to these writers, the state in Soviet-type systems was driven less by ideological or organizational imperatives than by the logic of its extractive, expansionist relationship toward society. They did not deny the existence of cleavages within state institutions, and indeed located differences in interest between top leaders and lower-level officials. The crucial cleavage, however, was to be found between the party-state apparatus and society. The state as a whole was regarded as more "monolithic" than "pluralist," and capable of great unity when confronted by potential challenges from below. Among exponents of this thinking, consensus did not develop over the proper conceptualization of state institutions. Fehér, Heller, and Markus conceived of the Soviet-style state as an institution *sui generis*, driven primarily by the urge to expand its *power* over society and to eliminate sources of societal autonomy, while writers such as György Konrad and Ivan Szelenyi conceptualized the apparat as a ruling class and the state as a monopoly capitalist.[34] Yet both sets of authors advocated what amounts to a predatory theory of rule and characterized the state mainly in broad sociological terms of its relationship to society.

The Soviet-type state, therefore, was regarded as "totalitarian" not primarily by virtue of its messianism, all-encompassing ideology, use of terror or mass mobilization, or distinctive organizational structure.

Rather, the essence of totalitarianism was found in the "elimination of any kind of recognized pluralism," manifested most clearly in the ban on free and autonomous association for political and economic ends. The destruction of "horizontal links" between individuals and groups of individuals, the creation of a vertical and comprehensive dependency of the individual on the state, and the étatization of all forms of public interaction were regarded as the dominant dynamics of totalitarianism. Thus, since the end of the Stalin period was not accompanied by reduction in étatization or opening of space for independent associational life, totalitarianism did survive Stalin's death. That official repression after Stalin no longer took the form of mass terror but became an automatic, reflexive bureaucratic response to organized expression of independence on the part of societal groups did not signal the liberalization or the end of totalitarianism suggested by revisionist works reviewed in categories II and III. Rather, it indicated that dependence and fear had become sufficiently institutionalized to allow for the use of means less crude and arbitrary than mass executions and imprisonment.[35]

In this analysis, official ideology and the belief systems of elites were regarded largely in Marxist terms: justificationist, instrumental, or irrelevant. Ideology functioned as the "language of domination," as "noise" that crowded out genuine information and communication and prevented society from gaining voice.[36] The state was regarded more as a repository of particular sets of interests than as the embodiment of charismatic authority. According to Leszek Kolakowski, the question of whether leaders take ideology seriously is unimportant. Leaders' behavior, after all, "is not altered by the degree to which they have internalized the official verbiage since they identify themselves with the interests that the ideology protects."[37] The state was concerned less with achieving "great projects" and "heroic combat tasks" than with eliminating autonomous subsystems that interfered with the expansion of its extractive capacity over society. Thus, it was unconcerned with whether or not the population actually believed its ideological claims; rote recitation of the dogma and refusal to challenge it publicly sufficed.[38]

Here, the relationship between state and society could not be conceived of as a "contract," which implies reciprocity and mutual freedom of action or at least choice. The logic of the "dictatorship over needs," moreover, differed considerably from that of the welfare state. In a welfare system the state provides goods and services to individuals to satisfy needs (need fulfillment is regarded as an end in itself), and/or to dampen potential popular discontent through the cooptation of social groups. The "dictatorship over needs," by contrast, aimed to destroy society itself by means of a comprehensive system of individual dependency on the state. The individual was not merely satisfied, pacified, or coopted; he or she was turned into a supplicant, a subject rather than a citizen. Policies and administrative structures that inevitably produced enormous waste and chronic shortages, and that appeared entirely at odds with economic rationality, were seen as consistent with maintenance of the system of dependence and the subjugation of society. Since the regime did not recognize the legitimacy of autonomous subsystems (excepting perhaps the family), what may have appeared as the state's efforts to "cultivate constituencies" in society were better understood as attempts at refining the system of dependency. The state was expansionist and extractive without being "inclusive."[39]

Society was not assumed to have internalized official dogma. Nor was it regarded as a willing partner in its own degradation, content to trade freedom and autonomy for subsistence. Rather, it was seen as having little choice in the matter, and the state was regarded as possessing a degree of control over the means of production, distribution, employment, communication, and coercion that could only have been dreamt of by Marx's bourgeoisie. Since society was neither content nor ignorant of alternative systems of rule and ways of life found in the West, the regime, in accordance with Weber's conception, experienced a constant and permanent crisis of legitimacy. Like Marx's working masses under capitalism, mass society under Communist rule was "radically excluded" from power but potentially restive and dangerous to the regime; the state properly regarded society as more of a threat than an opportunity.[40]

The scholarship in the fourth category produced highly systemic and consistent theories of state-society relations that successfully encompassed the economy as well as the polity and society, and it generated sophisticated and rigorous concepts. Yet it has been largely neglected by Western sovietologists. Reasons may include aversion to grand, abstract theoretical constructs and generalizations, especially those generated within a Marxist framework, and an unwarranted mistrust of the "objectivity" of East European and émigré writers. But other reasons may lie in shortcomings evident in writings in this category.

First, however interesting their theoretical designs and their insights into East European politics, writers in this category largely neglected the Soviet Union itself. To the extent that they dealt with it per se, they sometimes fell back on dubious political-cultural stereotypes that they avoided in their treatments of East Europe. "The Russians" were viewed as lying outside the traditions of "East-Central European culture" and as more willing than East Europeans to resign themselves to their status as supplicants of the state's beneficence.[41] Writers such as Fehér, Heller, Markus, Konrad, and Szelenyi enjoyed intimate familiarity with East European societies. Even without the extensive use of empirical techniques, they grasped both the logic of political domination and the prevalence of public cynicism in countries such as Poland and Hungary. They identified such phenomena as the "antipolitical politics" waged by individuals and groups intent on preserving some spheres of autonomy, and they comprehended the danger that it posed to even monolithic, "totalizing" state systems.[42] In Russia, however, a country with which they were less familiar, these writers discerned little potential for resistance. Some writers working within this approach did perceive the problems inherent in such a view. Zagorka Golubovic, for example, argued that Fehér, Heller, and Markus failed to account for the differential in levels of repression prevalent in much of East Europe, on the one hand, and in the Soviet Union, on the other. By so doing, they overlooked important, if latent and only potential, sources of societal resistance within Russia itself.[43]

Another shortcoming of this literature is its tendency to overestimate the monolithic nature of the state. However sophisticated their theory of the system of political domination as a whole, scholars seem to have misjudged the potential for the development of deep—and, for the system, ruinous—fissures within the leadership of socialist countries. They offered highly cogent theories of state-society relations, but they could not account for the rise to power in the Soviet Union of leaders whose reforms would set in motion processes that ultimately would undermine the system of domination itself. Despite their inadequacy for analysis of state-society relations, some of the revisionist state-centric approaches reviewed in category II better captured the dynamics of struggle within the official leadership. They left open the possibility that the rise to power of a "liberal" fraction might create the potential for breakthroughs that could not be anticipated by approaches that regarded the state as essentially monolithic.

A New Approach: Assumptions, Definitions, and Methodology

Despite some weaknesses, the literature found in the fourth category provides valuable ideas and concepts for analysis of transformations in state-society relations in Russia during the Gorbachev period. First, one may profitably borrow the highly systemic conception of state-society relations, which takes into account authority relations in many aspects of social life, including property relations, control over resources, and the structure of authority in the workplace. By focusing explicitly on state-society relations, this school overcomes some of the limitations found in the state-centric analyses of categories I and II, while careful attention to the state's role in obstructing and distorting the development of society provides a more balanced framework than found in works in category III.

Second, theorists in the fourth category furnish a useful conceptualization of the "state." They conceive of the state as the "system of domination," encompassing not only top leaders and formal institutions of the party-state bureaucracy, but also the structure of enterprise directors and managers. The fusion of political and economic power in Russia began to erode during the second half of the Gorbachev period. But the near-total étatization of the means of production and distribution and the inclusion of political and economic administration within a bureaucratic hierarchy of nomenklatura appointments remained largely intact in Russia until the time of the failed putsch. Nearly all enterprise directors, leaders of official trade unions, and employees of the state security apparat retained membership in the Communist Party and answered to higher party authorities. In this study, the "state" is understood as the party-state apparat, including the agencies of state security and the system of economic administration lying within the framework of the nomenklatura system. The "state" is conceptualized in institutional terms; thus, "rank-and-file" members of the Communist Party who do not hold any special responsibility for administration are not regarded as part of the state.

This definition is consistent with those employed in other areas of comparative politics. In writings on bureaucratic authoritarianism in Latin America, for example, scholars such as F. H. Cardoso and Guillermo O'Donnell define the state as the "pact of domination," which is understood to include the bureaucratic agencies of administration and coercion. These writers often conceptualize the pact of domination in terms of class relationships and include within it "fractions of dominant classes and the norms which guarantee their dominance." The "state," therefore, is sometimes understood to include the "upper bourgeoisie," consisting of the professional, managerial, and ownership elite that controls economic production.[44] This definition of the state, by including some actors positioned outside the formal structure of state institutions under capitalism, tends to blur distinctions between "public" and "private" power, indeed to produce a rather weak distinction between the very concepts of "power" and "state." In the Soviet case, however, the rough functional equivalents of the upper bourgeoisie—namely, the administrative and managerial elites

that controlled economic production—*were* found within the hierarchical, bureaucratic structure of formal state institutions. Thus, the concepts of "pact of domination" or "system of domination" may be
employed in the Soviet/Russian case in a purely institutional sense,
without the loss of definitional rigor inherent in inclusion of "fractions
of classes." Whether legislatures may be placed within the state poses
a more difficult problem. Before 1989, soviets were mere appendages
of party power that met infrequently and simply ratified decisions
made by higher authorities. But after 1989, when multiple-candidate
ballots began to appear in elections for soviets on all levels, some soviets actually became forums for the expression of public resistance to
the extant political system. In this study, the soviets will be regarded
as constituting something of an intermediate case, as lying within the
formal structures of power but not as full-fledged institutional members of the "system of domination." The role of the soviets and their
relationships with new independent political organizations will be examined in chapters 4 and 5.

In addition to generating a conception of the state useful for this
book, works included in the fourth category also have addressed theoretical issues useful in conceptualizing "society." "Totalitarianism" is
defined as the "ban on all pluralism," understood mainly as the pro-
scription of free and autonomous societal associations. Therefore, one
might infer that totalitarianism would reach its end at precisely the
moment that such groups emerged. Indeed, however important the
appearance of splits among state leaders for opening space for independent organized political activity, and however essential the attainment of some degree of socioeconomic "modernity" for creating a society capable of self-defense, it will be argued that the central dynamic
of the construction of a new political society lay in the struggle between emergent autonomous organizations and the institutions of
state power. Drawing further from the analyses reviewed in the fourth
category, it will be demonstrated that liberalization in associational
rights did not engender the formation of a "civil society" of the Western type. Rather, the persistence of structural barriers such as the system of dependency in the workplace and state control over property,
including the means of production and communication, strongly influenced the development of the new independent political institutions
and their relationship with the state. In Durkheimian parlance, these
structural factors shaped the transformation in the systems of solidarity and integration in the new society.

Certain assumptions found in the final group of writings, including
some that were appropriate for the pre-1985 period, will be relaxed or
discarded altogether. The state may scarcely be regarded as "total-

izing" or society as "totalized" after independent associations began to emerge in 1987 and 1988. Analysis will account for the importance of divisions within elites for the creation of public space for the emergence of social movements and organizations on both national and local levels. Yet, since this book does not focus on high politics, struggles and splits within the Communist Party leadership will be investigated only to the extent that they impinge directly upon the development of autonomous political organizations. It will be demonstrated that certain features of state behavior emphasized in literatures in categories I and IV, such as the urge to monopolization of power, intolerance of independent challenge, and a basic inability or unwillingness to share power and authority, persisted even under conditions of liberalization and profoundly affected the formation of democratic movement organizations. In the literature grouped into category I, analysts explained these features of state behavior largely in terms of ideological, psychological, and political-cultural features of the Leninist party. My assumptions regarding state behavior, by contrast, rest on institutional, structural and economic factors such as those stressed in the fourth category.

Just as ideology and belief systems will be deemphasized in treatment of the state, notions of popular political culture and psychology will play no part in explanations of the organization and behavior of societal actors. As pointed out above, even scholars whose ideas were grouped in category IV, who generated sophisticated structural analyses of East European societies and Communist systems as a whole, often fell back on tired and misleading notions of cultural exceptionalism in their treatment of Russia. In my own analysis, not all explanation will be reduced to macrostructural factors; the development of independent forces will be shown in some cases to be highly indeterminate. As will be demonstrated in chapter 5, which investigates the development of political groups on the local level, small groups of individuals sometimes strongly influenced the development—or underdevelopment—of independent forces at critical junctures. Yet, even in these cases, individual behavior will be explained in terms of political opportunity structures and political entrepreneurship, not political psychology or culture. Precisely the latter approaches, rather than use of meaningful comparative concepts such as "totalitarianism," checked the theoretical advancement of sovietology over the decades.

"Society" is defined in this study as organizations, groups, and individuals standing outside state institutions. The focus of this book is on independent organizations, especially the new alternative political parties and other "informal" (nonofficial) political associations. In the present framework, independent political society does not include "liberal" factions in the Communist Party, "reformed" official trade unions, or "reformist" leaders such as Gorbachev. It does include genuinely autonomous nonstate organizations, and many persons who, though in some sense products of the old system, broke fully with it and undertook the task of building alternative institutions. Most of the groups examined may be regarded as "revolutionary," even if they did not advocate violent methods. They fit Giovanni Sartori's definition of "antisystem" organizations, in that they rejected the limits of "within-system" reform and aimed explicitly to undermine the legitimacy of the regime they opposed. As Sartori points out, such organizations may or may not operate "inside the system"; they may or may not participate in elections and engage in other activities allowed or sponsored by the state.[45] In short, the present study focuses on a portion of the most significant *associations of the organized revolutionary opposition*.

Investigation centers on groups that may be labeled "democratic" or "progressive," in that they sought change in the direction of liberal or social democracy as these terms are commonly understood in the West. Such groups represented the predominant and fastest-growing tendency in Russia during the period of Gorbachev's rule. Independent conservative-Communist, "national-patriotic," and chauvinist groups did gain some following. But their size, popular support, and influence remained a tiny fraction of that achieved by progressive organizations.

The geographical scope of this study is limited to the Russian Republic. Most of the groups under investigation organized exclusively or mainly on the level of the Russian Republic, while ethnic popular fronts acted as the predominant revolutionary movement organizations in the non-Russian republics. Particularly in light of such centrifugal tendencies, Russia, rather than the Soviet Union as a whole, may be regarded as a distinct unit of analysis and serves as the subject of investigation.

Empirical inquiry is based largely on interviews and direct observation undertaken between June 1989 and October 1992, during which I spent a total of eighteen months in Russia. Publications, especially those issued by the independent organizations, serve as additional sources of information. The methodological limitations of reliance upon interviews and direct observation for social scientific analysis are well known. Yet given the shortage of secondary literature and scientific surveys, investigation of the subject at hand requires extensive use of such sources. If employed with circumspection, they provide a superior alternative to official sources of information and public opinion research. As Sidney Tarrow has argued in a review of research on social movements in East Europe, moreover, survey research in societies undergoing deep transformation is often misleading, as it focuses on attitudes rather than mobilization potentials.[46]

The following chapter presents an overview of the emergence of independent political organizations in Russia during the Gorbachev period. Chapter 3 introduces the theoretical framework of the study. Chapter 4 investigates how new groups forged identities, sought constituencies, built organizational structures, and formulated strategies for operation in the broader political arena. Chapter 5 examines group formation and development on the local level in four provincial cities. The final chapter considers the influence of the new independent political society on the prospects for democratization in post-Soviet Russia.

II

The Transformation of Politics: A Historical Overview

The Theory and Practice of Association under Socialism

Karl Marx's neglect of individuality, free association, and self-organization and his wholly negative critique of "civil society" are well-known features of his work.[1] Whether Marx's utopian vision of the end of conflict in communist society infused his theory with an authoritarian, statist logic is a point of debate among contemporary scholars. Yet Marx clearly attributed universality to the proletariat precisely by virtue of what he regarded as its capacity to transcend the realm of particularistic "interest" and to unite state and society. In his belief that social systems could be freed from conflict by abolishing the division between political and social power, Marx did not stand alone among early socialist thinkers. As John Keane has pointed out, the earlier "self-managing" socialism of Robert Owen and the state socialism of Ferdinand Lassalle shared "this deep ideology of homeostasis, of the possibility of constructing a society in which all particular interests are integrated into the whole."[2] To be sure, this view did not go unchallenged. Eduard Bernstein, for example, argued that the diversity of interests in a complex society was inevitable and even desirable. He regarded independent trade unions, political parties, productive associations, and cooperative retail shops as essential components of socialist society, and he warned that the urge to destroy civil society engendered a dangerous authoritarian impulse.[3]

As Bernstein himself acknowledged, however, this notion of association represented a minority view among socialists. It had little effect on the Bolsheviks, who regarded Bernstein as an apostate. Lenin considered the division between state and society to be meaningless in postrevolutionary society. Even Nikolai Bukharin, the "liberal" among the Bolsheviks, did not oppose étatization of social and economic life. He did advocate "an unprecedented flourishing" of "all kinds of workers' and peasants' organizations, press correspondents, and voluntary societies and associations." Yet he held that these groups, "together with Soviet power, in fact, form a single system, which embraces, enlightens, and reforms the broad mass of toilers."[4]

This tension between the desire for an active, variegated society, on the one hand, and the urge to totalization, on the other, was evident in Bolshevik thinking in general during the first decade of Soviet power. During the NEP period Lenin sought to secure the domination of the party over all political life. Yet he did countenance exchange and market societies that were only indirectly subject to state control, and he supported peasant cooperatives as an evolutionary alternative to the sudden imposition of revolutionary power in the countryside. Such formations, as well as the myriad "voluntary societies and associations" that Bukharin envisaged, were not conceived of as fully autonomous, competitive organizations of the type that Bernstein advocated. But they were regarded as intermediary in the sense that they were largely self-constituted, allowed for some organized social initiative from below, and lay outside the formal structure of the state.

With Stalin's rise to supremacy toward the end of the 1920s, however, the destruction of nonstate societal activity of every type became a crucial—indeed, *the* crucial—revolutionary imperative of the Soviet state. What space still existed for social initiative from below was abolished, and all organizations positioned between the individual and the state were destroyed. One of the most striking aspects of Soviet rule between the death of Stalin in 1953 and the rise to power of Gorbachev in 1985 is the persistence of purely statist theory and practice on questions of association. The end of the Stalinist terror was in no way accompanied by an opening of room for independent associational life. Official repression no longer assumed the form of mass terror—it did not have to. Rather, it became an automatic, reflexive, institutionalized bureaucratic response to any organized expression of social autonomy. The 1977 Constitution, to an even greater extent than Stalin's 1936 Constitution, asserted that all organized activity must conform to the substantive goals of the state. In practice, the Brezhnev leadership defined permissible organized activity solely as that taking place within the confines of state institutions.[5]

Despite the ban on extra-state political activity, some independent organizations managed to exist. Examples include the Orthodox Monarchist Union Order, which survived from prerevolutionary times, and the People's Labor Union (NTS), an underground dissident network with links to émigré groups abroad. Until the Gorbachev period, however, such groups operated surreptitiously and enjoyed no capacity for regular public expression.[6]

The change in leadership of the Communist Party in March 1985 marked the beginning of a new era in Russian and Soviet politics. It engendered a process of liberalization that sparked an explosion of organized extra-state political activity. The following account reviews the crucial events that shaped the emergence of the democratic movement and its organizations in Russia.

The Onset of Liberalization: 1985–87

The main development of the first phase of the Gorbachev period was a partial liberalization in official thinking and policy on questions of independent association. The phrase "socialist pluralism" entered the official Soviet lexicon during this time. In practice, the concept amounted to de facto toleration of the formation of some small, non-state citizens' organizations. Writers known to enjoy contacts with top leaders acknowledged publicly that diverse and even competing interests existed in Soviet society.[7] The principle of independent, organized intermediation of interests was not affirmed. But admission of societal diversity provided theoretical justification for limited tolerance of political activity outside the confines of formal state organizations.

Most of the pioneering associations were dedicated to preserving historical monuments, protecting the environment, or fighting alcoholism. Groups with clear political agendas began to emerge in 1987. In the spring a political discussion group, the Perestroika Club, formed in Moscow. In the summer, after several members of the club raised the idea of an association to investigate the crimes of Stalinism, preparations began for the founding of what would become Memorial. In August a group of non-Communist intellectuals started Citizens' Dignity, a small association pledged to promoting human rights in the USSR.[8] Also in August the first major conference of political discussion groups from around the Soviet Union convened in Moscow. Dubbed by its organizers "Social Initiative for Perestroika," the gathering caused alarm among some officials. But it enjoyed the blessing of the then head of the Moscow Communist Party Committee, Boris El'tsin, and was hailed by some progressive intellectuals as "a school of citizenship" and "an experiment in democracy."[9]

Such groups in no sense constituted a real opposition. At the time of their inception, they were dedicated to discussion and activism that were not incompatible with the goals of perestroika, as defined by top state officials. As of the end of 1987, glasnost' remained a thing of the future. The sudden disgrace and demotion of Boris El'tsin following his speech at a closed party meeting in November 1987, during which he criticized some of his colleagues for timidity in pursuing reform, illustrated the endurance of severe limitations on debate and dissent, even within closed fora and among top leaders.

Still the emergence and toleration of some small nonstate organizations was in itself a momentous development. It represented the birth, or at least conception, of a genuine public realm. If one accepts the definition of totalitarianism put forth in the previous chapter—the ban on all pluralism and the complete étatization of associational life—this form of regime, after six decades of ruinous existence in Russia, died quietly in 1987 in the apartments and small public conference rooms where the new political clubs convened.

Informal Groups, Glasnost', and the Advent of Public Debate: 1988

The year 1988 witnessed an expansion in the number of "informal" (nonstate) groups, the beginning of street demonstrations organized by these groups, and the emergence of several organizations whose goals and tactics placed them far beyond the bounds of official tolerance. In January the Perestroika Club divided into Democratic Perestroika and a smaller but more radical faction, Perestroika-88. In February a small but high-profile gathering of intellectuals that included Andrei Sakharov, Iurii Afanas'ev, and Ales Adamovich founded Moscow Tribune, a club that aimed to organize unofficial seminars on political topics in research institutes. In June a wider circle of liberal intellectuals intent on transcending political discussion and promoting activism founded the Moscow Popular Front. Such groups were loosely organized and possessed highly informal leadership structures. Memberships were fluid and overlapped substantially among groups.[10]

The stated goals of these and most other "informals" remained squarely within the bounds of the permissible during 1988 and focused mainly on generating and demonstrating support for perestroika. Yet any group whose activities included independent criticism of the regime—even aspects of it that top leaders claimed to oppose, such as the repressions and institutional legacies of the Stalin era—encountered official resistance. The Communist Party Central Committee pressured organizers of Memorial, who intended to hold their founding conference in October, into postponing the meeting until January 1989. The party also seized control of the group's bank account and obstructed its operations in a number of other ways.[11]

Memorial's aims and the official responses it encountered were moderate and measured compared to the principles espoused and reaction roused by the Democratic Union, which came into being in the spring and summer in Moscow, Leningrad, Sverdlovsk, and several other major cities. The Democratic Union was a small but diverse conglomeration of tendencies united by the objective of establishing Western-style multiparty democracy. It was the first group to declare itself an alternative political party and to pose an unvarnished challenge to the regime. Immediately after its formation, it began staging frequent street demonstrations. The manifestations, which even in Moscow normally included no more than several dozen activists plus as many sympathizers and curiosity seekers, often provoked violent repression and arrests. Activists were subjected to heavy persecution; many had their homes raided by the police, and several were sent to prison.[12]

While state action toward informal groups ranged from watchful tolerance to naked, forcible repression, independent politics became a prominent subject of public debate. Discussion focused on two closely related questions. First, was the emergence of independent groups due merely to the "insufficiency" or "weakness" of official mass organizations, or was it a natural and desirable consequence of liberalization? Second, were the informals temporary corrective phenomena or healthy, permanent components of political life? Gorbachev, in conformity with his plan of reviving the party by acknowledging its ossification and subjecting it to limited pressure from the outside, stated in April that informals "exist because existing [official] organizations do not satisfy people in their activities, atmosphere, and methods."[13] Gorbachev was not reflexively hostile to all independent organization as long as it conformed to the goals of perestroika. But he did not indicate whether he regarded it as desirable in and of itself. Some conservative leaders and commentators, reflecting the long-standing socialist hostility to extra-state political organization, regarded the informals as fleeting aberrations that would vanish upon the "completion" of restructuring. More liberal voices invoked Bernsteinian notions that diversity of interests was inevitable and that autonomous associations were normal building blocks of socialist society.[14]

Independent political organizations were not, of course, the only major topic of public discussion during 1988. As glasnost' took hold and strictures on freedom of expression began to soften, debate over the military in society, the Afghanistan war, interethnic relations, and the crimes of Stalinism began to appear in the press. Divisions among top leaders became increasingly apparent. In March the newspaper *Sovetskaia Rossiia* (Soviet Russia) published a letter from an ultra-conservative Leningrad schoolteacher, Nina Andreeva, that defended Stalinism and challenged the whole basis of glasnost' and perestroika.[15] The letter caused a sensation in the Soviet Union. Many regarded it as the work of disgruntled conservatives in the top leadership and feared that it portended a hard-line resurgence. While suspicions that high-level officials stood behind the letter proved justified, fears of an impending demise of glasnost' and liberalization did not. The Nineteenth Conference of the CPSU, held in late June and early July, included clashes among party leaders over the direction and pace of reform. Portions of the conference were broadcast unedited on national television, exposing ordinary citizens for the first time to the spectacle of open disagreement and genuine give-and-take among leading officials.[16] *Samizdat* publications issued by new autonomous associations added nonofficial voices to the debate over policy and social change. Still, print runs of such papers were very small, and information about autonomous groups was not widely available.[17] No media organs and few of the informals themselves—the Democratic Union being a notable exception—yet challenged the Communist Party's monopoly on power.

Organizational Growth and Mass Mobilization: 1989

In a number of respects, 1989 stands out as the crucial takeoff phase for autonomous political activity in Russia. Popular involvement in independent politics increased exponentially; informal groups whose activities had been limited largely to discussion evolved into far more serious political actors; and laborers in a crucial sector of the economy broke with decades of imposed quiescence.

The crucial event of early 1989 was the March ballot for the USSR Congress of People's Deputies. The vote was the first even partially open and competitive national election in the history of the Soviet Union. It was held under rules and conditions that strongly favored candidates loyal to the Communist Party regime. One-third of all seats were reserved for representatives of state organizations controlled by the party, and procedures for nomination of candidates from territorial districts concentrated most authority in the hands of those who already had it. The election therefore produced anything but a radical legislature. It did, however, allow for the election of some individuals—albeit a small minority—who harbored revolutionary agendas. It conferred on such persons the legitimacy of deputyship and lent them a public platform from which they could bring the era of debate-free lawmaking by faceless figures swiftly to a close. Perhaps of greatest moment, the balloting engendered the closest thing that the populace had ever known to a real election campaign.

Three tendencies existed in the nascent democratic opposition at the outset of the election campaign in late 1988–early 1989.[18] The campaign brought these tendencies into bolder relief; stimulated some popular mobilization on behalf of each of them; provoked some competition among them; and finally brought them together into a broader and more energetic movement. Persons who had been active in the Moscow Popular Front represented the first tendency. Successful candidates associated with this current included the historian Sergei Stankevich and the journalist Iurii Chernichenko. The Front served as the nucleus of their campaigns. This camp may be characterized as liberal-progressive. Few of its exponents had ever suffered harsh persecution for dissident activity. Many were still members of the Communist Party. Most were proto-radicals—individuals who to some extent had worked "within the system" to advance career goals, but who relished the opportunities that liberalization created for extending the bounds of the permissible. Their political and social philosophies were liberal and "Westernizing"; their preferred modes of operation competitive but not confrontational; their dreams for the country's future expansive; and their personal political ambitions boundless.[19]

The second tendency was more narrow and comprised a group of scholars who enjoyed little experience in politics, as well as a number of human rights advocates associated with Memorial, some of whom had suffered political persecution. The rallying point for these forces was the candidacy of the celebrated human rights activist Andrei Sakharov. Sakharov's victory as a representative from the USSR Academy of Sciences was attributable in large part to the tenacity, commitment, and newfound political acumen of several dozen young academics who organized support in research institutes and overcame the opposition of the academy's conservative administrative establishment.

The third current possessed wider and more amorphous social and organizational bases than either of the other two tendencies. Its ethos was personalist and vaguely populist; its central concerns were social justice, curbing power holders' privileges, and fighting corruption. This tendency found expression in the efforts that shaped the campaigns of Boris El'tsin and Tel'man Gdlian. The latter was a lawyer who had acquired wild and widespread popularity for his courageous personal crusade against governmental corruption and malfeasance. These candidates were not, at the outset of the campaign, tied to informal groups such as Memorial or the Moscow Popular Front. They enjoyed support from diverse sources, including "work collectives" in a number of factories. Their partisans were mainly ordinary people who hungered for justice and far-reaching change but did not necessarily possess clear political philosophies and agendas.

During the early stage of the campaign, relations among the three currents were cool and detached. Representatives of the first two tendencies viewed what appeared to be the populism and personalism of the third with suspicion. Supporters of El'tsin and Gdlian, on the other hand, had scant use for the culture of programmatic and philosophical discussion that pervaded the first current, and little understanding of the dissident tradition that made up the essence of the second. But in the course of the campaign, communication among organizers representing each of the three tendencies improved, particularly as control of the nominating process by forces ill-disposed to radical change—mostly the Communist Party and its affiliates—became increasingly evident. Thus, common progressive aims and shared experience in struggle engendered some convergence of the three main currents.

Shortly after the election, these forces worked together to found what became the first umbrella group of democratic forces, the Moscow Union of Voters (its Russian acronym, MOI, will be used here). The group's bland name, which according to a leading activist was adopted out of fear of provoking repressive action, concealed its true nature as the embryo of a broadly based opposition.[20] The organizers of MOI held two founding conferences and arranged compromises among diverse tendencies to ensure that each was well represented in the leadership, which took the form of a coordinating council. The structure of the association included, in addition to the coordinating council, about thirty groups, most of which were based in Moscow's territorial units (raion) and a few of which functioned in work collectives and academic institutes. MOI also took on affiliates from outside Moscow, mostly other progressive voters' associations from large provincial cities. Thus, while the group's name suggested that its operations were limited to the capital city, it actually functioned as a nerve center for communication and coordination among progressive groups from around Russia. The association was infiltrated heavily by agents who tried to provoke splits. But MOI held together. In the fall of 1989, it organized some of Moscow's first mass political demonstrations, including a gathering of some 50,000 in November.

The initial sessions of the USSR Congress of People's Deputies in the spring and summer of 1989 revealed that the new body as a whole would be a pliant servant of its creator, Mikhail Gorbachev. Still, convocation of the new legislature was an important and dramatic event. Progressive deputies, though overwhelmingly outnumbered by guardians of the old order, proved a vigorous and vocal force. During the inaugural session in late May, much of the Soviet population sat transfixed in front of their televisions as El'tsin excoriated the privileges of the apparat, which he termed an elite class, and Olympic hero Iurii Vlasov openly criticized the KGB.[21] In July about 250 deputies, or roughly 10 percent of the Congress's membership, formed a progressive fraction dubbed the "Interregional Group." Chaired by El'tsin, Sakharov, historian Iurii Afanas'ev, economist Gavriil Popov, and Estonian Academician Viktor Palm, the group quickly came to resemble an informal opposition. Though undisciplined and loosely organized, it served as a high-profile insurgency within an otherwise undistinguished legislature, and a rallying point for emerging democratic groups throughout the Soviet Union.[22]

While MOI provided some framework for cooperation among democratic forces and the Interregional Group gave progressives a foothold in the Soviet legislature, smaller, more tightly knit groups began to evolve into more coherent and mature formations. Some clearly resembled parties-in-waiting. In mid-1989 the Moscow Popular Front and Democratic Perestroika disbanded and spawned the Social Democratic Association and several other proto-parties. Citizens' Dignity became the Union of Constitutional Democrats, and members signed a document expressing intention to found a political party.[23]

The second half of 1989 witnessed a number of unprecedentedly large national conferences of new democratic movement organizations. In September representatives of over sixty groups from forty cities throughout the Soviet Union convened in Leningrad. In October a large constituent congress of local popular fronts from around the Russian Republic met in Iaroslavl'. Such conferences rarely stimulated organizational integration. They were often marred by bickering over minor procedural questions and by long-winded and insubstantial speech making. But they did lend activists from diverse associations across many regions a feeling of solidarity and seemed to embolden them. The Leningrad conference adopted a resolution calling for restoration of private property, inauguration of multiparty democracy, and removal from the constitution of Article 6, which guaranteed the "leading role" of the Communist Party.[24]

Such a public statement represented part of a broader radicalization of movement organizations' demands and actions. At the end of October, Memorial staged, in front of KGB headquarters in Moscow, the first sizable public demonstration against the KGB. Misleading official press reports notwithstanding, the manifestation aimed not only to commemorate the victims of the secret police during the Stalin era, but to protest the KGB's contemporary role as an agent of political repression and control as well.[25]

New professional associations also appeared in 1989. In February several hundred lawyers met in Moscow to form an independent union. In April "Sotsprof," a union of professionals' and skilled workers' organizations from ten cities that sought to foster American-style trade unionism, was founded. In July the Alliance of United Cooperatives was formed, bringing together regional and sectoral cooperative associations in an all-Union alliance. The demands of these organizations were not limited to parochial, particularistic concerns. The lawyers' group urged the end of the politicization of the advocacy. The cooperatives' alliance sought "economic democratization" and "the development of the market and market relations in the economy."[26]

A growth in independent publications helped give voice to emerging groups. During 1989 the number of periodicals issued by independent sources tripled, rising to over 600. Print-runs, while still extremely modest compared to those of official publications, increased considerably.[27]

One of the most remarkable developments of 1989 was the sudden emergence of a militant labor movement in the coal mining industry. Storm clouds began gathering in the spring, when several hundred miners in Vorkuta, Noril'sk, and Taimyr briefly stopped work to protest their compensation and their bosses' highhandedness.[28] In July massive strikes rocked the mining regions of the Kuzbass in western Siberia, Vorkuta, and the Donbass in eastern Ukraine. The strikes were spontaneous and, at best, loosely organized, but they spawned strike committees that quickly assumed the form of independent unions. In November the United Workers of the Kuzbass, a mass-based, nonstate association made up mainly of miners, was born in Novokuznetsk. The union's demands mostly related to pay and work conditions. Yet its program also demanded the restoration of private property.[29]

State responses to the birth of autonomous miners' organizations exemplified methods that were becoming standard operating procedure in official policy toward challenges from below. One tactic was establishing ostensibly independent organizations under official control parallel to truly autonomous groups. Another was obstructing autonomous organizations' operations by infiltrating groups, threatening organizers, and disrupting communication among activists. In the case of the United Workers of the Kuzbass, party leaders in Kemerovo first attempted to block the organization's formation by banning strike committees and starting a new union under the control of local and provincial authorities. After the ploy failed to win miners' support or to avert the founding conference of the independent union, officials initiated what activists called a "war" against the movement, launching a campaign against it in the local media, firing organizers, and deploying "reliable" workers to infiltrate the union's meetings and obstruct its operations.[30]

The birth of the United Workers' Front (its Russian acronym is OFT) of the USSR in July and of the same organization on the level of Russian Soviet Federated Socialist Republic (RSFSR) in September served as another illustration of state strategy. The union, which attempted to bring together both blue- and white-collar workers from many sectors, called for strict central planning, as well as strong opposition to private property, cooperatives, and the "young Soviet bourgeoisie." Whatever its pretensions to represent the interests of labor, the OFT was organized by the conservative Leningrad and Sverdlovsk city and oblast' party apparats and a handful of conservative academics. It gained only a small fraction of the working-class support enjoyed by autonomous workers' groups.[31]

The tactic of creating puppet organizations was also evident in the realm of professional associations. In June, several months after the founding of the new independent lawyers' group, the Ministry of Justice announced the formation of the USSR Union of Lawyers, whose stated purpose was to "create a rule of law state" and promote "communist self-management" in the legal profession.[32] In August, just weeks after the birth of the Alliance of United Cooperatives, the official national trade union organization started a new trade union of cooperatives.[33]

The rapid, concurrent growth of independent organized pressures and state resistance to these pressures exposed several deep, underlying trends in Russian and Soviet politics. First, it demonstrated that initiative for radical reform had shifted, in roughest terms, from state to society. Gorbachev's scheme for revitalizing the Communist Party state by curbing its worst abuses and subjecting it to limited pressure from below was, by late 1989, no longer viable. The lion's share of popular mobilization, from the urban voters' clubs and popular fronts to the Kuzbass strike committees, was no longer taking place in the name of restructuring the existing system. It now aimed at effecting what would amount to revolution—even if many actors did not yet describe their efforts in such terms.

The emerging struggle between state and society also evinced a growing inconsistency in official policy. In late November the Supreme Soviet of the USSR approved a draft law banning censorship of the media and legalizing publication by private individuals.[34] One month later the popular progressive television news program "Vzgliad" (Viewpoint) was suddenly canceled.[35] In July the chairman of the Ideology Department of the Communist Party Central Committee lauded the growing pluralism of Soviet society and raised the possibility of a future multiparty system.[36] In December the special police units trained for quelling civil unrest (forces known in Russian as OMON) were still violently repressing small, peaceful public demonstrations by groups calling for a multiparty system on the streets of Moscow, Leningrad, and other major cities.[37] The erratic policy of taking with one hand what had just been proffered with the other doubtless reflected differences among top leaders at the center as well as among officials across cities and regions. But it also betrayed a more profound and systemic tension between what state leaders said they wanted and what they were not willing to give up, between political pluralism and the statist and monopolistic essence of the regime. In short, the events of 1989—particularly when placed in the international context of the ongoing revolutions in neighboring East Europe—betrayed the profound contradictions inherent in "reform communism," "socialist pluralism," and other bedrocks of the Gorbachevian political project. Recognizing these contradictions and asserting that a quiet reactionary turn was already underway, Andrei Sakharov warned in a speech in December that liberalization could not be expected to continue indefinitely in the absence of enormous pressure from below. Without both much closer ties between democratic activists and mass-based workers' groups and a strong will and capacity to execute mass political strikes at crucial junctures, he argued, the "partyocracy, the enormous and all-pervasive party apparat which represents real power in the country and which relies on its armed wing, the KGB, and the army," would gradually and inexorably abandon liberalization. In the final analysis, it would never pass down a significant measure of power to society unless forced to do so by the threat of mass uprisings and total loss of control.[38]

Sakharov's prediction proved perceptive and prescient. Still, it did not capture the full picture of what had unfolded during the previous year. For, as one radical activist from Sverdlovsk stated at end of the year, 1989 "was the year when the anti-totalitarian movement entered the realm of serious politics."[39]

Political Polarization and Organizational Differentiation: 1990

The year 1990 witnessed an acceleration of trends evident during the previous year, as well as a number of new developments that rapidly polarized political life. The Communist Party began to show signs of strain; a new round of elections stimulated popular mobilization and produced substantial changes in some legislatures; alternative political parties came into existence and banded together under the banner of a national umbrella organization; and the process of rapid, if ambivalent, liberalization ground to a halt and was even reversed in some areas.

The first month of 1990 was marked by the dramatic emergence of a radical reform movement in the CPSU. Dissatisfaction with the pace of change among some party members was not new. Many members of the Interregional Group of People's Deputies, as well as some organizers of groups such as MOI, were party members. "Party clubs" of liberal Communists and Komsomol members had been gathering informally in many cities for several months.[40] The founding of the Democratic Platform of the CPSU in January 1990 lent organizational structure to a tendency within the party that desired far faster and more thoroughgoing transformation than that pursued by Gorbachev and the party leadership. The Democratic Platform sought to abandon the principle of "democratic centralism" within the party and to establish Western-style parliamentary democracy.[41]

At the time of the Platform's founding, some of its organizers believed that the CPSU could convert itself from a monopolistic state structure into a "normal" parliamentary political party.[42] By the middle of the year most members had given up such a hope. At its second all-Union conference, held in mid-June, the Platform issued statements condemning "the growing unity of conservative forces" and warning of a possible "return to totalitarianism." It noted the recent formation within the CPSU of the Russian Communist Party (RKP), which brought together many of the republic's most powerful party functionaries under the ultra-conservative leadership of Ivan Poloskov. The Platform demanded an end to three pillars of the party's dominance of state and society: its territorial and workplace structures, the nomenklatura system, and the ban on factions. Aware that their aims were as unrealistic as they were nonnegotiable, delegates sketched their plan to quit the party and found a new one if their demands were not met at the upcoming 28th Party Congress.[43]

To no one's surprise, they were not. The Congress, at which the Democratic Platform's representatives constituted only a tiny fraction of the roughly 5,000 delegates, only highlighted what the Platform's organizers had come to regard as the party's conservatism and institutional bankruptcy. The conflict between the orthodox majority and the small insurgent faction came to a head at the Congress when El'tsin announced his resignation from the party. Twenty-four other delegates followed him.[44]

The drama that unfolded in the CPSU was accompanied by equally significant events outside the party. In March elections were held for soviets on the republican, oblast', city, and district levels. Candidates who identified themselves with the democratic movement scored major victories in some places, achieving majorities in the Moscow and Leningrad City Soviets and sizable minorities in some other legislatures, including the RSFSR Congress of People's Deputies. Gavriil Popov gained election by fellow deputies as chairman of the Mossoviet; Anatolii Sobchak won the chairmanship of the Lensoviet. Soon after the elections, progressives in the new RSFSR Congress of People's Deputies founded a group called the Democratic Russia bloc. This fraction neither functioned as a political party nor constituted an absolute majority. But it was larger and more influential than the Interregional Group in the all-Union legislature, as was demonstrated by El'tsin's election as chairman of the republic's Supreme Soviet.[45] In June the new parliament adopted a declaration of republican state sovereignty; the Ukrainian legislature quickly followed suit. What would soon become known as the "war of laws" between the center and the republican legislatures had begun.[46]

Like the 1989 elections for the all-Union parliament, the 1990 elections spurred popular mobilization. The two months before the March 1990 vote were a time of huge public demonstrations in many Russian cities. In February several meetings in Moscow each attracted some quarter-million people. Speakers' oratory, as well as the placards carried and slogans chanted by participants, reflected a radicalization of the democratic movement. Invective was now aimed less at unpopular individual officials, the KGB, and "opponents of perestroika" than at the Communist Party regime as a whole. The stated goal of participants was not "reform" but rather democracy.[47] Some of the activists who had founded groups such as MOI and Memorial and who had organized progressive candidates' campaigns in 1989, such as Lev Ponomarev and Gleb Iakunin, themselves won election to the RSFSR Congress of People's Deputies in 1990.

During the four-month period between the March elections and the 28th Party Congress of the CPSU, a host of new political parties was born in Russia. Reacting quickly to the recent removal of Article 6 from the constitution, the Social Democratic Association became the Social Democratic Party of Russia (SDPR). The Democratic Party of Russia (DPR) and the Russian Christian Democratic Movement (RKhDD) came into existence. Lesser parties founded during this time included two groups of "Kadets": the Party of Constitutional Democrats (PKD) and the Constitutional Democrats/Party of Popular Freedom (KD/PNS). Several small anarchist parties and minor Christian Democratic organizations were born as well. In November some members of the Democratic Platform, many of whom had already quit the CPSU during or soon after its 28th Congress, founded the Republican Party of Russia (RPR).[48]

These groups, while political parties in name, by no means suddenly created a structure for a genuine multiparty system. Compared to the CPSU, parties in many Western and developing countries, or some new political parties in contemporary East Europe, Russia's new parties were very small. Only the DPR and the RPR, each of which numbered some twenty thousand at the time of their inception, enjoyed memberships of more than a few thousand. The founding of the RPR proved to be particularly disappointing. Despite its paltry representation at the 28th Party Congress, the Democratic Platform, according to polling data, enjoyed the support of some 40 percent of all Communist Party members in Russia during the summer of 1990. Thus, as they broke with the CPSU and planned the founding of what would become the RPR, the Democratic Platform's leaders expected their new party instantly to attract mass membership, perhaps several million people. They hoped to establish a weighty opposition to the CPSU on the basis of mass defections of disaffected Communists, and even to acquire a sizable portion of the party's property in the process. But rather than actually split the CPSU as planned, the RPR merely peeled off a tiny sliver of its membership and gained possession of none of the former's massive holdings. Some of those who declared their support for the Democratic Platform retained their Communist Party cards despite their opposition, though many quit paying dues and ceased participating in party activities. Others, including many prominent organizers of the Democratic Platform, quit the Communist Party but joined no other.[49]

Despite the new parties' humble and even disappointing beginnings, their geneses represented a remarkable development. After seven decades of pure monism, Russian politics now included bona fide institutions of opposition—even if not a "normal" multiparty system.

Soon after their founding, most of the new parties, along with other nonstate groups, began creating a framework for cooperation. Drawing on the fame and popular prestige of the Democratic Russia group in the new RSFSR legislature, deputies from that bloc as well as many activists outside parliament resolved to erect a broad umbrella over Russia's democratic movement organizations. In July they formed an organizing committee to begin working toward founding what would become the Democratic Russia Movement. In September three of the leading democratic organizations—the DPR, the SDPR, and the Democratic Platform (some of whose members were now planning the establishment of the RPR)—announced that they were forming a coalition, and that deputies from their groups would work together in soviets on all levels. In October the Democratic Russia Movement (hereafter referred to as Democratic Russia) held its founding conference in Moscow. Most prodemocratic parties and other political organizations joined as collective members. Many voters' associations and local popular fronts, such as MOI and its counterparts and affiliates in other cities, ceased existence as such in order to found local Democratic Russia chapters. Aiming to create a broad and inclusive organization, founders decided to offer membership on an individual as well as a collective basis. At their inaugural conference, organizers reckoned that their group encompassed about 100,000 individuals from the sum of collective memberships, plus about three to four times more individual members. Even these numbers, rather modest in a country the size of Russia, were probably overly optimistic. The group was loosely organized and riven by internal divisions even at its inception. It was, in short, no Solidarity. But it did represent by far the most formidable prodemocratic force in Russia to that time. It created a framework for cooperation among progressive groups, as well as some organized basis for competition between them and the Communist Party regime on all levels.[50]

The official policy of selective, erratic tolerance of popular mobilization evident in 1989 continued in 1990. A number of large-scale demonstrations held during the first half of the year, including many of the enormous public meetings in February, occurred without incident. Other demonstrations, however, continued to encounter repressive police action. In mid-March, for example, a meeting of the Democratic Union in Moscow was broken up violently by OMON troops, and thirteen participants were arrested.[51] In Saratov, police beat and arrested participants in a peaceful, prodemocratic May Day demonstration, including some deputies from local soviets.[52]

Another tactic evident in official policy was a press blockade of the opposition. Most large-circulation national, regional, and local newspapers, as well as Soviet television, rarely covered the democratic movement. When they did, information was often grossly distorted. Leaders of new autonomous organizations were smeared, or stories created the appearance that the organization in question supported "dialogue" or "consolidation" with the CPSU. Coverage of the Democratic Platform, which earlier had enjoyed some modest attention in the official press, virtually vanished after the group split with the CPSU after the 28th Party Congress.[53] Groups battled the information blockade by publishing their own newspapers whenever and wherever possible, and by recounting their activities orally at street demonstrations. Political barriers to information flow were lowered somewhat in 1990 as authorities in some places eased up on repression of independent publishing. But material obstacles grew more onerous. Specifically, the state paper monopoly "freed" prices on the paper it sold to independent sources, while maintaining "state" prices on that supplied to publishers of official newspapers. By the fall of 1990, the new "free market" rate for paper was ten times higher than that paid by state agencies.[54] The exorbitant cost of paper—not to mention the difficulties of gaining access to printing presses—dealt a strong blow to the independent press. Still, given the willingness of many citizens to pay many times more for independent publications in the few cities where they were readily available, financial problems failed to halt the growth of alternative newspapers, journals, and leaflets. The growing radicalism of several official newspapers whose editors and staffs had managed to break free from party control, notably *Moskovskie Novosti* (Moscow News) and *Moskovskii Komsomolets* (Moscow Komsomol), further alleviated problems of information shortage and disinformation, at least in the capital city.

As will be discussed in succeeding chapters, state resistance to pressures from below strongly influenced the development of democratic movement organizations. Still, through mid-1990, measures such as selective violence and intimidation aimed against activists, establishment of puppet organizations, and information blockade were also accompanied by some liberalizing policies. The removal of Article 6 from the constitution, which effectively lifted the ban on alternative parties, served as an example. State resistance neither shut down the democratic movement nor assumed the appearance of an about-face.

But in the fall, events began to lend credence to the warning that Sakharov had issued at the end of 1989. In September, at a plenum of the Russian Communist Party, a Committee of National Salvation was formed. The committee called for banning all alternative political parties, and even for freeing and arming prisoners willing to aid the cause of restoration. The conservative "Soiuz" (Union) fraction of the Union legislature backed the committee's demands.[55] Toward the end of the year, Gorbachev replaced a number of relatively liberal top officials with hard-liners. Interior Minister Vadim Bakatin, who had opposed use of troops to put down pro-independence demonstrations in the Baltics, was replaced by Boris Pugo, for whom the epithet "Stalinist" was scarcely too strong. On December 20, in a stunning speech before the USSR Congress of People's Deputies, Eduard Shevardnadze resigned his post as foreign minister and warned of an impending dictatorship.[56] In a televised speech before the same body two days later, the KGB chief, Vladimir Kriuchkov, assailed the growth of "antisocialist forces" and spun a series of bizarre conspiracy theories linking the Soviet Union's woes to domestic and foreign enemies.[57] During the same month, the chairman of the USSR Supreme Soviet, Anatolii Luk'ianov, made liberal use of his control of microphones in the legislature, cutting off deputies' speeches at the moment that they began to include criticism of the Communist Party or the Union government.[58] During the last week of the year, Interior Minister Pugo and Defense

Minister Dmitrii Iazov, acting on orders from Gorbachev, began deploying army troops alongside police units on the streets of some major cities, effecting what amounted to a kind of partial martial law.[59]

Reaction and Resistance: January–August 1991

The reaction that began in late 1990 intensified in early 1991. In January Gorbachev demanded and received a host of special decree powers from the USSR Congress of People's Deputies.[60] Much of the official media returned to stilted, preglasnost'-style reporting. A partial crackdown occurred against independent publications, several of which were at least temporarily shut down.[61] In mid-January troops sent by the central government struck out against the independence movement in Lithuania, seizing control of communications facilities and killing thirteen people during the ensuing demonstrations.[62] In further efforts to reassert its own primacy, the central government placed all republican banks under direct control of the KGB.[63]

The hard turn to the right elicited prompt, substantial popular resistance. While it failed fully to unify the democratic movement, it completed the process of polarization between the movement and the state. It reduced to an extremely low level what popular support the leadership and the regime might still have enjoyed, and it greatly enhanced the prestige of El'tsin and other figures associated with the democratic movement. It established a polarized antagonism between state and society that in some respects resembled that which prevailed in Poland during the 1980s. In immediate response to events in Lithuania, the Moscow chapter of the Union of Work Collectives, a broad coalition of workers' groups organized in 1990 at the initiative of coal miners' organizations, staged a brief political strike, demanding the resignation of Gorbachev and the Union government. In late January and February a series of prodemocratic public demonstrations on a scale not seen since February 1990 took place in many Russian cities.[64] In mid-February El'tsin, who despite his chairmanship of the RSFSR Supreme Soviet had for months been denied access to national media, was permitted to appear on prime-time television. He was not allowed to address the audience directly and was limited to an interview format. Yet he used the opportunity harshly to condemn Gorbachev, the CPSU, and the Union government, and to call for popular struggle against them and for full sovereignty for the Russian Republic.[65]

The spring of 1991 was marked by a flurry of political activity. In mid-March a referendum sought by Gorbachev on the future of the

Union was held. The measure, which asked voters whether they favored "a renewed Union," passed. Yet the referendum, in which one-third of the republics did not even take part, did nothing to stem the republican independence movements. And in the Russian Republic, voters were also asked whether they favored creation of a directly elected presidency of the RSFSR. A majority answered yes, setting the stage for the first national election for a chief executive in Russian history.[66]

March and April witnessed a massive new round of strikes by coal miners in the Kuzbass, the Donbass, the Mosbass, and other mining regions. The strikes of mid-1989 had centered mostly on economic demands. In 1991 the strikes were political. Demands included full sovereignty for the Russian Republic (in parts of the Donbass, for the Ukrainian Republic); the resignation of Gorbachev and the Union government and the formation of a "round table" of republican leaders to negotiate new interrepublican arrangements without leadership of the CPSU; and elimination of Communist Party organizations from the workplace (departiization).[67]

The timing of the miners' strikes stemmed in part from a desire to express support for El'tsin in advance of the third (extraordinary) session of the RSFSR Congress of People's Deputies, scheduled for early April. As they prepared for the session, conservative deputies made clear that they intended to bring El'tsin down with a no-confidence vote. But the session did not turn out as the conservatives had intended. The acrimonious approach of El'tsin's antagonists, El'tsin's own highly politic speech before the Congress, and pressures emanating from the streets and from the mines pushed many in the Congress's sizable bloc of waverers to side with democrats. El'tsin also benefited from the realization among even his detractors that avoiding an early, direct ballot for the presidency would be difficult given the result of the recent referendum, and that El'tsin's overwhelming popularity would almost certainly carry him to the new office. El'tsin therefore survived—though by a scant margin—as chairman of the Congress.[68]

In another development propitious to progressives, Aleksandr Rutskoi, a hero of the war in Afghanistan whom El'tsin chose as his vice-presidential running mate, started a group in the Congress dubbed "Communists for Democracy." The bloc's stated aims were as incongruous as its name, and only a small proportion of deputies formally joined it. Still its formation aided the democrats. Like the revolt of the Democratic Platform the year before, the move shaved another sliver off the body of the CPSU.[69]

During the spring and early summer of 1991, the democratic movement as a whole displayed encouraging signs of growth and maturation. Across the country, Democratic Russia became a real political force. It enjoyed great popular prestige and repeatedly exhibited an impressive capacity to organize public demonstrations at critical moments. In March, on the eve of the convocation of the RSFSR Congress of People's Deputies, it mobilized huge mass meetings in support of El'tsin in many cities.[70] As its ability to mobilize the populace grew, so did its capacity to mobilize resources. During one large two-hour demonstration in Moscow on March 10, it collected contributions totaling 170,000 rubles—at the time, no meager sum. By June it had established ties with several nascent sources of autonomous economic power, and had begun subsidizing local chapters in provincial cities.[71] In the meantime, several new parties emerged and placed themselves under its umbrella. Examples include the People's Party, lead by Tel'man Gdlian, and the Party of Free Labor, a gathering of aspiring entrepreneurs dedicated to economic liberalism.[72]

But the democratic movement also suffered from debilitating shortcomings. Despite considerable congruence of aims, Democratic Russia and its constituent groups, on the one hand, and the workers' movement, on the other, remained largely estranged; little framework for cooperation and coordinated action was realized. The workers' movement itself remained limited largely to the coal miners. While "workers' clubs" and independent unions of modest size and strength formed in pockets of some other sectors, only the miners achieved a level of organization and militancy that allowed for effective large-scale strikes.[73]

Despite its growing human and financial strength, Democratic Russia began to fragment in the spring and summer of 1991. Conflicts centered on issues such as whether mass demonstrations remained an appropriate mode of action, or whether the group should focus exclusively on organization-building and preparation for election campaigns; whether the umbrella group or its constituent parties should lead the democratic movement; and whether the republics should go their own ways or attempt to preserve some type of "non-Communist" union.[74] In April the DPR, RKhDD, and KD/PNS formed a bloc within the larger organization called "Popular Accord." While the bloc's leaders claimed that they did not intend to leave Democratic Russia altogether, the action did eventually prove to have been the beginning of the end of a unified democratic movement organization.[75]

Divisions within Democratic Russia blocked what many activists regarded as a crucial prerequisite to effective, sustained struggle with the regime: the emergence of a large, powerful, prodemocratic political party. El'tsin's lack of desire to found and lead such a party also checked its formation. After expressing some interest in the possibility in March, El'tsin dropped the idea and thereafter argued that his responsibilities in government prevented him from participating in such an endeavor.[76]

The parties that made up the nucleus of Democratic Russia suffered many of the same problems as the broader umbrella group. During the spring and early summer, internal quarrels among leaders enervated most of the new parties. The RPR and the SDPR were each bitterly divided over an effort made by some members of each group to achieve a full union between the two. Not only did a union of the two parties not occur, but each of them individually became deeply factionalized over the issue. The DPR experienced defections and serious divisions over what many members regarded as the dictatorial style of its chairman, Nikolai Travkin. By the summer the Democratic Union had split so many times that little was left of it save a few small chapters in a handful of major cities. Unsurprisingly, internal discord did not aid groups' efforts to expand membership and following. In contrast with initial expectations, none of the new parties experienced substantial growth. Several actually shrunk between the time of their founding and the coup attempt of August 1991.[77]

Despite quarrels and internal divisions, the democratic movement was united around several core goals and principles. The main aim was the destruction of the Communist Party system of rule and the transition to some form of democracy. Another was scrapping the command economy and moving toward a market system. By the spring of 1991 almost all democrats viewed opposition to "the center" and sovereignty for the Russian Republic as the best means to these ends. Due to the progressive profile of the RSFSR parliament (compared to its Union counterpart) and El'tsin's leadership, democrats envisaged what amounted to secession of Russia from the USSR— strange as the notion may seem—as the most promising route to revolution. Even democrats who wanted to preserve some form of Union and who opposed granting autonomy to small nations within the RSFSR, such as some leaders of the DPR, RKhDD, and KD/PNS, supported "full republican sovereignty"—that is, statehood—for Russia.[78] Democrats were also united by one overriding practical task: El'tsin's election to the Russian presidency. During the period between the referendum of mid-March and El'tsin's victory in the presidential vote of mid-June, the campaign served as a source of solidarity within and among democratic organizations.

The period leading up to and immediately following the election witnessed little real change in the direction of policy emanating from the center. Gorbachev's plan to sign the "9 plus 1" treaty, which would have ceded some authority to republican governments, did appear to represent some softening, at least on the part of the president on the question of decentralization. For the most part, however, the trend toward conservative reaction evident earlier in the year did not abate. In April Luk'ianov purged the USSR Supreme Soviet's committees and commissions of their progressive members.[79] A number of democratic activists, including the editor of a prominent alternative newspaper issued by the SDPR, were murdered in Moscow under very peculiar circumstances.[80] In May the Moscow apartment that served as the SDPR's national headquarters was ransacked and documents and equipment were destroyed.[81] In mid-June Prime Minister Valentin Pavlov requested special powers from the USSR Supreme Soviet; and KGB chief Kriuchkov, Defense Minister Iazov, and Interior Minister Pugo—who two months hence would attempt to impose their will by force—spoke out strongly against devolution of power to the republics and against liberalization in general.[82]

On the eve of the August putsch, the central government and the Communist Party continued to control the levers of real power in Russia: the means of coercion, production, distribution, and, to a lesser but still considerable extent, communication. But the force of the state had been reduced to *negative* power. The center and the party could prevent, obstruct, and coerce; but they could no longer even pretend to initiate, create, and convince. A motley conglomeration of autonomous societal organizations, spearheading a popular movement for democracy, had rendered power visible: that is, they had exposed the illegitimacy, brutality, and ineffectiveness of the existing political system. In doing so, they had begun to push it toward its demise. They did not yet possess the strength to destroy the system themselves. To accomplish that end, forces within the state itself, in a sudden, dramatic act of retrogression, would have to provide inadvertent assistance. Democratic movement organizations had closed the curtain on six decades of totalitarianism and demonstrated an impressive capacity to express and to mobilize. But their access to real power was still severely limited, and their ability to create an institutional basis for democracy remained very much in question.

III

Investigating the Phenomenon:
A Framework for Analysis

WHAT DID the groups examined in the previous chapter create? By the time of the abortive putsch, they clearly had forged a new independent political society and exerted substantial pressures on state institutions. How might the new society be characterized and its emergence explained? To what extent, moreover, did revolutionary societal organizations create the basis for democratic regime change in Russia?

Construction of the "dependent variable" stands as an especially complex part of this study, mainly because the study seeks to explain not a concrete, discrete event (e.g., a military coup, an electoral victory or defeat), but rather the emergence of a particular type of political society that heretofore has been poorly understood. The chapter therefore begins with close analysis of the phenomenon that will be explained. Did a civil society evolve in Russia, as many sovietologists argued? Or did something else emerge?

The Dependent Variable Defined

Conceptualizing Civil Society

"Civil society" is a slippery concept; there exist nearly as many conceptions of it as theorists who have examined it. Some definitions focus on concrete institutions, such as interest groups or the market. Others employ more normative or philosophical concepts such as individualism, privacy, and civility. Most theorists have defined civil society at least in part as the realm of independent, self-organized, and self-governing associations. Nearly all modern theorists of civil society, moreover, have insisted upon maintaining a distinction between state and society in their definitions.[1] In contrast with the literature on East Europe, most sovietology does not show the mark of close familiarity with modern or classical thinking on civil society. Though a number of sovietologists have applied the notion of "civil society" to Russia or the Soviet Union, only a sovietologist would include state agencies, or groups within state agencies, within the realm of civil society.[2] Such concept stretching, combined with the rapid pace of change in Russia, may have discouraged serious efforts at assessing precisely how far Russia had actually gone toward realizing a genuine civil society.

John Keane's definition provides a starting point for discussion. According to Keane, "Civil society may be conceived of as an aggregate of institutions whose members are engaged primarily in a complex of non-state activities—economic and cultural production, household life and voluntary associations—and who in this way preserve and transform their identity by exercising all sorts of pressures or controls upon state institutions . . . [its] units . . . are legally guaranteed and self-organizing."[3]

In its maintenance of the distinction between state and society, and its emphasis upon association, Keane's conception is consistent with most modern definitions. It is not, moreover, overly restrictive. It does not insist upon the presence of a "liberal tradition" or highly developed notions of "individuality" or "privacy" as prerequisites or diagnostic features—requirements that would rule out any discussion of civil society in Russia.

As Salvador Giner has argued, no paradigmatic civil society exists in the real world, only concrete individual civil societies, some more mature, or closer to an ideal, than others. Any comparative conception of civil society must, therefore, be ideal-typical.[4] To employ the concept for analytical purposes, several indicators of what might be regarded as a mature or "ideal" civil society are put forward here. Since this study examines concrete institutions in a given society (independent associations in Russia), the indicators are institutional, not normative. They focus on the nature of independent organizational forms. Since the indicators compose an ideal-typical model, they are continuous: societies may score "high" or "low" or somewhere in-between along different indicators in terms of "civil societyishness." One would expect a civil society of any degree of maturity to score high along at least several of the indicators. All Western and many developing countries would score high along all of them. The indicators do not, of course, provide a complete picture of society, nor do they fully capture all possible activities and institutions suggested in Keane's definition. They may, however, furnish an illuminating means of examining society's organizational forms.[5]

The first indicator regards groups' capacities for *aggregating* interests, which requires the definition and organization of interests. Capacity for interest aggregation depends on the identification of "cleavage issues" and the formulation of specific goals and agendas. It also involves the formation of a collective identity, which includes the identification of a membership. The aggregation of interests entails not only differentiation among groups' agendas and memberships, but also the formation of vertical and horizontal links among diverse social actors.

Interest aggregation helps make possible the *representation* of interests—the second indicator. Capacity for interest representation rests on what Claus Offe calls "solidarity norms" within associations, as well as on groups' "internal obligatory capacities." Effective organized representation of interests depends in part on the ability of groups both to acquire adequate resources from members (e.g., voluntary labor, donations) and to bind members and followers to strategic positions.[6] Interest representation requires that groups establish sufficient sway over members to articulate their goals in a larger political arena.

Interest *articulation*, the third indicator, is understood here not merely as the expression of group interests, but as their translation into concrete political claims and demands. Closely related to articulation are *access* and *control*, which will be considered together as the fourth indicator. *Access* requires channels for expressing demands and making claims and arenas for political competition. *Control* concerns groups' capacities for influencing outcomes and enforcing agreements. It refers to ability to offer sufficient incentives to state agencies, other groups, or the public as a whole to obtain recognition, protection, concessions, or other resources needed for the group's survival and effective operation.

The final indicator, *autonomy*, concerns associations' independence from the state and their ability freely to articulate members' interests. Legal guarantees enhance groups' capacities for independent action, though self-constituted associations may influence policy or public opinion even in the absence of legal protection. Property rights and free markets may contribute to the autonomy of groups by enabling them to establish independent resource bases and secure inputs without relying on the beneficence of the state. In addition to enhancing autonomy, independent resource bases may contribute to groups' internal obligatory capacities and thus enhance representative functions by furnishing group leaders with the means needed to provide "selective incentives" to members.[7]

Testing the Model

As of the end of the Soviet period, how did the new independent associations in Russia measure up according to these indicators? While exceptions to "rules" or central tendencies abound, examination of some of the most highly developed associations in light of the indicators presented here illuminates the extent to which they forged an institutional basis for civil society in Russia.

First, it should be noted that many of the independent organizations aimed to transform or overthrow the basic structure of domination, not just widen the sphere for independent activity in society. In this respect, they differed considerably from some of the associations that led the struggle against Communist rule in East Europe. For Solidarity in Poland and Charter 77 in Czechoslovakia, creating "public space" for autonomous social activity—that is, reducing the totality of state power by pushing the state out of certain realms of social life—for years took precedence over attempts actually to bring down the regime.[8] In the Russian case, most of the new political parties and trade unions, as well as other major political associations, aimed explicitly to destroy the power of the apparat, de-ideologize the state, and establish a market economy and democracy. Most groups focused less on the development of society than on transformation of the state. Indeed, many regarded democratization as a crucial prerequisite for the development of a vibrant and potent civil society.

The shared aim of rapid revolutionary change may have influenced the new groups' capacities for *aggregating* interests. Specifically, it contributed to a lack of differentiation in ideological orientations and policy prescriptions. To be sure, differences existed between democratic and "national-patriotic" or conservative forces. But among the progressive groups, who represented by far the strongest and best-organized tendency, programmatic goals differed very little. All favored a law-governed state and democracy. Yet the Democratic Party of Russia and the Party of Constitutional Democrats, both of which claimed to be purely liberal (in the European sense) in orientation, were little more "liberal" than the Social Democratic Party of Russia, and the latter scarcely more "socialist" than the former. As will be demonstrated in following chapters, some differences in outlook did exist among democratic groups. But these differences rarely found clear expression in groups' programs and were little known and poorly understood by the general public.[9]

Lack of ideological and programmatic differentiation among groups added to difficulties in targeting potential members and constituencies in broader society. One Soviet observer argued that the SDPR's stated goal of "capitalizing socialism"—a task that the party's leaders admitted was the opposite of that faced by their West European counterparts—would undermine its ability to attract urban skilled workers, the traditional stronghold of social democratic parties.[10] During its first one-and-a-half years of existence, the party's membership grew very little, and in August 1991 it stood at only about four thousand members, over 80 percent of whom classified themselves as "intellectuals." Another group of similar orientation, the Republican Party of Russia, had a similar social profile. Its membership actually *declined* during its first year, and in June 1991 membership figures were revised downward from original estimates of twenty thousand to about five thousand.[11] Even the largest of the new parties, the DPR, which in the summer of 1991 boasted a membership of 30,000, did not identify a set of concrete interests on which to build mass membership. The party's chairman held that his group's "social basis" consisted not of any particular class, occupational groups, or sets of interests, but simply of "those who agree with us and share our goals."[12] Not surprisingly, despite the declaration of one major independent trade union that "without strong connection with progressive intellectuals, there will be no real workers' movement," little vertical integration of democratic tendencies took place.[13] Nor did significant horizontal integration of democratic groups occur. Democratic Russia provided some basis for coordinated action. But it was plagued by internal divisions and did not engender the integration of like-minded tendencies.[14] In fact, between the summer of 1990 and the fall of 1991, most of the organizations that constituted Democratic Russia themselves experienced splits and mass defections.[15] In sum, vaguely defined programs and constituencies, weakly differentiated interests, inchoate organizational integration, and internal divisions remained substantial obstacles to effective aggregation of interests.

How far did autonomous associations go toward generating the internal "solidarity norms" and "obligatory capacities" necessary for *representation* of interests? To borrow Philippe Schmitter's criteria for representation, did the associations "structure themselves internally and engage in such relevant activities that they offer[ed] sufficient incentives to their members so that they [could] extract adequate resources in the form of dues, fees, taxes, donations, voluntary labor, compliance, etc. to ensure their survival if not their organizational growth"?[16] One may discern two major obstacles to effective representation. The first was the poverty of most organizations. The second regards groups' internal structures. While there existed a great diversity of organizational forms, few groups structured themselves in a manner that maximized their representative capacities. The organization of most groups was, in a word, hyperdemocratic. The new parties, trade unions, and umbrella organizations shunned hierarchy in favor of broad collective leadership. Lines of authority and responsibility were typically very poorly defined, often producing organizational paralysis and a leadership style that may be termed collective irresponsibility. Groups' conferences—typically anarchic marathons in which heated debates over whether to allot fifteen or twenty minutes to an agenda item could consume half an hour, and in which hard questions of organization, membership recruitment, and political strategy often went unaddressed—were exercises in hyperdemocracy. As if cognizant of Bernstein's admonition that "the idea of the limitation of the power of the state by means of groups, when the principle of subordination and centralization rules in these groups themselves is inconsistent, not to say contradictory," many activists regarded hierarchical structures and clearly defined lines of authority as incompatible with their aims in broader society.[17] From the standpoint of cultivating habits of democratic participation and competition—functions Tocqueville observed with approval in mid-nineteenth-century interest associations in the United States—hyperdemocratic structures and procedures may offer distinct advantages.[18] They may not, however, furnish an optimal basis for developing the solidarity norms and internal obligatory capacities necessary for representation of interests.

Problems of resource mobilization and organizational structure did not completely prevent groups from establishing some powers of representation. Some resource-poor organizations secured a remarkable degree of loyalty and substantial contributions of energy from their members, and several experimented with fund-raising techniques that would allow for the establishment of full-time, paid staffs. The formation of links with cooperatives' associations provided another possible avenue for overcoming poverty.

In sum, few of the independent organizations scored high on their capacities for effective representation of interests. The picture was mixed, however, and included instances in which groups achieved a great deal of member support and devised innovative, if not highly successful, strategies for overcoming obstacles to effective interest representation.

While some organizations demonstrated progress toward developing capacities for interest representation, their abilities to *articulate* interests, to open channels of *access* to the state, and to *control* the process of interest intermediation with state institutions remained severely limited. Mechanisms for gaining access to state agencies, including party committees, ministries, and soviets, were poorly developed. Independent organizations managed to have "their" representatives elected to soviets on all levels in 1989 and 1990, but only in rare cases did the new associations, *as organized groups*, manage to establish relationships with state agencies based on the interaction, negotiation, and bargaining that characterize pluralist, corporatist, or syndicalist intermediation. The very concept of "lobbying" in Russian parlance usually refers to the existence of advocates of certain interests *within* official organizations, not to the application of pressure by extra-state organizations.[19] This is not to argue that no real lobbying in the Western sense of the word took place. Through personal contacts with sympathetic officials, members of independent groups sometimes articulated demands and attempted to influence policy. Yet such activity was usually informal and ad hoc, and formal channels for access to policymakers remained poorly developed.

Lack of internal obligatory capacities meant that few groups could offer state institutions the inducements necessary to influence policy. Simply stated, few of the independent associations developed the strength needed to affect policy substantially *as groups*. Furthermore, throughout the Gorbachev years, state agencies demonstrated a persistent unwillingness, even inability, to recognize independent associations as legitimate vehicles for interest intermediation. Intermediation and power-sharing were foreign to the experience of most state officials in Russia; hence their efforts to coopt and "channel" the activities of independent groups toward "unity" with state agencies, and their creation of official bodies whose functions ostensibly paralleled those of certain autonomous organizations.

The negotiations that took place between striking coal miners and state officials during the summer of 1989, which resulted in promises of concessions, would seem to provide an exceptional case. Yet this case actually illustrates the difficulties autonomous organizations experienced in gaining official recognition as representatives of group interests. In September 1989 the Independent Mining Industry Workers Union failed to break with the official trade union after hundreds of representatives of the latter infiltrated a meeting and struck down a resolution calling for independence. Undaunted, representatives of strike committees vowed to form a committee to control the implementation of agreements drawn up with the government following the summer strikes.[20] But the group's ability to monitor and enforce the agreements was severely restricted by the intransigence of official unions and the unresponsiveness of central authorities. The strike committees initially secured an unusual degree of influence over their constituents (representation), translated grievances into concrete claims and demands (articulation), and even forced state officials to the bargaining table (access). But they were unable to sustain official recognition as representatives of their members. As the strikes of the spring of 1991 and the demands accompanying them demonstrated, the miners were also incapable of enforcing the terms of agreements with state officials (control). If the later round of strikes evinced the enduring representative capacity of strike committees, they also revealed the persistent inability or unwillingness of the state to enter into genuine bargaining with independent forces. During the 1991 strikes, for example, Prime Minister Valentin Pavlov, after much hesitation, finally agreed to meet with miners' representatives—but then only with "strike committees" that represented workers who were not on strike. The strikes ceased only when the Union government agreed to transfer control of the mines to the government of the Russian Federation. The move did represent an acknowledgment of the miners' power by the Union government. Yet workers finally returned to the mines not after genuine negotiations and settlement with either the Union or republican government, but simply on the promise of El'tsin that he, rather than the central authorities, would control proceeds from mining activities. Sporadic, uncoordinated strikes continued throughout the spring and summer of 1991, as many miners refused to regard El'tsin's promise as adequate redress of their grievances.[21]

To be sure, the history of the Gorbachev period is not lacking in instances of independent groups bringing pressure to bear on officialdom. In Bashkiria, for example, popular resistance, organized by an ecological group and a voters' association, led to the replacement of a hated party first secretary and some of his associates. But the case was typical of a number of "regional revolutions" in that the new leadership proved to be little more responsive to popular grievances—in this case, ecological concerns—than its predecessor. Street demonstrations forced personnel changes on nervous party committees but did not induce serious discussions with disaffected organizations.[22] Indeed, in the face of official unresponsiveness, the street—rather than the negotiating table—became the most highly developed and frequently utilized arena for the articulation of popular demands. Here, the intransigence of officialdom and the lack of well-defined agendas and constituencies on the part of independent organizations imposed less onerous constraints on societal activity. Street demonstrations revealed the depth of popular discontent; but they scarcely evinced the existence of a genuine civil society.

Assessing the *autonomy* of the new groups, the final indicator, poses a difficult task. Many associations jealously guarded their independence against official obstruction and attempts at cooptation. Yet, as of August 1991 most independent organizations in Russia still did not enjoy a genuine legal right to exist. In late 1990 and early 1991 the Union government and the government of the RSFSR adopted separate "Laws on Social Organizations." Though the new laws ostensibly offered organizations some legal guarantees, procedures for "registra-

tion" were complicated and subject to arbitrary interpretation by officials. The Union law required that all political parties desiring legal
recognition submit lists of at least five thousand members, complete
with addresses and passport numbers, to the Ministry of Justice by the
end of 1991. Some activists complained that this requirement retarded
the growth of their organizations, as many potential members were
loath to sign membership lists and supply personal information to central authorities, particularly in the atmosphere of crackdown prevalent
in early 1991. Not surprisingly, as of August 1991, no major independent organizations had yet received legal status on the Union level.[23]
Some groups survived even without legal protection. Most, however,
were acutely aware that they could be shut down at any time and
would enjoy no legal recourse. Absence of legal protection amounted
to what one leader of the SDPR called "the manipulation of fear, which
is a genetic feature of our system."[24] The disintegration of the Union
government following the failed coup attempt led to simplification
and liberalization of registration laws. Until at least August 1991, however, independent groups in Russia enjoyed few of the usual guarantees required for free associational life.

In conclusion, independent organizations in Russia did not score
high on any of the indicators employed here. Shortcomings in groups'
capacities for aggregating, representing, and articulating interests,
and influencing policy as organizations, were found in vague and undifferentiated agendas and constituencies; a low level of integration
of societal interests; weak internal obligatory capacities; narrow or
barely-existent channels of access to official sources of power; under-
developed mechanisms for exerting leverage over state institutions;
and a shortage of guarantees protecting groups against arbitrary state
intervention. In a number of cases, groups designed novel and even
effective strategies for overcoming these difficulties. In general, however, independent groups at the end of the Soviet period still faced an
uphill struggle in their efforts to acquire the capacities necessary for
effective collective action. If one regards strong, stable, autonomous
associations, capable of checking state power, as crucial components of
civil society, a genuine civil society had not been realized in Russia by
the end of the Gorbachev period. Significantly, while the term "civil
society" (*grazhdanskoe obshchestvo*) entered the lexicon of the autonomous associations' own publications and debates during the second
half of the Gorbachev period, few groups appeared to believe that a
civil society existed in Russia at the time. For example, in its founding
documents, New Forum, a "citizens' committee" of radical intellectuals, stated as a primary goal "the construction of an infrastructure for

civil society," defined as "a system of self-governing associations of individuals, independent of the state and formed from below, and the establishment of connections between them." It was precisely this "infrastructure," according to the group, that was lacking and must be created.[25]

An Alternative Conceptualization: The "Movement Society"

If the new independent organizations did not produce a civil society, or if they created one whose appearance, structure, and dynamics differed appreciably from those of many other civil societies, how might one characterize the new formation? The term "movement society" may capture the essence of the phenomenon.

Charles Tilly's conceptualization of alternative models of collective action furnishes a starting point for analysis. In his effort to distinguish social movements from other forms of organized political action, Tilly maintains that a social movement "actually consists of a series of demands and challenges to power holders in the name of a social category that lacks an established political position." The proper analogy to a social movement, he argues, is "neither a party nor a union, but a political campaign."[26]

In the Russian context, which of the new independent organizations posed challenges on behalf of "categories that lack an established political position"? In a compelling analysis of Soviet-style socialism, Marc Rakovski argued:

> In the majority of capitalist societies, every social group has the means of representing its own interests in relation to decisions of state power via its own political organizations. . . . The political rights of the individual are by and large the same in Soviet-type societies as they are in liberal democracies. But no special group, not even the ruling class, has either the right or the means to influence the exercise of their rights through organizations and means of information which are centered solely on the interests of that group. So the exercise of political rights becomes an empty ritual.[27]

Rakovski's analysis was written in the late 1970s and is not accurate as a description of Russia during the entire Gorbachev period. But his statement helps answer the question posed above: namely, that prior to the onset of the Gorbachev period, *no* social group enjoyed independent organizational rights. Thus, *all* of the associations that appeared after 1985 represented social categories that lacked an established political position. Given their newness and dearth of rights and resources, all of the new groups by their demands—indeed, by their very existence—continued until at least the failed putsch to fit this description and qualify, according to Tilly's conception, as social movements.

Indeed, the new political organizations in Russia resembled less political parties, unions, or interest associations, as these institutions are typically understood, than political campaigns. Mass demonstrations, rather than negotiations, served as organizations' main form of self-expression. Even the new political parties and trade unions, with their sweeping, often nonnegotiable demands and agendas, vaguely defined constituencies, lack of established rights, and emphasis on "transforming consciousness," embodied what may be termed "movement mentalities." Cooperatives' associations sought not only to advance members' interests, but to "democratize the economy"; parties' and trade unions' demands focused less on defense of partial interests than on "destroying totalitarianism," advancing "universal human values," and fostering the "spiritual rebirth of Russia."[28] Russia resembled less a civil society, with its established political parties, unions, and interest associations, than a movement society—that is, a myriad of complex, interacting, apocalyptic *political campaigns*.

Theorists of social movements in the West have discerned several distinct historical stages in organized social movement activity. The "old" movements, prominent during the stage of industrial capitalism, were bound up with the struggle for state power and the extension of political rights. With the achievement of full citizenship, the focus of social movement activity shifted to economic conflict. As Offe has noted, questions of production and distribution then dominated social movement activity in the West until at least the early post–World War II period. During this phase, socioeconomic interest groups often took the form of large-scale representative associations, characterized by a high degree of formal organization. Relations with state agencies and competition among interests assumed the form of pluralist or corporatist intermediation and political party competition. With the partial "solution" of the class conflict embodied in the social movement activity of this phase, the "new social movements," with their looser organizational structures and their emphasis on "postindustrial" or "postmaterial" issues and values such as peace, the environment, and personal autonomy and identity, began to emerge. In this final phase, societies spawned movements that focused on what Alberto Melucci has called the "democratization of everyday life."[29]

What is unique and most intriguing about the birth of Russian political society is the explosive, unprecedented, and *simultaneous* emergence of social movements based on all three types of conflict: citizenship, distribution, and "postindustrial" values. The "old" and "new" demands suddenly found expression not only within society as a whole, but also in the separate, individual programs and sets of demands put forward by nearly every major autonomous association. Few of the groups, including the unions, fronts, and political parties, failed to demand full voting rights and electoral reform (citizenship); deep structural reforms in the economy and an end to the privileges of the apparat (distribution); and major changes in policies on the environment and civil rights ("postindustrial" values).

The uniqueness of the current phenomenon can be understood only in the context of Russia's recent past, and by means of comparison with other countries, advanced industrialized and developing. Though issues of citizenship have not been fully resolved even today in many societies, principles of majority rule and universal voting rights have operated, *at least during certain periods*, even in many countries of the Third World. Whether or not one accepts the "totalitarian" label as a description of post-Stalin Russia, the obvious fact remains that the basic rights of citizenship won in past centuries and decades in many nonsocialist countries were not even a matter of public debate in Russia until after 1985. Similarly, problems of distribution and class conflict, which were partially resolved in the West over many decades and at least addressed during periods of working class rebellion and phases of relatively open rule in many developing countries, remained fully unresolved in Russia. That the official trade unions never served the interests of their members was by 1990 a truism, even among conservative state officials in Russia.[30] Some Soviet analysts by then spoke of the "serfdom of the working person" and the "fight against dependency that amounts to a Stalinist passport system."[31] One argued that in the absence of markets, "there is no way to calculate the rate of workers' exploitation by the state [in the Soviet Union]—but there is no doubt that it is the highest anywhere."[32] Accurate or not, this statement reflected a widespread belief in Russia that even the most limited gains on issues of distribution and production, including organizational rights, working conditions, and wages, lay not in the past, but in the future. And yet, even if the pre-1985 *political system* was in no sense capable of allowing for even partial resolution of problems of citizenship and distribution, *society* was indeed "modern" enough to spawn a plethora of even "new" social movements based on cultural, civic, and environmental concerns under conditions of liberalization. Analysis that stresses the importance of modernization in this instance appears convincing.

In sum, it was the "full unresolvedness" of even the most basic citizenship and distributive rights, as well as of "postindustrial" societal concerns, that produced a rare, if not unique, historical phenomenon.

And it has been precisely the sudden and simultaneous emergence of all three types of demands, not only in society as a whole but within many of its individual constituent organizations, that has given the birth of Russian political society its chaotic appearance and its dramatic character.

Even if this brief macrohistorical explanation helps provide some understanding of the emergence of the new political society, it scarcely explains the new society's specific features and development. Furthermore, while the model of the "movement society" provides a better description than other images and conceptualizations, it is too broad and amorphous in this form to serve as a concrete dependent variable. Thus the following section breaks the model down into a number of discrete questions that will serve as starting points for investigation in subsequent chapters.

The Dependent Variable Disaggregated

The Organizations

The first set of questions for investigation centers on the character of the autonomous organizations themselves. First, why did the new groups fail to secure mass membership and following? The situation during the late Soviet period stood in stark contrast to that which prevailed in pre-1917 Russia. In 1906, within one year after the onset of limited political liberalization, the Constitutional Democratic Party enjoyed a membership of at least sixty thousand. In the medium-sized provincial city of Briansk alone, the Social Revolutionary Party counted one thousand active members. By the end of 1905, moreover, emergent business associations had already become a powerful and well-organized independent force in Russian politics.[33] Some prerevolutionary parties were quite small. But, as Feliks Gross argues, parties such as the Bolsheviks were small precisely because they were conspiratorial and vanguardist.[34] Nearly all significant parties and other independent organizations in post-1985 Russia, however, operated openly and eschewed vanguardism of any type. The magnitude of the new Russian organizations also compares poorly to contemporary counterparts in East Europe. By February 1990, only months after liberalization in Czechoslovakia, the Czech Agriculture Party's membership numbered in the tens of thousands, and the new Green Party had received 300,000 applications for formal membership. By the same date, the new Social Democratic Party in Bulgaria claimed a membership of 30,000; in Hungary, the party of the same name included 17,000 members.[35] Even if such figures are not precise, they do, along with many events in the post-1989 politics of East Europe, reflect a qualitative difference between Russia and its former clients in the rates and magnitudes of organizational growth and consolidation.[36]

A functionalist hypothesis might suggest that groups other than political parties have performed the roles normally associated with parties in other political systems, particularly in structuring the vote and mobilizing public opinion. Indeed, Democratic Russia did serve as a vehicle for organizing dissent during 1990–91. But it could not and did not execute the functions either in society or in government of organized mass political parties. Given El'tsin's overwhelming personal popularity, moreover, it is unlikely that his margin of victory in the race for the Russian presidency would have been much less impressive without Democratic Russia's organizational support.

Other possible explanations also seem to exhibit shortcomings. A microeconomic rational choice approach, such as one based roughly on Mancur Olson's theory of collective action, might explain the smallness of groups in terms of lack of incentives for individual involvement. Such a theory could help explain why so few ordinary citizens joined groups, and therefore why groups failed to establish mass popular bases. It could also illuminate why so many celebrated progressive leaders, ranging from El'tsin to the mayors of Moscow and Leningrad, shunned membership in political parties—a fact that might itself be related to lack of popular enthusiasm for membership. As will be demonstrated, elements of such an approach hold considerable explanatory power. Yet one must also guard against injudicious application of Olson's principles. As Klaus von Beyme points out, the logic of Olson's approach to collective action rarely applies neatly to political parties, which typically lack the capacity to offer the "selective incentives" possessed by some other types of organizations.[37] And, as many analysts of social movements have shown, motivations for involvement in politics can scarcely be reduced to a desire to reap material benefits. Olson's "free rider" problem, moreover, may be expected to affect level of activism and personal commitment within organizations more than membership numbers. Even if autonomous organizations in Russia did lack sufficient incentives for membership, questions remain: *Why* did they lack incentives, *which* needed incentives were missing, and *what* prevented groups from securing them?

A sophisticated political-cultural or psychological explanation for the smallness of groups might stress the aversion that Russians may feel to collective involvement after decades of mandatory membership in a plethora of vacuous state-sponsored groups, ranging from the "Society for Environmental Protection," to which all schoolchildren belonged during the Brezhnev era, to the Komsomol, the Communist youth league that any student hoping to enter university was obligated to join. Given the images of authoritarianism, exclusivity, and empty rhetoric that the very word "party" doubtless conjures up after seven decades in which the term was used exclusively with reference to the CPSU, membership in a political party might be seen as especially unappealing. Yet in many other countries emerging from authoritarian one-party rule and étatization of organizational life, such psychological orientations have not ruled out the growth of autonomous political groups.[38] The very notions of "political party" and "interest group" are cherished in few societies. Such institutions are more often regarded as necessary evils than as positive goods; "bad reputations" need not prevent organizational growth and development.[39] In short, the functionalist, economic/rational choice, and psychological explanations outlined here seem to raise as many questions as they answer.

The second question concerns why groups were so ridden by internal disarray, infighting, and defections. Factionalism and internal conflict, particularly during early stages of organizational development, are hardly unusual. Observers of recent cases of democratization in Latin America, for example, may find the tales of organizational woe recounted in this study quite familiar. Yet in Russia internal conflict in organizations has been deeper, more pervasive, and more crippling in its effects than in most other cases. None of the major new parties avoided deep and corrosive internal divisions. Such splits, moreover, often took the form not of orderly and manageable factionalization, nor of division into two or more distinct but mutually cooperative groups, but rather of breakdown into several mutually antagonistic organizations. Interpersonal conflicts, rather than clear factional differences over program, policy, strategy, or tactics, have often appeared to create the deepest and most damaging divisions. Destructive internal conflict has hardly been limited to the parties. Even at the height of the Donbass miners' struggle against their bosses and what they described as the "totalitarian system of domination," chairmen of strike committees rarely retained their positions for long before being voted out by their coworkers, greatly complicating the task of organizing effective unions on citywide or higher levels.[40] Sotsprof, which until the end of 1990 was a promising and growing national union of white-collar workers, virtually destroyed itself over what may appear to an observer as a petty personal conflict among its leaders.[41]

Many explanations for factionalism and organizational breakdown found in general literatures on parties and other organizations apply, at best, only loosely to the Russian case. Giovanni Sartori holds that the "opportunity structure bearing on fractionalism" within parties can be reduced to organizational structure and to the electoral system, and ultimately to the latter.[42] Richard Katz attributes internal disunity largely to electoral competition within the party, particularly to the intraparty preference vote in which candidates for public office are nominated by party memberships.[43] In Russia, however, a plethora of even nonparty organizations held the right to put candidates forward for election to soviets; several candidates from a single party (except the Communist Party) rarely competed over a single office; and party affiliation normally did not figure prominently in candidates' electoral campaigns. In fact, parties did not—and could not—play substantial roles in the 1989 and 1990 legislative elections. Internal organizational structures and procedures for nomination and election of candidates for public office did play a part in the weakness of parties in Russia. But the actual operation of these factors differed substantially from patterns found in many other countries, as will be discussed in chapter 4.

Some scholars have stressed ideological or attitudinal explanations for internal disunity. In his study of the Green parties in Germany and Belgium, Herbert Kitschelt argues that division and disorganization tend to manifest themselves in proportion to the extent to which a group stresses broad, sweeping goals, such as the "democratization of society."[44] Most groups in Russia did emphasize such aims, and the factionalism, interpersonal conflict, and endless debates over ostensibly minor issues that Kitschelt observed in his subjects were evident in even greater measure in all of Russia's parties. Yet Kitschelt does not explain precisely how and why sweeping goals produce internal conflict. In Russia, moreover, one might have expected that the overwhelming power of "the enemy" (the Communist Party system), as well as commonly held revolutionary goals, would have served as unifying forces within new organizations, as they have during the struggle against authoritarian regimes in many other countries.

The third question centers on structural and operational features of autonomous organizations. Specifically, how might one explain the highly democratic and diffuse nature of groups' organizational structures and the high level of member participation? While relatively small and riven by internal divisions, groups strenuously resisted oligarchy. The oft-stated generalization that rank-and-file members play little or no role in internal will formation does not apply to autonomous political organizations in Russia. The level of what Maurice Duverger has described as "intensity of organization" was in some respects very high.[45] Ordinary members as well as leaders participated extensively in decision making. As will be discussed in chapter 5, organizations on the local level rarely consisted of one or several "local notables" and a mass of compliant members. On the contrary, groups often operated almost as collections of equals. On the national level, leadership plena and full membership conferences were usually well attended by members from around the country. Selection of national and local leaderships, which in most cases were collective, was carried out by voting of full memberships or all conference participants. And although important decisions were usually made by full memberships or plena at the national level, most parties and other groups did not enforce these decisions on local organizations. They explicitly permitted the latter to ignore decisions taken at higher levels, if activists considered these decisions inconsistent with specific local conditions and requirements of operation.

The highly democratic character of decision-making processes and internal will formation runs contrary to normal expectations. As both Kay Lawson and Feliks Gross point out, parties often reflect the system of rule under which they operate. Decentralized, federative governments, particularly in relatively open systems, tend to breed loosely organized, decentralized, and more "democratic" party organizations, while tightly centralized systems create conditions for the formation of parties with strict organizational hierarchies and strong control from above.[46] In prerevolutionary Russia, some parties did reflect in this manner the highly centralized and authoritarian state system that they opposed. Yet, in contemporary Russia, parties have mirrored less the authoritarian and hypercentralized state system that they sought to bring down than the ideals of the *future* state—and society—that they hoped to build. The character of the new parties and other associations also contradicts common political-cultural assumptions regarding Russians' longing for order, authority, and a strong hand.

The Organizations in Broader Society

The second set of questions focuses on the place and role of independent groups in broader society, and on relations among groups. The first issue regards groups' styles of operation and forms of action, and the surprising effectiveness of their efforts in certain areas. Whatever their shortcomings, parties, unions, and other organizations in some respects manifested impressive mobilization capacities. Even if unable to secure regular mass memberships, groups demonstrated aptitude for organizing large displays of public discontent and engaging in independent information provision. In many cities attendance at demonstrations organized by movement organizations stood in sharp and favorable contrast to groups' membership rosters and bank accounts. How did organizations so diminutive and in some respects ineffectual engage in significant radical action and cause so much trouble for a powerful state and an ostensibly firmly entrenched regime? Why, moreover, did they devote so much of their energy and resources to expressive and communicative forms of action, such as organizing mass demonstrations and publishing small-circulation newspapers, journals, and leaflets?

As one might expect, the strength, mobilization potential, and capacity for coordinated action of radical democratic organizations varied from city to city. A socioeconomic modernization approach might predict that such variation would be determined by differences in population size, industrial development, occupational structure of the work force, and level of educational attainment. As will be demonstrated in chapter 5, socioeconomic factors do help explain variation in the development of democratic forces across cities. But these variables often operated in ways highly inconsistent with conventional assumptions.

The second question concerns organizations' programmatic orientations and, more specifically, the lack of programmatic differentiation among groups. Why did differences over ideology, strategy, and social and economic policy not find coherent expression in groups' programs? Interviews with group leaders revealed genuine disparities on these matters. But differences were not clearly expressed in manifestos and programs. Most groups avoided explicit statements of what and whose interests they intended to advance and seemed to limit themselves largely to broad and often rather empty statements of good intent. It is unsurprising that the mass public was largely unaware of organizations' programmatic orientations. Widely held popular perceptions, often expressed by ordinary citizens in Russia, that "the democrats are all the same" and that "the democrats are better than the Communists, but both are all talk anyway" were understandable, even if inaccurate.

Is programmatic fuzziness simply a "modern" phenomenon? Some scholars, particularly those who see an "end of ideology" and a decline in class- or other group-based voting and political action in industrial democracies, might hold that a trend toward ideological and programmatic amorphousness is to be expected in any advanced industrialized society. Yet such arguments, which were quite popular during the 1960s and 1970s, are misplaced. Even if some limited programmatic convergence has occurred, ideological differentiation has declined only modestly, and the interest bases, if not the class bases, of modern parties have remained quite firm and stable. Political party affiliation has remained the most important determinant of electoral choice, and parties and other political organizations as a rule do target specific segments of the population for support.[47] At any rate, partial "resolution" of many issues of civil liberties and material production and distribution, to which the decline in ideology is sometimes attributed, has at best only begun to occur in contemporary Russia. A strictly "economic" explanation might attribute lack of programmatic differentiation to electoral competition and a general desire to broaden appeal to voters and potential members. But if parties in Russia were guided by such a logic, the strategy did not pay off, given the smallness and slow growth of organizations.

The third question on independent organizations in broader society concentrates on interrelationships and interaction among groups. Specifically, why did democratic movement groups experience such difficulties integrating and consolidating their efforts within a framework of unified organizations? While broad umbrella groups such as Democratic Russia sometimes fostered cooperation among like-minded groups, the extent of real organizational linkage and integration was very limited. The abortive efforts of the RPR and the SDPR to unite during 1990–91 provide an example. Many members of both parties regarded the separate existence of two small "social-democratic" groups with virtually identical programs as counterproductive and recognized that full union would probably produce a synergistic effect. Yet after nearly one year of heated debate over the matter within each party, which at one point actually threatened to destroy each separately, both decided to retain separate identities and to postpone integration indefinitely.[48] Organizations' inability to integrate or often even to "get along with each other" has sometimes been attributed to the underdevelopment of notions of reciprocity and principled compromise in Russian political culture. Yet in a land whose greatest popular hero is Andrei Sakharov and where many ordinary people are conversant in the philosophies of Semen Frank and Nikolai Berdiaev, such explanations cannot provide definitive answers.

The State-Society Nexus

The third set of questions centers on organizations' relations with the state. Why, even from what would appear to be positions of weakness, did relatively small and poorly integrated organizations display such a remarkable degree of radicalism and resistance to compromise with authority? The depth of intransigence varied across groups. The Democratic Union rejected participation in elections, while some other organizations believed that the soviets could provide footholds for forcing regime change. But autonomous groups that both favored democratic change and maintained good relations with officialdom were striking by their absence. By mid-1990 all major democratic movement organizations, though subject to official pressure and possessing memberships and resource bases incalculably smaller than those of their Communist adversaries, rejected any compromise with the Union government and the CPSU. Nor did poverty, organizational disarray, or intimidation prevent striking miners from demanding the resignation of Gorbachev and the transfer of power to a "roundtable" committee of republican leaders. If such demands appeared highly ambitious and even unrealistic, they were nevertheless taken extremely seriously by the strikers themselves.

Explaining the intransigence of independent forces, particularly given their overwhelming organizational weakness relative to state institutions, poses a difficult problem. Their behavior is inconsistent with the expectations of, for example, the resource mobilization theory of social movements.[49] This theory regards most social movement organizations as driven to some degree by desire for *inclusion* within the existing political system. This approach might predict that small and impoverished groups would not reflexively reject some form of compromise or at least peaceful coexistence with the institutions that controlled the lion's share of production, distribution, communications, and coercion.

The second question on relations between the state and independent groups concerns participation of democratic activists in the soviets. How did progressives, despite enormous disadvantages, capture so many seats in elections for soviets? And why did they then find converting electoral strength into real power so difficult? After the 1990 elections, "democrats" (or individuals who identified themselves with the democratic movement) made up sizable blocs in the RSFSR Supreme Soviet and in many city soviets. But while participation in the soviets lent voice to radical concerns and demands, democrats were able only in rare instances to achieve meaningful policy changes. In the 1990 elections for the Moscow City Soviet, democratic candidates won roughly three-quarters of the seats. But they enacted virtually no meaningful legislation during their first year "in power."

A frequent explanation for the inefficacy of democrats once in office is lack of political experience. It has been suggested that shortcomings in political culture might lie behind the inability of democrats in the legislatures to form and maintain a consensus. Again, however, given lack of programmatic differentiation among democrats on the basic tasks of democratization and marketization, lack of practice in working together ought not to hinder cooperation. In fact, one might expect that the enormity of the task of dismantling the old system would unite oppositionists. And, as will be shown in chapter 5, in some exceptional cases inexperienced progressive deputies did act in a disciplined and effective manner. Explanation for the failures of the democrats in legislatures must be sought elsewhere.

In sum, this section has broken down the central dependent variable—the "movement society"—into eight specific issues for examination. Questions focus on the size, organizational integrity, and organizational structures and decision-making procedures of independent associations; the effectiveness, forms of action, and programmatic orientation of groups, as well as relationships and interactions among organizations; and groups' political stances and tactics in their relations with the state and their participation in the soviets. The following section presents a framework for examination of these issues. It does not answer each of the questions, but rather introduces some of the key explanatory variables of the study and briefly outlines arguments that will be made in following chapters.

The Explanatory Framework

Elections and the Timing of Reforms

The timing and sequencing of liberalization and reform serve as the first major explanatory variable. Many developments that have spanned decades in some countries took place in Russia in the course of only a few years. Given the rapidity of change in Russia, one might expect that the timing of major events over even months could create conditions for propitious breakthroughs—or the formation of "birth defects"—in the development of the polity. This possibility recommends the usefulness of what Richard Katz refers to as "thinking backwards" over tightly related series of events and of Alexander George's method of microhistorical "process tracing."[50] The first section of this chapter noted the significance of the simultaneity of the emergence of social movement demands of every type. Examination of more specific questions outlined in the second section of the chapter calls for attention to the more proximate dialectic between changes effected "from above" and the development of independent societal forces.

The conditions under which elections were held, and in particular the timing of the convocation of elections and the "unbanning" of political parties, are of critical importance. In almost all cases of democratization in recent decades, multiparty "founding elections" have been a crucial moment in transition. The role of parties in such elections has varied. But in most cases, including those of Spain in the mid-1970s, Brazil and other Latin American countries during the 1980s, and East European countries since 1989, political parties, even if previously banned, operated relatively freely during campaigns leading up to "founding elections." They were able, to varying degrees, to discharge what Leon Epstein calls their "minimum function"—namely, "structuring the vote."[51] In the Soviet case, by contrast, the first elections for the USSR Congress of People's Deputies occurred in early 1989, over one year before political parties were allowed to organize as such and before Article 6 was removed from the constitution. Elections for the Congress of People's Deputies of the RSFSR and for soviets on lower levels were held in 1990, just before some political organizations proclaimed themselves parties. To be sure, "proto-parties" such as the Social Democratic Association (later the SDPR) and broadly based "voters' clubs" and "citizens' committees" such as the Moscow Union of Voters and Memorial helped organize campaigns for some radical candidates. But these organizations could not function as normal, programmatic parties. Indeed, in the first elections, they did not even have the right to nominate candidates for office, a privilege that was reserved for "territorial districts," the Communist Party and various state organizations, and "work collectives." In the second elections, they could put candidates forward, but nominations were still largely controlled—directly or indirectly—by the same agencies as in the first elections. At any rate, parties (other than the CPSU) could not play a major role in either election—much less acquire a functional monopoly over the nomination of candidates.[52]

Whether balloting held under such circumstances may be regarded as genuine "founding elections" must be left to question here. Of greater significance is how the timing of events affected parties and other independent political organizations. From the standpoint of optimal development of independent institutions and mechanisms for cooperation among democratic forces, the "opening" of 1989–90 was both *too sudden* and *too partial*. It strongly—and negatively—influenced the growth and effectiveness of alternative political parties. The timing of elections reduced incentives for ambitious radical leaders to join parties and encouraged a highly individualistic form of political entrepreneurship. The conditions under which elections were held also undermined progressive deputies' abilities to engage in united, effective action in soviets on all levels.

Structure and Character of State Institutions

The second major explanatory factor concerns the influence of state institutions (excluding the soviets). As Tilly argues, the development of social movements and the organizational forms through which their demands are expressed depend largely on the "process by which the political system shapes, checks, and absorbs the challenges which come to it."[53] During the period 1985–91, state institutions in Russia indeed demonstrated a capacity to "shape and check" challenges from societal actors. Yet the former also exhibited little aptitude for "absorbing" such challenges, and for formulating flexible, imaginative responses to independent pressures. Some analysts of democratization in Europe and Latin America have noted how *blandos* (soft-liners) have fortified their positions against *duros* (hard-liners) within the authoritarian state by forming alliances with emergent societal forces, in some cases facilitating devolution of authority to these forces and relatively smooth withdrawal of authoritarian governments from power.[54] In Russia, Gorbachev and other "reformers" did, at least through 1988, seek to "activate" social forces in support of their policies. Yet as many new groups emerged, grew, and radicalized in 1989, state leaders moved toward resistance and intransigence, which hardened during 1990–91.[55] To be sure, official policies and strategies toward independent challenges differed substantially from those of the pre-Gorbachev era. The directness and reflexivity of repression declined, indeed to a degree that made possible the emergence of independent opposition. But many other methods, including infiltration of independent groups and even soviets by agents of state security, sabotage of groups' activities, and harassment of and selective violence against group organizers continued and even intensified during 1989–91.

Repression was scarcely limited to the application of direct pressure on autonomous groups. It extended to the basic structure of domination and control in the workplace. Whatever divisions over policy developed among top leaders after 1985, control over enterprises by a hierarchical system of nomenklatura appointments remained largely intact through 1991, and citizens' dependence on goods and services obtained through the workplace increased dramatically as scarcity intensified. As will be demonstrated in chapter 5, authority relations in the workplace, combined with state action of many types, powerfully inhibited the growth and integration of autonomous political organizations. Official pressure also had unintended—and for the observer, perhaps counterintuitive—effects on groups' internal structures and patterns of operation. For example, as will be shown in chapters 4 and 5, infiltration and sabotage of organizations not only sometimes accomplished the intended effect of cultivating discord and mistrust among democratic activists. It also promoted a hyperdemocratic ethos and structure within their organizations. Inability to work secretly or conspiratorially, combined with the dangers of entrusting a great deal of authority to any one leader or group of leaders who might turn out to be "not with us," engendered tenacious resistance among members to concentration of power and closed decision-making procedures.

The state's structural inflexibility and intolerance account for only part of its influence on independent organizations. For during the years 1985–91, and especially during the second half of this period, not only were state institutions inflexible and incapable of sharing power and authority; they were also beginning to decay. The growing disorganization of the Communist Party was crucial to the emergence of autonomous—and revolutionary—loci of organized political activity. But the fragmentation of old structures of power and authority also in some respects *inhibited* the rapid development of the institutions of independent society. Just as effective intermediation requires that groups possess some leverage over the state, so must state institutions hold some resources and values sought by societal organizations.[56] Yet state power in Russia by the end of the 1980s had been reduced solely to *negative* power. Local officials had the power to shut down cooperative enterprises by the hundreds, as they did in many regions. But they could neither provide workers with attractive alternatives to employment in cooperatives nor extract dedicated performance from employees in state enterprises. Official trade unions could obstruct the formation of independent unions but could not represent workers' interests. Officials could interfere with the activities of democratic movement organizations but usually lacked the resources, imagination, and flexibility required for effective management of policy toward these groups. Given the disorganization of formal structures of power and the consequent blurring of lines of competence and responsibility, independent groups faced state institutions that were not merely intransigent, but also unsure of their own authority. Even upon gaining access to given state institutions, political activists often found that power had flowed elsewhere, or that no one actually knew where authority to resolve the issue of concern resided. This state of affairs hardly provided strong incentives for individuals to participate in independent politics or fostered links between state and societal institutions characteristic of relations between "modern" states and "mature" civil societies.

Property Relations and Socioeconomic Structure

The structure of socioeconomic relations serves as the third major component of the explanatory framework. The absence or extreme underdevelopment of markets in the Russian economy suggests the necessity of what Laura Boella refers to as "go[ing] beyond theories of 'bureaucratic societies'" and addressing "the concrete relation between politics and a form of production which, although it has abolished private property, has not done away with wage-labor but, rather, universalized it."[57] Although some loci of relatively independent economic power began to form during the second half of the Gorbachev period, the fusion of economy and polity in Russia for the most part persisted through 1991. The cooperative movement, which seemed initially to hold promise as a vehicle of economic change, did not create genuine markets or spawn an independent business class. Instead, the partial decentralization of authority on regulation of co-operatives led to the near-destruction of the cooperative movement by hostile local officials in several parts of Russia during 1989–90; and the introduction of onerous new rules on taxation and inspection during 1990–91 often forced cooperatives into corrupt "business relation-ships" with officials, creating "bureaucratic capital" and a "racket economy" rather than private capital and competitive markets. De-spite much fanfare, plans for "transition to a market economy," such as those embodied in the Shatalin Plan, were abandoned in early 1991 in favor of simple hikes in state monopoly prices. What little privatiza-tion did occur before the putsch, moreover, was in most instances car-ried out by enterprise directors for their own benefit, creating an alli-ance between traditional and "new" forms of parasitism, patronage and clientelism.[58]

The absence of a market economy strongly affected the emergence of independent political associations. Above all, it restricted groups' abilities to obtain needed inputs without reliance on political authori-ties and impeded efforts to establish autonomous resource bases. The hyperétatization of property presented groups in Russia with difficul-ties experienced less acutely by analogous organizations in societies in which property is less tightly and comprehensively controlled by the state. Theorists of social movements have shown that movements are often spawned by organizations that already possess adequate re-sources. The dynamics of growth in social movement organizations stem from how groups pool their resources and draw on funds pro-vided by associated groups to promote a common cause.[59] In Russia, however, possibilities for generating adequate resources internally or for drawing on resources provided by like-minded organizations were extremely limited. Groups in some instances devised innovative strat-egies for overcoming the difficulties that poverty imposed. In general, however, problems of resource acquisition restricted their capacities for organizational growth and integration.

The near-universalization of wage labor and the underdevelopment of private property and markets also exerted deeper effects via their influence on socioeconomic structure. These factors prevented the for-mation of a genuine middle class in Russia, or at least produced pat-terns of "class" and sectoral differentiation that differ dramatically from those found in the West. The absence of a genuine middle class, the relative lack of stratification among societal groups in terms of property ownership (accompanied by a stark differential between state and societal actors in terms of *control* over property), and the existence of structures of wage and skill differentiation across sectors that reflected the dictates of military-industrial production rather than the requirements of consumer demand strongly influenced patterns of development among new political forces. In particular, they help explain the weakness of programmatic differentiation among independent political organizations, including political parties, and the difficulties that groups faced in locating constituencies and sources of support in broader society. It will not be argued that the character of political organizations is fully "socially determined." But it will be shown, to paraphrase Otto Kirchheimer, that socioeconomic structure does establish "conditioning perimeters" within which those who strive to organize and represent interests must work.[60]

In sum, the causal argument put forward in this study constructs a *statist* approach to explain the emergence of the new *societal* institutions. All three of the major independent variables outlined above concern the environment created by the legacy and/or the immediate policies of state institutions. The study aims to demonstrate that the character and development of Russia's new autonomous political society has been shaped above all by the structure, nature, and policy of the state, rather than by socioeconomic modernization, political culture and psychology, or the cumulative weight of centuries of Russian historical tradition.

The New Political Society and the Transition to Democracy

The failed coup of August 1991 and the demise of the Soviet Union in its aftermath raise the possibility of a genuine transition to and consolidation of democracy in Russia. The prospect of regime change raises questions regarding the effects of the political development of society on the political development of the polity.[61] Specifically, for *what kind* of democratization or regime change did the institutions of the new political society create a basis?

As Giuseppe Di Palma points out, democracy is largely a matter of consent, and consent must be reproduced.[62] Even theorists who emphasize the importance of "nonelectoral" institutions in processes of interest intermediation acknowledge that in democracies, parties and party systems serve as the principal sites from which consent is extracted and reproduced.[63] Sartori argues that "partyless society cannot cope with politicized society."[64] In a similar vein, Katz maintains that without genuine programmatic parties to "structure campaigns, provide continuity from one election to the next, and provide links among candidates in different locales for different offices . . . elections are unlikely to be meaningful, even if they are technically free."[65] Modern democracy requires political parties. In industrialized democracies, most citizens are party adherents, even if not party members.[66] The configuration and degree of development of parties and party systems during early stages of transition may be of particular significance. As Alan Ware points out, during periods of social and economic transformation parties are in positions to "re-define lines of political cleavage, thus defining the sorts of wants citizens have."[67]

Democratic transition and consolidation also involve processes broader than those of party development. They raise more general problems of "stabilizing the system of representation."[68] Resolution of such problems requires formation of genuine, institutionalized links between state actors, on the one hand, and societal groups that command sufficient membership, following, or influence to serve effectively as agents of intermediation, on the other. Successful democratic transition typically involves "deals" among organized collectives that condition the uncertainties of transition with certainties regarding the effects of regime change on both societal groups and state actors. Bargains may take a multiplicity of forms and may be achieved through pluralist, corporatist, or syndicalist arrangements. Details of "deals" need not be fully worked out in advance; indeed, the transition process itself sometimes involves the striking of such bargains as a first step toward "institutionalizing uncertainty."[69] Yet the strength and character of autonomous societal institutions at the moment of the onset of transition may be highly relevant to eventual outcomes. The representative capacity of independent organizations strongly conditions the universe of the *types* of democracy from which political actors may choose. During a period of deep and rapid change, especially one instigated or hastened by sudden and unforeseen events such as the abortive coup attempt of August 1991, the question of "who speaks for whom" assumes particular urgency and importance. Given the small size, limited degree of integration, and weak representative capacities of most independent groups, as well as the highly uncertain nature of state power itself, the answer to this question in Russia is by no means clear.

One must not, of course, view democratization as the fulfillment of "prerequisites," and one must search for propitious as well as constraining circumstances. Dankwart Rustow is undoubtedly correct to argue that "democratic mindsets" are not prerequisites for democratic change. If they were, democratization would rarely if ever take place. Democracy often creates democrats, rather than the reverse.[70] At any rate, there is certainly no shortage of individuals holding "democratic" and "antiauthoritarian" beliefs in contemporary Russia. But few theorists fail to acknowledge the importance of the strategic interactions on which the main avenues toward democracy are built. The process of strategic interaction, if it is to generate some basis for "stabilizing the system of representation" and for "institutionalizing uncertainty," does require dense and vigorous networks of nonstate representative institutions.[71]

The transformations of the post-August 1991 period have already created opportunities for the expansion and integration of independent societal institutions in Russia, as well as conditions favorable for change "from above." Change is already visible in some of the factors included in the explanatory framework outlined above. For example, the destruction—or at least submergence—of the Communist Party apparat and the restructuring of the organs of state security may greatly improve the conditions under which independent associations operate. Radical economic reform promises to alter property relations in a manner favoring the growth and consolidation of organized loci of societal power. On the other hand, the timing and sequencing of elections and party formation during 1989–91 is an established occurrence and may have already created a birth defect in the electoral and party systems that will influence politics for years to come. Socioeconomic structure, moreover, may be expected to change only slowly, and political parties and party systems, once established, may not necessarily adjust quickly to socioeconomic change.[72] Addressing the issue of how the new political society will affect regime change necessarily involves speculation and prediction, as well as deduction from the explanatory framework outlined above. This question will be considered in the final chapter of the book. The intervening chapters focus on the emergence and development of autonomous political organizations during the Gorbachev period.

IV

Building Independent Political Society

THIS chapter examines the questions posed in the previous one by investigating six democratic movement organizations: the Social Democratic Party of Russia (SDPR), the Democratic Platform/Republican Party of Russia (RPR), the Democratic Party of Russia (DPR), the Russian Christian Democratic Movement (RKhDD), Democratic Russia, and the Democratic Union (DU). These groups were chosen for three interrelated reasons. First, they span a wide spectrum of organizational forms. Second, each was a "serious" major organization. Each enjoyed at least several thousand members and was organized on the national level. All possessed concrete organizational structures, purposive goals, and programs. Third, these groups represented the leading tendencies of the democratic movement. They accounted for only a small fraction of the thousands of autonomous political associations that emerged in Russia during the last several years of the Soviet period, yet they were, arguably, the strongest and most important of the new groups. Taken together, they constituted the core of the organized democratic movement.

This chapter is based largely, though not exclusively, on evidence gathered on groups' Moscow-based organizations. All groups made their headquarters in the capital, and most of their leaders resided there. The greater part of their publications were edited and issued in Moscow as well.

In the voluminous literatures on political organizations, conceptual distinctions among parties, unions, interest groups, fronts, and movements have received considerable attention. No consensus exists on precise definitions. Some analysts of social movements, particularly observers of "new" or "postindustrial" movements, define their subjects in ethereal, even metapolitical terms, while other authors stress more concrete organizational aspects. Even the seemingly "hardest," most readily identifiable entities—political parties—have been conceptualized in a plethora of ways. Some analysts have defined parties as any organizations that pursue the goal of placing representatives in government positions[1], or as any groups that nominate candidates for election to a legislature.[2] Some conceive of parties as those groups that translate mass preferences into public policy.[3] Still others emphasize the informational, educative, and/or mobilizational role of parties.[4] In fact, as Alan Ware points out, the boundaries between parties and other forms of political organization are, in practice, often fuzzy.[5]

Many of the distinctions and definitions found in the conceptual literatures, however useful for studying established democracies or systems with a recent history of at least some political pluralism, are of limited utility for examination of the Russian case. While some of the groups investigated here called themselves political parties, they did not participate as such in legislative elections or play major roles in structuring the vote.[6] Furthermore, if one accepts Douglas Rae's assertion that a party system is found not in parties themselves, with their persons, institutions, and activities, but rather in the competition among parties, Russia did not possess anything resembling a party system during the Gorbachev period.[7] The one organization that did function in at least vaguely "partylike" terms was Democratic Russia, the coalition of opposition forces that rejected the "party" label and defined itself explicitly as a "movement organization."

As asserted in the previous chapter, all of the groups under investigation are best conceptualized as *movement organizations*, insofar as they spoke for and acted on behalf of previously unmobilized constituencies and sought to advance goals and preferences that previously enjoyed no organized expression in the political arena. Regardless of the labels they adopted, all of the groups may be regarded as spearheads of social movements and as organizational components of the broader democratic movement.

Forging an Identity

All political organizations must form a collective identity. Some recent theoretical writings on social movements have directed considerable attention to the process of establishing a sense of "we" within movements and their organizations. Yet such writings, while often rich in intriguing abstractions, usually fail to address precisely how efforts to form a collective identity actually shape group formation and organizational structure and integration in practice.[8]

In newly emerging groups whose members enjoy little or no experience in autonomous self-organization, forming an identity—deciding who "we" are, what we believe in and stand for, and for whom we speak—poses a particularly important and complex task. Indeed, in the Russian case, simply establishing a sense of "I"—determining what one as an individual believes, where one stands on some political spectrum, and how one's own beliefs relate to those of others—

severely complicated collective identity formation within groups. Close examination of this matter would push analysis into the realm of political psychology and socialization and would reach beyond the scope of the present study. However intriguing the subject of individual political identity formation, discussion here focuses on groups and intergroup relations.

The Social Democratic Party of Russia and the Republican Party of Russia each experienced the vexing problems involved in forming a collective identity. Their experiences were typical of those of the democratic opposition groups. In a sense, the SDPR and the RPR serve as "hard" cases. Unlike many other opposition groups, each had enjoyed some organizational infrastructure for about one year before their formal founding as parties in 1990. For each, collective identity formation was—or should have been—less onerous than for groups that came into existence only during the last year or so before the August 1991 putsch. Since the two were born under the expectation that they would quickly combine their organizations, examination of them also illuminates how the process of identity formation *within* groups affected relations *between* them.

The Social Democrats

The SDPR was the successor to the Social Democratic Association (SDA), which in turn arose from several informal groups that formed in 1987–88. By the time of its founding in May 1990, the SDPR had already enjoyed over one year of life as a proto-party. The leadership of the new party at the time of its founding, moreover, was virtually identical to that of the group it succeeded. Some organizers of the SDA expected their association to evolve into two distinct parties: a "social-liberal" group and a more traditional, left-wing (in the Western sense) social-democratic organization.[9] But the Social Democrats held together, and they founded a single party shortly after Article 6 was struck from the constitution.

The division between the liberal and social-democratic tendencies evident in the SDA persisted in the SDPR. The left wing favored a language of discourse and policy positions consonant with traditional social democracy. In a speech at the party's Second Congress in November 1990, Pavel Kudiukin, one of three cochairs and a leading exponent of the left tendency, urged his colleagues: "Let's not turn away from traditional social-democratic culture. Let's keep calling each other comrade." But Kudiukin acknowledged that seven decades of Communist power had "completely discredited the phraseology of the left." He conceded: "We have to be realistic about the fact that the country is moving to the right, in the traditional Western sense of the political spectrum, and we must avoid language and phraseology that would alienate people."[10]

Debate over language and political posture continued through the end of the Gorbachev period. Still, from the time of the party's inception it was clear that the liberal tendency would predominate strongly. Understanding the group's political complexion is not difficult. The party was so concerned with establishing a sense of itself that it invited sociologists to conduct detailed surveys on members' social backgrounds and political orientations. Polls showed that about one-half of members classified themselves as "liberal"; one-tenth as "socialist"; and the remainder as "centrist."[11]

But what did these categories mean in the context of Soviet Russia? What did it mean to be an *esdek*—a member of the SDPR? The party expended a great deal of energy trying to find out. During innumerable hours spent at meetings, including leadership plena and small, local-level gatherings, I was struck by the quantity of time spent on ostensibly minor matters, such as discussing "the situation in the country" or preparing the latest press release on this subject. Indeed, meetings normally proceeded as follows: The agenda was established in advance or at the start of the gathering, with discussion on general topics such as "the situation in the country" and "party life" as the first orders of business. Such issues were allotted a limited block of time—say, the first half of the first day of a two-day conference. According to the agenda, attention would then shift to more substantial matters: organization, fund-raising, membership recruitment, political strategy, and so on.

In practice, however, the latter portion of the agenda—that is, something like three-quarters of it—was usually reached in earnest only in the closing hours of the conference, if it was reached at all. It therefore received only the most cursory and desultory treatment on the part of frazzled members. Ostensibly less weighty issues consumed the lion's share of time and energy. Typically, *every* or *nearly every* member in attendance (at leadership plena, some forty to sixty individuals) took their turn at the podium and offered lengthy, impassioned analyses of the general political situation and denunciations of the regime. Even minor differences of interpretation of current events often sparked heated, long-winded debate. The ritual frequently included solemn injunctions by presiding members that speeches be curtailed to allow for quicker transition to more substantive matters, as well as periodic interruptions from the floor urging a turn to more "concrete" issues. In fact, members often castigated themselves and each other for engaging in idle talk as the country outside the meeting hall fell ever more deeply into crisis and conditions demanded prompt and forceful action. And yet, as speaker after speaker mounted the rostrum, discussion inexorably turned back to seemingly less pressing concerns: How do you evaluate the "situation in the country" and how does your assessment differ from mine? How shall a Social Democrat characterize the regime under which the country has lived for over seventy years? How do we feel about the most recent incidence of official treachery, what baleful effects will it have on the people, and how shall we phrase our public response to it?[12]

Excursus: Identity Formation and Internal Operating Procedures

Such a style of operation was not limited to the SDPR. It prevailed in every one of the some dozen groups that I examined closely, including all six under scrutiny here. During the initial months of observation, I was baffled by the ostensible insubstantiality of debate at group meetings, as well as by the heated disagreements that differences over apparently minor issues provoked. When queried about such matters in interviews and informal private conversation, activists would often sardonically attribute their penchant for lengthy discussion of what were intended to be preliminary topics, as well as the highly fractious nature of intragroup relations, to a "Russian disease" or the "Russian psychology." Interestingly, however, most stated or implied strongly that *they*—in contrast to most of their fellows—were well aware that their groups' operational styles and procedures undermined capacity for effective, united action. *They*, moreover, recognized the "Russian disease" for what it was and understood the need to combat it in order to build organizations better equipped to do battle with the regime. But what could one do? This was, after all, Russia.[13]

In the case of the SDPR as well as other groups, however, something deeper—something unique to (or at least unusual about) the Soviet Russian political experience but not necessarily the "Russian character"—was at work. That "something," often invisible to participants themselves, was the search for a collective identity under conditions in which autonomous political identities had been submerged for over six decades. Only after observing groups for nearly one year did I realize that resolving crucial organizational, financial, and strategic problems—formal agendas and sincere aims notwithstanding—*was not the point of group activities*. Despite their intentions and their clear recognition of the urgency of more "concrete" problems, participants first had to discover and realize a collective identity. That such a process was extremely divisive and tortuous, and included many long speeches and much heated debate on the "situation in the country" and the character of the regime, was understandable—even if unfortunate in its consequences for organizations' cohesion and effectiveness.

Internal fractiousness and a proneness to long-winded debate over ostensibly insubstantial matters are scarcely unique to Russian organizations. They are evident in political groups in many other countries, particularly in young organizations. Yet such difficulties were especially intense, universal, and debilitating in the groups that spearheaded Russia's democratic movement. Why, in comparative terms, was this the case?

Embedded in the process of forming a collective identity was the task of creating a language of public political discourse and norms for group behavior. Under no other modern authoritarian regime have rulers—even where heavy-handed and brutal—monopolized political communication and association as completely and for as long as they did in the Soviet Union. In most countries undergoing transition, establishing an autonomous language of political discourse and norms for collective political action involved reviving that which had lain dormant for several years or several decades—and which in most cases had never been completely snuffed out.[14] Even in much of East Europe, pockets and networks of informal political communication were not shut down as thoroughly or for as long as they were in Russia. As of 1989, Poland had enjoyed for nearly two decades a vigorous, partially tolerated underground press that featured not only criticism of the regime, but even debates between different currents of opinion within the opposition movement. In Hungary, genuine—if not unbridled—debate over economic policy began appearing in scholarly journals and the official press in the late 1960s, and nonconformist political communication after that time was rarely dealt with as harshly as in the Soviet Union.[15] Czechoslovakia's four-decade-long period of communism was punctuated at its midpoint by a brief but remarkable opening that featured public discussion of radical reform. After the crushing of the Prague Spring, the tone of official political communication and the level of political repression for the next two decades mirrored conditions prevailing in Brezhnevite Russia. But tenacious and celebrated groupings of scientists, writers, and artists with strong ties to the West managed to keep alive some forms of alternative, "normal" political communication—even if their language and modes of action took the form of what the most illustrious of their numbers has dubbed "antipolitical politics."[16]

In Russia, open, genuine political debate and discourse had been buried for three generations by the time that glasnost' took hold in the late 1980s. The thaw of the Khrushchev era indeed represented a departure from the preceding period. Still, at no time did the thaw involve even limited tolerance of public debate regarding radical transformation of or alternatives to the existing regime.[17] Dissident activity during the Brezhnev era, moreover, was waged by isolated individuals or tiny groups on behalf of the basic human rights of other individuals. Dissident ranks included handfuls of self-avowed nationalists, liberals, and "Eurocommunists." But such individuals labored largely in isolation and under great pressure; they were scarcely as capable of preserving the notions and language of humanism, liberalism, and social democracy as their counterparts in much of East Europe. The relatively greater impoverishment of political communication and association in Russia is due not to disparities between "East-Central European" and "Eastern" political-intellectual traditions over the centuries. Rather, it is best explained by differences in the stringency and duration of the regimes under which societies labored during the current century.

The near total loss in Russia of "normal" forms of political communication, and the disappearance from political life of philosophical and organizational categories taken for granted in much of the world—social democracy, trade unionism, liberalism, nationalism, Christian democracy, and so on—meant that forming autonomous group identities, once it was possible to do so, posed a particularly difficult challenge. It meant that declaring one's own affiliation, naming one's group, creating a common language, and reaching agreement on shared principles involved few if any "givens"; nearly everything had to be borrowed or created from scratch.[18]

Returning to discussion of the case at hand, it may be noted that one "serious" organizational matter actually was the subject of much debate and action within the SDPR. This was the question of whether or not to amalgamate with another party of similar orientation, the RPR. Before this matter is discussed, however, the RPR itself will be examined.

The Republicans

The RPR grew out of the Democratic Platform of the CPSU, the radical-liberal faction that formed at the beginning of 1990 to protest what its adherents regarded as the conservative intransigence of the party leadership. The atmosphere that surrounded the organization of the RPR in the summer and fall of 1990 was one of considerable optimism. Roughly 40 percent of the membership of the CPSU—though only a tiny fraction of its leadership—had expressed sympathy with the

Democratic Platform in opinion surveys conducted on the eve of the 28th Party Congress. Although the RPR counted only twenty thousand members at the time of its founding in the fall, leaders expected an early, massive inflow of members, particularly given the large number of resignations and "deactivations" that the CPSU suffered during 1990.

To attract defecting CPSU members, the RPR labeled itself a "party-movement" of noncommunist, but not anti-Communist, orientation.[19] To distance itself from its origins, however, it also strongly eschewed communist or socialist ideology. In fact, it renounced all ideologies of any type. Still the group, like the SDPR, was overwhelmingly liberal in outlook and professional in composition.[20]

What, then, was to be the party's raison d'être? Why did its adherents, upon quitting the CPSU, not simply join the SDPR, the DPR, or another of the already existing alternative parties? During the months preceding the party's founding, its organizers debated these points. They arrived at two reasons for starting a party of their own. First, according to Vladimir Lysenko, a deputy in the Russian parliament and the author of the documents on which the Democratic Platform had based its founding, former Communists needed their own party since separately they might not gain entry to other groups "as equals."[21] Second, according to Stepan Sulakshin and a number of other leaders, only by retaining their organizational integrity and status as a breakaway fraction of the CPSU could members of the Democratic Platform lay claim to a portion of the CPSU's property. Indeed, some members of the Democratic Platform/RPR held out hope until the spring of 1991 that the Communist Party would cede some of its massive holdings or might be forced to do so by the courts. The RPR intended to return the property it acquired to "the people" by turning it over to the control of soviets and perhaps even charitable organizations. Such hopes proved unjustified, and, as some activists later conceded, rather naive.[22]

The history of the RPR between its inception and the putsch was one of disappointment, declining expectations, and internal discord. The anticipated expansion in membership did not occur. On the contrary, initial estimates of membership numbers proved overly optimistic. At its Third Congress, held in June 1991, the group revised its estimate of members downward, to about five thousand.[23] Like the SDPR, the RPR experienced difficulty solving or even addressing problems of recruitment, propaganda, and fund-raising. It also suffered from serious internal divisions. By the summer of 1991, two of the group's cochairs, Lysenko and Viachislav Shostakovskii, were no longer on speaking terms. Factions had grown up around the two that threatened to destroy the party, though the group did avoid a formal split. The central source of strife, which also became a crippling point of contention within the SDPR, was the controversy over whether the two parties should form a single organization. The conflict within each party and the groups' failure to unite show how the struggle to form collective identities affected not only groups themselves but also relations between them. It illustrates the difficulties involved in realizing broader, unified organizations within the democratic movement.

Group Identity and the Conundrum of Union

The question of a full union of the SDPR and the RPR was on both parties' agendas even before the latter's formal founding conference in the fall of 1990. Many members and observers assumed that the two would not long retain separate identities. There seemed to be little point in doing so. Their programs were virtually identical; the social composition of both was overwhelmingly professional and intellectual; some leaders of the two were personal acquaintances; and neither group alone was large or well-endowed enough to pose a formidable challenge to the Communist Party regime. The only compelling "objective" reason not to unite was the hope of some Republicans that by maintaining a separate identity, they might acquire a slice of the CPSU's property. By the spring of 1991, however, such hopes had largely evaporated. The SDPR and the RPR appeared to be headed toward full consolidation in late 1990 when their members who served as legislators formed "unified RPR-SDPR fractions"—usually a handful of deputies—in soviets on all levels.[24]

But the union never occurred. In each party the proposal had its backers and its opponents; indeed, by early 1991 the matter became the main source of division within each party. Figures on the proportion of members in each party that favored consolidation varied wildly depending on the bias of the individuals issuing estimates and the ways in which the question was phrased in surveys.[25] In the end, opponents of union won the day, and plans for amalgamation were scrapped. The issue remained a source of discussion and controversy through the summer of 1991. As early as April, however, a commentator in an SDPR newspaper recognized that "there are no objective reasons for us not to join together, but the matter has become such a serious point of division for us both that it should be abandoned."[26]

Advocates of union, who included SDPR Cochairman Oleg Rumiantsev and RPR Cochairman Lysenko, appeared to have a strong case. They portrayed the separate existence of two small "liberal social-democratic" organizations as an unaffordable luxury at a time of official reaction and sharply rising political tensions.[27] Sergei Markov, head of the SDPR's program committee, argued that union was vital not only for effective struggle against an increasingly conservative Communist Party and Union government, but also "to convince the people that we democrats are serious and disciplined contenders, that we are not just up here playing games."[28]

So why did the union, so apparently sensible and even inevitable from organizational and strategic points of view, provoke such deep opposition within both parties, and why did it fail? Some opponents adduced matters of political principle. The RPR's Sulakshin and Shostakovskii both contended that the "social-democratic idea" had no place in Russia's political future. Given the devastating effects of the command economy and the extent to which the idea of "socialism" had been discredited, only a liberal approach based on Western-style capitalism could both attract popular support and rescue the country from ruin. Only in the unforeseeable future, after a market economy had begun to function normally, could "social-democratic" concerns for more equitable distribution be addressed.[29] Some of the SDPR's members who disfavored union expressed misgivings regarding this stance. They feared that some Republicans were so anxious to expiate their Communist political heritage that they had begun to swing to pure libertarianism.[30]

Upon examination, however, differences in principle between the two parties appear insubstantial and cannot explain their failure to join forces. The SDPR was dominated by avowed liberals who favored market capitalism; even Kudiukin, who identified with the party's "left wing," acknowledged this fact and asserted that the party would "orient itself on contemporary social democracy as it is now practiced in the West."[31] Both parties favored massive privatization and European-style mixed economies. Both, as will be discussed in the following section, sought their constituencies in the "new middle class." Both, of course, strongly espoused civil liberties of every type. Indeed, on these and all other points, their programs and public statements were virtually identical.[32]

The real source of opposition lay elsewhere. Namely, it was found in members' fervent desires to maintain the precarious and hard-won senses of collective identity that they had established within their groups. The cardinal significance that members attached to preserving their groups' identities was demonstrated clearly at party meetings. At the SDPR's Second Congress, held in October 1990, some delegates expressed fear that since the RPR appeared to be larger and stronger than their own party, the former would "swallow us up" in the event of full union. Many members stated that they supported union, but only in the event that their party could retain its own identity—a proposal scarcely consonant with genuine amalgamation.[33] Indeed, this inconsistent position became a well-worn litany at party gatherings. At the SDPR's leadership plenum in December 1990, speaker after speaker argued that there was no good reason not to unify the two groups and that progress toward doing so must begin at once—provided, that is, that SDPR's "party life" (*partiinaia zhizn'*) and "identity" (*litso*) could be preserved.[34] This view helps explain how 85 percent of delegates could respond in a survey taken at the party's June 1991 congress that they still favored union—without real progress toward union having taken place.[35]

The importance that members attributed to preserving their *litso* was also expressed frequently in private conversation. Aleksandr Obolenskii, an SDPR cochair and radical deputy in the USSR Congress who gained wide fame for daring to run against Gorbachev for the presidency in 1989, stated: "We [the SDPR and the RPR] do seem a lot alike, we share much common ground. But a full union threatens us with a loss of our own identity. . . . If we can find a way to unite without losing our identity it will be fine with me, but otherwise I cannot support it."[36] Virtually the same situation obtained in the RPR, with many members proclaiming the need to join ranks, but stopping short of endorsing what would amount to giving up their separate existence. Valerii Lunin, a member of the RPR's coordinating soviet, deputy in the Russian Congress, and leader of the democratic movement at Moscow State University, echoed Obolenskii's view: "Of course we must cooperate closely, that's desirable. But each organization, not just ours but theirs as well, must establish its own identity before there can be any progress toward union."[37]

Yet, given their closeness on matters of principle and organization, one might expect the Social Democrats and the Republicans to have regarded their own identities as entirely compatible and therefore to have felt that amalgamation would cost them very little. Explanation for resistance to union might be found in members' desires to preserve the feeling of "belonging" that they derived from participation in their organizations. Some analysts have demonstrated that while convictions and purposive goals often motivate individuals to join political organizations, members often remain active due to the satisfaction gained from social contacts and feelings of personal solidarity.[38] Thus, members of each party may well have wanted to avoid risking or diluting the comradeship they enjoyed with their colleagues. One might expect such a feeling of group belonging to be particularly precious to those who lived in an environment that had long suppressed free and independent association.

Political convictions and a desire for solidarity were indeed the primary motives for participation in movement organizations in Russia. Groups were too poor in both resources and access to power for material incentives to have served as compelling reasons for joining and staying active. And if activists were driven *solely* by *political principles*—by desires to act on one's convictions, to "make a difference" in forging a new society and influencing policy—uniting the SDPR and the RPR would not have been difficult. The two parties, after all, shared the same goals, and probably would have constituted a more formidable force as a single organization. The solidarity benefits that members derived from participation therefore did matter, and were at the root of the failure to unite.

But what aspect of their group identity were members afraid of sacrificing, and how would union have threatened the solidarity benefits that they enjoyed? Understanding the abortive union requires looking beyond programs and public statements. The real source of opposition to union lay in the meaning that members attached to their personal backgrounds and the relationship between their backgrounds and the identities of their organizations.

In the case of the SDPR, a crucial source of identity was members' non-Communist pasts. Few Social Democrats had any quarrel with allowing defectors from the CPSU into their organization. Several former Communists, such as RSFSR deputy Leonid Volkov, even held leadership positions. Yet "formers" constituted no more than about 20 percent of total membership, and none of the three original cochairs (Obolenskii, Rumiantsev, and Kudiukin) had ever been members of the CPSU. Given their intellectual and professional backgrounds, many had been invited to join the CPSU and refused, or had joined as young people and then quit long before it was "safe" to do so. While the SDPR was by no means a party of former dissidents, some of its members had suffered political persecution. Kudiukin, for example, spent over one year in a KGB prison for underground publishing—at a time when RPR Cochairman Shostakovskii presided over the Moscow Higher Party School, an ideological training ground for aspiring apparatchiks. One leading member of the SDPR stated at a plenum in December 1990: "It was tough for me not to be a Communist. I have nothing against [the Republicans] personally. But in the eyes of some people they appear repainted."[39] Obolenskii echoed these sentiments:

Each who joined the [Communist] Party overstepped, inside himself, an invisible internal boundary. He accepted the party's internal rules and blind subjugation. The majority in our party could not violate our own individuality and join the CPSU. For many of us refusal to join began the erection of obstacles that prevented us from realizing our own personal and career goals. Even now it's hard, before it was impossible, fully to realize oneself without joining the party. The Republicans are all formers; things changed, and then they left.[40]

Like most other Social Democrats, Obolenskii did not oppose admitting "formers" to the SDPR. But to unite with an organization made up almost exclusively of recent defectors from the CPSU would have meant that the large majority of his compatriots would suddenly become individuals who had benefited from the system that they now decried as a totalitarian dictatorship. Thus, union would have cost the SDPR an important component of its own identity: its status as a truly "non-Communist" organization, most of whose members had for years or decades demonstrated personal courage and integrity.

The question of former political status was also significant to the Republicans. But it influenced identity and contributed to opposition to union somewhat differently than in the SDPR. In the RPR, the crucial aspect of group identity that blocked union was the belief that members' origins as Communists, and as renegades who had initiated a radical reform movement *within* the CPSU, accorded them special status within the democratic movement. Specifically, many members regarded their origins as proof of their superior intellectual and organizational attainment. References to their own group's "high intellectual and scholarly level" recurred frequently in speeches, documents, and interviews with leaders. Anatolii Tretiakov, one of the RPR's main organizers in the city of Orel, explained that his party "differs from others insofar as it brings together the intellectual and highly active forces in society."[41] Valerii Lunin maintained that "the main thing is not our numbers but our intellectual strength and our potential to unite democratic tendencies."[42] During a meeting of the RPR's coordinating soviet in the spring of 1991, Cochairman Sulakshin made his argument against union with the SDPR by referring to the latter's "lower intellectual level." To drive his point home, Sulakshin even gestured in the direction of SDPR Cochairman Rumiantsev, who was in attendance as a guest![43]

To be sure, many Republicans experienced deep ambivalence over their Communist pasts. They also feared that their origins might reduce their new party's popular appeal. To avoid the nightmare, expressed by an activist prior to the party's founding, that "a year from now, no one will remember that we were the Democratic Platform, only that we were Communists," they assiduously distanced themselves from Communist ideology and organizational practices.[44] Lysenko, while asserting that the party had no ideology, claimed for it status as "the most liberal of all the parties."[45] The group stated that its choice of name not only expressed the high priority it assigned to republican sovereignty, but also "remove[d] the problem of our Communist past, which would have remained had we retained the old name [the Democratic Platform]."[46]

On the other hand, the Republicans were former Communists who had become acquainted with one another while working within the CPSU—even if as rebels. Furthermore, however strongly they renounced their previous political affiliation and rejected the Communist Party as a hegemonic ruling structure, many harbored a residual, grudging pride at having been members of the organization that assembled—by inducement, inspiration, or threat—most of the country's most able and accomplished citizens. They also felt that they really had something to lose by joining the democratic movement. They therefore regarded their own failed attempt to "democratize" the CPSU, followed by their full break with it, as demonstrations of a boldness that democrats who had never been Communists could not appreciate or understand.

In both of the groups under discussion, the struggle to establish collective identities served as a crucial source of three interrelated phenomena: the inordinate time and energy expended on ostensibly inconsequential matters and the consequent failure to resolve more substantial problems; the divisions that appeared within the groups, often provoked by small differences among members over semantics or interpretation of current events; and the intractable difficulties that the parties experienced in realizing organizational union. The complete absence in Russia for over six decades of autonomous associations and independent means of political communication meant that the search for collective identities—deciding who we are, what we believe, and how we are to conduct our business—proved particularly vexing and tortuous. To a far greater degree than in other contemporary transitions, the most basic elements of collective political identity had to be invented and assembled entirely from scratch. Political-organizational "inexperience" therefore played its role. But answers to *how* inexperience affected group formation and *why* it proved such a serious impediment to organizational development and consolidation are found in the process of identity formation. Finally, the irreducible and irreconcilable kernel of each group's *litso* that undermined plans for union had little to do with objective factors such as program, principles, strategy, or organization. It lay, rather, in a subjective factor that may appear relatively insubstantial to the observer but nevertheless carried profound meaning for the actors themselves.

The Russian Experience in Comparative Perspective

Some of the problems discussed above, including organizational disarray and a tendency to focus on seemingly minor issues at the ex-
pense of far more pressing ones, were particularly intense, pervasive,
and enervating in the organizations of the democratic opposition in
Russia. But such difficulties are scarcely unique to Russian organizations. For example, in his fine study of the Green Parties in Germany
and Belgium, Herbert Kitschelt observed that "militants expend un-
told hours on reaching small decisions, siphoning off political enthusiasm." He was struck by the parties' "unpredictable internal decision
modes," as well as the "factionalism and endless procedural debates
. . . and interpersonal conflict" that prevailed within them. As part of
his explanation, he offers an intriguing proposition: "Factionalism
tends to increase the more a party emphasizes the democratization of
society as one of its overriding goals."[47]

While Kitschelt does not indicate conclusively the possible direction
of causation, his analysis implies that the sweeping and nonnegotiable
nature of group demands itself somehow helped produce the disorder
and lack of discipline he observed. The hypothesis is prima facie convincing. Certainly the problems he witnessed among the Greens are
neither as strikingly conspicuous nor as debilitating in their effects in
the German Social Democratic Party or other groups whose aims, at
least in the contemporary period, are far more concrete and circum-
scribed than "the democratization of society." In the Russian case, *all*
of the organizations of the democratic movement indeed put forward
"the democratization of society" as their central demand; and they suffered—arguably, in even greater measure—from all of the factionalism, interpersonal conflict, endless debates over apparently insubstantial issues, and unstable or ineffective internal decision modes that
Kitschelt witnessed in the subjects of his study. Taken together, these
dysfunctional traits and behaviors will be referred to here as the "syndrome of ineffectiveness."

Kitschelt's hypothesis may be illustrated in the following simple
model:

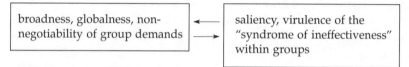

The possible direction of causality is not firmly specified; causality
may run in either direction or in a reciprocal, mutually reinforcing
relationship.

Analysis of Russia's opposition groups suggests the need for elaboration and refinement of this hypothetical model. It indicates that while sweeping demands and a "syndrome of ineffectiveness" are indeed correlated, no necessary causal link exists between them, and both may be caused by another factor.

It was argued above that the complete and long-term absence in Russia of associations capable of pressing and expressing social demands and engaging in autonomous political communication greatly complicated the task of forming collective identities within the groups that emerged in response to liberalization. To a greater extent than in other cases, Russia's new opposition organizations had to invent their identities *ex novo*. The very act of associating freely and independently for political purposes was entirely new. For more than sixty years, no collective political identities of any type other than those created and sponsored by the Communist Party had been tolerated. No societal interests or causes had enjoyed autonomous voice.

In the SDPR and the RPR, it was precisely all the matters that were bound up with creating a collective identity that engendered the pathologies that prevented the groups from getting on with more serious business. Identity formation includes deciding what we believe, how we understand our country's plight and our role in reversing it, and how we are to conduct our business. Creating an identity does *not* include tackling the more substantive problems of strategy, tactics, agitation, and resource mobilization. Indeed, the latter are best conceived of as "second order" problems that can be addressed effectively only after the former set of issues has been resolved and a meaningful group identity established. In other words, members must decide who "we" are before they can decide what we are to do and how we are to do it. The more difficult and complex the process of creating identity, the more virulent the "syndrome of ineffectiveness" and the greater the difficulty of even reaching the stage of actually "getting things done."

Furthermore, the sweeping demands that groups put forward in the Russian context did not themselves *cause* internal dysfunction. To be sure, groups did issue global, nonnegotiable demands—including and especially the "democratization of society," in all of its meanings and ramifications. But the grandiosity of demands, like the complexity and tortuousness of collective identity formation, stemmed from the novelty of the groups themselves and of the identities around which they organized, as well as from the prior absence in society of voice for the interests and causes groups championed. As discussed in the previous chapter, the long-standing prior ban on autonomous association and communication plus the state's previous refusal to confer even the most fundamental rights of citizenship—much less to address distrib-

utive or "postindustrial" concerns—meant that all the new progressive political organizations put forward demands of every type. Taken
together, these demands amounted to—in fact, required—the "democratization" of just about everything. Since all demands of every type
had been pent up for three generations, it is unsurprising that, once
their expression became possible, they appeared to be—and were—
sweeping, global, and seemingly limitless.

In the German and Belgian cases, the act of associating freely for
political purposes was of course not new. Free communication and
open competition for influence among autonomous, self-constituted
organizations had long been normal features of political life. But the
principles around which the Greens attempted to construct their identities—those of "deep ecology," which envisions fundamental transformation of the relationship between humans and the natural environment—were indeed novel; and they previously had enjoyed no
strong, organized voice in the political system. It was precisely the
novelty of the groups' identities and the newness of their voices in the
political arena that both engendered the expression of sweeping demands and vexed the process of forming a sense of "we" within the
parties. And the struggle to form a coherent identity quite naturally
produced many of the pathologies also visible in Russia's new organizations. It similarly undermined capacity to "get things done" and operate effectively in the broader political arena. It is noteworthy that,
given the novelty of their identities and their voices, *all* of Russia's alternative political parties and other autonomous political associations
experienced the same conundrums as the European Greens, and for
similar reasons.

The argument may be summarized roughly in the following scheme:

```
┌─────────────────────────────────────────────────────────────────┐
│     novelty of groups' identities and voices in the political arena (A) │
└─────────────────────────────────────────────────────────────────┘
              ↓                                    ↓
┌──────────────────────────────┐   ┌──────────────────────────────┐
│ broadness, globalness, non-  │   │ complexity and difficulty of │
│ negotiability of group demands (B) │   │ collective identity formation │
│                              │   │ within groups (C)            │
└──────────────────────────────┘   └──────────────────────────────┘
                                                   ↓
                                   ┌──────────────────────────────┐
                                   │ saliency, virulence of the   │
                                   │ "syndrome of ineffectiveness" │
                                   │ within groups (D)            │
                                   └──────────────────────────────┘
```

All variables are continuous; all relationships are positive; and causality runs in a single direction. The probability that B and D will be correlated is high, since both are the product of A. But the relationship

between B and D is not causal. C serves as the intervening variable by which A exerts its effect on D.

The scheme may provide a more differentiated and less opaque picture of the dynamics of new organizations than is commonly found in the literature on social movements. Analysts have long noted that new organizations, and particularly those that aim to speak for previously unmobilized constituencies and interests and that put forward sweeping demands, conduct their operations differently from those that are more "established" and/or that speak for causes and groups that already enjoy voice in the political system. Some have also observed that the former appear to be more "disorganized" than the latter. Some scholars, moreover, have placed a great deal of emphasis on questions of "identity" within social movement organizations. Indeed, an entire body of writing on social movements is widely known as the "identity school." But within this literature, the questions of *why* "identity" matters, *what* shapes it, and *how* the process of its formation influences groups' operations are rarely addressed squarely. Causal relationships among variables are hardly ever specified clearly. Analysis is often blurred by an obscurant argot that stresses "conflicts around control of cultural patterns" and "intersubjective understanding" rather than political struggle, explication of concepts, and comparison across cases. The analysis presented here may point the way to a more fruitful and precise approach to understanding the role of identity formation in the development of social movement organizations.

In its examination of the sources of organizational dysfunction and the difficulties groups experienced in joining forces, this section has emphasized problems of collective identity formation. The legacy of total state control over associational life influenced strongly the progress of identity formation within the groups that emerged in response to liberalization; and the process of identity formation, in turn, engendered a host of difficulties for new organizations. Another important environmental factor—namely, the climate of suspicion and mistrust within groups created by the threat of infiltration and sabotage—also vexed intra- and intergroup relations. This factor will be discussed later in the section on organizational structures. The following section investigates organizations' searches for support in broader society.

Locating a Constituency

Russia's autonomous political groups, like their counterparts anywhere, faced the task of cultivating membership and support. Debate has long raged in the literatures on parties, organizations, interest groups, and social movements over whether the class basis of organizational affiliation, voting behavior, and collective political action in general has changed substantially in Western democracies in recent decades. Related questions regarding the extent to which "objective" social cleavages between classes, sectors, denominations, ethnic groups, and communities find expression in representative political organizations have also stirred much controversy. Yet most analysts agree that political organizations, however "accurately" they reflect "objective" cleavages, do target certain social groups for support and formulate their programs and appeals accordingly. Furthermore, even most scholars who emphasize the role of elite behavior and human agency, and/or regard the relationship between political-organizational affiliation and "class" position as loose and indeterminate, would concur with Otto Kirchheimer's assertion that social structure establishes the "conditioning perimeters" within which political leaders must work.[48]

Russia's insurgents characterized their attempts to locate constituencies and attract support as the search for a "social base." If their efforts to establish collective identities centered on the questions of "who are we?" and "what do we believe?," their searches for social bases addressed "whom do we represent?" and "who shall join us?" The slow growth and modest magnitude of opposition organizations demonstrated that the latter set of questions proved no less vexing than the former. The difficulty of finding a social base—and, consequently, of realizing substantial and robust organizational development—stemmed from the peculiarity of the contours of the social-structural perimeters that defined the environment in which organizers operated.

In recent years many Western scholars have emphasized what they regard as the growing sophistication and stratification of social structure in Russia. Some hold that even before 1985, industrialization had given birth to a "new middle class," engendered subtle graduations within that class, and stimulated growing stratification within the "working class" as well. According to this argument, Soviet social structure in the post-Stalin period converged with the social structures of Western or relatively advanced developing countries.[49]

Yet, as discussed in chapter 1, such scholars confuse cause (industrialization) with effect (growing class differentiation). They fail to explain how industrialization could have given rise to Western-style social differentiation in a society in which bus drivers and unskilled laborers often earned more than university professors or skilled laborers, where the state served as the sole major proprietor and employer, and where political authorities tightly controlled the professions. Such analysts also typically treat urbanization and growing educational attainment of the population as a whole as evidence of deep and growing social-structural variegation within society—as if the first inexorably and concomitantly produced the second.[50]

Most writings that emphasize social-structural differentiation use diachronic rather than cross-country empirical referents. Thus, contemporary social structure in Russia is usually compared to that which existed during the Stalin era or even in prerevolutionary times, not with social structures in Western or developing countries. Russian society has unquestionably undergone substantial differentiation over the past half-century. Still it continued through the end of the Soviet period to differ starkly from nonsocialist societies.[51] The Brezhnev-era policy of *uravnenie* (equalization) of wages, combined with the long-standing ban on private property and entrepreneurship and near-total state control over employment, production, distribution, and services, limited severely the social-structural effects of economic change. Finally, neither the black market nor the corruption and privileges of the apparat induced genuine class formation and differentiation. Black markets do not create middle classes; and, as one scholar has remarked, "The embourgeoisement of the political elite is not the same as the rise of a Soviet bourgeoisie."[52]

In industrialized societies, most major political associations, including parties, unions, and interest groups, are based in large part on material interests. The concerns and programs even of associations that represent ethnic communities are usually rooted to some degree in economic demands and aspirations. The weak and peculiar stratification of Russian social structure therefore established very different "conditioning perimeters" around political life than those evident in many other—particularly nonsocialist—cases. Opposition leaders in Russia were acutely aware of the challenges that socioeconomic circumstances posed. These conditions both limited public involvement in the new autonomous organizations and shaped the latter's programs and political strategies.

The Social Democratic Party of Russia and the Republican Party of Russia: The Search for the Elusive Middle Class

Like some other groups, the SDPR and the RPR initially intended and expected quickly to become mass organizations. Yet neither party experienced the anticipated growth in membership and support. Both were forced quickly to adjust their expectations and ambitions.

The SDPR explicitly claimed the "middle strata" of the population as its social base. At its Second Congress, held in October 1990, the party declared that "our social base is the new middle class, though we seek to foster social partnership and want to help all strata adjust to the market."[53]

Where was this new middle class to be found in a society shaped by the command economy, in which only the first and most tentative steps toward market formation and small-scale privatization had been taken? Leaders quickly grasped that the stratum they targeted existed in only the most inchoate form. They recognized the need both to adjust their expectations and to appeal to the broadest possible segment of public opinion. At a meeting of the program committee in March 1991, one activist pointed out that "we must recognize that the structure of our society is not really normal. Our skilled workers sometimes make less than our unskilled ones, and then we have the problem of the lumpen intelligentsia."[54] Cochairman Obolenskii noted in February 1991 that "the paradox is that in our country we probably don't yet have a stratum that can serve as our social base. So we probably now should abandon our efforts to gain mass membership and just use our intellectual potential to work out a sensible program that will attract people and use it to win elections."[55]

But what of a more traditional social democratic strategy, one that aimed to build working-class support? Certainly the party would have welcomed close links with the coal miners, whose strike demands, which included massive privatization, departiization of the workplace, and parliamentary democracy, were as unabashedly liberal as those of the SDPR. Several party members did, in fact, attempt to forge ties with miners' and other workers' groups. But the effort was largely unsuccessful, and the party as a whole invested little in it.[56] Leonid Volkov expressed the dominant view when he stated at a party gathering that efforts to entice workers were premature: "I see little reason to try to direct our activities toward workers. The fact is that workers don't need us now, and they won't until we have a market system. The working class hasn't clarified yet in our country."[57] One of the party's few leaders who did advocate a traditional social democratic strategy, Galina Rakitskaia, echoed Volkov's assessment, albeit inadvertently and from a different point of view. Rakitskaia stated that she objected to the party's "idea to foster a new middle class, then represent it but also be a party of class compromise." Rather, her group should concentrate more on "representing the interests of hired labor." Yet she admitted that it would be difficult to determine what this approach would mean in practice: "Of course it's hard to say what it means to represent 'hired labor' under our conditions. I, as a professional scholar at this institute, am no less a 'hired laborer' than any manual worker. Most people are in this category in our country, and we all work for the same employer."[58]

The difficulty of locating a constituency led the Social Democrats to a position that Kudiukin characterized as "socioeconomic realism."[59] This stance, which was expressed in the party's program, amounted to maintaining focus on the "new middle class" but addressing appeals to the broadest possible audience and formulating them on the basis of "general human interests." It also meant that the group to a large extent came to view itself as an actor that would struggle for democratization in the present, but that would realize mass membership and assume genuine representative functions only in some unforeseeable future.

The experience of the Democratic Platform/RPR paralleled that of the SDPR. The former openly stated its aim to represent virtually all interests and all strata of the population. Cochairman Lysenko defined the party's constituency so widely as to include virtually everyone but the general secretary of the CPSU. He asserted that the RPR "is striving to realize its program working for the interests of workers, military personnel, entrepreneurs, pensioners, intellectuals, and other strata of the population."[60] Yet, as its founding documents stated, the party intended to represent "above all the interests of middle strata." Explicitly omitting calls for equality of station or outcome, the group expressed its intention to strive "for equality before the law and equality of opportunity" for all, and for the creation of a nation of genuine citizens.[61]

Yet, as Cochairman Shostakovskii stated in an interview in May 1991, the elements on which the party intended to base itself had, at best, only begun to emerge. Speaking in the future tense, he explained: "As for our social base, I think we will be a party of intellectuals and of free labor, and will represent the interests of alternative [nonstate] sectors of the economy, cooperatives, commercial banks, and a segment of skilled labor."[62]

The quandary in which the SDPR and the RPR found themselves was summarized effectively by Andranik Migranian in an interview held in late 1990. Speaking to a leader of the Party of Constitutional Democrats (PKD), a small group that like the SDPR and the RPR strove to promote liberal democracy, Migranian argued that the obstacles to the growth of opposition parties were to be found as much in broader society as in the parties themselves. He told his interviewer from the PKD: "All right, let's look at your party as a liberal-democratic party. In that case it must be a party that relies on middle strata of the population. But in today's Russia such strata do not exist. . . . Of course, if there occurs a transition to a market [economy], it will give birth to new social strata, and these will seek to express themselves politically." At the present stage, political groups needed to rely on the leadership of "famous people" to attract mass support. According to Migranian, however, they lacked such celebrated individuals.[63]

The Democratic Party of Russia: From the Party of Labor to the Party of Travkin and Other Anti-Communists

The one opposition party that defied Migranian's generalization regarding the absence of famous people was the Democratic Party of Russia, headed by Nikolai Travkin. Several other parties, most notably the RPR and the SDPR, did include several prominent radical parliamentarians. Yet only the DPR was led by a figure of real public renown.

The DPR, as originally conceived by those who planned its founding in the spring of 1990, was to be a broad-based democratic movement organization that would stimulate mass public participation in opposition activity. Travkin, however, angered many of the dozen or so other prominent activists involved in preliminary organizational work with what they regarded as his authoritarian and egomaniacal style. Travkin's insistence, put forth suddenly and unexpectedly at the party's founding meeting, that the group be governed by a single chair rather than a group of cochairs further alienated many of his colleagues. Due to his celebrity, acquired in part through his impassioned speeches before the USSR and RSFSR parliaments (he was a deputy in both bodies), his plan prevailed and he was elected chairman. Some prominent organizers, including Lev Ponomarev, Vera Kriger, and Leonid Bogdanov, immediately quit the party and turned their energies toward building what would soon become Democratic Russia.[64] Others, including Garri Kasparov and Arkadii Murashev, stayed in the DPR, though these two figures later left after personal disputes with Travkin.[65] Whether an unrent DPR could have achieved a genuine mass base—and perhaps even have performed the role to which Democratic Russia later aspired—must be left to question.

Despite its rocky and inauspicious founding, the DPR subsequently pursued the goal of gaining broad support with greater intensity than either the RPR or the SDPR. Like the others, it experienced setbacks and disappointments, and secured only a fraction of the members that its leaders had hoped for and anticipated. It nevertheless fared somewhat better than other parties, attracting over thirty thousand members by the summer of 1991.

The DPR's leaders initially regarded radical workers' groups as their natural allies. During the spring and summer of 1990 Travkin courted labor aggressively. In one interview he stated that "the workers' movement is our social base." He held that his party's and workers' groups mutual aim of rapid departiization of the workplace served as a strong basis on which to unify forces. He expressed optimism that radical labor would soon see the need for involvement in an opposition party and maintained that the DPR would prove a natural magnet. Acting forcefully on his statements, he traveled to the Kuzbass in an attempt to enlist miners' groups as collective members of the DPR.[66]

By early 1991 Travkin had changed his position. In January he stated: "We're not a party of workers, of intellectuals, or of any other group. We say that the economy doesn't work, so let's found a market system. We see the need for democratic structures, so we seek to build them. People who feel the way we do—that's our social base. Maybe interest-based organizations will emerge in time, that's fine. But that's for tomorrow. Right now we have to change this regime."[67] What induced the change of strategy? Early failures to achieve a mass inflow of workers very likely contributed to the shift. While the Kuzbass miners received Travkin warmly, they were loath to associate themselves closely with the DPR or any other democratic movement organization and rejected appeals for joining as collective members.[68]

The shift was also rooted in leaders' assessments of class-based recruitment strategies. In an interview held in June 1991, Mikhail Tolstoi, one of the DPR's three deputy chairmen and a member of the RSFSR Congress of People's Deputies, raised the issue of why opposition political organizations "don't really represent concrete popular interests." Asserting that "to understand all of our parties' problems in terms of lack of experience would be facile and unsatisfactory," he offered a sophisticated and elegant—if somewhat hyperbolic—explanation:

> Our population is simply not highly stratified according to interest. It is still a homogeneous, faceless mass. The communists destroyed classes; their idea was that the population would be made uniform, and then the party would represent this uniform mass, this abstract people, as its vanguard. This was the Bolshevik scheme, and it was, to a large extent, realized. Now we see the beginning of some differentiation of interests in society. But only after we have had real free commerce and entrepreneurship will we be able to speak of distinct interests of hired labor, entrepreneurs, bureaucrats, military personnel, and so on. . . . We must first become structured as a society, and only then as a polity.[69]

Another of the party's deputy chairmen, Aleksandr Terekhov, offered a similar assessment. Defending his party's eschewal of pursuing a certain social stratum in its program and public appeals, he stated:

"We could adopt a social democratic strategy, and pretend to defend the interests of labor. But doesn't social democracy emerge in response to the inequalities produced by a market economy? We don't have a market economy."[70]

But the DPR adapted to the social-structural environment differently than the SDPR or the RPR. While the other groups backed away from their original hopes for quickly achieving a mass base, the DPR clung to such hopes. Alone among the alternative parties, the DPR continued to maintain, in the words of Tolstoi, that "massiveness is absolutely necessary to do battle with the regime." According to Tolstoi, "the tremendous informational, technical, and financial problems that a movement faces in this enormous country" meant that only strong, sizable organizations could "develop the infrastructure necessary for effective operation."[71] The SDPR and the RPR largely resigned themselves to status as "parties of the future." They remained active in the struggle for democracy, but accepted that they would flourish and undertake substantial representative and mobilizational responsibilities only after genuine transition to a market economy had begun. The DPR, by contrast, decided to portray itself, in Travkin's words, as "a party of today."[72]

To this end, the DPR abandoned entirely a commitment to any social stratum. By the end of 1990 references to "the working class" disappeared from its documents and public statements. Its program, which was published in early 1991, explicitly eschewed plans to represent any class or social group. It maintained that the DPR was a party for all "socially active people who refuse the world of illusions . . . [a party that seeks] the social, economic, and spiritual rebirth of Russia."[73]

To stimulate mass involvement, the DPR highlighted what it perceived as its two most attractive features. The first was its leader. The DPR became known in popular parlance as the "party of Travkin," and the party itself did nothing to discourage use of this epithet. While Travkin was widely regarded in the democratic movement as an unprincipled opportunist, he did enjoy a high degree of public recognition. Furthermore, he enjoyed a public reputation as a committed organizer, as a bold "doer" in a movement—and a polity—that seemed to have more than its fair share of "talkers." He and his party did not shy away from exploiting his celebrity to recruit members. When asked if he feared that his group would degenerate into personalism, Travkin replied: "If it takes personalism quickly to realize a real mass party right now, that's fine. Later on participation can be based on programs and principles."[74]

The second card that the DPR played was its anticommunism. All organizations of the democratic opposition were, by definition, anti-

Communist. All sought to bring down the regime and to promote transition to democracy and market capitalism. But many groups, including the SDPR and the RPR, did not place "anticommunism" per se at the center of their agendas and public appeals. Most of their leaders regarded it as an insufficient basis for building "constructive" programs. Despite their revolutionary demands, many had little taste for fighting bolshevism with what they regarded as Bolshevist tactics.[75] The DPR had no such compunctions and regarded "anticommunism"—however loose and vague as an orienting principle—as a strong basis for mobilizing the disaffected. While taking care to avoid condemning Communists "as people," the DPR did cultivate a reputation for vehement opposition to the CPSU and all that it stood for.[76]

To some degree, the strategy worked. The DPR became the largest of the alternative parties. Its relative strength was particularly evident in the provinces, though Travkin's claim that "50 kilometers outside Moscow and Leningrad we are the only group with a presence" was a gross exaggeration, as will be shown in the following chapter.[77] The DPR's social composition was relatively diverse. The party did not undertake extensive sociological research on its own membership. During attendance at numerous party gatherings, however, I found that the DPR was less overwhelmingly intellectual, professional, and middle-aged than other parties. It spawned a modest—but in comparative terms, not unimpressive—youth organization. At its Second Congress, women comprised 30–40 percent of delegates—compared to about 10 percent at the meetings of the SDPR and the RPR.[78]

In sum, the DPR operated in the same social-structural environment as other opposition groups, and it similarly failed to achieve the mass involvement that its founders had desired and anticipated. Yet its continued commitment to mass participation, along with its decision to forsake soliciting particular social strata in favor of personalist and anti-Communist appeals, enabled it to achieve relatively high levels of organizational growth.

The Russian Christian Democratic Movement: A Community of Believers

The Russian Christian Democratic Movement was the main Christian Democratic organization of the democratic opposition. The RKhDD declared its existence as a party in the spring of 1990, though it preserved the term "movement" in its name and declared that members were free to continue their participation without formally joining the "party within the movement." In early 1991 its leaders estimated—

very likely with considerable exaggeration—that the RKhDD comprised about fifteen thousand activists, roughly one-third of whom had chosen to join the party. While the RKhDD was not the sole Christian Democratic organization in Russia, it was the only one of any real significance. Others included the Christian Democratic Union (KhDS) and the Russian Christian Democratic Party (RKhDP). The former was organized in 1989 by Aleksandr Ogorodnikov, who had spent more than a decade in prison for religious activities. Ogorodnikov was well known among human rights activists in the West and religious dissidents in Russia. But his eccentricity and modest organizational skills alienated most of his original followers. By early 1991 most KhDS groups throughout Russia had renounced their association with him and joined the RKhDD. For its own part, the RKhDP never grew beyond a few dozen associates of its organizer, a young scholar named Aleksandr Chuev.[79]

Like the SDPR, the RPR, and the DPR, the RKhDD espoused sweeping democratic goals, roundly condemned the regime, and urged transition to market capitalism. Hints of Russian nationalism occasionally surfaced in the statements of a few of the RKhDD's leaders. But the group strongly denounced "national-patriots" such as those active in Pamiat'. Nationalism was clearly subordinated to universal, liberal goals. Only after the putsch of August 1991 scattered and transformed the democratic movement would a virulent, illiberal form of Russian nationalism show its face clearly in the RKhDD.[80]

In contrast with the other three parties discussed above, the RKhDD never aspired to mass membership nor sought a social base among particular economic or occupational strata. It regarded itself instead as a community of believers. It espoused a clear division between church and state, but its ethos was less secular than that of contemporary European Christian Democratic parties. The group was not confessionally exclusive. In several central Russian cities activists recruited among the small but growing communities of Seventh Day Adventists.[81] Most members of the RKhDD, however, were adherents of Orthodoxy. Two of its cochairs, Viktor Aksiuchits and Gleb Anishenko, were Orthodox philosopher-publicists. The third, Viacheslav Polosin, was an Orthodox priest. Another leader, Gleb Iakunin, was an Orthodox priest and celebrated human rights activist who had suffered persecution for religious activities during the Brezhnev era.

One might expect religious belief to have furnished a firmer basis for recruiting members than economic interests. Perhaps well-defined classes did not yet exist in Russia. But certainly there were religious believers. The RKhDD clearly sought its social base among the faithful, without regard to economic interests or station. Viktor Aksiuchits, an

RKhDD cochair and a deputy in the RSFSR Congress, declared: "We are Christian publicists, philosophers, historians; we are those who have studied and who know our nation's best spiritual traditions, and we seek to bring these back to life." Aksiuchits expressed pride in his movement's makers, asserting that "our base, the religious intelligentsia, is the flower of the Russian intelligentsia." Yet he stated, with regret, that such a base could not give rise to a broad mass movement:

> Other democrats, and indeed the people as a whole, have largely lost touch with our national and religious traditions. Most of society has, tragically, forgotten what we talk about. We are, under current circumstances, pioneers. . . . We know we are the exceptions, espousing ideas that have to a great extent been lost. Maybe in the future we will have a mass base, but we do not have one now. We cannot develop a mass social base now relying as we do on Christian public-mindedness [*khristianskoe obshchestvennost'*] since this has been destroyed and depoliticized in our society. So, you see, our social base is vigorous and free-thinking, but it is really very narrow.

Thus, just as leaders of the SDPR and the RPR acknowledged that their own chosen constituencies—portions of the "new middle class"—were still inchoate and did not yet furnish foundations on which to build substantial organizations, so did Aksiuchits regard his association's social base as poorly defined and articulated. Only in some still uncertain future, after "Christian public-mindedness" had reestablished itself in national life, could his movement expect to become a formidable political force in its own right.[82]

The Democratic Union: The Few and the Bold

The Democratic Union (DU) was the first organization in Russia to confront the regime directly. From the time of its inception in 1988, it denounced the CPSU in the harshest terms and demanded full civil liberties, Western-style multiparty parliamentary democracy, and capitalism. It was the first group to declare itself a political party. It did so as an act of defiance against the ban on alternative parties. Alone among democratic movement organizations, the DU, or at least a large majority of its members, renounced participation in any activities sponsored by the state, including soviet elections. At its Fifth Congress, held in January 1991, activists debated whether to drop the "party" label in favor of "movement" or some other term. They agreed that their association was not in any normal sense a party. But a majority voted to keep the original label as a badge of their early—and initially, solitary and perilous—resistance to the regime.[83]

The DU was the ultra-radical flag of the democratic movement. It refused to join Democratic Russia. It regarded fellow democrats from other organizations as weak-kneed compromisers, ever importuning the authorities for permission to engage in opposition.[84] According to Eduard Molchanov, the editor of the DU's main newspaper, *Svobodnoe Slovo* (Free Word), Unionists sought, above all else, to enjoy and exercise "freedom without prior permission."[85] The DU was profoundly anti-Communist, but it did not build an ideology around "anticommunism." It refused even to recognize the CPSU as a legitimate force worthy to be reckoned with.

The DU sought above all else to foster the birth of a "citizen's consciousness" in Russia. It offered an extremely harsh critique of Soviet society as well as of the regime. It held that totalitarianism had erased any notion of citizenship and even independent personality. Much like the émigré writer Aleksandr Zinoviev, Unionists maintained that individuals had become slavish accomplices in their own degradation. Unlike Zinoviev, however, they believed that the "Soviet mentality" could be overcome. The route to recovery of citizenship lay in civil disobedience, in what the group called the "civic path" (*grazhdanskii put'*). Unionists exhibited a singular talent for attracting the blows of police clubs and for landing in jail. They reveled in their arrest records and in the barrage of attacks that the official press leveled against them.[86]

For the Unionists, praxis was everything. Opposition was a way of life rather than a form of organization. The group did nothing to identify and cultivate a social base. The only meaningful social distinction was that between those who lived *po-sovetskii* (in the Soviet way) and those who had recovered their individuality and acquired a citizen's consciousness. Class, religious, and ethnic distinctions were of little importance. The notion of a "social base," which figured prominently in the discourses of other movement organizations, was rarely broached by Unionists. The DU saw its role not as structuring movement activity and representing interests, but rather as demonstrating to society that the regime could be challenged, that "one does not have to live by the lie." It never really sought a mass membership or following.[87]

Nor did it achieve one. It never grew beyond about two to three thousand adherents throughout the Soviet Union. Its "social base," such as it was, comprised bold, disgruntled, antipragmatic individuals from all walks of life. Many of its members were intellectuals, though the group did nothing to attract intellectuals per se. Some had histories of dissident activity; many were students, teachers, and writers who had lost their jobs for political reasons. In terms of membership, influence, and notoriety, the DU probably peaked sometime in mid- or late 1989. By the time of the coup attempt, the DU's numbers had dwindled and its role had largely been played out. Given its maximalism, and the considerable—indeed, foolish—courage that defined it members' approach to political liberation, the group's smallness was scarcely surprising. Yet its influence outweighed its numbers. By challenging the regime openly before others dared to do so, and by repeatedly absorbing the blows of police truncheons in the name of principles that others would only later espouse openly, the DU forged substantial public space for independent political activity during the initial phases of liberalization.

Democratic Russia: The Great Umbrella

The formation of Democratic Russia in October 1990 represented the culmination of efforts to build a framework for coordination among democratic forces. The decision to found such an organization was taken at a meeting of the Moscow Union of Voters in June 1990.[88] In some respects, the founding of Democratic Russia represented a fallback strategy. Had the DPR not suffered mass defections of strong leaders at the time of its founding; had celebrated democrats such as El'tsin or Tel'man Gdlian launched parties or broad popular fronts of their own in 1988 or 1989; or had the Democratic Platform/RPR rapidly realized its original plan to attract hundreds of thousands of defecting liberal-minded Communists, Democratic Russia might never have been conceived, at least not in the form that it assumed in the fall of 1990. As it was, however, the difficulties of public mobilization and party-building, along with the increasingly conservative cast of the Communist Party and the Union government, convinced democratic leaders of nearly all stripes of the need to pool their efforts, at least temporarily. In short, Democratic Russia was largely an ad hoc response to the needs for public mobilization, intergroup cooperation, and coordination among progressive deputies in soviets. In its charter, Democratic Russia declared its intention to unite "all progressive forces" and to promote the emergence of a civil society in Russia.[89]

Democratic Russia was principally a coalition of groups. At its founding conference, 16 percent of delegates came from the DPR; 10 percent from the Democratic Platform/RPR, 8 percent from the SDPR, and so on.[90] As an organization of organizations, Democratic Russia cannot really be treated as a distinct, separate entity of its own. But it did constitute a force larger than the sum of its major constituent associations. Assessing actual membership in Democratic Russia is exceedingly difficult, if not impossible. Clearly, however, many hundreds of thousands of citizens who would never consider joining more formalized groups associated themselves in some way with Democratic Russia. Many attended its demonstrations, purchased its membership card for a few rubles, and contributed small sums to its general funds in cities and towns throughout Russia.

The leadership of Democratic Russia was broader than a collection of the leaders of its constituent groups. While each major collective member of Democratic Russia enjoyed representation on its coordinating soviet, some activists who did not represent other groups also served in the leadership. Thus, while Democratic Russia's leadership organs included Vladimir Lysenko of the RPR, Viktor Aksiuchits of the RKhDD, Nikolai Travkin of the DPR, and so on, it also included Iurii Afanas'ev and Vladimir Bokser, whose only real organizational allegiance was to the umbrella group itself.

Differences between leaders who represented other organizations and those who did not were often evident in Democratic Russia's internal debates. Leaders who had built independent organizations prior to the formation of Democratic Russia were often reluctant to subordinate their groups to the "general will" of Democratic Russia. They tended to regard Democratic Russia as a temporal marriage of necessity and argued that it must limit its activities to consultation, coordination, and information provision. On the other hand, some of those who had refrained from independent organizational work prior to the umbrella group's founding regarded it as a force superior to its collective members. They sought to expand its functions and its authority to speak for the movement as a whole.[91] In practice, while Democratic Russia did foster cooperation among progressive groups, its leaders from the parties ensured that it never acquired the authority to discipline members and make decisions binding on them.

Democratic Russia never sought a constituency on the basis of class, confession, ideology, or any other category save opposition to the regime. It aimed for maximum inclusion, though it restricted its own numbers to self-avowed democrats. In early 1991, at a time of growing official conservatism, a debate broke out in Democratic Russia over how widely the group should cast its net. At a meeting of the coordinating soviet in late January, the RPR's Lysenko urged building a "broad antireactionary coalition" that would include "not only democrats, but all those opposed to harsh dictatorship." Comparing Democratic Russia with the Lithuanian popular front organization, Lysenko argued: "Let's face it: We are not Sajudis. In Russia we do not have a widely supported national movement. We are now living through a dangerous official reaction. We should make common cause now with even those apparatchiks who oppose dictatorship." Most leaders rejected this strategy. Vladimir Bokser, expressing the view of the majority of the coordinating soviet, asserted that Democratic Russia would lose its meaning and its muscle if it reached out even to those who did not call themselves democrats. While "ordinary" members of the CPSU were welcome, the movement could scarcely accommodate all but the most reactionary custodians of the regime.[92]

Still, as its founding documents stated, Democratic Russia embraced all "progressives"—that is, anyone who opposed the regime and favored democracy. Its "social base" was its collective members plus anyone who identified with its goals. It intentionally avoided appeals or activities that suggested dedication to anything but the most general, universal goals of democratic revolution. Any pretensions to interest representation or to mobilizing or appealing to particular sectors or strata were left to its collective members. To avoid usurping its collective members' functions or alienating individuals who might be put off by a highly structured organization, Democratic Russia insisted on maintaining its status as a "movement." El'tsin's fleeting suggestion, made in a speech in March 1991, that Democratic Russia consider converting its status to that of a "superparty" was immediately quashed by the group's leaders.[93]

This section has discussed how social conditions in Russia, shaped by the legacy of Communist Party rule, influenced the growth and development of autonomous political forces. The cleavages and interests around which political organizations normally form were only weakly present in Russia during late communism. Opposition leaders themselves were acutely aware of the obstacles that the country's peculiar social-structural conditions posed, and their assessments on this matter shaped their political behavior and strategies.

The weakness of socioeconomic differentiation, caused by decades of étatization of property and employment, the absence of markets, and policies that compressed wage differentials and divorced material compensation from occupational station and economic performance, limited severely the potency of appeals and programs based on economic interests. No classes, no class-based politics. The eclipse of Orthodoxy and other confessions over seven decades of repression reduced the potential of religion and spiritual commitment as bases for political organization. It inhibited the growth potential of groups that sought to base themselves, as did the RKhDD, on "Christian public-mindedness." Finally, ethnicity and nationalism could not, of course, play the same defining political role that they did in non-Russian republics or even in East Europe. Due to Russia's status as the maker and central entity of the Soviet regime, as well as ethnic Russians' overwhelming numerical preponderance in the RSFSR, a powerful ethnic movement based on aspirations for national liberation did not emerge. All democratic movement organizations did, by mid-1990, call for "sovereignty" for the Russian Republic. But this effort to withdraw Russia from the Soviet Union was a tactic used to weaken the "center" and the Communist Party regime. It did not represent an ethnic movement for national independence in the sense that a group such as Sajudis—or for that matter, Solidarity—did. In short, the interests, issues, and divisions around which political organizations normally form and develop were less evident and differentiated in Russia than in most other cases.

Russia's social terrain created incentives for political organizations to abandon quickly or to avoid altogether appeals and strategies based on economic interests or other categories that typically serve as bases of organization. Given the shape of Russian society, "passions"—rather than "interests"—constituted the motor of autonomous political organization; and all major movement organizations shared the single overriding passion for democracy. Groups' programs therefore differed very little. The programs of all of the organizations discussed above condemned the regime in broad, caustic strokes; stressed "freedom of the individual" as the greatest good; and touted "general-human values" and "common sense" as core principles. All were long on generalities and sweeping statements of liberal philosophy; all were short on specifics and concrete proposals for action.[94] The SDPR's Kudiukin offered an incisive diagnosis and explanation: "In almost all programs general-democratic and general-liberal goals predominate. We all share a common goal: to transit from an essentially pre-industrial socio-political structure to a modern society. In such a situation it is unsurprising that one program hardly differs from another."[95]

Those groups that did not entirely abandon a commitment to particular social strata—the SDPR, the RPR, and the RKhDD—either never held or quickly retreated from hopes for rapidly acquiring mass membership. They came to phrase their statements of organizational aspiration in the future tense. Those groups that maintained a strong commitment to mass membership and participation—the DPR and Democratic Russia—ruled out any appeals based on socioeconomic, religious, or other interests. They formulated their appeals exclusively on opposition to the regime or on personalism. These groups did achieve a relatively high level of popular involvement. Finally, the

Democratic Union neither sought to build a distinctive social base nor to achieve mass membership. Rather, it simply served as a magnet and an outlet for expression of profound discontent with the political system.

Crafting Organizational Structure

The Commitment to Internal Democracy

Most of the organizations of the democratic opposition enjoyed—or suffered from—a high level of internal democracy. The hierarchical structures and oligarchy typically found within political organizations, in democracies as well as authoritarian systems, were rarely seen in Russia's democratic movement. Indeed, from the standpoint of the requirements of efficacious decision making and action, organizations were excessively democratic. Given its corrosive effects, hyperdemocracy may in some sense be regarded as part of the "syndrome of ineffectiveness" discussed above in the section on identity formation.

Intensely democratic and participatory structures and practices were evident in the earliest of the informal groups that emerged in 1987–88. True to the label they adopted, most of the informals lacked any real leadership organs—much less formal hierarchy and discipline. For instance, one typical informal group, *Aktivnaia Positsiia* (Active Position), which was founded by several dozen activists in the far northern city of Apatity in 1988, self-consciously operated as a gathering of equals. According to one organizer, there was simply no room for hierarchy in an organization committed to overcoming the stultifying effects on the individual and society of decades of subordination and blind obedience.[96] Such a commitment to egalitarianism was visible in larger informal groups as well. The Moscow Popular Front also functioned as a loose collection of equals. The Moscow Union of Voters (MOI) did form a leadership structure. But its governing organ took the form of a broad, nonhierarchical coordinating soviet of some nineteen individuals.[97]

The organizations examined in this chapter were more highly structured than the informal groups that preceded them. Yet the former were also loosely assembled and possessed collective leadership structures. In all of the groups, most major decisions were made at congresses of full memberships. All were governed by a body of some twenty to sixty members in which all regions were represented. Groups adopted different names for this body. The SDPR called it the "governing board" (*pravlenie*); the RKhDD borrowed the prerevolutionary term "Duma"; others referred to it as the coordinating soviet.

At the top level, most of the groups were headed by an assembly of cochairs. Only the DPR, which will be discussed separately below, was led by a single chairman. The SDPR, RPR, and RKhDD each had three cochairs; Democratic Russia had six. The DU had no chair or cochairs at all, only a coordinating soviet. In none of the groups were well-defined, discrete tasks actually apportioned among leaders. Leaders were not cochairs *for* anything in particular; they were simply cochairs.

Activists often criticized these features of organization. The leader of the SDPR in Tula called the cochair system a license for "collective irresponsibility."[98] Mikhail Astaf'ev, a leader of the KD/PNS, inveighed against Democratic Russia's sexpartite chair and remarked that "it is not surprising that Democratic Russia can hardly ever agree on anything."[99] The collective leadership structure and the irresponsibility that it bred was even ridiculed at group meetings. At a February 1991 leadership plenum of Democratic Russia, Leonid Babkin, a scholar who was widely regarded as a sage of the democratic movement, raised the issue in a speech. At one point he called for all cochairs in attendance to identify themselves. The request betrayed that only one of the six was present—and this at a crucial leadership conference convened to devise strategy on the upcoming referendum on the status of the Soviet Union and the future of the Russian presidency. Though the revelation scarcely shocked activists in attendance, it predictably prompted groans, hoots, and much sardonic shaking of heads.[100]

For all groups except the DPR, discipline of any type was anathema. It was rarely if ever in evidence at meetings. As discussed above, conferences normally featured countless hours of lengthy speeches by every or nearly every member in attendance—an operating procedure that consigned the formal agenda to irrelevance. Other forms of discipline were also shunned. Expressing a position common among democratic groups, the RPR declared in its founding documents that its members who served as deputies in soviets "work for their voters only." In no case would the party attempt to enforce a "line" on its members. In practice, group leaders scrupulously observed this principle.[101] Additionally, none of the groups considered the decisions of leadership organs or even full congresses binding on local organizations. Chapters were in all cases free to undertake their own activities and take their own positions in accordance with the requirements of local conditions. Most associations, including all of those under examination here, simply required that no person or group claim to speak or act on behalf of the organization at large if its position or action plainly contradicted the principles and rules adopted at congresses and leadership plena. Thus, Viktor Kuzin remained a respected member of the Democratic Union even while he served as a deputy in the Moscow City Soviet—despite the Union's strong opposition to participation in elections or service in elective office. The DU's rejectionist position on participation in "official" activities, adopted and reaffirmed by overwhelming majorities at congresses, was strictly regarded, in the words of Eduard Molchanov, as a "nonbinding recommendation."[102]

No organization, of course, was perfectly democratic in practice. Groups exhibited some of the traits identified with Samuel Eldersveld's model of "stratarchy," insofar as control from the top over local organizations remained minimal, while authority to speak for the organization often resided de facto with an "elite echelon."[103] As will be discussed in the following chapter, "central" offices—for reasons of geography, communications, resources, and external threat, as well as ideals—exerted virtually no control over chapters in the provinces. The "elite echelon" that claimed to speak for the group and that made mundane, week-to-week decisions was in all cases the Moscow-based, or "central," chapter. These bodies were quite large, encompassing a circle far wider than the cochairs alone. In the case of the RPR this group numbered twenty-one members and called itself the party's "working colleagues" (*rabochie kollegy*). This group, which brought together the roughly one-third of members of the national coordinating soviet who resided in Moscow, met weekly and managed the party's affairs between meetings of the coordinating soviet and between congresses. The analogous organ in the case of Democratic Russia had no special title or form, but in practice also brought together members of the coordinating soviet who lived in the capital. It numbered some twenty-five to thirty persons.[104]

Even the modest degree of centralization and hierarchy involved in such arrangements frequently came under fire from non-Muscovites. Since central bodies did not control local chapters, protests regarding interference from Moscow were rarely heard from provincial organizers. Yet the latter did often contest the authority of Moscow-based chapters to speak on their behalf and to direct group affairs between plena or congresses. Pleas from provincial activists for full inclusion in decision making were often heard at leadership plena and meetings of coordinating soviets or their analogues. In the spring and summer of 1991, the RPR experienced serious internal discord over what some provincial leaders regarded as "Moscow's" arrogance and alleged tendency to ignore their preferences.[105] The internal bulletin of the SDPR frequently included articles by local leaders urging that if certain decisions must be made before the next full congress, the full membership somehow first be canvassed on the matters under consideration.[106]

Only the DPR deviated from this pattern. It eschewed—or attempted to eschew—hyperdemocratic internal norms and procedures. It established a hierarchical authority structure, the top levels of which consisted of a single chair and three deputy chairs, each of whom was assigned a distinct area of competence. As was the case with other organizations, the party's central organs in fact exercised little control over provincial chapters. But the DPR's leaders did adopt a somewhat less laissez-faire approach to provincial organizations. Not only did they attempt more aggressively to recruit members outside the capital city, but they sought more assiduously to maintain close links and frequent communications between Moscow and everywhere else. To this end, Chairman Travkin traveled frequently and extensively throughout Russia, exhorting potential recruits and encouraging—or, perhaps more to the point, ordering around—the faithful, however modest their numbers might be in a given location.

The DPR's leaders regarded full pluralism and democracy within opposition organizations as antithetical to advancement of these same values in society as a whole. Party discipline, according to Deputy Chairman Tolstoi, "is dangerous and undesirable only when there is only one party." In any polity, he argued, only hierarchical organizations, run by professionals, can effectively mobilize citizens, structure political competition, and offer the public real choice.[107] Travkin never tired of attributing the collective impotence of progressive deputies in the legislatures—particularly in the Moscow and Leningrad soviets, where radicals held majorities but produced little to show for it—to the absence of strong, disciplined parties.[108] In fact, according to Travkin and the DPR's other leaders, discipline and hierarchy were even more urgently needed under Russian conditions than in democratic polities. Given the foe's—the Communist Party's—immensity, authoritarianism, and hegemonic position, progressive groups could hope to survive and compete only if they realized a high level of coherence and capacity for united action. Fire could be fought only with fire; the opposition, Travkin asserted, would have to form "analogous structures"—that is, adopt some of the enemy's features—in order to do battle with it.[109]

Travkin's principles were certainly not always realized in practice, and they often divided the party. Indeed, his attempt to establish less-than-democratic internal structures encountered considerable resistance and caused the defections of Garri Kasparov, Arkadii Murashev, and several other leading activists. The DPR's meetings were sometimes more orderly than those of other movement organizations, but not much. Many members objected to hierarchy but stayed in the party only because they admired Travkin's pugnaciousness, or because the DPR seemed to them to be the most clearly "anti-Communist" of the new parties.

Within the democratic movement, in any event, the DPR's organizational structure was exceptional. The following sections examine the two major causes of the hyperdemocracy that prevailed within most groups: activists' desires to depart from the traditional Soviet style of organization; and intragroup mistrust and fear stemming from the threat of hostile infiltration and sabotage by state authorities.

Breaking with "Bolshevism"

Alberto Melucci has noted that the organizational form that a social movement adopts may be "an end in itself," as well as a "message, a symbolic challenge to dominant codes."[110] The organizational forms found in Russia's democratic movement indeed represented symbolic challenges to traditional Soviet forms of organization, with their subordination and sham participation. Activists' fervent desires to escape from the culture of "democratic centralism" that pervaded not only the CPSU but all Soviet "public organizations" lay at the root of the participatory and nonhierarchical ethos evident in most opposition groups. The groups were in a literal sense "reactionary," insofar as they took shape in self-conscious antithesis to the regime they opposed.

Within most groups, the concentration of individuals committed to highly participatory forms of organization was even higher than it might have been had there been substantial material incentives for joining. As discussed above, opposition groups' lack of access to resources or real power meant that most individuals who joined were motivated by matters of principle and personal solidarity rather than by material inducements. Joiners sought to participate in and direct group affairs, not merely to "get along" and passively to reap "benefits." The structure of incentives for participation therefore reinforced the normative commitment within many groups to participatory and democratic procedures.

In their organizational practices, democratic groups (except the DPR) strove above all to break with what they habitually termed "bolshevism." The term, as used by oppositionists, was understood as "democratic centralism" in all of its manifestations plus an amoral "ends justify the means" mentality. "Undemocratic" associations, according to most activists, could not forge democracy; intragroup democracy was a necessary concomitant of the democratization of the broader polity. A commitment to internal democracy and a critique of traditional "Bolshevist" methods was evident in the earlier writings of some of those who would go on to organize political associations. For instance, at the time when the first of the "informals" were making their debut, Oleg Rumiantsev published a lengthy tract that attacked the prevailing "bureaucratic model of the neofeudal type" with its "hierarchy, centralization, and disallowance of horizontal ties or spontaneous development" within organizations. Drawing on both Gramsci and Tocqueville, Rumiantsev argued that the new autonomous groups, with their highly decentralized, nonhierarchical, and participatory character, might effect a laudable "revolution in public consciousness."[111]

The desire to break completely with "Bolshevist" organizational principles was evident in most of the groups that succeeded the informals. The Democratic Platform of the CPSU was originally founded largely to protest the lack of democracy *within* the party and to press for abolishing democratic centralism.[112] Not surprisingly, the party that the Democratic Platform spawned, the RPR, vigorously eschewed traditional organizational ways. The RPR's Lunin, expressing a widely held reservation concerning the DPR's style of organization, asserted: "Although I respect Travkin, we democrats should not and ultimately cannot build organizations that resemble the CPSU but that work against it. It's not consistent, it's not democratic, and it doesn't make good sense."[113] The Democratic Union's Molchanov echoed, in even stronger terms, Lunin's sentiments. Molchanov regarded his group's antitraditional organizational structure as one of its proudest achievements: "We thought for a long time about how to destroy hierarchy. Our solution was the coordinating soviet. We invented this broad and nonhierarchical structure. Now almost everybody, including the MDG [the Interregional Deputies Group of the USSR Congress of People's Deputies] has adopted it."[114] The veracity of Molchanov's suggestion that other groups modeled themselves on the DU must be left to question. But his observation that others also sought to purge the demons of subordination and centralization was essentially accurate.

Internal democracy was not only a moral imperative; according to many democrats, it was also a practical necessity. The RPR's Shostakovskii held that organizations that exhibited features associated with the Communist Party and its affiliates would, in the final analysis, only repel people. "Given our history and the popular mood," Shostakovskii stated, "most people are not going to be attracted by tough discipline."[115] RKhDD leader Aksiuchits shared this view. He argued: "Right now we need a movement, we need parties without rigid (*zhestkie*), Bolshevist structures. Most people just don't like the idea of having more of what we've had for so long."[116]

The Hidden Hand of the State and the Politics of Mistrust

Activists' convictions, shaped largely in opposition to the negative example furnished by official organizations, served as the first cause of hyperdemocracy within organizations. The second cause derived less from democratic principles than from the exigencies created by external threat. Specifically, it stemmed from the mistrust created within opposition groups by the fear of surveillance, infiltration, and sabotage by the organs of state security. The presence—demonstrable or merely suspected—of state agents within associations engendered strong resistance among activists to concentration of authority and closed decision-making procedures.

Autonomous political organizations comprised individuals who in most instances became acquainted with one another only in the course of working together in their groups. Everyone, moreover, lived in a society in which the state habitually monitored in myriad ways even persons with no history of political dissidence. These factors insured that strange or inexplicable occurrences or the appearances of sharp divisions within groups often raised the specter of sabotage and bred uneasiness and suspicion among activists.

Indeed, the threat of infiltration by individuals who were, in the vernacular of the opposition, "not with us" weighed heavily on democratic movement organizations. In the case of the SDPR, for instance, one member urged at the December 1990 leadership conference that the party create a "special service" for "defending ourselves against infiltration from the outside." While the idea was rejected by a majority as impracticable and potentially self-defeating, its proposal did illustrate the depth of anxiety over the external threat.[117] Sergei Belozertsev, a deputy in the USSR Congress and a leading member of the SDPR, voiced similar concerns in an article published in the summer of 1991. Adducing examples in the SDPR and in Democratic Russia of projects strangely gone awry, mysterious disappearances of funds from the coffers of local organizations, and the frequent, sudden appearances of divisions within groups over "matters that had already been settled," he asserted that "if we consider more why we haven't gotten things done, we would better understand the presence of the KGB in our organizations in the democratic movement."[118] Given the extremely suspicious murder of the editor of one of their publications and the ransacking of their main offices in the spring of 1991, few Social Democrats failed to recognize and feel the threat from outside.[119]

The specter of infiltration and sabotage in some cases complicated relations between as well as within groups. It was noted earlier how the struggle to create and protect group identities helped undermine efforts to unite the SDPR and the RPR. The external threat also contributed to the failure to unite. Some members of the SDPR feared that unification risked bringing a spate of KGB agents into the party. The Republicans' status as former Communists heightened anxieties. Concerns over the issue at one point led SDPR leader Leonid Volkov, himself a former Communist and at least for a time an avowed advocate of union with the RPR, to explain to his colleagues: "We shouldn't worry that union [with the RPR] will bring in the KGB. The KGB uses non-[Communist] Party people anyway to infiltrate our groups."[120] Volkov's assertion that one should not confuse former party affiliation with propensity to work for "the other side" was almost certainly on target. But his decision to make an explicit statement to this effect during a leadership plenum showed that the danger of sabotage was of concern to many activists and contributed to their reluctance to join forces with the RPR.

The RPR also sensed a threat from "the outside," though it did not seem to fear that union with the SDPR would exacerbate that threat. Cochairman Shostakovskii stated: "Everyone knows that these supposedly secret workers, an army of millions, are in all organizations, big and small. We definitely feel the pressure. . . . Strange things happen in our Moscow organization, and many occurrences are not accidental. And some of our leaders have come under direct pressure."[121] As in many associations, the fear of infiltration bred suspicions and poisoned intragroup relations. At a meeting of the RPR's coordinating soviet in the spring of 1991, several leaders openly and heatedly accused one another of working for the KGB.[122]

The RKhDD, according to Cochairman Aksiuchits, similarly suffered heavy infiltration and sabotage. Aksiuchits attributed "periodic, utterly inexplicable blow-ups" within the organization, as well as arbitrary police action against the small publishing cooperative that the group founded to raise funds, to intentional acts by agents of state security. He asserted with great confidence that Aleksandr Chuev, leader of the tiny Russian Christian Democratic Party, was a KGB agent, planted to discredit and divide supporters of Christian Democracy. He held that the head of the Christian Democratic Union, Aleksandr Ogorodnikov, was not a KGB agent, though "the KGB knows very well how to use such inept people." Aksiuchits claimed that he and some of his colleagues knew such things with absolute certainty, adding: "We're old human rights activists. We've dealt with them [the KGB] before. We know how they work."[123]

Gauging the accuracy of such assertions is impossible. Participants themselves—not to speak of observers—could not always know for certain which "blow-ups" and other myriad difficulties stemmed from "normal" intragroup politics and which were perpetrated by infiltrators. The hand of the security agencies was very often truly invisible. As the DPR's Tolstoi explained, "The KGB uses others, and works in such a way that it cannot be seen or traced or directly felt. All sorts of things happen. But where's the KGB? Nowhere, it seems."[124]

Given the magnitude and operational style of the agencies of state security, activists' own accounts and experiences, and documentary evidence that has come to light since August 1991, the degree of infiltration of many groups was indubitably extensive. Indeed, during the period of official reaction that began in mid- and late 1990, the KGB itself abandoned the pretense that it did not monitor and interfere in the affairs of the opposition. Its chief, Vladimir Kriuchkov, announced in a speech delivered to the USSR Congress of People's Deputies in December 1990 that his agency "does not adopt the stance of an onlooker" in its dealings with "antisocialist forces."[125]

Yet, for the purposes of present discussion, the actual extent of infiltration was less important than oppositionists' perceptions and beliefs regarding the threat of it. As the statements and incidents adduced above reveal, activists were acutely sensitive to the dangers of covert intrusion. Their perception of threat kept them in a constant state of suspicion regarding many of their fellows. Unsurprisingly, suspicion created a climate of mistrust—or at least wariness—within groups.

Still, why and how did mistrust caused by external threat engender "hyperdemocratic" organizational structures and styles of operation within groups? The causal relationship might seem counterintuitive. Threat of hostile infiltration by the authorities has often given rise to tightly knit, closed, secretive, and highly centralized oppositions. Tsarist Russia, after all, bore the Leninist revolutionary party; and oppositions working in other authoritarian police states have frequently imitated this organizational form.

Explanation for the link between external threat and internal hyperdemocracy is found in activists' extreme reluctance to delegate authority under conditions of rampant suspicion, as well as in the situation created by the presence of a state so penetrative and secret police so pervasive that no opposition group could even hope to escape their gaze. The logic of the argument is explicated in the next chapter, which analyzes in detail the effects of official resistance and repression on the democratic opposition.

The following and final section of this chapter departs from discussion of the internal dynamics of opposition groups and considers their place in the broader political arena. In particular, it investigates groups' struggles for sway over policy and public opinion and their relationship with official power.

Struggling for Influence

Confronting Official Power: Closure and Decay

According to some contemporary analysts, the "political opportunity structure" that shapes the environment for social movement activity exerts even greater influence over the development and behavior of movement organizations than do macrosocial phenomena. Some scholars who adopt such a view, such as Sidney Tarrow, argue that the degree of openness of formal political institutions is a crucial—perhaps *the* crucial—component of political opportunity structure.[126]

In comparative terms, the degree of openness of state institutions in Russia during the Gorbachev period was, at best, extremely limited. Despite liberalization, central authorities and the party demonstrated little interest in or aptitude for establishing mechanisms and channels for devolving power to emergent societal forces. In contrast with many other political transitions, little if any negotiating or "pacting"—implicit or explicit, secret or public—occurred between representatives of the authoritarian state and the opposition. Unlike many military governments in Latin America or Southern Europe—or for that matter the Jaruzelski government in 1988–90—the Gorbachev leadership never intended to withdraw from power. It anticipated—indeed, initiated—changes *in* the regime; but it never planned for or intended a change *of* regime.

During the middle years of the Gorbachev period, it appeared that Gorbachev and other "softline" leaders might, like their counterparts in many other transitions, ally themselves at least partially with opposition forces. Some of Gorbachev's public statements, most notably his oft-cited injunction to ordinary citizens that "we will push from above, and you push from below," led some observers to believe that he intended to split the party and initiate genuine power-sharing and democratization. Had Gorbachev turned resolutely against the regime's "hard-liners" and embraced the emerging democratic opposition in 1989 or perhaps even 1990, the subsequent history of Russia—and perhaps the Soviet Union as a whole—might have been different than it was in fact. By mid-1990, however, Gorbachev had begun openly and consistently to express only contempt for the "so-called democrats" and had unambiguously declared his allegiance to "socialist choice."

At no time did he attempt to cultivate ties with or recognize the demands of any democratic movement organizations in Russia. The only meaningful negotiations or serious discussions that ever took place between the central government and forces external to it were undertaken with republican governments, and then only during the last several months of the preputsch period.

To be sure, central authorities did at times enter into discussions with a number of new parties and other organizations—but only with "reliable" groups that had been created by the state. The official tactic of establishing puppet organizations parallel to real autonomous groups, discussed in chapter 2, extended to political parties in 1990. In the spring, as the DPR, the RKhDD, and the SDPR came into existence, so too did groups such as the Liberal Democratic Party (LDP). Led by the eccentric demagogue Vladimir Zhirinovskii, who earlier was expelled from several democratic movement groups on suspicion of working for the KGB, the LDP received ample attention in the official press. Its founding was announced on the front page of *Pravda*, which did not report the founding of other alternative parties.[127] In June, the LDP and several other tiny parties with names such as the "Party of Peace" and the "Party of the Person" coalesced into the "Centrist Bloc." Soon after the coalition's founding, its representatives, none of whom were known in the democratic movement or had gained election to any soviet on any level, were featured on television and radio programs. They were shown meeting with officials such as the head of the KGB, Vladimir Kriuchkov, the chairman of the USSR Supreme Soviet, Anatolii Luk'ianov, or Prime Minister Nikolai Ryzhkov, none of whom ever met, formally or informally, with leaders of other new parties. After discussions on topics such as "our multiparty system" or "the dangers of Left extremism," a leader from the Centrist Bloc— often Zhirinovskii—would meet with the press to laud the government's "cooperative stance," its commitment to pluralism, and its eagerness to enter into "constructive dialogue" with alternative parties.[128]

The Union government's response to the massive miners' strikes of early 1991 further illuminated the state's unwillingness to open channels for negotiation with its opponents. Gorbachev's response was limited to scolding the miners for undermining the economy. Prime Minister Pavlov met with "strike committees" that were actually representatives of official unions that were not on strike. In the surreal "negotiations," which received coverage in the national media, the "workers" put forward modest economic—but no political—demands. The government promptly "met" them, and both parties walked amicably away from the table. Since miners in most regions had already dropped their economic program in favor of purely political demands, and since the government's negotiating partners represented no one, the talks did nothing to settle the strikes.[129]

While these stratagems lent an already bewildering political theater a touch of the absurd, they failed to discredit, divide, or co-opt the democratic or workers' movements. They did demonstrate the utter inability and/or unwillingness of power holders to deal seriously and imaginatively with autonomous political actors. They helped convince broad segments of public opinion that the regime was unreformable, that democracy could scarcely develop on the Communist Party's watch.

What formal contacts did develop between central authorities and genuine opposition groups were for the most part limited to relatively low levels. The Communist Party apparat did include agencies responsible for relations with "social-political organizations." Responsibility for such contacts was normally invested in low- and mid-level officials in the ideology departments of local party organizations. Contact between officialdom and autonomous groups normally took the form of "roundtable discussions" organized by authorities. One official in the Moscow city Communist Party apparat who maintained relations with independent groups, a young self-proclaimed "Gorbachev man" who expressed distaste for the party's most conservative elements and who scarcely fit the stereotype of the colorless and tight-lipped party functionary, described his work in the following terms:

> We organize roundtable discussions as well as media campaigns. Organizations and movements have their own documents and programs in which they present their ideas for the development of society. We invite them to roundtables. At our discussions, we find weak spots, illogical places in their programs. We correct them, and show that on a given proposal that nothing good for the people will come of it. We offer frank criticism. . . . We say, "Look here, this point we accept, but there you're wrong. Let's change it and find common language." We make our case in the media as well. Unfortunately, however, in today's conditions, the opportunities for finding common points are very few, since a sharp polarization has taken place in society.[130]

Not surprisingly, such discussions neither created channels through which autonomous organizations could articulate demands and influence policy nor elicited the enthusiastic involvement of democratic activists. Oppositionists, in any event, were under no illusions. Expressing a view shared by nearly all democratic movement leaders during the latter stages of the Gorbachev period, the SDPR's Obolenskii stated: "At this point I doubt that the party can actually maintain full control over society indefinitely. But I also doubt that it has any intention of doing otherwise."[131]

But the intransigence of state institutions represented only one aspect of their closure. Their disorganization—indeed, by 1990, advanced state of decay—also inhibited the formation of channels between the state and societal organizations. Some disintegration of the state provided a crucial opening for the growth of opposition. But, paradoxically, the rapid erosion of state institutions' authority during the second half of the Gorbachev period in some respects presented opposition organizations with difficulties no less challenging than those posed by direct official interference and sabotage. The indispensibility of stable and responsive state institutions for the growth of civil society is recognized by many modern theorists. Andrew Arato and Jean Cohen point out that "a modern civil society . . . is in a complementary relation to at least some version of the modern state." A state that lacks effective economic and administrative steering functions, structures permitting for the intermediation of interests, and a capacity for the universalization of law can actually impede the emergence of the organizations of civil society.[132] State and society do not necessarily stand in inverse relationship. The power of each may even rise and fall together.[133]

Yet, by the end of the 1980s, the state in Russia possessed only *negative* power—that is, the ability to control, obstruct, harass, and coerce. As will be shown in detail in the following chapter, these powers remained formidable through the end of the Soviet period. But any remaining capacity to bargain, compel, and convince evaporated during 1989–91. Independent political forces faced state institutions that were not only unwilling to negotiate, but also to a large degree unable to deliver.

The Opposition's Response: Frustration, Radicalism, and Expressive Mobilization

The reality of official closure was not lost on the democratic movement—nor, for that matter, on society at large. Official closure strongly influenced the development of the organized democratic opposition. Above all, it discouraged mass membership and participation in— and therefore retarded the growth of—autonomous organizations. Groups' lack of access to power quite naturally reduced incentives to join them. Political conviction and a desire to engage in struggle and to enjoy the company of like-minded fellows of course drove some to take up building organizations anyway. Yet, given groups' lack of influence over policy, along with overwhelming (and justifiable) public skepticism regarding prospects that the party and its nomenklatura intended to devolve power or could be forced to do so in the near future, it is unsurprising that only a tiny fraction of the Russian population ever sought involvement in independent political organizations.

Groups' dearth of influence not only limited their attractiveness to ordinary citizens; it also reduced incentives for holders of private wealth to invest in them. The deficit of autonomous economic power in Russia presented movement organizations with material constraints far more acute than those faced by analogous groups in countries where property has been less completely controlled by the state. The quantity and availability of what some analysts of social movements call "potential support groups" were very low.[134] But even among those holders of private wealth who were present in Russia at the time, incentives to invest in organizations whose clout was so modest were normally not strong. There were exceptions. Garri Kasparov, the world chess champion, implacable anti-Communist, and one-time activist in the DPR contributed one million rubles to help start up what became a leading independent publication, *Demokraticheskaia Rossia* (Democratic Russia).[135] Leonid Bogdanov, the chief of Democratic Russia's financial operations, claimed to have forged gainful ties with some organizers of the Moscow *Birzha* (a nascent commodities exchange) as well as with several other wealthy individuals.[136]

But such contributions from a relatively small number of highly motivated actors were hardly adequate to build flush organizations. They did help enable Democratic Russia to establish an office in Moscow, publish several small-circulation newspapers, and begin offering subsidies to some local chapters. Only in the summer of 1991, however, did Democratic Russia acquire the means to hire a tiny staff of paid full-time workers.[137] Most of what limited resources were available to the movement, moreover, flowed directly and exclusively to Democratic Russia. Its constituent groups, as well as other associations such as the DU, enjoyed little if any access to substantial material resources. For the most part, such groups labored in poverty. As of early 1991, the largest of the alternative political parties, the DPR, had yet to secure funds adequate even to rent an office for its headquarters in Moscow.[138] Thus, movement organizations' lack of access to power set in motion a vicious circle. It reduced their attractiveness to potential members as well as investors. Their consequent smallness and poverty, in turn, vexed their efforts to establish the infrastructure and provide the incentives needed to attract mass membership.

The closure of state institutions affected not only the development, but also the behavior and style of operation of opposition groups. It provoked a remarkable degree of radicalism and intransigence. Some theories of social movements, particularly those found in the resource mobilization paradigm, emphasize that movement organizations, whatever their stated goals and intentions, normally strive for some degree of *inclusion* within the existing political system. But the manifest impossibility of genuine inclusion, coupled with the utter incompatibility of the aims of the opposition and those of the regime's custodians, only bred intransigence among democratic groups. That intransigence, moreover, intensified in proportion to the growth of official conservatism during 1990–91.

The Democratic Union had always preached civil disobedience and noncompromise. By mid-1990 the public rhetoric of all other democratic organizations closely resembled that of the DU. On the eve of its full break with the CPSU, the Democratic Platform denounced "the party leadership's refusal of dialogue with progressives," warned of "a real threat of a return to totalitarianism," and called for what amounted to dismantling the regime.[139] Particularly following the events of late 1990–early 1991, Democratic Russia ruled out any possibility for compromise or productive contact with the party and central authorities. It endorsed civil disobedience and called for political strikes against Gorbachev, the CPSU, and the Union government.[140] At a meeting of Democratic Russia's coordinating soviet at the end of January, one leader warned of the impending threat of a "Polish or Chilean solution" and successfully argued that "we must adopt the most radical possible language now."[141]

A similarly high degree of radicalism and intransigence was evident in miners' organizations. After enduring over a year and a half of unfulfilled pledges and bizarre "negotiations" between central authorities and agents who did not represent them, strikers from all major coal mining regions dropped all economic demands in favor of purely political ones, which included Gorbachev's resignation, departiization of the workplace, and transfer of power to republican governments. Their actions reflected an understanding that little could come from further attempts to deal with the party and central authorities, and that nothing short of regime change could ameliorate their circumstances. The perception that state officials "can't deliver what we want even if they wanted to, so why even deal with them," expressed often by striking miners, grew out of recognition that state institutions, even at their most benign, had little to offer them other than cold tolerance.[142]

The regime's obvious and growing unpopularity also encouraged radicalism within the opposition. The Leningrad section of the SDPR, writing in the party's internal bulletin, notified other chapters that intransigence was good politics. It stated: "The Leningrad Organization of the SDPR fully rejects any cooperation with the Communists. . . . The leadership of the Leningrad Organization believes that if Social Democrats were to undertake any such cooperation, their [public approval] rating would fall."[143] Notwithstanding the fact that most Leningraders—not to speak of Russians in general—were at best only vaguely aware of the SDPR's existence, this stance reflected a belief that intractability was an essential component of the effort to gain esteem.[144]

The closure and decrepitude of the state not only frustrated the growth of opposition groups and provoked them to intransigence; it also stimulated a style of operation that may be labeled "demonstration politics." This mode centered primarily on mobilizing expressions of discontent, struggling for sway over public opinion, and fighting the information shortage posed by state control over mass communications. Given the poverty of autonomous organizations and the absence of established channels for interest representation, groups were left with few options other than demonstration politics.

The organization of *mitingy* (mass public manifestations) was the centerpiece of demonstration politics. Autonomous groups became highly adept at mobilizing sizable and peaceful shows of opposition, as shown by the waves of demonstrations that swept Russia in 1990–91—and finally, by the effective resistance that Democratic Russia hastily organized around the White House on August 19–21, 1991. Democratic leaders regarded *mitingy* as one of the few avenues open to them for influencing official thinking. According to Vera Kriger, a member of Democratic Russia's coordinating soviet, the regime's custodians, despite their refusal to recognize the opposition, could not fail to notice gatherings of tens or hundreds of thousands of citizens in the streets. She stated: "Here's how Mikhail Sergeevich looks at it: He sees a huge crowd at a demonstration, and he thinks that means strength; if he sees only a few, he sees weakness. . . . We hope to create pressure. They have sixteen million in the [Communist] party, and say that they reflect the opinion of the people. We want to show how many people oppose the socialist path."[145]

Large demonstrations of course displayed the popularity of democracy not only to its opponents, but also to the mass public and to democratic activists themselves. As in any analogous situation, they fostered a spirit of solidarity and self-confidence within the opposition. Perhaps to a greater extent than in many other cases, demonstrations in Russia also played a crucial role in disseminating information and raising funds. They offered activists opportunities to publicize their demands, report information not covered in the official press, read out their telephone numbers for those who might want to join their groups, and collect contributions from sympathetic crowds. The role of protest demonstrations will be examined further in the following chapter.

Another form of action in which opposition groups could and did engage was independent publishing. Issuing their own newspapers and leaflets enabled them to advertise their demands and programs and thereby to circumvent the blockade that most official news sources erected to coverage of the democratic movement. Indeed, progressive groups regarded battling information shortage as one of their most difficult and important challenges.[146] The appearance of independent, nonpartisan (but prodemocratic) newspapers such as *Nezavisimaia Gazeta* and *Kuranty* helped alleviate information problems toward the end of the Gorbachev period. Yet such newspapers were exceedingly difficult to obtain outside Moscow. Much of the job still fell to movement organizations. As one activist asserted in *Gospodin Narod*, the main newspaper of the RPR: "We're not in Chicago; we're not even in Prague, and in Russia the populations of entire regions can be cut off from information about democratic forces." Under such conditions, "only [independent] party structures with their organizations, publications, and alternative systems of distribution" could fill in the omissions and correct the distortions transmitted through the official media.[147]

Most opposition organizations vigorously took up the challenge. The DU, despite its small membership and minuscule resource base, published over two dozen different newspapers in nearly as many cities throughout the Soviet Union, though only one publication, *Svobodnoe Slovo* (Free Word), was printed both on a regular basis and in runs of more than ten thousand copies. The Social Democrats, beginning in 1989 in their first incarnation as the SDA, also published extensively. By late 1990 the SDPR published, in addition to its internal bulletin, three newspapers in Moscow, as well as several dozen papers that were issued irregularly in various cities. In late 1990–early 1991, as television and radio reporting returned to a style reminiscent of the preglasnost' era, democrats stepped up their publishing efforts wherever possible. The SDPR, for example, resolved in the spring to begin printing El'tsin's decisions and statements, which were rarely reported in the state-controlled media, on leaflets to be posted in public places.[148]

Autonomous groups' capacity to produce and distribute information was, of course, dwarfed by that of the state media. Poverty, the difficulty of securing access to printing facilities, and repression of independent publishing conspired against the opposition's efforts. Only one newspaper published by a movement organization—*Demokrati-cheskaia Rossia*, named for its publisher—achieved print runs over 100,000. This and most other publications, moreover, were often inaccessible outside Moscow and Leningrad—though, as will be discussed in the next chapter, groups in some provincial cities demonstrated great resourcefulness in issuing their own publications.

Still, despite their relatively modest magnitude, the media that independent political groups created contributed powerfully to breaking the state's monopoly on communications and information provision. They pushed glasnost' far beyond the confines of mere official "openness." That opposition groups expended much of their energy and meager resources on publishing was scarcely surprising: it was, after all, one of the few ways by which they could express their demands, mobilize public support, and make themselves known to a broader audience.

Organizing demonstrations and publishing were the chief means opposition groups used to mobilize and express popular discontent, but they were not the only means. In the spring of 1991, and particularly during the campaign for the Russian presidency, Democratic Russia established cells in enterprises.[149] In cities dominated by highly conservative apparats or in military enterprises even in localities where less repression prevailed, organizing such cells was often impossible. But in some workplaces in a number of cities, including Moscow, employees active in the democratic movement formed small working groups. They did not, nor did they intend to, rival or resemble the Communist Party's workplace organizations. Their chief role was informational. According to Democratic Russia's Kriger: "We now supposedly have freedom of speech, but radio, TV, and the newspapers don't exactly report everything of interest. Our cells—and their size isn't even important, since three people in a workplace of one thousand can inform the others of what we're doing and of El'tsin's pronouncements—can help overcome the shortage of reliable information."[150]

In sum, the character of state institutions, and in particular their closure and decay, helped frustrate autonomous political organizations' efforts to secure mass involvement and substantial resource bases. But it also engendered a remarkable degree of radicalism and intransigence on the part of those same groups. Finally, since the state's closure and decrepitude meant that movement organizations could not possibly acquire meaningful representative and negotiating functions, groups turned their energies toward expressive and communicative forms of action, which included independent publishing and mobilizing mass public displays of discontent.

Electoral Politics and Legislatures: "Democratization" without Liberalization

The elections for the USSR Congress of People's Deputies in March 1989 and for the RSFSR Congress of People's Deputies and all soviets on lower levels one year later would seem to provide an exception to the policy of closure. The elections might have been expected to have mitigated the unfavorable political opportunity structure that opposition organizations confronted. They were the first even partially competitive legislative elections in Soviet history. The elections did spur popular mobilization on behalf of candidates of all stripes. They opened legislatures for the first time to some opponents of the regime, creating opportunities for public expression of discontent within elective bodies. They relegated to the past the sight of wooden, anonymous figures raising their hands reflexively and in unison on each and every vote, and they converted at least some of the soviets into fora for genuine debate.

Still, the elections neither opened channels for the organized representation of societal interests nor engendered a genuine multiparty system. The timing of the elections was critical. The first round of elections was held well *before* alternative parties were legalized, and the second round at roughly the same time that parties were beginning to receive some still murky legal right to exist. In comparative perspective the reforms therefore followed a highly atypical pattern, with partial "democratization" (free—or at least freer—elections) *preceding* "liberalization" (the unbanning of political parties). This peculiar sequence influenced both the character of the new legislatures and the subsequent development of nascent parties.

Several interrelated facts stand out as particularly significant. First, parties played little role in Russia's first multiple-candidate-ballot elections for soviets on all levels. Second, the independent organizations that did participate in campaigns were broad, loosely organized "citizens' committees" and "voters' clubs" whose activities were limited largely to promoting the nomination by official agencies and "work collectives" of any candidates deemed "progressive." These groups did not enjoy the right to nominate their own candidates at all in the first elections. In the second round, in 1990, some of them did have such a right, but then so did a multitude of types of organizations, most of them official. Thus, parties (with the exception of the Communist Party) never acquired a significant role—much less a functional monopoly over the nomination of candidates—in either round of elections. Nominating procedures, moreover, were controlled by "electoral commissions," dominated in most cases by state officials, often Communist Party functionaries. So, not surprisingly, the elections did not produce anything resembling "party government" or the opportunity for "alternation in power" among competing parties. Finally, the soviets were by no means structured in a manner that facilitated their execution of government functions. Since their previous role was limited to providing some appearance of popular legitimacy for party decisions, the soviets were very large; even the soviet of a city of one-quarter million, for example, typically had about two hundred members. These basic structures were preserved after the elections of 1989 and 1990. Significantly, however, the "new" soviets convened far more frequently and in much longer sessions than the old rubber-stamp legislatures. While the old soviets convened for a few days at a time several times per year to ratify party decisions, the new ones began to act more like permanent legislative bodies, which met frequently and in some cases engaged in genuine debate.

So at precisely the time when independent political associations were beginning to emerge and develop but before they enjoyed any real organizational rights, many thousands of democratic organizers— and, perhaps even more importantly, *potential* democratic organizers—suddenly faced unprecedented opportunities for participation in official elective bodies. The USSR Congress of People's Deputies, which numbered over 2,200 members, suddenly included several hundred of the country's democratically minded and most celebrated cultural heroes, former political dissidents, and radical activists. Some of these individuals subsequently gained election to the USSR Supreme Soviet, the smaller standing body that the Congress of People's Deputies elected from among its own membership. In 1990 many "democrats" won election to soviets on the republican, oblast', city, and district (*raion*) levels. In Poland, Brazil, Spain, and many other countries, opposition leaders as well as many ordinary citizens spent years, if not decades, struggling "from below" before they ever enjoyed the opportunity to serve in public office. Their Russian counterparts entered legislatures suddenly and usually without such long experience—and largely unbeholden to political parties or other organized societal forces. The sudden appearance of "office-seeking" opportunities and experience as deputies did not "deradicalize" such individuals. But it did often turn their energies away from the task of building alternative institutions and engaged them in long and often fruitless debates in legislative bodies that were too large and unwieldy to execute real government functions.

Thus, the conditions under which elections were held affected the development of independent political organizations, especially parties, in a number of ways. It is impossible, of course, to ascertain how many prodemocratic politicians would have invested their efforts in party-building had elections been held after parties had been legalized, had full "liberalization" preceded partial "democratization" by, say, one or two years. But it is clear that the sudden appearance of opportunities to seek office—and, for successful candidates, to serve in it—directed the attention of many budding radical political entrepreneurs away from the relatively unglamorous task of building independent political organizations and toward the higher-profile work of legislators. The structure of incentives helps explain why so many talented democratic leaders—Sergei Stankevich, Anatolii Sobchak, and Boris El'tsin, to name only a few highly celebrated figures—sought their fortunes and built their reputations in the legislatures rather than in autonomous political organizations. The soviets provided platforms from which political unknowns could—normally by means of stirring, sometimes televised speeches—acquire instant fame, be it on the national, provincial, or local level. The soviets therefore quite naturally depleted movement organizations of potential sources of talent and energy.[151] The elections themselves, moreover, provided scant incentives for ordinary citizens and voters to affiliate or identify themselves with alternative political parties.

Had the new soviets greatly empowered progressive forces, the price they exacted on movement organizations by drawing talent away from them might have been worth it. The soviets did serve as important fora for the expression of movement demands. After the spring 1990 elections, even the most conservative soviets included at least a handful of prodemocratic gadflies who used the opportunities for public exposure that deputyship provided to call for revolutionary change.

On the whole, however, democratization through "soviet power" did not come to pass. Three reasons stand out. First, since the elections did not encourage party formation, they produced amorphous legislatures bereft of discipline. So even where democrats achieved majorities or near-majorities, there usually existed little basis for disciplined action and cooperation among deputies. Whatever one might think of Nikolai Travkin's political rhetoric and behavior, his argument that legislatures without parties were doomed to impotence, regardless of how "progressive" their composition, unquestionably held a great deal of validity. Second, the soviets were in any event not constituted in a manner that enabled them actually to govern. They were too large and tended to be dominated by their executive committees, which in many cases were made up of unelected holdovers from the old soviets.[152] Third, the soviets never acquired great power and authority in the precoup period. They became far livelier and marginally more powerful than they had been before 1989. But control over material production and distribution, communications and information, coercion, and the other sources of real power remained largely with the party-state apparat, even as the latter began to decay.[153] The soviets and their relationship to the democratic movement will be discussed in greater depth in the following chapter.

Many democrats were well aware of the weakness of the legislatures in which so many invested their energies. Referring to—and addressing—fellow democrats who had won deputyships and achieved some public recognition, Leonid Babkin remarked in a speech at Democratic Russia's February 1991 leadership conference: "Those of us who have gotten somewhere have gotten carried away with it. Our parliamentary victories aren't doing us any good. Our legislatures are really facades of legislatures anyway, as we now know."[154] Babkin's admonition spoke to a problem larger than the institutional weakness of the soviets. It also illuminated the tension between the responsibilities of deputyship and those of building independent societal organizations. It suggested that the latter task was being neglected in favor of the former, with inauspicious consequences for the democratic movement.[155]

Indeed, the sudden availability of office-seeking opportunities and the conditions under which offices were sought not only siphoned off human capital that might otherwise have flowed to independent organizations. They also encouraged a type of purely individualistic, free-lance political entrepreneurship even among those persons who *did* both win deputies' seats *and* work in autonomous associations. To be sure, many leaders of independent groups who gained election to a soviet remained active in their respective groups. Yet such individuals owed their parties little. Their electoral success—and, in the minds of many, their budding political careers—depended mainly on their own efforts and popularity. Most leaders of opposition groups who also gained election to soviets acted without responsibility toward their organizations.[156] So while many soviets *included some members of parties*, the parties themselves *were not represented* in the soviets. Thus, while Social Democrats could take pride that two of their own, Oleg Rumiantsev and Leonid Volkov, served on the Russian parliament's Constitutional Commission, the party in no way influenced the behavior of its "representatives." In some soviets, rules conspired further to separate deputies from their groups outside the legislature. Members of the presidium of the RSFSR Supreme Soviet, for example, were forbidden also to serve as chairpersons of societal organizations. Thus, Viacheslav Polosin, following his election to the parliament's presidium, was obligated to forfeit his position as cochair of the RKhDD.[157] Many deputies, including democrats, considered such a rule appropriate, as it was intended to guarantee the "independence" of parliamentary leaders.

In a speech given in the spring of 1991, Viktor Sheinis, a member of Democratic Russia's coordinating soviet and a deputy in the RSFSR parliament, captured the quandary in which democrats found themselves. According to Sheinis, "heading some parliamentary commissions and committees, many activists in the democratic movement turn out to be lost for the task of political work." In the absence of responsibility to larger organizations, moreover, deputies worked entirely free-lance. The consequent disorganization and lack of accountability produced "an utter lack of any discipline. In the best case [progressive] parliamentarians vote the right way, but not all of them and not always . . . And in their work on committees and commissions, democrats end up carrying responsibility for decisions that are at best poorly thought out, and at worst simply disgraceful."[158]

To say that the elections decapitated the new parties and other independent groups would be too strong. Some activists remained committed to both their deputyships and their organizations. Still, the elections and the legislatures they produced did not, for reasons discussed above, stimulate the development of parties and other autonomous groups in the same way that they have in many other cases. Nor did the presidential election of the spring of 1991 have this effect. The campaign galvanized democrats and provided a source of unity within the movement. Democratic Russia assembled an "apparat" of volunteers who took charge of promoting El'tsin across Russia. Yet, as one observer of the election has pointed out, El'tsin's personal aloofness from the organization that managed his campaign in some ways actually "disorganized" it. The election left Democratic Russia and its constituent groups themselves little stronger, larger, or better organized in the wake of the successful effort than they had been before it.[159]

The elections opened government to a degree unprecedented in Soviet history. The legislatures that the elections produced included for the first time avowed opponents of the regime and served as fora for the expression of radical demands. But, due to the conditions under which they were held, the elections did not, in contrast with "founding elections" in many other countries in transition, stimulate the growth of a substantial multiparty political system. Whether Gorbachev and his associates—the creators of the new electoral and soviet system— intentionally designed and timed reforms in such as way as to dampen the development of the opposition, or whether the whole process and its consequences unfolded haphazardly, must be left to question.

Whatever the intentions of the authorities, the soviets elected in 1989 and 1990, by virtue of their combination of institutional weakness and their attractiveness to democratic activists, functioned less as working legislatures than as a multitiered modern Versailles.

Conclusion

This chapter has investigated four of the most important aspects of the development—and underdevelopment—of the organizations of the democratic opposition: groups' efforts to create collective identities; their attempts to identify "social bases" and attract membership and support; their creation of organizational structures; and their operations in the broader political arena. The preceding analysis reveals the determinative power of the regime under which the opposition emerged. Groups' struggles to form a collective identity were deeply affected by the long-term prior erasure of alternative identities in the political system. Their efforts to locate a constituency were impeded by the peculiarity of social structure in Russia, which in turn was shaped by the prior étatization of property and policies designed to eliminate social classes as such (even while creating a small privileged stratum whose status was based on political position rather than economic production). Organizations' internal structures were formed largely in reaction to what oppositionists regarded as the negative example of the Communist Party, and in response to the threat of hostile infiltration and sabotage by state agencies. Finally, opposition groups' modes and styles of operation in the broader political arena were determined by the political opportunity structure they confronted, which in turn was shaped by the rigidity, closure, and decrepitude of state institutions and by the sequencing of reforms undertaken from above.

The following chapter, which examines the democratic movement in several provincial cities, focuses more specifically on the immediate effects of state repression on the development of democratic movement organizations. Several of the determinative factors analyzed in this chapter, including the history of submergence of alternative political identities and the timing of elections, varied little or not at all across localities in Russia. Yet differences did emerge among cities in the level of official control and repression of movement activity. These differences engendered disparities in the political opportunity structures that opposition groups confronted, and made possible substantial variation in the progress of movement organizations across cities.

V

The Struggle in the Provinces: A Tale of Four Cities

MOST WORKS on revolution, including those on contemporary Russia, focus primarily on the national level. In Russia, as in many other cases, the capital city is properly considered the main locus of both opposition activity and regime resistance. During the period 1985–91, Moscow remained the undisputed center of policy-making authority in Russia. The headquarters of most independent organizations were located in the capital, and groups' national conferences were usually held there. Most leaders of national (all-Russian) organizations resided in the capital, and the "Moscow" and "national" leaderships of many groups were virtually identical. The primacy of the "center" was underscored by the events of August 1991, when the fate of all of Russia, and perhaps even the Soviet Union as a whole, seemed to hinge on a short-lived showdown in the heart of the capital between a clique of reactionary putschists, on one side, and a small group of democratic leaders, protected by a crowd of courageous supporters, on the other.

Yet, like many other "national" (as opposed to strictly regional-separatist) revolutions, the transformation of Russian politics may be conceived of as a composite of microrevolutions, occurring simultaneously but at divergent rates and under discrete local conditions. However centralized the traditional model of Soviet rule in Russia, the partial erosion of central authority and the fragmentation of the party-state apparat after 1985 produced significant variation in the integrity and repressiveness of official power across cities and oblasts and created dissimilar environments for the growth of democratic movements. Furthermore, most of the insurgent organizations under consideration adopted highly decentralized structures and modes of operation. Local activists retained great autonomy and freedom of action. They were subject to little if any discipline—and enjoyed scant financial support—from their Moscow-based leaderships. In short, the partial decentralization and disintegration of state power and the autonomy of local democratic movement organizations, as well as the sheer size of Russia, gave rise to significant discrepancies in the progress of revolutionary politics across cities.

This chapter investigates the struggle for democracy in four provincial capitals: Sverdlovsk (now Ekaterinburg), Tula, Volgograd, and

Orel. While the chapter does not furnish a "thick" description of local politics, it helps provide a richer portrait than a study limited to "national" developments and the politics of the capital city. It also substantiates and elaborates some of the more general propositions advanced in previous chapters.

All four of the cities under consideration are industrial centers, and each is the capital of its respective oblast'.[1] The four differ in size and proximity to the capital. Sverdlovsk has a population of roughly 1.2 million; Volgograd, 1 million; Tula, 600,000; and Orel, 350,000. The smaller cities, Tula and Orel, are located in central Russia and are closer to the capital: the former three hours by train from Moscow; the latter, six hours. Sverdlovsk, in the Urals, and Volgograd, in the south of Russia, are roughly twenty-four hours by train from Moscow. As provincial capitals, all enjoy significant cultural and intellectual life; all are sites of institutions of higher education. Inhabitants of none of the four enjoy the cultural life and access to information available in Moscow or Leningrad/St. Petersburg. In each of the four cities, however, the full complement of official newspapers and journals with national circulations are readily obtainable. While no reliable figures on variation in literacy rates are available, none of the cities should be expected to deviate from the national norm of near-universal literacy. All contain large factories, though there do exist some differences in the cities' industrial profiles. Industry in Sverdlovsk and Tula is oriented heavily toward weapons and munitions production, with military-industrial production accounting for 75–85 percent of industrial output. Military-industrial production constitutes roughly 40–60 percent of output in Volgograd and Orel; both cities also contain significant construction and light industries.[2]

Unlike many large industrial centers, such as Novosibirsk, Cheliabinsk, and Magnitogorsk, which were built largely from scratch during the Stalin period of force-paced industrialization, none of the subjects of this study is a "new city." The histories of Tula, Orel, and Volgograd stretch back four or more centuries; Sverdlovsk was founded in the early eighteenth century. Although all of the cities were subject to the dislocations and demographic tumult of the Stalin period, each is home to some residents who trace their local roots back several generations. None of the four is a "mining town." While some mining activity takes place in Tula and Sverdlovsk Oblasts, the cities themselves are not home to large numbers of miners. The politics of none of the four cities, therefore, were affected directly by miners' strikes; unlike mining centers such as Donetsk and Novokuznetsk, none generated powerful organized labor movements. Ethnic Russians, moreover, constitute overwhelming majorities in each of the four cities. None of the cities is located in an autonomous republic or has large non-Russian minorities or communities of foreigners; none has experienced serious interethnic conflict during recent years.

In sum, the subjects of investigation may in some sense be considered typical medium-sized provincial Russian cities. Despite the obvious difficulties and limitations of controlling for demographic factors, the four may be regarded as sufficiently similar to allow for meaningful comparison among them.

Difficulties of measurement and causal determination inherent in analysis of politics at the national level are just as acute in investigation of local politics. Incontrovertible evidence and hard data are exceptionally hard to come by. Even ostensibly quantifiable information, such as membership numbers, can rarely be expressed precisely; leaders of independent organizations were themselves often unsure of the exact size of their groups.[3] Assessing the extent, incidence, and harshness of official repression and evaluating the policies of local organs of power also present methodological challenges. The only sources of fully reliable information on such matters—local KGB and police records—are not open for investigation. The strength and influence of democratic organizations are similarly difficult to measure. As will be discussed in the final section, indicators drawn from election data, such as "fraction democratic" in local legislatures, serve as neither satisfactory measures, significant determinants, nor reliable predictors of the progress of democratic forces on the local level. Interviews with activists and officials, direct observation, and review of what reliable published sources do exist serve as the best—even if imperfect—sources of information on movements on the local level.

Opposition Movements in Four Cities: An Overview

Sverdlovsk

Popular political mobilization and independent political organizations emerged earlier in Sverdlovsk than in most other cities in Russia. The first major informal group, Discussion Tribune, came together in early 1987. Although members of the local Communist Party organization founded the club, participation was not limited to Communists. The group served as an early forum for future democratic organizers to become acquainted, exchange information, and discuss matters of mutual concern.[4]

The first incidence of mass mobilization in the city took place in November 1987. It took the form of a remarkable popular reaction to the demotion of Boris El'tsin following his controversial speech before a closed meeting of top party officials in Moscow. El'tsin was born in

Sverdlovsk Oblast' and began his political career there. He had gained wide popularity and a reputation for probity during his tenure as first secretary of the Sverdlovsk Oblast' party organization in the 1970s— rare feats for any official holding such a position during the Brezhnev years. Many in Sverdlovsk therefore regarded El'tsin's disgrace as both a blow to perestroika and an affront to a local hero. News of the event sparked spontaneous, uncoordinated, and sustained street gatherings of several thousand people, who demanded publication of El'tsin's speech and full official explanation for the cause of his demotion. Demonstrations began in mid-November and continued on an almost daily basis for nearly a month.[5]

El'tsin's demotion was not reversed, and his spectacular political resurrection would not begin until late 1988. But the "El'tsin Incident" and the demonstrations that followed in its wake triggered public politicization and autonomous political activity in Sverdlovsk. As one local organizer recalled, "He was one of ours, and his example woke us up, made us realize that we could and must get involved. And at those demonstrations people made contacts and friendships and found that they were not alone, that many others felt as they did."[6] In January 1988 Miting-87 was founded by several dozen radical activists dedicated to preserving the spirit of the demonstrations. The group organized weekly political discussion meetings on the city's main square. In the fall of 1988 most members left the group to found a local chapter of the Democratic Union. Some activists from Miting-87 who desired a nonconfrontational, but still radical, approach to politics founded Iskra (Spark), a club dedicated to studying Russian history and philosophy and reviving liberal national traditions.[7] In mid-1988 a small but vigorous informal press sprouted in the city. Noteworthy among the new independent publications was a monthly journal, *Slovo Urala*. Edited by a group of former political dissidents from Sverdlovsk and the neighboring city of Nizhnii Tagil, the journal printed information unavailable in the official press on the democratic movement in Sverdlovsk and the Soviet Union as a whole.[8] In late 1988 the journal's editors founded their own political association, Vozrozhdenie (Rebirth). Like Iskra, Vozrozhdenie advocated vigorous political engagement but eschewed direct confrontation with the authorities whenever possible. It conceived of its own role in terms of fostering moral rebirth by means of studying and disseminating literature on national history and the contemporary democratic movement.[9]

As in many other cities, elections for the USSR Congress of People's Deputies in early 1989 prompted the formation of local "voters' clubs" dedicated to promoting the nomination of progressive candidates. In Sverdlovsk, such groups focused largely on extolling and promoting the nomination of El'tsin. These voters clubs survived the spring elections and in the summer of 1989 joined ranks with several other associations to found the Movement for Democratic Choice (DDV). Thus, nearly one year before the founding of Democratic Russia on the national level, Sverdlovsk enjoyed an umbrella organization of democratic forces. The DDV promoted progressive candidates in the spring 1990 elections for soviets on the republican, oblast', city, and district levels. Due in part to the group's efforts, progressives captured roughly half of all seats in the Sverdlovsk City Soviet. Following the founding of Democratic Russia in Moscow in mid-1990, the DDV formally identified itself as Sverdlovsk Oblast's chapter of Democratic Russia, though the group retained its name as a symbol of its autonomy and as a mark of pride in its early founding. In the summer and fall of 1990, the Democratic Party of Russia, the Republican Party of Russia, and the Social Democratic Party of Russia established organizations in the city and joined the DDV.[10]

In some respects, Sverdlovsk manifested an impressive record of social mobilization and organizational development. Even before the elections of early 1989, the city had achieved a high level of mass involvement in street demonstrations and a relatively rich associational life. It developed a lively alternative press, which gave voice to democratic aspirations even before the formation of the DDV and alternative political parties. El'tsin's overwhelming popularity helped sustain mass involvement. In March 1991 demonstrations in support of El'tsin, who was facing a conservative challenge to his chairmanship of the RSFSR Supreme Soviet, drew as many as 100,000 people—nearly one-tenth of the city's population.[11]

Yet the democratic movement's success was not unambiguous. Of the three major alternative parties, only the DPR founded a significant presence; as of the summer of 1991 it counted 150–200 members in the oblast', about one-third of whom resided in the city of Sverdlovsk. The SDPR and the RPR together attracted only a few tens of members in the city and established little if any presence in the oblast' outside the capital. The SDPR, after establishing an organization and beginning publication of an impressive radical monthly newspaper, was decimated in 1991 by the emigration of several of its leading members. The Democratic Union, after a fast start in 1988, by early 1991 had dwindled to a handful of rather eccentric militants. The Russian Christian Democratic Movement enjoyed no representation at all. While the DDV proved a formidable force in the 1990 elections, corrosive fissures appeared in early and mid-1991. Activists from the DPR assumed what leaders from some other groups regarded as disproportionate influence within the DDV, appropriating most leadership positions and control over the group's scarce resources. Several organizations that had joined the DDV as collective members, including Vozrozhdenie, came to regard the DDV's leaders as dishonest opportunists and withdrew from the DDV in mid-1991.[12]

Tula

Organized democratic activity commenced much later in Tula than in Sverdlovsk. The first informal organization in Tula, Civic Initiative, appeared in late 1988. The group, which was fully independent though organized by a handful of liberal Communists who later founded a chapter of the RPR, waged an unsuccessful campaign against the candidacy of a well-known conservative general in the 1989 elections for the USSR Congress of People's Deputies. The founder of Civic Initiative later recalled that the campaign had amounted to something of a success for the nascent democratic movement, as the military leader, whom the local apparat supported strongly, won by only a narrow margin against a relatively unknown progressive candidate.[13] The Democratic Union founded a small organization but never established the presence that it enjoyed in Sverdlovsk, and it faded shortly after its birth in mid-1988.

The first signs of mass mobilization in Tula became apparent at the end of 1989, when a handful of activists from Civic Initiative began organizing weekly demonstrations in the city's central square. As in other cities, the demonstrations furnished a means for activists—and future activists—to became acquainted and to exchange information. According to one organizer, the meetings, which by the time of the elections of March 1990 regularly attracted several thousand participants, also helped demonstrate to the people of the city that "the regime could be opposed, it could be done. [The demonstrations] helped a significant part of the people here to begin escaping from fear."[14]

The first real breakthrough for democratic forces came in the elections of the spring of 1990. Progressive candidates, who during the campaign signed onto a list they dubbed "People's Power," captured about half of all seats in the city soviet. People's Power did not possess a strong organizational structure; unlike the DDV in Sverdlovsk, it served merely as a way for progressive candidates to identify themselves. It neither brought together independent democratic organizations under a common umbrella nor developed its own cadre of activists outside the local legislature. But the strong showing of candidates who identified themselves with People's Power animated the local movement. In June 1990 the DPR was organized. By the spring of 1991 it boasted about one hundred members in the oblast', over half of whom resided in the city. The RPR and SDPR founded organizations in the fall of 1990, and by the spring of 1991 they had achieved growth commensurate with that of the DPR. The RKhDD established a somewhat smaller group. Immediately after their founding, the new parties formed a local chapter of Democratic Russia. While the Tula chapter of Democratic Russia did not realize the mass involvement achieved by its counterpart in Sverdlovsk, the DDV, the former enjoyed a better balance among constituent groups. No one party assumed disproportionate influence, and the organization was somewhat less subject to internal conflict and defections than the DDV in Sverdlovsk.[15]

Tula's democratic organizations did not manage to create a weighty alternative press. But the "capture" of the local Komsomol newspaper by a group of radical young journalists lent voice to democratic forces. In 1989 the newspaper *Molodoi Kommunar* (Young Communard) contrived to loosen its dependence on Communist Party financing and direction and began reporting—often sympathetically—on the local democratic movement. The paper retained nominal ties to the Komsomol and often subdued its reporting to pacify the authorities. Still, one of its leading correspondents admitted: "We regard our job as that of liberating people from fear of the Communists and the command-and-administer system. . . . We are in fact tied closely to Democratic Russia; everyone who works on the paper in whatever capacity has their connections to the organization."[16]

Popular mobilization in Tula differed in both magnitude and focus from that in Sverdlovsk. During the months preceding the failed coup attempt of August 1991, Sverdlovsk witnessed huge demonstrations, some of which amounted to outpourings of popular support and affection for El'tsin. Even accounting for the difference in the cities' sizes, demonstrations in Tula were comparatively small. Furthermore, while El'tsin did acquire in Tula the strong popular support he enjoyed throughout Russia, demonstrations in Tula often focused on matters other than El'tsin. One cause that gained significant popular support during 1991 was expression of solidarity with striking miners. Few miners lived in the city of Tula. Unlike in cities such as Donetsk and Novokuznetsk, the miners' movement did not affect local politics directly. But strikes in the neighboring Mosbass region helped rally democrats in Tula, who organized demonstrations to express support and to collect money, food, and cigarettes for the miners during the spring strikes.[17] Another issue around which democratic forces rallied—indeed, an issue that they themselves created—was a minor corruption scandal involving the use of dachas in a neighboring town by Tula's Communist Party officials. Democratic Russia organized several demonstrations at the sites of the vacation homes, demanding that they be relinquished for use by children's recreational camps. The controversy enabled local democratic groups to attract public attention and support by opposing official privilege.[18]

In sum, despite late and humble beginnings, the democratic movement in Tula assumed meaningful proportions by mid-1991. Tula never experienced the levels of mass mobilization found in Sverdlovsk, but it did develop significant independent associational life.

Volgograd

As in Tula, the democratic movement started late in Volgograd. The latter city experienced little noteworthy independent politics until early 1989, when a group of teachers and engineers at the local polytechnic formed a progressive voters' club on the eve of the March elections. In the fall several leaders of the club tried to organize public demonstrations. Their efforts were largely unsuccessful. One later noted: "We rarely got more than a few hundred at our demonstrations at first. Not many people listened to us; most talk of democracy still took place in peoples' kitchens. But at least people did begin talking among themselves."[19]

At the beginning of 1990 political discussion moved suddenly from kitchens to the streets. The incident that sparked mobilization was the publication in *Ogonek* of a damning exposé on the regal lifestyles and heavy-handed rule of the first secretary of the Communist Party committee of Volgograd Oblast', V. I. Kalashnikov, and his lieutenants.[20] Appearing in a celebrated national magazine, the piece caused a sensation in Volgograd and handed democratic organizers an explosive issue around which to rally public discontent. Shortly after the article's publication, organizers of the voters' club called a public forum at the local polytechnic and invited Kalashnikov and several other officials from the city and oblast' party apparats to address the charges. The officials made the mistake of accepting the invitation. To the delight of its organizers, the forum degenerated into a rancorous exchange of accusations among top party officials. Detecting an opening and recognizing the political potency of the corruption charges, organizers redoubled their efforts to mobilize public opposition. Now the task was far easier than it had been one year past. During January 1990 several tens of thousands took to the streets on an almost daily basis, surrounding the headquarters of the oblast' and city party committees and demanding Kalashnikov's ouster. At the end of the month, after several weeks of public outcry, Kalashnikov and several of his top deputies were removed from their positions.[21]

Following what Volgograders came to call the "February Revolution," organized democratic activity rapidly picked up momentum. In February several activists founded the Social Democratic Organization, which immediately began publishing its own newspaper. In June the organization became the Volgograd SDPR. In March emergent political organizations and representatives from local cooperatives formed the Civic Initiative Committee, the first umbrella group of democratic forces in the city. During the summer and fall the RPR, DPR, and RKhDD established organizations and, together with other groups, founded a local chapter of Democratic Russia. In late 1990 and the first half of 1991 these organizations experienced remarkable growth and development. The SDPR and the DPR each quickly established organizations of several hundred members in the oblast', most of whom resided in the city. Democratic Russia functioned smoothly; relations among its constituent groups were largely free of the friction evident in the DDV in Sverdlovsk and other umbrella organizations in many other cities.[22]

Democratic organizations did not establish an independent press comparable in size and diversity to that found in Sverdlovsk. Yet problems of information provision were mitigated by several progressive newspapers founded or edited by radical journalists. As in Tula, the Komsomol newspaper in Volgograd shook loose from its ideological overseers and began publishing on democratic forces. At the end of 1990 a group of young journalists from the paper *Molodoi Leninits* (Young Leninist) went a step further than their counterparts in Tula, quitting the Komsomol newspaper and founding their own semi-weekly publication, *MIG*. Although initially beset by financial difficulties, the fledgling paper, with its unabashedly radical bias and featured weekly local public opinion surveys that invariably embarrassed Communist Party authorities, enjoyed an early, explosive growth in sales of subscriptions. By mid-1991 it had become one of the city's most popular newspapers and had established itself as a profitable enterprise with a small but well-paid staff.[23] Thus, after "sleeping through" 1987–89—years when organized opposition germinated in places such as Sverdlovsk and Moscow—Volgograd experienced an explosive and sustained period of politicization and organizational development.

Orel

The history of insurgency in Orel was the opposite of that of Volgograd. Activity started late but blossomed once it commenced in Volgograd; in Orel, opposition emerged early but never achieved substantial

mobilizational capacity or strong organizational footing. Like Sverdlovsk, Orel was home to a small but energetic group of persons whose
political dissidence predated the Gorbachev era. One such individual
had founded a union of *samizdat* writers and since 1984 worked for
Ekspress Khronika, an underground newspaper that surfaced in 1987
and became one of the Soviet Union's leading sources of information
on the democratic movement. The Glasnost' Society, a small, Moscow-
based circle of radical journalists, established a chapter in Orel in 1985.
In 1987 a young biologist who since the late 1970s had convened secret
weekly Bible discussion meetings in his apartment founded a society
dedicated to aiding shut-ins and invalids. These and a handful of other
activists constituted the early nucleus of the democratic movement in
Orel. In early 1988 they formed a local chapter of Memorial, the society
committed to documenting and redressing the crimes of Stalinism, and
initiated a campaign to collect signatures in support of erecting a mon-
ument to victims of repression in the city. In the fall of 1988 they organized the city's first demonstration, a small commemorative gathering at the wall of a prison in Orel that had been the site of massacres
during the 1940s. In what was to become part of a consistent pattern
of behavior by local authorities, the meeting was broken up by the
police.[24]

The first notable success for fledgling democratic forces in the city
was the election of V. I. Samarin to the USSR Congress of People's
Deputies in early 1989. With the organizational help of democratic activists, the radical populist Samarin soundly defeated an old appa-
ratchik who enjoyed the support of the local nomenklatura. The campaign afforded local oppositionists the chance to become acquainted
and to acquire experience mobilizing public opinion.[25]

During the second half of the Gorbachev period Orel witnessed spir-
ited efforts by local democrats to win public support and stern official
reaction to any activity that smacked of opposition. During the summer of 1989 a half-dozen activists formed a provisional coalition of
democratic forces, the Orel Popular Front (ONF). In August, when the
group tried to organize a demonstration to publicize its intentions and
mobilize support, the meeting was disbanded by the police. Undaunted, leaders reorganized a brief meeting on the outskirts of town
later in the day, and the crowd of several hundred proclaimed the
founding of the ONF. Lacking any hope for securing use of a public
building for a conference, the ONF adopted a program by voice vote
during its open-air meeting. In early 1990 the ONF did manage to convoke several demonstrations that attracted crowds of a few thousand,
which were sufficiently large to discourage strong police action
against demonstrators.[26]

Several independent organizations managed to issue their own newspapers, but on an irregular basis and in very modest print runs.[27] The Komsomol paper *Pokolenie* (Generation) began printing information on the democratic movement in 1989, but it never displayed the independence or boldness of its counterparts in Tula and Volgograd.[28]

Democratic activists were able to create some basis for meaningful associational life. In July 1990 Gleb Anishenko, a cochairman of the national organization of the RKhDD, traveled to Orel and helped establish a local chapter of the party. The DPR also founded an organization in July; and a few months later several dissident Communists broke with the party and established a local RPR. In late 1990 these groups, which worked together in the ONF, disbanded the latter and declared the founding of the Orel chapter of Democratic Russia. But the new parties realized meager public involvement. In the summer of 1991 the RKhDD and the RPR each had about twenty members in the city; neither founded a significant presence in the oblast' outside the capital. The DPR managed a membership about three times that size and did establish several small organizations outside the provincial capital. The SDPR was absent in Orel. Democratic Russia provided some basis for cooperation among democratic forces. But relations among groups were strained, complicating the task of organizing effective, united action.[29] Despite an early start, the democratic movement in Orel did not achieve a high degree of mobilization or organizational development.

While all four cities were influenced by national events and trends, and while all were sites of organized democratic activity, review of local histories reveals ample diversity in movements across cities. The following sections explain the causes of variation. They demonstrate that the development of democratic movements depended largely on two major, sometimes interrelated factors: the nature of the local "breakthrough event" and the severity of a number of forms of state resistance and repression.

The Breakthrough Event

The breakthrough event is defined as a discrete watershed or tightly bundled sequence of occurrences that served as the "first success" for local democratic forces. In each city I found virtual unanimity among activists within and across insurgent groups on the question of which event amounted to their first major success, though activists sometimes differed in their interpretations of the event's meaning and consequences. The *timing*, *site*, and *type* of breakthrough in each city influenced social mobilization, the political identity of local activists, political entrepreneurship, and even state repression in ways that altered the momentum and force of democratic movements.

Sverdlovsk: The El'tsin Incident

The crucial breakthrough for the democratic movement in Sverdlovsk was the disgrace of El'tsin and the sudden outpouring of public opposition it prompted. Of particular significance were the context in which the event occurred—a function of its timing—and the fact that the catalyst for the event was a single personality who was far removed from the local scene.

The timing of the breakthrough in Sverdlovsk substantially influenced the subsequent development of democratic forces in the city. The "El'tsin Incident" took place very early in the life of the democratic movement in Russia. Few independent organizations capable of expressing social movement demands yet existed in Sverdlovsk, or indeed anywhere in Russia. Debate in the official press over the compatibility of autonomous political activity with "Soviet values" and "Communist life" had appeared only recently; the idea of political expression outside the bounds of state institutions was still novel. Official tolerance of independent activity was still severely limited.

Two major currents prevailed in the nascent democratic movement at this time. The first found expression in "political discussion clubs," such as Discussion Tribune in Sverdlovsk and Democratic Perestroika in Moscow, which were dedicated, at least ostensibly, to advancing Gorbachev's program of perestroika and glasnost'. Although the discussion clubs were organized for the most part by liberal intellectuals, their aims were shared by many ordinary citizens who had yet to engage in any political activity. Difficult as it may be to remember or comprehend from the vantage of the late or post-Soviet periods, these were times of considerable optimism in Russia. Gorbachev was not yet widely unpopular, and many felt the excitement of forward motion after decades of political freeze and economic decline. The second current was more radical. Its adherents included old political dissidents and others who were profoundly hostile to the regime, persons who regarded the reforms as ruses meant to shore up a decaying but fundamentally immutable system of domination. In late 1987 and 1988 this tendency was expressed by a number of small organizations that advocated civil disobedience and confrontation with the authorities. It also resonated in groups that eschewed direct, public encounters with the police in favor of "spiritual" or "moral" resistance through private revival of national traditions, religion, and culture.

It was in this environment, which still lacked parties, fronts, or indeed any substantial organized "radical middle ground" between a soft, vague, "pro-perestroika" disposition and a highly intransigent tendency, that news of El'tsin's sudden demotion transpired in Sverdlovsk. The event animated the two existent tendencies and accelerated their organizational development and institutionalization in Sverdlovsk in a manner that influenced politics long after the breakthrough occurred. It stimulated the rapid emergence of small groups of highly radical and visible—but largely ineffectual—political entrepreneurs. The activists who formed Miting-87 and the Democratic Union in the aftermath of the demonstrations were genuine radical malcontents who sought to convert public discontent over El'tsin's demotion into sustained, structured opposition. They viewed El'tsin's disgrace as evidence of what they had always known: that Gorbachev and other Communist leaders regarded liberalization in strictly instrumental terms, and that reform would be abandoned whenever it was regarded as threatening to the regime. Nor did these early radicals lionize El'tsin, whom they saw as very much a creation of "the system," even if a relatively liberal and courageous one. They regarded his fall less as a slap to a hero than as an opportunity to fire and radicalize public opinion.[30]

But the demands of the great majority of those who filled the streets of Sverdlovsk in late 1987 were quite modest. Most simply insisted that El'tsin's speech be made public, and that Gorbachev explain why it had provoked El'tsin's demotion. Many feared an impending conservative turn and felt offended by the fall of a local hero. Yet, as the failure of groups such as Miting-87 and the Democratic Union to attract mass public support revealed, few citizens in 1988 were prepared to undertake civil disobedience and risk persecution. Many regarded the early radicals skeptically, as people who had "little to lose." Indeed, many early radical organizers were highly alienated, disgruntled individuals who had suffered greatly under the Brezhnev regime. The courage and commitment of such activists cannot be denied; but nor can the possibility that they were not the individuals, nor theirs the cause, most capable of attracting ordinary citizens to the democratic movement at the time.

While they did not manage to win extensive popular backing, these groups did rouse a great deal of official hostility. Clashes, sometimes violent, between groups such as the Democratic Union and the police frequently punctuated the politics of Sverdlovsk during 1988–89, quickly establishing a pattern of antagonism between intransigent opposition forces and equally obdurate authorities. Not surprisingly, the "softer" tendency, represented in part by the efforts of voters' clubs on behalf of El'tsin, proved far more popular in Sverdlovsk during 1988–89.[31]

Thus, well before the local and republican elections of 1990, two distinct tendencies had become entrenched in the democratic movement in Sverdlovsk: maximalist, or "extremist," and pragmatic, or "soft." The former waned as the Democratic Union faded, and as more "pragmatic" groups such as the DDV and its constituent organizations began to appropriate more radical rhetoric. But the maximalist current was preserved in associations such as Iskra and Vozrozhdenie, which, while unenthusiastic about open confrontation with the authorities, regarded some "softer" activists as latecomers, political opportunists, and pseudo-democrats. Though the two currents did manage on occasion to find bases for common action during 1989–91, fissures in the movement resurfaced toward the end of the period, when Vozrozhdenie and other groups withdrew from the DDV.[32]

If the *timing* of the breakthrough stimulated the emergence and institutionalization in Sverdlovsk of currents that reflected the basic division in democratic identities prevalent in Russia in 1987 and 1988, the *type* of issue that created the event wedded much of the local movement—particularly the "softer" tendency—to a single individual. To be sure, personalism had its advantages. The cause of a local hero was easily grasped by ordinary citizens. It expedited popular involvement in voters' clubs, election campaigns, and public demonstrations. But El'tsin's cause became such an obsession that it sometimes "crowded out" other matters, including developing strong and viable organizations and meaningful party programs.[33] In early 1991, as ultraconservatives were staging a virtual takeover of the Union government and moving violently against separatism in the Baltics, the DDV expended considerable time and energy attacking and mounting a recall campaign against a deputy whose election it had supported, but who subsequently criticized El'tsin in a speech in the RSFSR Supreme Soviet.[34] As of the summer of 1991, the largest independent organization in Sverdlovsk was a group called the "El'tsin Club." One of its cochairs, who in July 1991 was still a member of the CPSU and had no intention of quitting, explained that "people of all orientations and beliefs come to our group, which is based on affection for Boris Nikolaevich and not on any specific program or ideas."[35]

El'tsin's distance from Sverdlovsk at the time of his demotion exacerbated the drawbacks of personalism. The El'tsin Incident was very much an *external* shock. It centered not on local issues or persons, but rather on an individual who had long ago left the scene for national politics. Though the event prompted the rapid emergence of local democratic organizations, it was not engineered by local forces. It therefore not only focused attention on a single individual, but also directed it away from concerns closer to the city and oblast' themselves. As will be discussed below, breakthroughs that centered on more immediate issues may have provided better opportunities for effective local political entrepreneurship.

In sum, the earliness, personalism, and "externality" of the El'tsin Incident promoted the emergence and institutionalization of militant but largely ineffectual, and popular but somewhat personalistic, tendencies. These currents persisted and divided the movement in the city until the end of the period under examination. Furthermore, the radical aims and tactics of the "early movers" quickly established a highly confrontational relationship between the authorities and segments of the democratic movement.

Tula: The 1990 Soviet Elections

While Sverdlovsk was rocked by a spectacular early breakthrough, Tula never experienced a sudden, dramatic, defining event. The first major success for the democratic movement in Tula, and the event that local activists themselves considered a milestone, was the strong showing of progressive candidates in the spring 1990 elections for the city soviet. This event differed substantially from the El'tsin Incident.

The breakthrough took place far later in Tula than in Sverdlovsk. Sverdlovsk had experienced over a year of independent political activity before the first small informal group assembled in Tula. In conversations and interviews held in the spring of 1991, many activists in Tula expressed embarrassment that their city, despite its proximity to Moscow, had slept through the early years of political ferment in Russia and stirred only on the eve of the 1990 elections. Indeed, Tula in some respects never caught up with cities such as Sverdlovsk in terms of social mobilization and organizational development. During the period between the spring 1990 elections and the failed coup attempt of August 1991, even accounting for the difference in the sizes of the two cities, mass demonstrations of popular resistance in Sverdlovsk dwarfed those held in Tula. While Sverdlovsk gained a reputation as a stronghold of insurgency, Tula seemed to remain a political backwater, influenced by, but hardly at the vanguard of, the democratic revolution.

But closer examination reveals that the tardiness of the breakthrough in Tula held consequential advantages. The historical context in which movement activity commenced is again significant. By late 1989 the democratic movement in a number of cities in Russia, most notably Moscow, had already begun to spawn voters' clubs and proto-parties, such as the Moscow Union of Voters and the Social Democratic Association, that sought revolutionary change but employed tactics and forms of expression more sophisticated than those of groups that emerged during the first wave in 1987 and 1988. Thus, by the time nascent democratic forces experienced their first major success in Tula, the range of organizational options available to activists was far broader and richer than it had been two to three years before. A portion of the tortuous and chaotic path toward the creation of democratic identities and organizations had already been traversed in places like Moscow and Sverdlovsk. Democrats in Tula did not have to retrace that path completely. As they charted their courses in the months following the March 1990 elections, they enjoyed the opportunity to found local chapters of the SDPR, the DPR, RPR, and Democratic Russia. The lateness of its rouse enabled the city to skip the stage when oppositionists could pin their hopes only on celebrated individuals or on groups such as the Democratic Union. The founding of Democratic Russia in Tula only months after the onset of major organized oppositional activity meant that democrats were able to establish a forum for cooperation and coordination early in the life of their local movement.

The city's late start not only eased the process of organization-building and mitigated the danger of corrosive splits within the democratic camp; it also encouraged relatively nonconfrontational relations between the democrats and local authorities. As will be discussed in the following section, official repression was hardly unknown in Tula. But naked attacks on associational rights, such as police action against peaceful demonstrators, were exceedingly rare. Politicians on both sides recognized a link between the timing of the movement's nascence and the state of relations between opposition and apparat. The leading local organizers of both the RPR and the SDPR held that the late emergence of the opposition reduced the potential for "extremism" in the city and facilitated tolerable—though scarcely amicable—relations with the authorities.[36] Interestingly, an official from the local apparat who was responsible for relations with independent organizations shared this view.[37]

The type and site of the breakthrough event also influenced the city's political development. Sverdlovsk again furnishes a useful counterpoint. As discussed above, the El'tsin Incident infused an element of personalism into the democratic movement in Sverdlovsk. The event was, moreover, an "external shock" that stimulated, but was not induced by, local movement activity. Tula's watershed differed along both dimensions. It was neither a consequence of nor a stimulus to personalism. The victories of candidates who composed "People's Power" in the 1990 elections resulted from the collective efforts of local activists. No single individual, either during or after the election campaign, emerged as a paramount force or symbol of the movement. Furthermore, the election itself, though a relatively mundane occurrence that lacked the drama of the El'tsin Incident, was an "internal" affair rather than an "external" shock. Local figures, rather than a person far removed from the scene, played the leading roles in Tula. Mobilization focused more on local issues of immediate relevance to the city's population than the cause of an individual or the fate of "reform" in the nation as a whole.

Volgograd: The February Revolution

The milestone in Volgograd was the removal from power of Kalashnikov and his deputies in early 1990, an incident that local democrats invariably referred to as "our February Revolution." The event spurred rapid growth of organized political activity. Of the breakthroughs in the four cities discussed here, the dismissal of Kalashnikov in Volgograd exerted the most powerful—and, from the standpoint of democratic forces, most propitious—effect on local politics.

Several features of the Kalashnikov incident are particularly important for understanding its impact. Like in Tula, the breakthrough occurred rather late. Democratic activism had been modest in Volgograd prior to early 1990. Once the breakthrough ignited public interest in progressive politics, Volgograd enjoyed the same advantages associated with "late development" that Tula did: the opportunity to borrow models of political organization developed in Moscow and other locations, as well as the ability largely to skip the tortuous and divisive earlier period of democratic identity-formation and open conflict with local organs of state power. The breakthrough in Volgograd, as in Tula, was nonpersonalistic. The object of public wrath was a group of apparatchiks; but an *issue* (official corruption and privilege) rather than a *person* (the adulation and defense of a particular hero) propelled public action. The breakthrough was, moreover, an "internal" affair. The *Ogonek* article that exposed official corruption in Volgograd was to some extent an "external shock," since it appeared unexpectedly in a national magazine. Nevertheless the issue the article addressed was very much a local one for Volgograders. The accessibility, immediacy, and sensational quality of the article furnished local democrats with an explosive issue around which to organize public dissatisfaction. The exposé enabled them to step forward as champions of the average townsperson, who endured interminable privation while unelected higher-ups grew fat off the public purse.

The outcome of the incident created an extraordinary sense of empowerment among local democratic forces. It accorded the organizers of the January demonstrations instant local fame and popular reputations as dragon slayers. Ordinary townspeople who participated in the demonstrations, moreover, could feel that they themselves had helped throw out the entire leadership of the oblast' party apparat—a success unlike those experienced by local forces in Sverdlovsk or Tula. In Sverdlovsk, demonstrators' demand that the contents of El'tsin's speech be publicized eventually were met, but El'tsin's demotion was not reversed in response to public outcry. In Tula, the strong showing of democrats in the 1990 elections for the city soviet did represent a genuine accomplishment. Yet few regarded the soviet as a seat of real power. But with the ouster of the top level of the oblast' party apparat following public protests, Volgograders felt that they had dealt a real blow to the state. The exhilaration the affair produced was still palpable in Volgograd in mid-1991 and helps account for the relative ease with which democratic activists mobilized public involvement in new organizations in the months after the February Revolution.

Public protest was actually not the only cause of Kalashnikov's downfall. A split in the apparat itself was also crucial. Although only a handful of democratic organizers knew it at the time, some of the compromising information in the *Ogonek* piece was leaked by the first secretary of the Volgograd City Communist Party Committee, A. M. Anipkin. Anipkin coveted the oblast' first secretary's post and sought an opportunity to pose as an enemy of corruption on the eve of elections. The ploy worked. Not only did the party appoint him to replace Kalashnikov, but he won election to the RSFSR Congress of People's Deputies in March. While the split in the party apparat was a crucial ingredient of the breakthrough, most Volgograders were not aware of how important it was. According to several leading democratic organizers, most of the city's residents knew that some strains had surfaced among local officials before Kalashnikov was dismissed but were unaware that Anipkin had actually passed damning information on Kalashnikov to the journalist who wrote the exposé.[38] Most residents viewed Kalashnikov's dismissal as more the result of popular pressure than the consequence of a schism in the leadership; they still regarded the February Revolution as their own triumph.

Whatever its "true" source, the February Revolution not only heightened public politicization; it also induced a sudden, steep decline in repression in the city and the oblast' as a whole. Kalashnikov had ruled as a petty tyrant, incapable of tolerating signs of political or economic independence in Volgograd or surrounding towns. His successor had hardly established a record as a liberal during his tenure as city party first secretary. But after the incident thrust him to the first secretaryship of the oblast' party organization and the RSFSR Congress of People's Deputies, Anipkin apparently regarded repression as inconsistent with his newfound role as popular hero and presided over a sharp retrenchment in official coercion and harassment of independent forces.

Orel: The Samarin Election

Unlike Sverdlovsk and Volgograd, Orel never experienced a spectacular defining moment. The watershed in Orel, like in Tula, took the form of an electoral success. While progressive candidates' strong showing in the 1990 elections for the city soviet forged Tula's breakthrough, Orel's first success took place a year earlier, in the 1989 elections for the USSR Congress of People's Deputies. It centered on the election of a single democratic candidate, V. I. Samarin.

The context in which the breakthrough occurred in Orel in some respects resembled that which prevailed at the time of the watershed in Sverdlovsk. Although the El'tsin Incident happened earlier than the Samarin election, the latter may also be regarded as an early breakthrough. It took place just as voters' clubs and other such associations were organizing, and one year before local and republican elections and the formation of political parties. As in Sverdlovsk, the groups that emerged during and in the wake of the event comprised many individuals of rather limited organizational aptitude. One leading progressive journalist in Orel, who specialized in coverage of local democratic organizations as well as the affairs of the city soviet, summarized the consequences of the timing of movement emergence with remarkable clarity and candor:

> We need organized social movements, since we must struggle with the regime and try to change it. But oppositional organizations are very small in our city, and they haven't attracted much popular support. When movements started here, which was really quite early compared to many places, many of the first out were people like [E. A.] Chernov and [Iu. V.] Karpeev, people who felt offended by the system and wanted to lash out. . . . By the time more serious people like [V. D.] Tokar started working in 1990, the movement here had already been discredited to some extent in the eyes of the people by those who clearly were out for themselves and had little ability to attract good people to the cause.[39]

The "early movers" not only partially "discredited" democrats in the city but also helped to create—as they did in Sverdlovsk—fissures in the movement. The division between eccentric, if courageous, ultra-radicals and those who joined the movement in later stages was manifest through mid-1991.[40]

As in Sverdlovsk, some of the regime's opponents stirred early in Orel, with lasting effects on the local democratic movement. But in Orel some insurgent activity was evident well before the breakthrough event, and the latter was the product not of an "external shock" but rather of an "internal"—that is, local—election campaign. To say that nascent radical organizations engineered Samarin's victory in early 1989 would be an exaggeration. With his radical populist rhetoric and oratorical flair, Samarin may have prevailed even without the support of groups such as Memorial and the Glasnost' Society, though their work on his behalf, which included putting up campaign posters, distributing literature, and organizing gatherings to express support and publicize his positions, did help him gain wider public recognition. Samarin himself, at any rate, certainly did not feel deeply indebted to his strongest backers. Most of those who openly organized support for him were harassed by local authorities after the campaign. Upon being informed of the persecutions after taking up residence in Moscow, Samarin displayed little interest in aiding his own supporters and indeed sought to distance himself from them rather than attempt to use his authority to protect them against official abuse.[41]

The election campaign did bring citizens together in a common cause, and local activists regarded it as a formative moment. In the final analysis, however, the Samarin election proved a rather inauspicious breakthrough. Though the event was created locally, it was in some sense "externalized" when Samarin, the personification of local progressive achievement, left for Moscow shortly after his election to join the Congress of People's Deputies. Breakthroughs in Tula and Volgograd created democratic leaders who remained "at home." In Orel the sole local hero left the scene before he could help build a movement, and he dissociated himself from those who had worked hardest and sacrificed the most to assure his victory. In addition to failing to defend his supporters after the election, Samarin refused to join the ONF after its founding later in 1989. He told local activists during a visit home that once the group had achieved a strong structure and mass membership, he would be glad to sign on.[42] That Samarin's behavior was unprincipled and destructive cannot be denied. But given the status of the local movement, it cannot be regarded as irrational or surprising. Samarin's aloofness was all the more damaging given how closely the breakthrough was tied to him personally.

In sum, the earliness, "externalization," and personalism of the break-through in Orel proved an inauspicious combination and reduced the event's potency as a stimulus to the growth of the democratic movement in the city.

Breakthrough events, or "first successes," thus strongly influenced the subsequent development of democratic movements. In two of the cities in particular, *fortuna* played a large role: El'tsin just happened to be from Sverdlovsk; and the exposé on Volgograd's rulers could have been written about the party chiefs of any oblast' or city in Russia. In all cases, the timing (early/late), type (personalistic/nonpersonalistic), and site (external/internal) of the breakthrough were of particular importance. Perhaps paradoxically, "late developers" (cities that did not experience substantial movement activity until relatively late in the Gorbachev period) enjoyed some advantages over "early movers." Breakthroughs based on a single individual, such as those in Sverd-lovsk and Orel, were less propitious than those that were not. Events that centered on "internal" or local issues and/or that spawned local political entrepreneurs (Tula and Volgograd) were superior to those based on issues or persons removed from the local scene (Sverdlovsk) or on local individuals who left town after the event (Orel). The subject of democratic political entrepreneurship will be addressed in greater depth in the section that discusses the impact of repression on the evolution of democratic forces.

State Responses to Independent Challenges

Direct Repression of Insurgent Forces

While breakthrough events helped define the courses of movement activity, the relationship between democratic groups and the state influenced even more strongly the development of organized opposition forces. Indeed, in one case—Volgograd—the breakthrough assumed particular importance due in part to its powerful effect on the integrity and repressiveness of local and provincial organs of state power.

Official policies toward independent challenges exhibited certain common features across cities. In all of the cities, liberalization proceeded far enough to open some space for independent opposition; in none did repression and official interference disappear entirely. Official agencies everywhere were influenced by statements and policy emanating from Moscow. Yet close examination reveals consequential diversity in official policies across cities.

The *Sverdlovsk* oblast' and city apparats were firmly controlled by conservative officials throughout the Gorbachev period.[43] The oblast' party committee underwent a change of leadership in early and mid-1990, but the shakeup produced little change in the orientation of the party apparat and the organs of state security.[44] State power employed the full complement of repressive and obstructive tactics against the opposition. Official large-circulation newspapers in the city and the oblast' for the most part refused to report on democratic organizations. The programs of progressive candidates for soviet elections were sometimes printed, but often with distortions and omissions. The official press sometimes featured forebodings of the impoverishment that supposedly would accompany empowerment of democrats and a transition to a market economy.[45]

Official resistance also took the form of repression of street demonstrations and group meetings organized by Miting-87, the Democratic Union, and other radical organizations. Although surprised authorities tolerated the initial round of spontaneous demonstrations in support of El'tsin, the police often broke up subsequent demonstrations during 1988 and 1989 and arrested, threatened, and fined organizers. In December 1988 Sergei Kuznetsov, an organizer of the Democratic Union in Sverdlovsk, was arrested on charges of anti-Soviet agitation. Kuznetsov's case became a cause célèbre for activists in Sverdlovsk and across Russia. Kusnetsov, who staged a hunger strike in prison during 1989 to protest beatings that he claimed he received while in confinement, was finally released in January 1990.[46] Incidence of forcible repression of association declined after 1989, when the Democratic Union and Miting-87 faded and organizations such as the DDV came to the fore of the democratic movement. Police action against such relatively "moderate" groups was not unknown. For the most part, however, state agencies relied on softer methods, such as denying permission to hold demonstrations and refusing to register progressive candidates for soviet elections, in dealings with voters' associations and most alternative parties.[47]

Infiltration of independent groups by agents of state security was another method employed by the authorities. Attempts at infiltration appear to have been aimed particularly at groups such as the Democratic Union and Vozrozhdenie. In the case of the Democratic Union, infiltration—or the fear of it—complicated organizational work; one activist recounted that the regular appearance of unknown and suspicious individuals at group meetings promoted mistrust within the group and reluctance to entrust anyone with leadership responsibilities.[48] Infiltration or the fear of it did not always induce organizational paralysis. Members of Vozrozhdenie, for example, felt confident that they could identify and marginalize infiltrators. Remarkably, in one case they even obtained the admission of an infiltrator that he had been hired by the KGB to gather information on the group and disrupt its operations.[49] Leaders of larger organizations, such as the DDV and several of its constituent parties, reported that infiltration of their groups and tapping of their phones was commonplace, but not sufficiently onerous as to destroy groups' operations.[50]

In short, the level of repression in general in Sverdlovsk was significant but not extremely high. Direct action was targeted mainly against groups whose tactics and messages authorities regarded as particularly offensive. Demonstrations held by radical organizations such as the Democratic Union and Miting-87 were often broken up by the police, while some large-scale demonstrations, particularly those organized by groups such as the DDV, were tolerated. Most groups suffered the threat of infiltration as well as the difficulties of disseminating information in the face of an official press that was controlled almost wholly by conservative authorities. Yet direct repression of independent political activity did decline perceptibly between the time of the "El'tsin Affair" and the coup attempt of August 1991.

Like in Sverdlovsk, the party-state apparat in *Tula* was conservative, but not so repressive as to foreclose the emergence of opposition. Like Sverdlovsk, Tula experienced a change in the leadership of the oblast' Communist Party committee in 1990, with no visible effects on the general orientation of the apparat.[51] There was "less to repress" in Tula than in Sverdlovsk. As discussed above, Tula for the most part slept through the early stages of the country's democratic insurgency. When the movement did begin to emerge in late 1989, its makers concentrated more on election campaigns and relatively quiet organization-building than on civil disobedience and open confrontation with the authorities. Incidence of open repression of street demonstrations and group meetings was low. While local organs of power scarcely embraced democratic groups and causes, they did exhibit some flexibility and desire to at least appear reasonable in their relations with opposition forces.[52] By mid-1991 autonomous organizations experienced relatively little difficulty in their efforts to register with local authorities. Most democratic activists expressed concern that their groups were infiltrated. Many asserted the usual—and highly plausible—claim that the KGB tapped and recorded their telephone conversations. Still, few felt that infiltration and monitoring undermined their organizational work completely. Problems of information dissemination eased somewhat in 1990 when the Komsomol newspaper began printing information on the local democratic movement.

Direct repressive action and intimidation were not unknown in

Tula. Igor' Liubimov, a journalist who worked for the progressive Komsomol newspaper, reported in the spring of 1991 that he regularly received anonymous telephone calls threatening him and his children if he continued to report on the democratic movement and to criticize the Communist Party. He also recounted that he and his staff had received several recent visits from Communist Party officials who threatened to take "certain actions" against the paper if it did not change its "extremist" ways.[53]

On the whole, the level of direct state repression against democratic activists and their organizations in Tula may be regarded as moderate. Evidence suggests that local officialdom did not experience a strong sense of threat and was able to accommodate at least some modest growth of opposition forces in the city.[54]

In *Volgograd*, a high level of repression reigned until early 1990. An attempt in 1987 by a group of students at the local polytechnic to organize a students' association independent of the Komsomol provoked a KGB campaign to root "extremists" out of the school.[55] The local and oblast' apparats did not feign liberalism in their policies toward independent activism, political or economic. Kalashnikov organized bands of thugs to destroy nascent cooperatives.[56] Authorities tolerated the formation of a voters' association in early 1989, but the group initially was heavily infiltrated by the KGB.[57] Until early 1990 officialdom maintained a level of fear sufficiently high to discourage acts of civil disobedience and mass demonstrations.

But the "February Revolution," which culminated in the dismissal of the top echelon of the oblast' apparat, transformed the environment in which democratic forces operated. It seems to have destroyed the will—perhaps even the capacity—of local organs of power to repress and obstruct the opposition. Not only did *all* democratic leaders interviewed in Volgograd report that interference and repression had nearly disappeared in early 1990; remarkably, some also expressed a belief that local party and state security officials had resigned themselves to at least some erosion of their own authority and to the inevitability of democratization. Valerii Zenin, the deputy chair of the city's DPR, stated:

> Of course it's hard to give a general assessment, but things are much better here than in other cities and oblasts. We now feel no interference from the KGB. The [Communist] Party doesn't love us, that's for sure, and they control most of the press, but that's a problem everywhere. We [representatives of democratic organizations] met with several dozen [Communist] Party workers recently in an auditorium. We argued openly and heatedly. . . . the struggle continues . . . but I saw in many of their faces an understanding that democracy is inevitable.[58]

Father Dimitrii Nesterov, the flagrantly anti-Communist leader of Volgograd's Christian Democrats, similarly claimed that he encountered no interference, and he attributed the authorities' leniency to the effects of the February Revolution: "At our last demonstration, Colonel Targashov, the head of the Constitutional Department [of the KGB] even walked up to me and said, 'Congratulations, Father Dimitrii, you spoke well.' . . . That February Revolution really had its effect. It showed that if we can throw out even such a big bird as Kalashnikov we've really got some power. Even the conservatives here understand this now."[59]

The sudden liberalization that accompanied the February Revolution extended to economic as well as political life. In many cities in Russia, including Tula and Sverdlovsk, cooperative enterprises established a modest presence by the end of the Gorbachev period. Yet most successful "private" enterprises were, at best, semiprivate. "Privatization" often took the "spontaneous" form of appropriation of property by enterprise managers, who drew their power from their status in the nomenklatura. Inputs were usually financed and acquired through semiofficial channels, involving "cooperation" with state enterprises, police, and state security agencies. Most cooperatives not founded by apparatchiks were quickly forced into "business relationships" with local organs of power and labored under crippling rules and restrictions, both formal and "informal." Unimpeded profit-making by truly independent entrepreneurs was unusual in most parts of Russia,[60] but it became relatively commonplace in Volgograd after the February Revolution. Mikhail Tsagoianov, an entrepreneur and member of the SDPR who earned over five million rubles[61] in the first half of 1991 speculating agricultural goods, asserted that his business experienced no interference or pressure from local authorities: "*Vlast'* works for itself, and we for ourselves. . . . After February 1990, *vlast'* knows what the indignation of the people can do, and it does not bother us."[62]

In short, a high level of direct repression persisted in Volgograd until early 1990, after which repression declined suddenly and dramatically. By mid-1991, it had almost disappeared from the city's politics.

In *Orel*, by contrast, repression of every type remained strong and unremitting. The authorities sanctioned no public demonstrations, though activists did manage to stage several gatherings that were surrounded but not dispersed by the police. As a rule, however, even small demonstrations encountered police action. The KGB monitored democratic activists so closely that any planning of demonstrations by telephone assured that police would arrive at the intended site in advance of the activists themselves. Many of those who worked for Samarin's election were arrested and held for brief periods and/or threatened following his victory in early 1989. As of mid-1990 the Orel

Popular Front could state, with little exaggeration, that "our citizens enjoy no freedom of association and little freedom of speech. . . . Perestroika has not yet touched our city or oblast'."[63]

Nor did repression decline substantially in 1990–91. Independent publishers continued to encounter heavy obstruction.[64] Activists managed to found a chapter of Democratic Russia in late 1990, though the level of fear in the city was still so high that many who attended the founding conference signed pseudonyms in the meeting's register. The prosecutor's office summoned and fined leaders of the DPR, the RKhDD, and Memorial on a regular basis during 1990–91. Organizers also frequently received threatening anonymous telephone calls. Unsurprisingly, some believed that the security organs infiltrated their groups. Yet given the extent of direct repression of association and the closeness with which activists' communications were monitored, authorities may have even regarded infiltration of organizations as unnecessary.[65]

Local CPSU officials did little to hide their contempt for democratic forces. In contrast with Communist Party presses in many cities, which often merely refused to publish information on the democratic movement, the press in Orel featured open attacks on the city's "so-called democrats," and thinly veiled suggestions that oppositionists were involved in dark conspiracies to undermine the local economy.[66] In an interview with the author in mid-1991, the city's party official in charge of relations with independent organizations could not name a single individual or group identified with the democratic movement, on the local or national level, whom he respected. Deriding local democrats as "children," he dismissed the notion of a multiparty political system in Russia and expressed admiration for the ultraconservative leader of the Russian Communist Party, Ivan Poloskov.[67]

Vladimir Ziabkin, a leading organizer of the DPR and Democratic Russia in the city, offered a concise summary of the situation in Orel: "The [Communist] Party controls everything here. We democrats can only work as partisans."[68]

Repression's Hidden Hand: Control and Dependency
in the Workplace

The species of state action discussed to this point—violations of associational rights, infiltration of organizations, information blockade, threats against and intimidation of oppositionists—may be regarded as forms of *direct* repression. They were aimed explicitly at democratic activists and organizations and represented deliberate responses by local officialdom to independent challenge. Levels of such types of official pressure varied over time and across cities depending on the policies of the local and oblast' apparats. Another form of repression, less direct and visible, but also less mutable and even more profoundly *systemic*, was the political control the state exerted over the workplace. Assessing the extent and effects of such a factor is difficult. Thorough investigation of variation in workplace repression across cities would require extensive surveying and long-term observation of employees in a variety of workplaces and industries in a number of locations. Even lacking such a comprehensive data base, a study of the democratic movement and social mobilization in Russia cannot ignore the role of repression in the workplace. The persistence of control over enterprises by a unified, hierarchical system of nomenklatura appointments, controlled by the Communist Party, chilled mobilization across Russia even as direct repression against insurgent forces waned in some locations.

The administration of enterprises by what Soviet workers dubbed the "triangle" (the party committee, the official trade union organization, and the enterprise director and his deputies) is a well-known feature of the Soviet system. Its nature and consequences have received most extensive treatment in the literature on Soviet-type economies; the political effects of this structure of administration have attracted less attention. And while several studies have considered the political role of authority relations in the workplace in the pre-1985 period,[69] few have investigated its influence on popular mobilization during the Gorbachev era.

Neglect of this topic by Western analysts may be traced to chronic tendencies both to overestimate the extent to which the nomenklatura system eroded under Gorbachev and to confuse official statements of intent with genuine reforms and policy changes. To be sure, some top Soviet leaders abandoned the "nomenklatura principle" in name, and even denounced it publicly, as early as 1989. Some loosening of the system was indeed evident by the end of the Gorbachev period. To adduce a rather mundane example offered by a factory worker and democratic leader from Tula, under the old system a factory director could not promote an individual to any administrative position, including to foremanship, without the signature of the city party first secretary; by 1990 such formal approval was often considered unnecessary. As the worker pointed out, however, "consultation" between local party officials and the director remained the rule, even on such routine matters.[70] In fact, while such relationships did become less "formal" during 1989–91, their essence changed little. The Communist Party continued to control the appointments of enterprise administrators. The latter remained as firmly positioned within the nomenklatura system as the administrations of the KGB and the police.

Underestimation of the nomenklatura system's tenacity has often led observers to a mistaken view of Soviet enterprise directors as an elite apart, somehow more "pragmatic" and "performance-minded"— and, by implication, more liberal—than the party officials who appointed them. Informed by the persistence of a "red" versus "expert" image of the Soviet economy, analysts have sometimes viewed enterprise managers as a potentially progressive force, impatient with political control and eager for liberalization of any type that might rationalize production and release employees' creative energies. Thus, some observers regarded passage of some authority over *production* decisions from party officials to enterprise managers as indication of a broader "depoliticization of the workplace," with obvious implications for political as well as economic life.[71] This view, however, fails to distinguish between party control over production decisions, the directness of which indeed declined during the Gorbachev years, and political control over the workplace in general, which could scarcely ebb as long as the party controlled the appointments of enterprise directors. Given the persistence of the nomenklatura system, it is unsurprising that enterprise managers, including those appointed after 1985, rarely proved to be strong proponents of political liberalization, in their own enterprises or in society as a whole. Many democrats considered enterprise directors "our worst enemies" or "the worst conservatives of all."[72]

Enterprise managers and, by association, the Communist Party, used two main levers to control employees' political behavior. The first was the power to dismiss, demote, or refuse promotion. The second involved the ability to deny access to goods obtained through the workplace. These methods could be employed overtly, as punishments, or latently, as threats. In the first instance, employees could be demoted or denied access to products as retribution for political disloyalty; in the second, the mere possibility of sanctions might be used to enforce political quiescence.

The system's efficacy depended on the degree of employees' mobility and dependence. Had citizens enjoyed greater freedom to change jobs, and residences if necessary, the threat of dismissal or demotion might not have acted as a strong deterrent. Likewise, had individuals' dependence on goods provided through the workplace declined, the potency of the threat of denial of access would have diminished accordingly.

Neither of these conditions obtained during 1985–91. The growth of cooperatives created some new employment opportunities outside the state sector. But for the vast majority, particularly those who lacked specialized skills and knowledge, escape from state enterprises was hardly an option. And the specter of a deep contraction of the labor market that loomed as plans for "transition to a market economy" took shape in 1990 offset whatever liberating effects that the growth of non-state enterprises might have generated. Indeed, the threat of mass unemployment inherent in rationalization of production and marketization of exchange handed employers a fresh and puissant instrument for enforcing political loyalty. The possibility that those who had quit the Communist Party and/or engaged in radical activity would be the first to go in the (very likely) event of layoffs and the uncertainty of finding alternative employment in a shrinking labor market were lost on few workers. Had the *propiska* system, which required citizens to obtain official permission to change place of residence, been abolished, opportunities for finding employment in another location would have enhanced labor mobility and mitigated the threat of job loss. But this highly salient vestige of totalitarianism remained virtually unchanged during the Gorbachev era. It continued to subject those who sought to change residence to a highly uncertain and often lengthy and expensive process of securing official permission. The difficulty of acquiring a new apartment under conditions of acute and worsening housing shortage, along with state control over allocation of dwellings, further restricted labor mobility. Nor did employees' dependence on goods obtained through the workplace subside. While no reliable figures are available, the ratio of food and other goods distributed through workplaces to those sold in stores almost certainly increased substantially as shortages grew more acute and as items vanished from state shops during 1989–91. Deterioration of the economy created a tyranny of want that only strengthened enterprise directors' leverage over employees.

The extent of control over employees varied across enterprises and industries. In general, employers enforced political loyalty most forcefully in enterprises that specialized in production for military purposes. The vast majority of enterprises in the Soviet Union, including collective and state farms, produced *something* for use by the military. But those that specialized in weapons systems, munitions, and defense technologies were placed in a special class, the aptly named "first category." Workers in first-category sectors were often better educated and more highly skilled than those in nondefense industries. As a rule, the former enjoyed higher wages and better access to scarce goods. They were also subject to special regimes that involved less tolerance for independent organization and deviant political behavior, within or outside the workplace.

Socioeconomic modernization theory would suppose that cities whose work forces enjoy relative advantages in education, skills, and income would present particularly fertile soil for the growth of social movements and opposition to authoritarian rule. In Russia, however, universal étatization of large-scale enterprise, the primacy of military production and the militarization of the economy, and the high level of political control over employees in defense enterprises conspired to blur or even reverse the expected relationship between sophistication of work force and mobilization potential. Thus, mobilization was more extensive in mining cities such as Donetsk and Novokuznetsk, whose inhabitants were relatively poorly educated but also subject to less political pressure in the workplace, than in Tula and Sverdlovsk—or, for that matter, Cheliabinsk and Voronezh—where military industries dominated local economies.

How did city size influence patterns of mobilization and political action? Socioeconomic modernization theory posits a strong positive relationship between urbanization and political development. Larger cities, by virtue of the richer opportunities they create for educational, associational, and cultural life, are considered more likely sites for the emergence of a well-informed and politically dynamic populace than smaller cities and towns.

Assessment of the effect of control and dependency in the workplace does suggest a positive relationship between a city's size and its potential for generating social movements. Yet when the influence of the state is placed at the center of analysis, as it is here, size and "political potential" are linked by a different logic than that postulated by modernization theory. The present approach suggests that larger city size presented two major advantages for the growth of insurgent political forces; modernization theory captures neither of these factors. First, persons residing in larger cities enjoyed greater anonymity. The risk that their participation in this or that political organization or demonstration would be found out and reported to their employers was lower than in smaller communities in which coworkers, employers, and local organs of state security enjoyed closer familiarity with individuals' private activities. Second, larger cities afforded a greater number and range of alternative sources of consumer goods, so employees' dependence on items furnished through the workplace was less acute. A Muscovite threatened with denial of access to vodka or meat supplied through his or her workplace stood a better chance of finding them elsewhere than did a resident of Ivanovo, a city of some one-half million. An inhabitant of a small town would very likely enjoy no alternative source of supply at all, particularly under conditions prevailing during 1989–91.

The extent of "workplace control" in the cases under examination cannot be known precisely. The preceding discussion, however, furnishes a framework for deducing hypotheses on variation across cities; and evidence drawn from observation and interviews provides an opportunity—however imperfect—for departing the realm of speculation and deduction.

First, one would expect the hidden hand of workplace control to weigh slightly more heavily on democratic movements in Sverdlovsk and Tula than in Volgograd and Orel. Military-industrial production dominated the economies of the former pair of cities. The lion's share of the work force employed in industry worked in enterprises that specialized in production for military purposes. The proportion of industry devoted to defense production was somewhat lower in Volgograd and Orel. Fewer factories therefore operated under the special regimes found in first-category enterprises. Second, one would expect differences in sizes of population to accord advantages to movements in Sverdlovsk and Volgograd. Maintaining anonymity and locating sources of sustenance outside the workplace were harder in the smaller cities of Tula and Orel, though Tula's proximity to Moscow might have served as a mitigating factor. In sum, one would conjecture that state control over the workplace exerted its effects least onerously in Volgograd. Sverdlovsk, with its large population and heavy concentration of military industry, and Orel, with its smaller size and lower proportion of military production, would serve as intermediate cases. The political effects of state control over enterprises might have been most pronounced in Tula, which was smaller than Sverdlovsk or Volgograd and dominated by military industry.

The evidence on workplace control, or at least how local democratic leaders experienced and perceived such control, is *roughly* consistent with these propositions. While several democratic leaders in *Volgograd* raised the issue as an enduring problem and as partial explanation for the absence of a strong workers' movement in the city, none feared for their own jobs or experienced significant harassment at work after February 1990, though several stated that they had encountered difficulties before that time. Since the February Revolution undermined the local apparat's coercive capability, or at least spoiled its taste for monitoring and repression, even enterprise directors who might have wished to control the behavior of their employees outside the workplace very likely lacked the information needed to do so after early 1990. In other words, the absence of a commitment on the part of the party and the KGB to direct repression, including infiltrating group meetings and public demonstrations and recording the identities of democratic activists, reduced employers' ability to keep tabs on employees, particularly in a large urban area such as Volgograd. Thus, a decline in forms of *direct* repression, aimed explicitly at organized democratic forces, automatically triggered a diminution in *indirect*, *structural* repression, exercised through the workplace and directed at the populace as a whole—though one would hardly expect fear in the workplace to evaporate overnight. Furthermore, the economic liberalization that ensued after the February Revolution created better opportunities for the growth of nonstate enterprises, and thus for escape from the state sector, than existed in the other three cities or indeed in most other Russian cities at the time.

In *Orel*, the apparat's commitment to thoroughgoing repression, its vigilant monitoring of independent opposition, and the relatively small size of the city canceled whatever advantages the lower proportion of military industry may have posed. In advance of demonstrations planned on the national level, such as those which democratic forces across Russia organized in February 1990, the oblast' and city party committees in Orel often ordered enterprise directors to forbid employees to attend any public gatherings for political purposes.[73] Many activists encountered persecution in their workplaces; some were fired for their political activities.[74] Anatolii Tretiakov, one of the few residents of Orel who left the Communist Party to organize a local chapter of the RPR, regarded fear for one's job as a crucial obstacle to mobilization in Orel and in Russia as a whole. He explained:

> For seventy years, fear has been our mother's milk, and for the majority, this remains. . . . Now everyone knows that movement toward a market economy means unemployment. At many enterprises here, word has gone out that political troublemakers and those who leave the [Communist] Party or stop paying dues will be the first to go. . . . The democratic movement is very weak here. But don't forget the threats we are under, and that we have no social guarantees for the unemployed."[75]

Control and dependency in the workplace weighed heavily on the democratic movement in *Sverdlovsk*. Many of the earliest activists who formed groups such as Miting-87 and the Democratic Union confronted sanctions at work.[76] The large size of the city, in addition to gradual reduction in direct repression there during 1989–91, probably lightened pressure in the workplace. But the heavy concentration of military industry insured that workplace control continued to exert substantial influence. Tamara Alaiba, an organizer of the RPR in Sverdlovsk and a leading member of the party's national coordinating soviet, attributed the absence of a strong workers' movement and the difficulty of achieving mass involvement in democratic organizations in part to the city's industrial profile. She pointed out, moreover, that administrators of enterprises specializing in military production not only imposed especially stiff penalties for political disloyalty; they also could provide attractive positive incentives for compliance:

> Our whole city is part of the military-industrial complex; 85 percent of our industry is tied to it. I can explain the political significance of this in a single word: barter. All these military enterprises have something valuable to trade around. They can get things unavailable to others, like imported products, good shoes, and cars. And then the enterprises parcel them out. The military-industrial complex preserves distributive socialism. The ruble doesn't buy much, so power is in the hands of the enterprise administrators, those with access to goods. It keeps the people [who work in such enterprises] passive. . . . There's a lot of corruption, but the system does work as it's designed to.[77]

Democrats in *Tula*, particularly the few workers who joined and achieved leadership positions in the local democratic movement, offered similar assessments. Their participation in opposition politics demonstrated that "it could be done"; but their explanations for why few of their fellows followed their example shed light on the broader effects of control in the workplace. Vitalii Zaivyn, a factory worker who was elected to the city soviet in 1990, and whose formidable abilities quietly to promote democratic causes without offending conservatives helped him win election as the legislature's deputy chairman, phrased the problem bluntly: "Workers in Tula do seem conservative. It's really quite simple: Bosses here have their workers by the [expletive omitted]. They tell them if you do this, you won't get that."[78] Nikolai Matveev, a worker at the huge Kirov arms factory who was elected to the oblast' soviet and became a local populist hero for his sharp tongue and willingness to challenge officialdom, asserted: "Workers here are paralyzed by fear. Over 80 percent of production in Tula is for the military, and all of us who work in this complex are completely dependent upon it." Matveev described an intricate network among enterprise directors in the oblast' that enforced blackballing of politically unreliable workers desiring to change jobs. The system insured that "if you have clear democratic political convictions and you seek work in a defense factory, the director will call around to find out about you, and you will be, well, politely turned away." To facilitate provision and dissemination of information on employees, the oblast' soviet, a majority of whose members were enterprise directors and party functionaries, established its own "sociological research department." In 1990 defense factory directors in Tula oblast' formed their own "Union of Directors," which, according to Matveev, "enabled them both to pursue their economic interests and enforce politi-

TABLE 2
Intensity of State Repression And Control In Four Cities

	City			
Type	Sverdlovsk	Tula	Volgograd	Orel
"Direct" forms				
Repression of association	medium	medium-low	high until 1990; then low	high
Information blockade	medium	medium	high until 1990; then low	high
Repression of private eco-nomic activity	medium	medium	high until 1990; then low	high
Infiltration and sabotage of groups	medium	medium-low	high until 1990; then low	medium-high
"Indirect" form				
Control and dependency in the workplace	medium-high	high	medium-low	medium-high

cal persecution in a better-organized fashion." Even deputyship in a soviet did not shield individuals from pressure at work. Matveev maintained that while administrators "deal with me with a bit of care, since I have a certain popularity at my factory and some others, most workers [who are soviet deputies] come under enormous pressure at work. Their bosses make it very costly for them to support democratic positions in the soviet."[79] Levels of state repression and control in each of the four cities are summarized in table 2.

Consequences of Repression and Control

Political Opportunity Structure, Political Entrepreneurship, and Popular Mobilization

Repression and state control of all types molded the political opportunity structures political activists—and potential political activists—confronted on the local level. These political opportunity structures, in turn, largely determined the type and quality of progressive political entrepreneurship that emerged in each of the cities. Political entrepreneurship has been the subject of considerable attention in the literatures on organizations, interest groups, and social movements. Most studies focus on elites, either high officials or top leaders of large organizations and mass movements. The following discussion examines how political opportunity structures established by the state shaped the relatively small-scale, micropolitical entrepreneurship that emerged in the cities under investigation. Some of the assumptions that normally inform rational choice approaches, such as that which regards all politicians and especially leaders of political parties as "office-seekers" motivated solely by desire for election (or reelection), cannot be taken as universal "givens" in the cases under consideration, in which uncertainty was great and opportunities for pursuing public office were only beginning to arise. Even without the benefit of such an assumption, examination of the opportunity structures insurgent leaders faced exposes sources of variation in political development across cases.

Guillermo O'Donnell and Philippe Schmitter have noted the importance of "exemplary individuals," distinguished by their extraordinary commitment, courage, or ambition (or some combination thereof) during the initial stages of movement against authoritarian regimes.[80] Such persons test—and sometimes redefine—the bounds of the permissible. The political opportunity structures they encounter are determined largely by the strength and type of state resistance and repression prevailing at the time. Yet in many cases, such as those of redemocratization in Latin America or of escape from Communist rule in some countries of East Europe, the existence—or at least memory—of independent social movements softened the strictures of the opportunity structure that the regime established. The makers of Poland's revolution in 1989 emerged or benefited from Solidarity's infrastructure; some leaders of the Czechoslovak revolution were associated with Charter 77. These groups composed elements of genuine—if tenuous and beleaguered—independent political societies. The opportunity structures revolutionary leaders faced were not set by the state alone; *society* had already had some say in establishing the bounds of the permissible. In some East European countries, the risings of 1989 did not actually constitute the first waves of revolt. Other waves had preceded them; the waters had been choppy for years.

By contrast, independent organizations and movements were virtually unknown in pre-1985 Soviet Russia. To be sure, the "exemplary individuals" who defied authority after 1985 themselves altered the bounds of the permissible. But they had no predecessors, or at least none who had managed to invent an *organized* challenge to the state.[81] The state alone had established the political opportunity structure. The bounds of the permissible had been fixed for decades. No Solidarity or Charter 77 had ever challenged and altered those boundaries. Thus, Russia's democratic entrepreneurs were in all instances the initiators and creators, never the products, of organized movement activity. On the national and local levels, they were engaged in a struggle to build independent society—and democracy—from scratch. They therefore emerged either from "nowhere" (they enjoyed little or no previous political-organizational experience) or from within "the system" (they came/defected from the party-state apparat). If the word "entrepreneur" evokes one who starts operations with a certain fund of independent capital, perhaps the term "pioneer" better captures the role democratic leaders played in Russia. For the purposes of discussion, however, the term "entrepreneur" will be used here.

While the struggle for democracy spawned political entrepreneurs of every conceivable type, most may be grouped into one of four categories. The first may be labeled *compromisers*. This category comprised two types of political entrepreneurs. The first was represented by an individual who held somewhat "progressive" beliefs and goals, but who remained firmly "within the system." He or she made a reputation as an advocate of "democratic reform" but retained membership in the Communist Party and did not actually challenge the party's paramountcy in state and society. Some such individuals declared themselves proponents of "revolutionary" transformation but in practice did not promote genuine regime change. The second type of compromiser was one who espoused truly radical views, but who refused to ally with any organization of the independent democratic opposition. Many such individuals were office-seeking opportunists who were eager to capitalize on public discontent and the organizational support of democratic groups during election campaigns but unwilling to commit themselves to support for the organized democratic movement after elections. While they differed substantially from "conservatives" or proponents of the pre-1985 status quo, compromisers of both types in fact contributed little to the development of democratic movement organizations.

The second type of entrepreneur was the *pragmatic radical*. He or she was either never a member of the Communist Party or quit it by or around the time of the 28th Party Congress in the summer of 1990. These individuals advocated genuine regime change, and they dedicated time and energy to building alternative political institutions—a voters' club, an alternative party, Democratic Russia, and so on. While in every sense a revolutionary, the pragmatic radical placed exigencies of organization and action above ideological purity. For this type of entrepreneur, the measure of any mode of action or expression was its utility for hastening democratic transition. Like the compromiser, the pragmatic radical may have been motivated strongly or even exclusively by "self-interest." Unlike the former, the latter realized his or her own ambitions in the struggle against the regime and labored to establish a record and a reputation that would befit a political career in a future, transformed—perhaps even post-Soviet—Russia.

The third type of democratic entrepreneur was the *saint*.[82] Such a person placed purity of intention, righteousness of action, and the cause of moral rectification above political expediency. He or she regarded regime change and democracy as necessary, but not sufficient, conditions for personal and national salvation. Such individuals attached great meaning to symbolic action, such as a vigil to commemorate victims of Stalinism. They sometimes preferred work in groups dedicated to cultural or intellectual revival to the task of building competitive political organizations. The saint often at least appeared to place the dictates of conscience above personal gain or even safety. He or she may be regarded as a "rational actor" only if preference ordering is adjusted to account for the possibility that one may derive more satisfaction from promotion of cause than from personal advancement. While the saint might be an effective political entrepreneur, he or she often did not possess the personal ambition, organizational skills, and stomach for intrigue needed for mobilizational tasks and usually found in larger measure among pragmatic radicals. The saint's advantage was ability to persevere even while enduring any manner of hardship.

The final category consisted of *fanatics*. Though strongly committed to democracy, such persons were often motivated primarily by grievance and hatred of the system. They relished confrontation and preferred dramatic expressive action to the more mundane grind of institution-building. The fanatic may have proven adept at civil disobedience but often rejected any institutions associated with the regime, even elections for soviets. He or she was courageous and daring. But other democratic activists and ordinary citizens often regarded the fanatic not as an "exemplary individual"—either an effective organizer or an attractive role model—but rather as one who had "little to lose." Fanatics distrusted fellow democrats who did not share their beliefs and commitment to radical tactics, and they typically failed to distinguish between compromisers and pragmatic radicals, both of whom they regarded as associates of the regime. The fanatic therefore sometimes created divisions within the democratic movement.

Political entrepreneurs of all four types could be found throughout Russia by the second half of the Gorbachev period, though saints, as in any society, were probably in shortest supply. On the national level, the compromiser was typified by Gorbachev's leading "liberal" adviser, Aleksandr Iakovlev; the pragmatic radical by Nikolai Travkin and Aleksandr Obolenskii; the saint by Andrei Sakharov; and the fa-

natic by the Democratic Union's Valeriia Novodvorskaia. The historical record of the Gorbachev period demonstrates that the second type
of political entrepreneur was the most skilled at mobilizing public
opinion and building autonomous organizations. As a rule, pragmatic
radicals were more dedicated revolutionaries than compromisers, but
better organizers than saints or fanatics. Yet, since saints were driven
primarily by moral considerations and fanatics by grievance, they
often "emerged" earlier than pragmatic radicals. Saints and fanatics
were willing to oppose the regime openly even under strong threat of
persecution, so even the slightest liberalization making some expressive action possible was enough to "activate" them. As suggested in
the above section on breakthrough events, the most "rational" and politically talented individuals—pragmatic radicals—often did not enter
opposition politics until they perceived a real possibility for advancing
democratic causes. For the purposes of this chapter, questions remain:
How did the political opportunity structures established by local organs of power shape local political entrepreneurship; that is, how did
they determine "who led" the democratic movement? How, in turn,
did the various forms of emergent entrepreneurship affect popular
mobilization? For the purposes of clarity and brevity, examination will
focus only on the city with the highest level of repression, Orel, and
that with the lowest, Volgograd.

Repression and control determined what types of political entrepreneurship were possible and profitable in a given city. It therefore
influenced both *who* emerged and *what entrepreneurial role* a given individual was capable of assuming. In *Orel*, with its heavy-handed authorities, opportunities for the second type of entrepreneur, the pragmatic radical, were severely limited. Like elsewhere, many of the
"early movers" in Orel were saints or fanatics. It was mainly these individuals who organized support for Samarin's election campaign,
and who paid with their jobs, personal security, or peace of mind. The
persecution of Samarin's supporters did not go unnoticed by potential
pragmatic radicals, by those inclined to initiate opposition but averse
to persecution and unwilling to act without some real possibility of
making a difference. Many such individuals held valued jobs, such
as teaching posts at local institutes or white-collar positions in local
enterprises. They could be expected to undertake democratic political
entrepreneurship only after the threat of reprisal diminished substantially and sufficient public space existed for sustained popular participation in independent politics.

But since only the most modest and limited liberalization occurred
in Orel, those who under less severe conditions might have become
pragmatic radical entrepreneurs had to explore other options. One

was to remain silent and do nothing. The second was to work quietly within a democratic organization without calling attention to oneself. Neither of these alternatives, of course, amounted to launching oneself as a political entrepreneur. The third possibility was to assume the part of a compromiser and work explicitly within the bounds of the permissible for whatever "progress" might be possible under existing constraints. An example of such an individual was Aleksandr Kisliakov, who became chairman of the city soviet in 1990 and who retained membership in the Communist Party through the end of the Gorbachev period. According to local democratic activists, including several who knew him personally, Kisliakov was a "closet democrat" who sympathized with the movement, but who realized that association with movement organizations would discredit him with the apparat and the soviet's conservative majority, and almost certainly cost him his position as chairman. In an interview with the author, Kisliakov stated that he considered himself a "democrat" and favored radical political change. But he also intimated that he saw little possibility for the growth of a serious democratic movement in Orel or in the oblast' as a whole. The best he could do for his city, he asserted, was to try to improve the supply situation.[83] Samarin was another type of compromiser. As discussed above, he benefited from the work of democratic activists during his campaign for the USSR Congress of People's Deputies, but after election he refused to participate in the Orel Popular Front or even to shield his supporters from persecution.

Whether Kisliakov and Samarin *would have* become pragmatic radical organizers and undertaken building alternative political organizations had Orel been a more liberal place must be left to question. Two conclusions, however, may be drawn from these cases. First, Kisliakov's and Samarin's actions—and inactions—constituted perfectly rational responses to the political opportunity structure that existed in Orel. Conditions compelled ambitious individuals, including advocates of democratization, to compromise with established authority and/or to avoid association with and accountability to the democratic movement. Second, the refusal of energetic, politically adept individuals such as Kisliakov and Samarin to associate themselves with local democrats robbed the movement of sorely needed organizational skills. Aleksandr Romash, who worked for Samarin's election and later helped to found the ONF and the RKhDD, remarked that Samarin's offer to participate in the ONF only *after* it had become a strong organization with mass membership amounted to "a professor telling you he will decide on whether he will serve as your dissertation adviser after you write your dissertation and he's read it. But how can you write your dissertation without an adviser? It leaves you in a lurch."[84] Indeed, the paucity of highly skilled, well-known organizers left the movement in Orel in a lurch, largely bereft of pragmatic radical organizers and in the hands of saints, whose numbers were small, and fanatics, whose propensity for conflict with the authorities and frequent trips to the prosecutor's office hardly fomented enthusiasm among ordinary citizens for participation in opposition politics. Even some of the leaders of the main alternative parties in Orel hardly fit the profile of the pragmatic radical. In contrast with his counterparts in many other cities, the leading organizer of the DPR in Orel better fit the description of a fanatic. He stated that he had decided to enter democratic politics and found a party "not because I think there are a lot of good, honest people in the movement, because I think there are actually very few. I joined because I wanted to spite the KGB. The KGB is setting up its own agents in the new parties, and I wanted to start a DPR here before the KGB came in and established a phony one of its own."[85]

Unsurprisingly, the few organizers who might be termed pragmatic radicals were often reluctant to ally themselves closely with some of the city's other democratic activists. For example, Valerii Tokar, who quit the Communist Party and helped organize a chapter of the RPR and Democratic Russia, sometimes shunned other democratic leaders and groups, frequently sitting aloof during organizational meetings of the ONF. Tokar, a politically ambitious teacher of engineering at a local institute, very likely felt that strong, unqualified association with the city's poorly organized democrats would subject him to persecution without necessarily enhancing his public image. His unsuccessful campaign for the RSFSR Congress of People's Deputies, during which he received the support of local democratic forces and was smeared in the official press for his alleged ties with some of the movement's less savory characters, cannot have heightened his desire to assume the role of a forceful, visible, and unapologetic democratic organizer.

In *Volgograd*, the dramatic decline in repression that followed the February Revolution in 1990 deeply altered the local political opportunity structure. It created ample space for pragmatic radical entrepreneurs. Igor' Lukashev, an army officer and instructor at a local institute, and Dimitrii Nesterov, an orthodox priest, serve as examples. Both men worked quietly and unobtrusively until early 1990, but then exploited the collapse of the apparat and sudden liberalization in a manner that aided both the local democratic movement and their own personal political fortunes. The public demonstrations against official corruption that accompanied the February Revolution afforded Lukashev, Nesterov, and others the chance to attract wide public notice and establish reputations as orators and organizers. The apparat's disarray and the decline in repression after the breakthrough presented fresh opportunities for mobilizing public opinion and expanding the democratic movement. Capitalizing on the chance to build their own organizational bases, Lukashev quit the Communist Party and launched a chapter of the SDPR; Nesterov, who had never been a Communist and who had worked underground as a *samizdat* publisher during the Brezhnev period, founded the RKhDD in the city. The presence of such effective and respected organizers attracted capable—and, as will be discussed in the following section, wealthy—individuals to the new parties. Both Lukashev and Nesterov, in turn, tapped their groups for organizational and financial support.

Would Lukashev have played the role that Kisliakov did in Orel—that of a compromiser who made his way within "the system" and contributed little to the growth of the movement—had he experienced the same constraints that the latter faced? Would Nesterov have been forced into the role of the saint, unwilling for reasons of religious and ideological conviction to compromise with Communist authorities, but similarly incapable of mobilizing extensive organizational support, had he lived in Orel? Answers require venture into the realm of the counterfactual and cannot be known with certainty. But the timing of the leaders' political debouchment indicates that the radical shift in political opportunity structure strongly affected their calculations.

Effective entrepreneurship spurred public involvement. The magnitude of mobilization and participation should not, of course, be exaggerated. Even in Volgograd, autonomous groups' sizes and growth rates were hardly spectacular compared to those found in major cities in many other countries in the throes of political upheaval. The only cities in Russia other than Moscow and Leningrad/St. Petersburg that witnessed sustained mass involvement in independent politics during the Gorbachev period were mining centers such as Novokuznetsk and Kemerovo. There, specific local conditions—including the potential for at least partial escape from the heavy hand of the authorities in the workplace—expedited levels and forms of mass action not seen elsewhere. The persistence of fear and dependency in the workplace undoubtedly continued to dampen mobilization potentials in most Russian cities, including Volgograd. Yet, of the cities under review here, Volgograd did achieve the most impressive levels of participation in independent political organizations.

In sum, differences in intensity of state repression created disparities in the political opportunity structures that democratic activists encountered and thereby produced significant variation in the quality of democratic entrepreneurship. Quality of entrepreneurship, in turn, strongly affected levels of popular participation.

Resource Mobilization

The second factor that state repression and control largely determined was the ability of local democratic organizations to acquire resources. Like political entrepreneurship, resource mobilization capacity may be conceived of as an intermediate or intervening variable, determined in large part by the policies and actions of local organs of power, and itself, in turn, partially determinative of the general development of democratic movement organizations.

Students of parties, interest groups, and movements have long recognized a strong, positive relationship between groups' resource mobilization potentials and their capacities for growth, development, and effective action. Some analysts who work within a "resource mobilization" paradigm have shown that movement organizations often are born and grow in alliance with preexisting organizations, which provide crucial financial, technical, and human support, especially during the start-up phase.[86]

One of the most salient and important differences between social movements in Russia and those in many other, particularly nonsocialist, countries lies in the opportunities groups enjoyed for securing material support. During its early stages, the German Green Party was able to tap preexisting environmental protection organizations. The civil rights movement in the United States relied during its early years on resources furnished by or channeled through churches. During democratization in Brazil in the mid- and late 1980s, the Workers' Party, whose leader nearly captured the presidency in the first direct elections, drew on funds and talent contributed by trade unions and built up over nearly two decades. In Gorbachev-era Russia, however, the legacy of étatization of associational and economic life created conditions for the growth of social movement organizations that differed considerably from those found in other cases. In a word, since the organizations examined in this book were the first major autonomous groups to emerge in Russia during the entire Soviet period (at least after the late 1920s), they enjoyed only the barest opportunities for locating and drawing on resources from other like-minded independent organizations. Examination of the problem of resource mobilization, like study of political entrepreneurship, illuminates differences between empowering and enriching independent society, on the one hand, and creating it from scratch, on the other.

Due to the étatization of association and the fusion of polity and economy, nearly all independent groups were born and continued throughout the Gorbachev period to live "on a shoestring." Provincial groups faced even more severe constraints than their counterparts in Moscow. Organizations operating in the capital sometimes received donations from abroad. But foreign contributors rarely channeled support to provincial groups, which usually received, at best, only a small "trickle down" from contributions to their national organizations. Aid from abroad often took the form of indivisible gifts, such as a copy machine or a personal computer, which as a rule remained in possession of headquarters in Moscow.[87] Even pecuniary contributions rarely found their way to provincial chapters. Acute scarcity and the imperative to concentrate resources where they could be most effectively exploited, rather than greed or corruption on the part of Moscow-based leaders, usually determined internal distribution of funds. There simply was not enough to go around. Democratic Russia did by mid-1991 establish a fund large enough to enable its headquarters to begin offering modest subsidies to some provincial chapters.[88] For the most part, however, local organizations generated their own sustenance, made their own decisions, and relied on their own wits.

Three sources of funds were available to groups on the local level. One was members' dues. Given groups' small sizes and their reluctance to restrict participation, this source yielded scant income. Few organizations on either the national or local level required members to pay dues on a regular basis. Some requested a one-time membership fee, but only cooperatives and business associations charged more than about twenty-five rubles. Most groups charged only a few rubles, and subsequent contributions were usually voluntary.

Collections taken up at public demonstrations brought in more money. In provincial cities, to an even greater extent than in Moscow, the large wooden collection boxes that circulated at demonstrations, into which ordinary citizens stuffed spare kopecks and small-denomination notes, served as the lifelines of the democratic movement. Usually money was collected for umbrella organizations that enjoyed broad appeal and recognition, such as the local voters' club, popular front, or, beginning in mid-1990, Democratic Russia organization, rather than for a particular party. In all societies in which they occur, mass public demonstrations function as media for expressive action and collective oath-taking, for the creation of solidarity and shared identity. In few places, however, have they served as important a fund-raising role as they did in Russia.

Ties with what sources of nonstate economic power did exist in Russia—with independent businesses and their associations—served as the third possible wellspring of material support. Relationships such as that which developed between Democratic Russia and the Moscow *Birzha* were possible, albeit on a smaller scale, on the local level.

Resource mobilization potentials of local movement organizations therefore depended on the degree of associational freedom, particularly the freedom to assemble public demonstrations; the extent of official tolerance of private economic activity; and the ability of local democratic activists to obtain contributions from holders of private wealth.

Only in Orel was repression of association sufficiently severe to foreclose mass demonstrations as major sources of income throughout the entire Gorbachev period. Authorities often refused to sanction demonstrations in the other three cities as well. By early 1990, however, activists in the other three cities were able to secure permission or at least tolerance often enough to organize occasional mass meetings. Sums collected at demonstrations were modest during the early stages, but later grew substantially. Viacheslav Andriianov, a leading organizer of Democratic Russia in Tula, reported that in 1990 local rallies usually generated only several hundred rubles; but in March 1991 one yielded three thousand rubles.[89] Mikhail Borisov, cochair of Sverdlovsk's DDV, recounted in July 1991 that one recent demonstration had generated seven thousand rubles, "not a small sum for us."[90]

Such sums did not liberate local organizations from want. In Tula, as of the spring of 1991, Democratic Russia did not even possess a typewriter or photocopy machine, much less a personal computer or a printing press. Yet, given the dearth of alternative sources, money raised at demonstrations played an important role. It helped groups purchase paper, occasionally rent public buildings for group meetings, organize public discussion seminars, and engage in other relevant activities. It enabled Democratic Russia organizations in Sverdlovsk and Volgograd to hire a few full-time, albeit temporary, staffers to work on El'tsin's presidential campaign. In addition to the material support it provided, such "popular financing" boosted activists' morale by furnishing evidence of broad public support.[91] Contributions were particularly welcome given the difficulties that activists confronted in achieving mass involvement in their associations. Dependency and fear in the workplace, lack of personal time and energy free from obtaining the means of subsistence, and dubiety regarding the prospects for genuine political transformation may have checked participation and membership in new parties and other independent organizations. But activists could take heart in the willingness of many thousands of their fellow townspeople to sacrifice money, in a time of great hardship, for the democratic cause.

One might expect ties with cooperative enterprises, even if less morally gratifying than contributions from a mass base of supporters, to have furnished the most lucrative source of support. Demonstrations were usually held irregularly and were sometimes banned or harassed. The amount of money they generated could not be known in advance, and sums did not reach meaningful proportions until relatively late in the period under examination. In many Western and developing countries, connections with businesses and their associations provide political organizations with more profitable and stable sources of income than small contributions from individuals. But in only one of the four cities under review did insurgents manage to forge close, highly gainful links with new holders of independent economic power.

Democrats enjoyed little opportunity for aid from private business in Orel. While tenacious political-associational repression restricted contributions from individuals, official intolerance of cooperative activity ruled out private enterprise as a major source of support. Given the weakness and disorganization of democratic forces—itself due largely to state repression—what few cooperatives did operate in Orel did not have a strong interest in close ties with oppositionists. Thus, democratic organizations in Orel never managed to establish substantial resource bases. As one democratic leader stated in May 1991: "We democrats are very low on means here. We do everything only on desire and initiative."[92]

Official tolerance of private economic activity was greater in Tula and Sverdlovsk. In both cities businesspersons founded local cooperatives associations. In Sverdlovsk, a citywide union of cooperators was founded in late 1989; in early 1990 an oblast'-wide association was formed, and later in the year the oblast' organization joined with others in the region and founded the Urals Regional Association of United Cooperatives.[93] In Tula, the cooperative movement was neither as large nor as well-organized as in Sverdlovsk. Still, some modest cooperative activity did develop in Tula, and in the spring of 1991 local entrepreneurs founded an association.[94]

With respect to the development of private business, Sverdlovsk and Tula were "typical" Russian cities. In neither was private economic activity banned entirely; but in neither did it develop freely and without official interference. The authorities in neither city were as intolerant as those in Orel. Officials in both Sverdlovsk and Tula, however, were not loath to enforce the stream of burdensome rules on cooperative activity that emanated from the center, nor to take full advantage of the opportunities for graft and predation that the murky and mercurial legal status of private business afforded. In the summer of 1991 Viktor Chupriianov, a leader of the cooperative movement in Sverdlovsk, stated that his main tasks remained promoting the "registration" of cooperative enterprises by local officials and protecting the former from the latter, as well as promoting "equal treatment under the law for all forms of property."[95] Some loci of relatively independent economic power had begun to take shape in the city, but private enterprise had hardly cast off its fetters.

Relations between the cooperative movement and the democrats in Sverdlovsk were friendly; indeed, the cooperatives association joined the DDV as a collective member. But the cooperatives and their associations did not serve as the main sources of funds for democratic political organizations. Democrats maintained that while they were working to establish ties with the cooperatives, efforts had not yielded rich rewards; collections taken at demonstrations remained their chief source of income.[96] According to Chupriianov, the cooperatives association leader, most businesspersons advocated democracy but did not see compelling reasons to contribute heavily to movement organizations. "Of course the DDV expects some material support from us," he stated, "but I've made clear that we expect the democrats to help us concretely. . . . Our alternative parties all say they support entrepreneurs and a market economy, and no doubt they do, but so far we don't see concrete steps."[97] Similarly, in Tula, where the cooperative movement was weaker than in Sverdlovsk but not entirely prostrate, entrepreneurs supported democratic goals (which of course included transition to a market economy) but for the most part were unable or unwilling to subsidize democratic groups. As of late March 1991, support was limited to a one-time, one-thousand-ruble contribution by a small group of entrepreneurs to the local Democratic Russia organization.[98]

Only in Volgograd did democratic organizations establish highly profitable links with emergent private business. The formula for success consisted of a radical reduction of state interference in private economic activity; the presence of skilled political entrepreneurs capable of drawing businesspersons into their organizations or at least gaining their financial support; and a perception on the part of some holders of wealth that the democratic movement was worth investing in, that the benefits—immediate or eventual—of contribution would outweigh the costs.

The first ingredient, radical economic liberalization, was discussed above in the section on state responses. As noted previously, repression of private economic activity fell dramatically in Volgograd in early 1990, indeed to levels lower than those prevailing in the other three cities. That entrepreneurs in Volgograd operated under the same fluid and nebulous laws on private property and enterprise that their counterparts in other cities did was of little real consequence. Far more significant was the relative reluctance or inability of the apparat in Volgograd, after the February Revolution, to shut down, squeeze, or restrict the independence of local entrepreneurs. In Gorbachev-era Russia, after all, "the law" was certainly not "the thing"; what mattered was how the local apparat interpreted it. Volgograd officialdom's relatively laissez-faire approach to private enterprise eased the urgency of securing "registration" and buying the tolerance of local authorities. While corruption, extortion, and "business relationships" between cooperatives and officials were probably not uncommon in Volgograd, entrepreneurs did enjoy an unusual degree of autonomy. Such independence was evident during the founding conference of the Volgograd Oblast' Union of Entrepreneurs in June 1991, when business leaders rejected calls by officials from the oblast' apparat for a "union of efforts on behalf of our common goals of transition to a market economy."[99]

But liberalization per se merely created space for independent economic power; enrichment of democratic forces required links between entrepreneurs and democratic organizations. Only skilled *political* entrepreneurs could forge such ties. As discussed above, effective democratic political entrepreneurship—the possibilities for which depended largely on abatement in repression and coercion—did emerge in Volgograd. Leaders such as Lukashev of the SDPR, Nesterov of the RKhDD, and Vladimir Sosipatrov of the city's voters' association— successful, "respectable" professionals who possessed formidable political-organizational skills—convinced a number of newly rich business entrepreneurs to invest in the democratic movement. The spirit of optimism that the February Revolution sparked aided democrats' efforts; they could, after all, make the case that they stood a good chance of soon being "in power." So in contrast with their counterparts in Sverdlovsk and many other cities, most of whom as late as the summer of 1991 were still awaiting "concrete actions" on behalf of their interests, some businesspersons in Volgograd regarded the *future* utility of *current* support for the democrats as very high. One successful businessman, Mikhail Tsagoianov, explained his association with the SDPR in the following way:

> We decided to chose a rising group of leaders, and I liked the Social Democrats, so to facilitate contacts I naturally joined the party and started working. . . . We don't have formal agreements, but we do give the party a lot of aid. When the campaign for the mayoralty comes up later in the year, Lukashev will probably run, and he stands a good chance of winning. We'll pay for radio time, for advertisements, for renting concert halls, for posters and campaign literature. We hope that if he wins, he'll be good to us. We're trying to act as a lobby, as a source of support for those who will support our economic interests. I think we will succeed pretty quickly.[100]

Thus, some organizations in Volgograd quickly achieved a rare level of material endowment. The SDPR had access to as much money as it could use. The Christian Democrats also enjoyed lucrative ties with local entrepreneurs. While he would not disclose fully the sources of his party's funding, Nesterov explained: "For financing, we've got millionaires—I mean real entrepreneurs, not Communists, people who don't love 'the comrades' and who help us out. They tell me, 'Don't worry, Father Dimitrii, you politicians should do your business, we ours, and since business is not such a clean affair, we'll do that, you stay clean, and we will take care of you.'" Lest his claims be dismissed as braggadocio, Nesterov showed me to a room in his apartment that contained a fax machine and an expensive photocopier, both purchased abroad for hard currency—items rarely seen in possession of democratic political organizations even in Moscow.[101]

In sum, resource mobilization capacities differed substantially across cities and were correlated strongly and positively with associational rights, particularly freedom of assembly, and with freedom of private economic activity. Quality of political entrepreneurship and business entrepreneurs' expected future utilities regarding investment in the democratic movement—factors that themselves were determined mainly by levels of repression prevailing on the local level—were also closely associated with groups' resource mobilization potentials.

Internal Structures of and Relations among Democratic Organizations

The third major factor that state control and repression shaped was the internal structures of, and relations among, democratic groups. Political entrepreneurship was determined by the level of repression in general, and resource mobilization capacities by the degree of associational and economic repression in particular. The dimension of state action that most strongly influenced organizational structures of and relations among opposition groups was infiltration and sabotage— and fear thereof. The argument may seem counterintuitive and requires explanation. Before the effect of infiltration and sabotage is discussed, however, several related issues should be addressed.

First, the distinction between intragroup relations (organizational structures) and intergroup relations (the structure of the democratic movement in general) in practice was not clear-cut. In most places, including the cities under examination, umbrella organizations, most notably Democratic Russia, subsumed alternative parties and other independent organizations. While relations among members of a party were clearly "internal" matters, patterns of interaction among alternative parties may be conceived of as either intergroup relations, on the one hand, or internal affairs of the local Democratic Russia organization, on the other.

Second, democratic political organizations in Russia during the Gorbachev period did not lack internal democracy. As discussed in the previous chapter, many established organizational structures, operational procedures, and habits of discourse that bordered on the anarchic. This state of affairs characterized parliamentary fractions as well as independent political associations. However commendable activists' desires to avoid oligarchy, internal hyperdemocracy often paralyzed organizations and sapped their capacity for united action. "Good" or "desirable" internal structures and relations therefore entail a degree of authority and hierarchy sufficient to allow for effective making and execution of decisions, and for cooperation and some unity of action both within groups and among organizations within the broader movement.

Third, it must be noted that internal structures and intergroup relations were not molded by state action alone. It was argued above that differences in levels of certain types of repression largely *determined* variations in quality of political entrepreneurship, levels of popular mobilization, and resource mobilization capacities. The influence of repression on the internal workings of and interactions among groups was more modest. As discussed in the previous chapter, endogenous factors, such as activists' ardent desires to break with "bolshevism" and to "be democratic," indubitably influenced organizational life as well. "Breakthrough events" also exerted their effects. As shown above, the timing of breakthroughs helped shape the subsequent evolution of relations among groups. In Orel and Sverdlovsk, which experienced relatively early watersheds, individuals who had confronted authorities openly during the early stage of movement activity often resented more cautious latecomers, while the latter often regarded the former as inept dreamers incapable of working judiciously within existing constraints. "Late developers" such as Volgograd and Tula experienced less conflict and division within their local movements. Still, examination of cases suggests that infiltration and sabotage—or fear and anticipation of them—also influenced the internal lives of opposition groups and the movement as a whole.

Fear of infiltration and sabotage engendered mutual suspicions within groups, both in Democratic Russia and inside its constituent organizations. Expectation that one's fellows might be working for "the other side"—collecting information for use against oneself, quietly sabotaging group efforts, and so on—did not foster trust and collegiality. That considerable mutual mistrust prevailed among democrats in Orel was not surprising; many "democrats" in the city very likely *were*, after all, working for the "other side." Similarly, the high level of mutual trust among Volgograd's democrats was due in part to the perception that one had little to fear from one's colleagues. The liberal turn in official policy that followed the February Revolution signaled that hostile infiltration would probably diminish or even disappear.[102]

Mutual mistrust within organizations was associated, in turn, with hyperdemocratic internal structures and divisive competition for leadership. In Orel, despite the smallness of movement organizations, most groups were led by two or more cochairs; only the RKhDD had a single chair. Within Democratic Russia, struggle for leadership crippled operations. Debates over who would serve on the coordinating soviet and control the organization's tiny purse were constant sources of contention; arguments over and balloting for leadership positions consumed far more time and energy than questions of political strategy, program, propaganda, and recruitment combined.[103] In Volgograd, not only was conflict over selection of leaders less severe, but most of the groups that constituted Democratic Russia themselves enjoyed effective organizational structures, with a single chair, often several deputy chairs, and relatively clearly defined lines of authority. Tula and Sverdlovsk, where the threat of infiltration and sabotage was lower than in Orel but higher than in Volgograd, again served as intermediate cases. As of the spring of 1991, relations among the organizers of Democratic Russia in Tula were good, though the organization was preoccupied with the vexing question of whether its recently formed coordinating soviet, composed of fifteen members, should elect *three* or *five* cochairs.[104] In Sverdlovsk, the DDV by mid-1991 had established a more effective structure than the Democratic Russia organization in Tula. In the spring of 1991 the former settled on a structure that included two cochairs and that concentrated most of the authority within the oblast' organization in the hands of the leaders from the city of Sverdlovsk (i.e., activists from the city took over the leadership of the entire oblast' organization). As discussed above, however, the centralization of power met with strong opposition and provoked mistrust on the parts of some of the DDV's collective members. As part of the reorganization, moreover, the coordinating soviet actually doubled in size, becoming a bloated board of over forty members that seldom met and that experienced difficulty engaging in disciplined action. Resistance to hierarchy and exclusion of members from decision making remained strong.[105]

To this point, a relationship between fear of infiltration and sabotage, on the one hand, and mistrust and conflict among insurgents, on the other, has been posited. Observation of a rough empirical relationship between mutual mistrust and hyperdemocratic operations and structures has been put forward. But the *logic* of the latter link—that between lack of trust within the movement and absence of effective organizational structures—remains to be explicated. The relationship might appear improbable. One might expect mutual mistrust produced by fear of official obstruction to engender highly centralized and disciplined organizations. Opposition groups working in hostile environments have rarely been models of internal democracy. The Leninist principle of "democratic centralism," so long on centralism and so short on democracy, and so often adopted by oppositionists engaged in struggle with centralized authoritarian regimes, evolved precisely out of the needs both to operate effectively and decisively and to protect the organization from infiltration and destruction by hostile state authorities.[106]

But working secretly and conspiratorially was not an option for movement organizations in Russia during the late Soviet period. In the late nineteenth and early twentieth centuries, parties struggling against tsarist rule sometimes managed to organize secret conferences, often of several hundred people. Similarly, in some countries experiencing revolutionary or separatist struggles in the present-day world, opposition forces are sometimes able to operate outside the gaze and reach of the state. The structure and technology of state control in contemporary Soviet Russia, built over many decades, precluded such modes of operation. The chainlike networks in which dissidents worked in the pre-1985 period, wherein each activist communicated with only a single other person, reflected an understanding of the impossibility of working in groups of more than a few and escaping the notice of the authorities. Liberalization broke the ban on independent association—thereby ending totalitarianism in Russia—and cleared space for groups dedicated to radical transformation. But the technology and institutions of state control remained; the possibility that groups of more than a few persons could operate outside the purview of officialdom still did not exist. The state could repress or tolerate opposition; agents of state security could infiltrate and sabotage autonomous organizations or leave them alone. But in any case, officialdom knew that the groups were there; it was well aware of their activities.[107]

The opposition therefore had no choice but to work "openly." Everyone knew that they were being watched and that there was little they could do about it. The problem was how to minimize the damage of possible infiltration and sabotage within the constraints imposed by an "omniscient" state.

Herein lies the link between fear of infiltration and hyperdemocracy. The formation of functional, effective organizational structures requires *delegation*—of power, authority, and responsibility. Who says organization says leadership, and who says leadership says delegation—even if, contrary to Michels's maxim, who says organization does not *necessarily* say oligarchy. The risk for groups under threat of infiltration was that authority might be delegated to one who was not "with us," to one who was "sent" or even hired or blackmailed after joining the group of his or her own volition. Since activists as a rule did not enjoy a long history of mutual acquaintance and usually met for the first time in the course of their work in the movement, shortage of information on "who was who" within groups was often acute.

An infiltrator could be either a full-time employee of the KGB or an ordinary citizen who performed piecework. The number of professional KGB agents involved in such tasks, not to mention individuals in the latter category, probably will never be known with certainty. But if revelations from East European countries provide any guide, several million citizens in Russia were, by choice or necessity, linked in some way with the security organs, and many were engaged in infiltrating and informing on the party's enemies. If an outside agent did not gain a position of authority and responsibility, the harm he or she could do might be limited to collecting information and disrupting group activities in subtle but not fatal ways. But the elevation of such persons to a leadership positions imperiled a group's integrity and ability to function. The "wrong" person in the "right" place—by intentionally squandering scarce resources, sabotaging the execution of decisions and the planning of activities by inaction, fomenting conflicts with other organizations, pitting group members against each other in a variety of ways—could endanger a group's existence, particularly during its inception and early stages. Thus, resistance to delegation of authority, even at the cost of organizational efficacy and efficiency, was not entirely illogical. The stronger the feeling of duress and fear of infiltration and sabotage, the greater the reluctance to delegate. It is unsurprising that organizational chaos was more severe, and hyperdemocracy more acute, where insurgent groups had more to fear from the authorities.

This section has examined the influence of the state on the development of the democratic opposition. It has been demonstrated that variation in the maturity and magnitude—in short, the success—of democratic forces across cities is best explained by dissimilarities in the political opportunity structures faced by local movements. These opportunity structures, in turn, were determined by degree of state repression and resistance. Specifically, causal relationships have been traced between several different types of control and repression, on the one hand, and democratic political entrepreneurship, levels of popular mobilization, groups' capacities for resource mobilization, and internal structures of and relations among groups, on the other. The relationships are summarized in figure 1.

The Paradox of "Soviet" Democracy

To this point, this chapter has analyzed democratic organizations and examined sources of variation in the evolution of movements across cities. This final section shifts attention to local soviets. It does not furnish a complete treatment, but rather offers several observations and tentative conclusions, some of which are at odds with conventional thinking, on the operation, organization, and composition of the soviets, as well as on their roles in local democratic movements.

In chapter 4 the relationship between the timing of elections and the emergence of autonomous organizations was explored. The following discussion focuses more explicitly on the role of the soviets and election campaigns in the progress of the democratic movement on the local level. How did local legislatures, elected by the populace rather than appointed by the party for the first time in the spring of 1990, contribute to the democratic movement? What constrained the soviets and prevented them from "seizing power" on the local level?

Local election campaigns stimulated popular involvement in opposition politics. They spawned voters' clubs that often later served as the nuclei of parties and broader organizations such as Democratic Russia. As discussed in the section on breakthrough events, elections for the city soviet in Tula constituted the first tangible success for democratic forces in that city. Across cities, election campaigns not only stimulated popular involvement; they also "introduced" previously unacquainted individuals to each other. They helped partially to "dealienate" or "deatomize" society.

Once convened, local soviets themselves also contributed to the development of the democratic movement. Above all, they served as fora for the expression of democratic aspirations. Progressive deputies' speeches and public statements, sometimes covered in the local media, brought home the radical demands voiced by several insurgent legislators during the nationally televised proceedings of the USSR Congress of People's Deputies in 1989. Using the rostra of soviets as

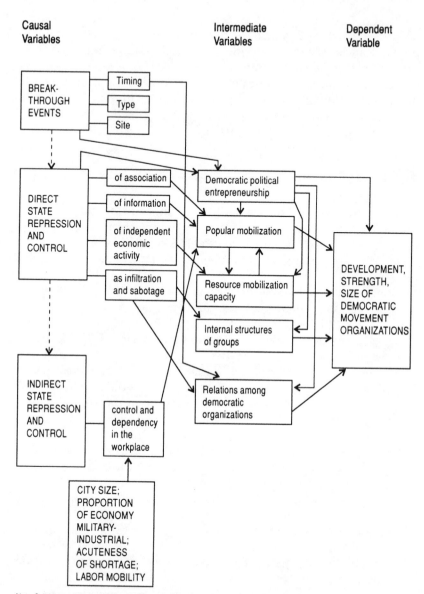

Causal Variables · Intermediate Variables · Dependent Variable

BREAK-THROUGH EVENTS
— Timing
— Type
— Site

DIRECT STATE REPRESSION AND CONTROL
— of association
— of information
— of independent economic activity
— as infiltration and sabotage

Democratic political entrepreneurship

Popular mobilization

Resource mobilization capacity

Internal structures of groups

Relations among democratic organizations

DEVELOPMENT, STRENGTH, SIZE OF DEMOCRATIC MOVEMENT ORGANIZATIONS

INDIRECT STATE REPRESSION AND CONTROL

control and dependency in the workplace

CITY SIZE; PROPORTION OF ECONOMY MILITARY-INDUSTRIAL; ACUTENESS OF SHORTAGE; LABOR MOBILITY

Note: Solid bars without arrows represent enumeration of aspects of causal variables.

Dotted lines with arrows show causal relationships that obtain in some cases; solid lines with arrows show causal relationships that always obtain.

The arrows from "Breakthrough Events" and "Direct State Repression" to "Democratic Political Entrepreneurship" indicate that all aspects of each of these causal variables affect entrepreneurship.

FIGURE 1. Causal Model of Democratic Movement Development in Four Cities

pulpits, democrats localized challenges to power holders. After March 1990, animadversion within elective bodies not only would issue from the center and strike at "the system" as a whole; it would now emanate from every corner of the land and focus on officials and offices with which most citizens enjoyed intimate familiarity, under whose authority they had always lived and worked.

But while the soviets lent voice to the democratic movement, they did not, and could not, govern. Multiple-candidate ballot elections partially "democratized" the legislatures. But the soviets were neither invested with great power nor restructured in a manner that would have enabled them to seize power themselves. Since the apparat retained control over the means of production, distribution, and coercion, the soviets could not themselves carry out radical political transformation on the local level, even while they did furnish platforms for protest. That the weakness of the soviets was due largely to the intransigence of the "pact of domination" on all levels and its unwillingness or inability to devolve real power and authority cannot be denied. But comprehending the enigmatic parts local soviets played in 1990–91 requires closer examination of the institutional arrangements that hindered legislative empowerment.

First, while the content of the legislatures changed after March 1990, the form did not. The soviets were far too large to govern. They were designed to furnish trappings of popular support for party decisions, not to make decisions themselves. The soviet of even the smallest city under examination in this chapter, Orel, had two hundred members. Such a parliament could scarcely run the municipal government of a city of one-half million, even under the best of circumstances. A council of, say, ten to twenty members would in any society be far better suited for the job.[108]

Second, while soviets were formally invested with a wide array of powers, their decisions could be "made for them," reformulated, or ignored by their executive committees, which as a rule were composed of holdovers from the pre-1990 period. Before 1990 the executive committee was made up of several deputies from the soviet and served as the permanent standing body that implemented the party apparat's decisions. The soviet at large, known as the "session," met only a few times a year to endorse unanimously whatever was placed in front of it. All members of executive committees everywhere and on all levels, of course, were Communist Party members. Many were themselves party officials; there was extensive overlap in personnel between party committees and soviets' executive committees. After the elections of March 1990, these same executive committees remained in place in most cities and oblasts'—even if their members were not elected to the soviet. So while the membership of the session changed, in some cases dramatically, the executive committee often changed little or not at all. The session was not formally subordinate to the executive committee; the former could make any law it desired. But neither was the executive committee in practice usually subordinate to the session. A typical executive committee therefore implemented those laws and rules with which it agreed, and it did so in ways that suited itself. Laws with which it did not agree it simply sabotaged by neglect. Budgetary decisions and economic policy, including policy on local enterprises, remained in most cases at least de facto under the control of executive committees. In short, unelected executive committees retained great power and autonomy from the soviets whose decisions they were supposed to carry out. So what authority that *did* devolve from party committees to soviets passed not to elected deputies but to executive committees, which were usually dominated by—not coincidentally— Communist Party officials. This state of affairs produced what one progressive deputy in the Sverdlovsk Oblast' Soviet called "a paradoxical situation" in which "real power in the oblast' is exercised mainly by the old organs of executive power, while responsibility for their actions rests with elected deputies, including democrats."[109]

Such conditions often touched off conflict between elected deputies—particularly progressive deputies—and executive committees. Debates over whether and how to control executive committees seized many soviets.[110] Indeed, controversies concerning division of power dominated the attention of deputies of all stripes in many legislatures during 1990–91. One institutional innovation introduced after March 1990 was the presidium. Elected by full sessions from their own memberships, presidia were generally composed of 5–10 percent of total membership and were meant to provide some direction and leadership for soviet affairs. While the powers and functions of presidia were poorly defined at the times of their formation, radical deputies hoped that presidia might be more progressive than executive committees, and perhaps capable of challenging executive committees' powers in a number of areas.

In many cities, including all of those under examination, battles over division of labor and authority were inconclusive and of Byzantine complexity. While such conflicts defy meaningful generalization, in most cities they were not resolved in a manner that enabled progressives to subdue executive committees. By means of deft subterfuge, democrats in the Tula City Soviet did make some progress on this score. Several progressive deputies managed to organize elections for the presidium soon after the convocation of the soviet in the spring of 1990. In the words of one: "Before anybody knew what was going on, we held elections and got a presidium that was over half our people, 20–25 percent waverers, and 10–15 percent conservatives. After that, the conservatives didn't even have any interest in working on the presidium." After achieving control of the presidium, democrats pushed through a rule that amalgamated the functions of the presidium and the executive committee, effectively enhancing the control of the session over the executive committee. As of the spring of 1991, division of power in the soviet was still extremely poorly defined.[111] Yet, while democrats had not actually seized control over execution of the soviet's decisions, they had demonstrated an impressive understanding of the sources of the legislature's weakness and considerable aptitude for maneuver.

The balance of power between, and the composition of, city and oblast' legislatures served as the third structural obstacle to democratic empowerment in the soviets. The division of power and responsibility *between* city and oblast' soviets was as uncertain and contested as the division among sessions, executive committees, and presidia *within* soviets. In general, however, the balance of power strongly favored oblasts. The executive committees of oblast' soviets—which in practice were usually subordinated to the oblast' Communist Party committee—exerted great influence over city budgets and controlled material supply and distribution within the entire oblast', including the food supplies of cities. Oblast' soviets thus held potent tools for quashing shows of radicalism or independence by cities. Not only did oblast' soviets possess a great deal of de facto veto power over decisions made by city soviets, but the threat of retaliation by the former for "democratic decisions" exerted a chilling preemptive effect on progressive action within city soviets. One leading democratic deputy in the Tula City Soviet remarked: "The cities are trying to get more power, but the oblasts can strangle our efforts. . . . Here we even hear things from the oblast' like, 'If this planned demonstration [by democrats] is allowed in Tula, the city will soon be without meat.'"[112] In all cities except Volgograd, I repeatedly heard such complaints from leaders of democratic organizations and progressive deputies in city soviets.[113]

The disparity in power would not have presented such a serious problem for democrats were oblast' soviets no more conservative than city soviets. But in most cases the former were indeed much more conservative, with the majority of their deputies typically drawn from the ranks of factory and collective farm directors and local Communist Party secretaries. Precise determination of "fraction democratic" and "fraction conservative" in soviets is impossible. Some deputies elected on the basis of radical platforms turned out to be fair-weather democrats at best, conservatives at worst. Many were "waverers" who sided now with conservative, now with progressive positions. Others started with no clear convictions and underwent radicalization after their elections. In every soviet, at least a few Communists sided with the "democrats." Some who entered soviets as members of the CPSU quit after the elections but did not announce it publicly, so gauging even how many Communists sat in a given legislature is difficult. In roughest outline, however, individuals of democratic orientation occupied about half of the seats in the city soviet and 10–15 percent of seats in the oblast' soviet in Tula; about half of seats in the city and 20 percent in the oblast' in Sverdlovsk; and about 30 percent in the city and 10 percent in the oblast' in Orel. Only in Volgograd did the composition of the city and oblast' soviets differ little, with progressive deputies holding 30–40 percent of seats in each.[114]

Why was the "fraction democratic" so much lower in oblasts than in the provincial capitals? The short and obvious answer is that rural and small-town voters elected more conservative deputies than urban electorates. Indeed, the ratio of the population of the provincial capital to that of the oblast' as a whole was a fairly reliable predictor of the political profile of a given oblast' soviet. The cities of Tula, Sverdlovsk, and Orel accounted for only about a quarter of the populations of their respective oblasts, while the city of Volgograd contained nearly half the population of Volgograd oblast'.

Yet may one assume, as have some analysts who employ a modernization approach, that inhabitants of rural areas and towns held a stronger preference for Communist Party tutelage than their more sophisticated and liberal city cousins?[115] Full discussion of the sources of voting behavior would require an examination of authority relations, public opinion, and electoral processes in small towns and rural areas that goes beyond the scope of this investigation. But the arguments made and evidence adduced in this chapter suggest the need to avoid two facile premises: that voting behavior "accurately" reflected public opinion in Russia during 1989–90; and that the outcomes of elections demonstrated a certain nonurban "conservatism." Such notions presuppose that (1) voters in general possessed a rich and diverse choice of candidates; and (2) they enjoyed roughly equal opportunities across population centers of various sizes to express genuine preference.

Both are highly dubious assumptions. A link was drawn above between fear and dependency in the workplace and city size. Residents of larger cities enjoyed both better opportunities for personal anonymity and more diverse and extensive alternative sources of scarce goods outside the workplace. Just as fear and dependence in the workplace placed harsher constraints on the abilities of residents of smaller communities to engage in radical activity, so they also imposed more severe limitations on their freedom of expression at the ballot box. Much of the process for nominating candidates for soviets was carried out in "work collectives." In practice, employees were often "requested" to nominate their directors, on whose beneficence they relied for access to food and, in many towns and rural districts, housing and other essentials. Many therefore voted "as they were told" by their bosses and district Communist Party leaders; opportunities for progressive candidates were often very limited. Following the nominating process, voters in rural areas and towns often did not enjoy a diverse choice of candidates. Far more often than in larger cities, there was no "democratic" alternative on the ballot at all.[116]

Even in cases in which voters enjoyed real choice, enterprise directors possessed formidable advantages. Their access to an enterprise's funds and outputs gave them something of value that could be promised to voters in exchange for support. Electoral rules allowed candidates to run in any district; they were not obligated to run in the place of their residence or work. This rule enhanced the mobility of slush capital by enabling directors to pick districts in which the goods they could promise to deliver in exchange for votes were in shortest supply. A director of an asphalt factory or construction enterprise in a city could run for office from a rural district whose roads were badly in need of repair. A director of a small-town enterprise that manufactured pipes might run in a district of a larger town or city whose water supply system was broken down.[117] Urban and nonurban voters alike might be swayed by such promises. Yet one might expect the latter, who have been relatively economically disadvantaged, to be more susceptible, regardless of personal political convictions. Needless to say, an individual who held a deep personal commitment to progressive goals would not be won over by promises of better roads or pipes. The point here is that it may have been perfectly rational and understandable for even "nonconservative" individuals, for those who actually opposed the regime but who also valued parochial concerns and interests—one need not speak in terms of parochial *attitudes* and *beliefs!*—to vote for conservative candidates. Such patterns of barter between candidates for public office who control resources and voters are, of course, familiar to students of politics in many developing countries.

This short excursus hardly confutes the possibility that many voters in Russia sincerely supported conservative candidates, and that nonurban voters generally held less progressive views than inhabitants of major cities. It does suggest the wisdom of extreme caution in using voting behavior as a measure of popular preferences in the situation that prevailed in Russia in 1989–90.

The obstacles to democratic empowerment through and within the soviets discussed to this point—the size of soviets, the power and independence of executive committees, the subordination of cities to oblasts, electoral arrangements favoring conservative candidates—may be regarded as structural or institutional factors. They were exogenous to the democratic movement insofar as they were features of the political-institutional environment established by the state, and they were largely beyond the control of democratic forces themselves. But several factors endogenous to the movement also influenced the progress of radical forces within legislatures. The first concerned the highly imperfect quality of information available not only to voters, but to democratic activists during election campaigns. Progressive voters' associations often simply could not determine "who was who" during the chaotic few months leading up to elections. In some places, endorsement by the local voters' organization was a valued commodity. Some voters' groups sent lists and even photographs of endorsed candidates to Moscow, where the Moscow Union of Voters or another of the groups that would soon coalesce into Democratic Russia made and sent back campaign posters with the names and pictures of local candidates alongside a photograph of El'tsin. The poster typically was emblazoned with a caption such as "For Democracy! For El'tsin and [name of local candidate(s)]!" Thus, candidates of every stripe— particularly in Sverdlovsk, which was home to both El'tsin and a strong voters' association in the form of the DDV—sought endorsement from progressive voters' groups. But most aspirants had yet to establish political reputations. Voters' committees, however sincere and committed, often simply could not know how "democratic" candidates were or if they had the slightest qualification to serve as legislators. So they endorsed many who turned out after winning election to be conservative, inept, or both. Iurii Davydov, a leader of the DDV, recalled:

> At the time of the election, the DDV supported a big group of candidates. Naturally, we [the leadership of the DDV] didn't have time to listen to each of the candidates present their cases in detail, so many of the people we supported turned out after the elections not to be democrats at all. They just wanted our support, to be affiliated with us and with El'tsin. They would come to us and say, "Look at this great democratic program I've got!" We would say, "So, you're a democrat?" "Yes I am!" "Great!" That was it. So, as you can imagine, a lot [of insincere candidates] slipped through.[118]

Despite such problems, many genuine and reasonably competent democrats were elected to oblast' and, in greater numbers, city soviets in early 1990. Yet even in many soviets that included a high proportion of progressives, sessions were often characterized by paralysis and deadlock. The inability of relatively "democratic" soviets to seize real power and revolutionize local politics was understandable, for the reasons discussed above. But the frequent incapacity of their sessions even to enact progressive legislation—execution and implementation aside—reflected a shortcoming in democratic fractions themselves. This problem, which represents the second "endogenous" check on effective democratic action within legislatures, was simple absence of discipline among progressive deputies. Observers of the Moscow City Soviet are well aware of how a body initially famous for its progressive profile—three-quarters of its deputies were elected on radical platforms—quickly became infamous for its chaotic proceedings and inability to legislate. Much the same thing happened in other, less celebrated cases. Among soviets in cities under examination, the city soviet in Sverdlovsk was noteworthy for its resemblance to its Moscow counterpart. Progressive deputies occupied a large proportion of seats. But, bluntly stated, they rarely ever accomplished anything. Despite their impressive numbers, democrats experienced extreme difficulty coordinating action on voting and submission of legislative proposals. Some deputies attempted to organize a coherent bloc under the DDV banner. They tried to call meetings of the "DDV fraction" in advance of floor votes to establish a common plan of action and a binding democratic "line." But organizers of the "fraction" could rarely even convoke the number of deputies needed to reach agreed upon, binding decisions. The leadership of the DDV (outside the soviet), moreover, exerted little effort to foster strong ties between the organization as a whole and its proponents in the soviet. Consequently, in the words of Aleksei Goncharenko, an organizer of Iskra and a leading democratic deputy in the city soviet, "Each deputy represents only himself. Among the democrats . . . there are no groups, no unity, and no real representation of interests. . . . Like cats on the prowl at night, each representing only himself—that's the way our deputies work."[119] Any possibility of effective logrolling with conservatives in the absence of discipline and strategic planning within the democratic camp was, needless to say, out of the question. In fact, even achieving the quorum needed to take votes in the session (one-half of all deputies) usually proved difficult. On proposals made by democrats that carried some chance of passing, Communist deputies would often exit the floor prior to the vote, and vice versa. Given the roughly even split between liberals and conservatives, and the fact that no more than 140 of 200 total deputies ever attended a session, lawmaking became a virtual impossibility. The soviet was therefore reduced to a debating society, replete with stirring speeches and calls for revolution—and devoid of authority. Democrats in the Sverdlovsk Oblast' Soviet were slightly more unified. But given the numerical preponderance of conservatives and their dominance of the soviet's executive committee and presidium, the body could not serve as a vehicle for radical reform.[120]

Explaining the utter absence of discipline among democrats in many legislatures poses a difficult task. Simple "lack of experience" undoubtedly played a role. Psychological-cultural explanations, which attribute fractiousness to the "Russian mindset" and/or the persistence even among democrats of "Bolshevist characteristics"—inability to listen, aversion to compromise, unfamiliarity with notions of reciprocity—are often heard among Russian observers and elected deputies themselves.[121]

But exceptional cases reveal the inadequacy of such explanations. Volgograd's oblast' and city soviets were such cases. About 30–40 percent of deputies in each soviet identified themselves with progressive programs. Yet, while they constituted minorities, in both bodies democrats worked well together, often voting in blocs and achieving a rare degree of consensus on strategy. Their discipline meant that their minority status did not prevent them from pushing through a number of important pieces of progressive legislation. In mid-1990, even before the RSFSR Supreme Soviet adopted its law on parties and social organizations, both of Volgograd's soviets had begun registering groups of every stripe, thereby granting them at least some legal protection and the right, for example, to establish bank accounts. In early 1991 the oblast' soviet passed a law allowing privatization of land. By the middle of the year some nine hundred private farms had been established in the oblast'. It also adopted legislation that devolved a significant degree of authority to the Volgograd City Soviet and established an unusually clear division of power between the two bodies—extraordinarily progressive measures. In both soviets, democrats not only worked relatively well together on the floor, but established impressive attendance records. In contrast with many of their counterparts in Sverdlovsk's soviets, they almost always showed up for sessions. Their discipline guaranteed that a quorum was usually reached, and that they often constituted absolute majorities during votes. In cases when they did not form majorities, they sometimes engaged in logrolling, trading what they regarded as relatively minor concessions for progress on issues of greater concern.[122] In short, democratic forces, to a rare degree, controlled the agendas of both soviets.

The effectiveness of Volgograd's democrats was due to several factors, some of which have already been discussed. The relatively large proportion of democrats in the Volgograd Oblast' Soviet, attributable to the favorable ratio of the sizes of the city to the oblast' as a whole, naturally contributed to democrats' abilities to get things done in the oblast' legislature. The liberalness of the oblast' soviet, and in particular its willingness to share power with soviets on lower levels, in turn facilitated democratic action in the city legislature. Other factors are closely related to those discussed in previous sections of the chapter. The low level of repression and the progressive momentum created by the February Revolution very likely reduced the obstinacy of executive committees in both soviets, thereby creating the (well-founded) impression among democrats that real change could be effected through legislatures and providing incentives for investment of time in substantive legislative work. The high quality of democratic leadership also played a role: Sosipatrov, Lukashev, Nesterov, and many others were soviet deputies as well as leaders of autonomous organizations. The strength of and good relations among Volgograd's democratic groups *outside* the soviets almost certainly facilitated solidarity and effective action *within* the soviets. Volgograd's progressive deputies suffered from the same lack of experience and partook of the same political culture as their fellows in other Russian cities. But a combination of auspicious factors—both human and structural—enabled them to establish a relatively impressive record of discipline and effectiveness.

But Volgograd was indeed the exception. Democratization by means of legislative empowerment remained a promise unfulfilled through the end of the Gorbachev period. Whatever the sources of their inefficacy, the soviets, even in the eyes of many democratic deputies, had been largely discredited as governing institutions by the time of the August coup attempt. Sergei Kireev, a career military officer and democratic leader in the Tula City Soviet, expressed widely held sentiment when he stated in the spring of 1991: "I've worked here for a year and come to the conclusion that the system of soviet power is unsound. It doesn't work—or, rather, it works in a way that makes change impossible and that leads to irresponsibility."[123] The connection between the performance of the legislatures at the end of the Soviet period and the growth in executive power and the bankruptcy of legislatures in post-Soviet Russia will be addressed in the final chapter.

VI

Democracy from Scratch

A CENTRAL argument put forward in this study is that the character of state power furnishes the key to understanding the independent political society that emerged in Russia during the Gorbachev period. It has been argued that the conditions under which elections were held, state repression and control of popular political participation, and the fusion of polity and economy—all of which were shaped by *vlast'*—determined the scope of popular mobilization, the content of social movement demands and the organizational forms through which they were expressed, and the behavior and strategies of independent political associations. The causal argument has accorded primacy to the structure and character of state power rather than the beliefs, ideas, and policy orientations of particular power holders; domination, resistance, and struggle rather than modernization and development; fortuitous breakthroughs and "path-dependence" rather than evolution; and political opportunity structures and political entrepreneurship rather than ideology and culture. If the *statist, institutional* approach to *political-societal* change constructed here furnishes a powerful and robust explanation for social movements and their organizations, one would expect the regime changes that followed the abortive putsch of August 1991—the ultimate "breakthrough event"—to alter the development of autonomous political organizations, even in the absence of immediate changes in political culture or level of economic development. On the other hand, one might expect the legacy of the late Soviet period to leave a deep and lasting imprint on post-Soviet Russian political life. The present approach would also recommend examining precisely what changes the coup attempt induced—and did not induce—in state power and particularly in the causal variables employed in analysis of the Gorbachev period before considering the prospects for democracy.

A full understanding of the political changes that have occurred since the failed coup is impossible at such an early stage, and at any rate it is beyond the scope of this study. Brief examination of several of the central tendencies that defined politics during the first year or so of the postcoup period may nevertheless illuminate how the legacy of the Gorbachev era—the crucial first stage of posttotalitarian politics—is shaping post-Soviet Russia. It may provide some clues to the future of both the new Russian regime and the intermediary institutions linking the state with broader society.

The Collapse of Communist Power and the Post-Soviet Russian State

The New Course: The Ghost of the Recent Past and Elite Choice in the Postcoup Crisis

During the months following the coup attempt, El'tsin and his associates faced a bewildering set of conflicting imperatives: dismantling the Soviet Union while preserving some framework for interrepublican cooperation; banning the Communist Party and consolidating some degree of control over the means of coercion without provoking organized resistance; and launching far-reaching economic reforms under conditions of economic disintegration. The unexpectedness of the coup attempt and the suddenness of its collapse exacerbated the crisis of emergency power that followed in its wake. Storm clouds had been gathering for some time. In retrospect, the coup attempt may appear as a logical and even inevitable culmination of a conservative turn that had been evident for over a year. And yet, while few were surprised that the old order refused to give up without a fight, the form that the reaction took and its timing caught most in Russia unawares. Opposition forces possessed no contingency plan for operations following a sudden, successful coup—much less a scheme for "assuming power" and implementing reforms in the event of the collapse of the Union government and the Communist Party.

The unpreparedness of the opposition for power, the presence of a president of Russia who emerged from the coup attempt with extraordinary prestige and authority, and the immediacy and severity of the economic crisis defined the environment within which the new post-Soviet Russian polity was born. These factors placed a tremendous measure of power in the hands of El'tsin and created formidable pressures for him to put the dictates of economic crisis management and reform above considerations of political change and democratization.

The central thrust of the new political course consisted of a harsh policy toward the Communist Party as an organization combined with extreme leniency toward and accommodation of the officials who made up the administrative mainstay of the old regime. A presidential decree issued in the early days following the collapse of the putsch banned the activities of the Communist Party on Russian territory, but arrests of individuals were limited to a tiny number of cases and were aimed only against the coup plotters. Persecution or even removal from positions of authority in government and enterprise administrations of those appointed under the nomenklatura system was ruled out. El'tsin also failed to call new elections for soviets, effectively leaving in place at all levels the legislatures that were elected in March 1990. Most of his appointments to the cabinet and other high-level positions, moreover, went to individuals who had acquired substantial administrative experience during the Gorbachev and earlier periods.[1]

El'tsin on a number of occasions has portrayed restraint and clemency toward the guardians of the old order as signs of healthy tolerance and a spirit of liberalism.[2] The absence of mass repression and persecution indeed may be regarded as a laudable departure from the practices of the predecessor regime and those of "postrevolutionary" governments in many other cases. But the real reasons for quickly reaching an implicit settlement that was highly uncostly to the custodians of the old system were rooted less in lofty principles than in practical exigencies and pragmatic political considerations.

El'tsin inherited an economy that was not merely "on the brink" of collapse; in many respects it had already collapsed. Production had been declining steeply for several years; supply networks, for both intermediate and consumers' goods, had broken down; and shortages of even basic food products had become dangerously acute in many cities. By the fall of 1991 crucial reforms that the Union government had long resisted, above all the elimination of price controls, could be put off no longer, at least not without risking mass privation. Yet such measures, however urgent and necessary, promised to spark price inflation that would greatly outstrip wage inflation. El'tsin and his advisers were well aware that economic reform would be painful and unpopular—all the more so given the cumulative effects of the preceding several years of prodigious economic mismanagement and official procrastination and obstinacy on issues such as price liberalization, privatization, and monetary and credit policies.

Of equal importance in understanding El'tsin's course was the political situation he inherited. Three interrelated circumstances, each discussed in previous chapters, were of particular importance. First, the new government presided over a society and an economy that were far more deeply and pervasively penetrated by the state than those of most other countries that have experienced transitions from authoritarian rule. The only other countries whose levels of étatization under the antecedent regime have compared to that of Russia have been others emerging from socialism. Among the latter, only other former Soviet republics had endured such a high degree of étatization for as long as Russia; the duration of total rule in East Europe was briefer by a generation. And within East Europe, several countries, most notably Poland and Hungary, never reached the level of étatization found in Russia. Second, little genuine, systematic power-sharing took place during the Gorbachev period. To be sure, the strength of society grew and the regime began to fragment and decay during the late 1980s. But arrangements and mechanisms for controlled devolution of power and authority to organized societal forces were conspicuous by their absence in Russia. Gorbachev and other Soviet leaders intended to modernize and revitalize the existing system of rule and were prepared to subject the state to considerable stress to achieve this end. But they never conceived of their own policies as preparation for withdrawal from power and transition to a post-Soviet, post-Communist system. Third, while the opposition movement organizations established substantial infrastructure for the expression of antiregime demands, they did not, for reasons explained in previous chapters, create strong and effective institutional bases for representation of societal interests.

How, then, did these conditions constrain elite political choice in the early postcoup period? The *severity of the crisis in material production and distribution* meant that economic reform would have to take precedence over all other considerations. The *depth and extent of étatization* meant that real change of *vlast'* in human terms would require not only the replacement of several thousand officials in public administration and the armed forces, as sometimes has been the case in other transitions, but rather massive purges and personnel changes at all levels and in all realms of political and economic life. Unlike in most nonsocialist countries, the administrations of all large-scale and most small-scale productive enterprises were fully continuous parts of the state; all enterprise and "trade union" directors were state officials and Communist Party members. All were appointed by the party itself. Thus, real supersedure of the state would have necessitated replacement of the apparat, of the several hundred thousand officials who controlled the institutions of government, coercion, mass culture and information, education, and material production and distribution. Such a change would have been momentous, destabilizing, time-consuming, and of highly uncertain result, even under the best of circumstances. Under conditions of economic collapse, the initiation of such a process cannot but have appeared daunting, even unfathomable.

The *inability and/or unwillingness of the state to establish power-sharing arrangements in the precoup period* meant that little of the "pacting" among elite representatives of competing social groups and interests often in evidence in other transitions could take place in Russia before

August 1991. No terms, implicit or explicit, for a settlement of any type among various state and societal actors had been drawn up. The stewards of the Soviet state never accepted the need to establish such terms since they never planned on withdrawing from power. And nearly all organizations of the democratic opposition were convinced by about mid-1990 that notions of "restructured" or "soft" communism were absurd contradictions in terms. These groups were united by—if nothing else—their unwillingness to consider any compromise that included the perpetuation of Communist Party control over state institutions. Furthermore, the *incapacity of the opposition to establish the institutional bases for mass interest representation during the Gorbachev period* meant that Russia entered the postcoup period with the question of who shall speak for whom entirely unanswered. As of August 1991 the alternative (non-Communist) political parties enjoyed neither mass memberships and followings nor the capacity to structure competition in the soviets. Thus, unlike in Spain or Hungary, political parties could not step forward as the guiding forces of transition. The workers' movement was strong only in coal-mining regions. Even there, loose coalitions of strike committees rather than coherent union organizations predominated, and the movement enjoyed only the most tenuous organizational connections to Democratic Russia and its constituent groups. Independent interest and professional associations were everywhere still in their infancy and scarcely capable of speaking for a mass base of members. So in contrast to Poland and some Latin American cases, no organization or coalition of groups could credibly claim to speak for entire sectors or classes. Finally, unlike many East European countries and nearly all non-Russian Soviet republics, Russia lacked a large popular front or other movement organization based on ethnicity that united mass opinion in the cause of "national liberation" and escape from imperial tutelage.[3] In short, the country entered the postcoup period with neither blueprints for an orderly, controlled transition on the table nor the broad, large-scale representative organizations necessary for negotiating such a transition.[4] Nor, moreover, given their small sizes, fractiousness, and highly uncertain social bases, could opposition forces offer El'tsin a credible promise that *they* could replace the apparat and effectively staff en masse the myriad agencies on which power in the country is based—administrative offices, security services, enterprise and institute directorships, and so on. Herein lies the gravest consequence of the state of affairs captured by Vladimir Bukovsky's simple and penetrating observation that "while there were far too many revolutionaries in 1917, this time there are too few."[5]

In sum, immediately upon acquiring emergency powers in the aftermath of the failed coup, El'tsin embarked upon a course that included swift action against the Communist Party organization. But his policy also placed immediate economic considerations above problems of democratization. It failed to include measures rapidly to restructure or replace many of the institutions upon which the old system was based or to "democratize" extant institutions through wholesale supplanting of sitting officials. The constraining conditions that shaped El'tsin's course, each of which represented a piece of the legacy of the preceding period, were an acute and worsening economic crisis; an economy and society deeply and thoroughly penetrated by the state; the absence of preexisting plans or arrangements for a controlled transfer of power; and a deficit of revolutionary organizations sufficiently large and powerful to speak for mass interests, control mass political behavior, and remold the offices and replace the cadres that constituted the human infrastructure of the old regime.

El'tsin

The explanation presented to this point for the new government's course, like the explanatory framework of the book as a whole, has focused on political opportunity structures. Yet, given the extraordinary role that the Russian president played during the coup attempt and the enormous authority he enjoyed in its aftermath, no explanation for elite choice can be complete without a word on El'tsin himself.[6] El'tsin's personal beliefs and convictions have been the topics of much discussion in both Russia and the West. Whether or not he is a genuine "democrat" and if so, what kind, must be left open here. Such a question at any rate is of only limited relevance to the topic at hand and probably has no definitive answer.

Yet it might be pointed out that however courageous his behavior before, during, and after the coup attempt, El'tsin is, at least by personal and career experience, no Vaclav Havel, Lech Walesa, or Zhelyu Zhelev. During times of crisis such as El'tsin experienced following the coup attempt, individuals often fall back on old habits and the counsel of persons with whom they enjoy long and close familiarity. In El'tsin's case, these habits are sometimes those of the oblast' party first secretary, and these individuals often those whom he has known for many years during his long career in government. In contrast with the bodies of advisers that surround the leaders of many countries of East Europe and the former Soviet Union, El'tsin's cabinet and inner circle

include no individuals who were earlier persecuted for dissident political activity. El'tsin did acquire the status of the leading figure in the
democratic movement during the Gorbachev period. But his connection to the movement was more complicated and less intimate than
many observers and even democratic organizers themselves realized
at the time. Though an advocate of radical democratization, he was
more a patron than a creator—or a creation—of the organizations
under investigation in this study. They latched on to him rather than
the reverse, as was starkly evident in the spring of 1991, when Democratic Russia and each of it constituent parties nominated El'tsin as
"their" candidate for the presidency while demanding little or nothing
in return. El'tsin always maintained his independence. He never incurred pinioning debts to his supporters. He initially helped lead the
"Interregional Group" of progressive deputies in the USSR Congress
and later associated himself loosely with Democratic Russia. But he
never launched a party of his own nor involved himself directly in the
life of any autonomous movement organization.

El'tsin's stance vis-à-vis the democratic movement and his previous
career as a party functionary scarcely preclude the possibility that he
holds at least some truly "democratic" convictions. Still less do they
support the mistaken image of him, widely held in the West, as a populist demagogue. Populists do not launch harsh economic liberalization programs, publicly assume personal responsibility for the hardships to come, and refrain from scapegoating once the pain sets in and
personal popularity begins to wane—all of which El'tsin has done. But
his career experience and political independence prior to August 1991
may help explain his actions—and inactions—in the months following
the coup attempt.

The Consequences of Elite Choice

The course that El'tsin chose during the fall and winter of 1991–92 affected profoundly the subsequent evolution of the new post-Soviet
polity. First, it set off what was to become a cycle of mutual disappointment between the president and many of those who had supported him so ardently before the putsch.[7] Despite the limited sizes,
structural weaknesses, and uncertain constituencies of the organizations they created, many activists hoped that El'tsin would apportion
cabinet posts and other top positions among leading organizers from
Democratic Russia and its constituent groups. El'tsin's decisions in the
early postcoup period frustrated such expectations. El'tsin included
some leading democrats in the group of roughly two thousand people

that formed his Moscow-based apparat. But their numbers were quite modest, and El'tsin entrusted most top positions either to holdovers or to less experienced technocrats whom he regarded as competent to devise and implement economic reform. Furthermore, most of the limited number of democrats who were included in some capacity were leaders such as Sergei Stankevich, the deputy mayor of Moscow in the Popov administration, and Gennadii Burbulis, with whom El'tsin enjoyed acquaintance from his days as party leader of Sverdlovsk Oblast'. Such individuals had acquired their celebrity and democratic credentials during service in office and/or through personal association with El'tsin. Like the president, they were former Communists and free-lance political entrepreneurs who did not join an alternative political party or devote great time and energy to building autonomous political organizations.

If El'tsin disappointed many of those who had supported him most fervently before the putsch, the reverse was also true. Before the coup attempt an unabashedly liberal bent distinguished the programs and positions of the parties that made up Democratic Russia and the parliamentarians who associated themselves with the democratic movement. On economic issues, most espoused liberalization in all spheres: decontrol of prices, massive privatization, elimination of restrictions on capital and labor mobility, liberalization of laws on foreign investment—in short, crash de-étatization of the economy and rapid transition to capitalism. After many decades of social pauperization and privation under a system that called itself "socialist," even most of those who called themselves social democrats placed liberalization above economic equality. So as El'tsin unveiled his plan for economic reform in the fall of 1991, the first stage of which centered on freeing prices, he had good reason to expect strong and virtually unanimous backing from the old regime's democratic opponents.

But most democrats had never actually considered the costs and consequences of economic liberalization. Their agendas and programs were more wish lists and philosophical treatises than plans of action. When the moment finally arrived to enact and implement reform and to face the hardships and dislocations involved, many opponents of the command economy underwent a remarkable overnight conversion from pure liberalism to traditional social democracy. Some suddenly discovered the advantages of "social protection" and moved quickly to oppose at least elements of the unvarnished liberalization that they had long supported in the abstract. Pressing his case vigorously and wielding the threat of his decree powers, El'tsin did push through the essentials of the first stage of his program. His success, however, rested less on strong support of democratic parliamentarians and organizations than on the inability of any other group, progressive or conservative-Communist, to offer anything resembling a workable alternative. Given the cold embrace with which many democrats received his program, El'tsin had good reason by the spring of 1992 to regard his loyal allies-in-opposition as fair-weather partners in government.[8]

The second major consequence of El'tsin's policy course resulted specifically from the decision to forgo both fresh elections and replacement of the old apparat. This policy left the old guard in place in two crucial sets of institutions. The first was the soviets. The elections of 1990 did change the composition of some soviets substantially, and in several major cities they even produced progressive majorities. Still, as recounted in chapter 5, the conditions and rules under which elections were held strongly favored the candidacies of guardians of the old order, particularly on the oblast' level. Since their personnel often did not change even after the 1990 elections, soviets' executive committees tended to be even more conservative than full soviet sessions. El'tsin's failure to call new elections in the aftermath of the coup left the old soviets and their executive committees entrenched on all levels. The second set of institutions in which custodians of the previous regime remained ensconced was enterprise administrations. El'tsin's inability or unwillingness to replace enterprise administrations left this crucial stratum of the nomenklatura in charge of most productive units.

By the fall of 1992 the soviets, from the Supreme Soviet of the Russian Federation to legislatures on the district level, and enterprise directors, particularly from the huge monopolistic units that constitute the mainstay of the national economy, had become the most formidable and tenacious sources of resistance to the government's economic reform program, as well as the most influential opponents of rapid democratization. The Supreme Soviet, under its erratic and despotic chairman, Ruslan Khasbulatov, moved on issues such as fiscal policy, privatization, and press freedoms toward more conservative positions.[9] Nearly half of the body's deputies joined Russian Unity, a coalition of Communists and nationalists. Oblast' soviets and particularly their executive committees, by their influence over the implementation of presidential decrees, became weighty institutional hindrances to reform of all types.[10]

Enterprise directors, for their own part, became an assertive force for preserving or resurrecting elements of the command economy. Their most impressive organizational creation, the Union of Industrialists and Producers (the political arm of which was called "Obnovlenie"), was founded in June 1992. The group's members were drawn from the ranks of the old nomenklatura. They presided over more than half of total industrial output, including the lion's share of military-industrial production. At the time of its creation, the group's aims included the resignation as prime minister of the architect of the government's economic reform program, Egor Gaidar; immediate assumption by the state of responsibility for all interenterprise arrears, totaling 1.5 trillion rubles; massive government emission of low-interest credit to heavy industry, without regard for solvency; exemption of entire sectors, including the energy industry, from privatization; and enactment of provisions that would effectively grant directors themselves controlling interest in enterprises that are privatized. By the fall of 1992 the Union had achieved considerable influence. Between June and October its efforts contributed to major shifts in the government's reform program, including partial restoration of financing of military production, appointment of several of its own members to cabinet posts, and selection by parliament of a new Central Bank chief who was sympathetic to the Union's concerns and who actually supported the August 1991 coup attempt. At the end of the year it helped bring down Gaidar and secure his replacement by a veteran manager of the energy industry, Viktor Chernomyrdin.[11]

In sum, the second major consequence of El'tsin's postcoup policy course was that forces of the old order maintained firm footholds in both legislatures and units of production. Large, hard pieces of the ancien regime therefore remained lodged deeply and extensively in the body politic; and these pieces proved adept at putting themselves back together again and resisting radical reform.[12] El'tsin's choices in the early postcoup period—which according to the explanation offered above were at least in part forced upon him by the situation he inherited—quickly returned to haunt him.

El'tsin responded by seeking expanded powers for himself. His policy consisted of ruling by presidential decree; attempting to establish a structure of presidential appointees on all territorial levels to execute his decrees; and seeking a constitutional mandate for measures that would effectively grant him emergency powers and reduce the legislatures to "consultative bodies" until the end of his term in office in 1996.[13]

El'tsin's efforts raised a cruel dilemma for Russia's liberals. On the one hand, the entrenchment and resiliency of reform's antagonists, particularly in the soviets and units of production, seemed to necessitate strong executive rule. And no matter how disappointed some democrats were with El'tsin's performance as president of post-Soviet Russia, most continued to regard him as vastly preferable to his conservative and nationalist critics and to view his presidency as a shield against harsh authoritarian reversion and erosion of hard-won civil rights and freedoms.[14] But overweening executive power raises the specter of dictatorship; and absolute power, even if vested in a popularly elected "democrat," has a way of begetting tyranny.

Independent Political Society after the Coup

Depolarization and Identity Crisis

Like elite politics and state institutions, autonomous political organizations were influenced deeply by August 1991 and its aftermath. The collapse of the Union government and the Communist Party transformed the conditions under which groups' searches for identity and influence took place, broke up existing coalitions, and stimulated the emergence of new organizations and alliances. But post-Soviet society, like the post-Soviet state, bears the imprint of the Gorbachev era and has been characterized by a considerable degree of continuity. The experience of autonomous political associations during the turbulent early postputsch period defies precise generalization; and the groups themselves and alliances among them remain fluid and unstable. Several trends, however, are discernible.

Soon after the coup attempt, Democratic Russia began to unravel. In the fall of 1991 the parties that made up the Popular Accord bloc (the DPR, RKhDD, and KD/PNS) withdrew from Democratic Russia. The subsequent history of Democratic Russia is one of further divisions and a search for a new role. In mid-1992 it split over its relationship to the El'tsin government, with one part of the group in favor of "critical support" and the other urging full opposition.[15] By late 1992 Democratic Russia's days as a broad and formidable coalition of democratic forces clearly had passed.

Most of the organizations that made up Democratic Russia survived but did not flourish. The DPR experienced a modest growth in membership, rising to about fifty thousand by late 1992. Most other parties saw membership numbers stagnate at precoup levels. Within many groups, however, a certain process of maturation took place, with leadership structures becoming somewhat better defined. The SDPR switched from the amorphous collective leadership of the precoup period to a single chairmanship. Most new parties founded after the coup opted from their inceptions for pyramidal leadership structures and clearly defined lines of authority. They include the People's Party of Free Russia, a self-proclaimed "centrist" party chaired by Vasilii Lipitskii and closely associated with Vice President Aleksandr Rutskoi, the Economic Freedom Party, an association of economic liberals and entrepreneurs, and the Socialist Party of Labor, a left-wing social democratic organization.[16] The cause of this development cannot be known with certainty. But it is noteworthy that it occurred in tandem with a general decline in fear of repression, infiltration, and sabotage by the organs of state security. The change is highly consistent with the argument made in previous chapters regarding the relationship between external threat and hyperdemocratic internal organizational structures and procedures. The shift may also be due in part to a waning of the obsession with shunning "Bolshevist" styles of organization now that the Communist Party has lost its hegemonic force.

While some departure from prior organizational patterns is evident in leadership structures, a countervailing tendency, which represents a continuance of a Gorbachev-era trend, may be observed in relations between central (Moscow-based) organizations and provincial chapters. Here, the autonomy of local and regional chapters and disjuncture between them and their Moscow-based leadership, as well as the close cooperation that often characterized relations among various democratic organizations on the local level during the previous period, appear to have become even more pronounced. While considerable variation exists across cities and regions, in many localities activists from the groups that composed Democratic Russia maintained close personal ties and working relationships, even as Democratic Russia as a national organization fragmented.[17] The development corresponds to a broader trend toward the regionalization and localization of power that accelerated after August 1991.[18]

On the national level, the demise of the Communist Party, the fragmentation of Democratic Russia, and the advent of new groups gave rise to fluid and novel coalitions. The Popular Accord bloc began to break up soon after leaving Democratic Russia in the fall of 1991. In June 1992 the DPR, the People's Party of Free Russia, and Obnovlenie joined together to found the Civic Union. In August a motley conglomeration of conservative Communists and "national-patriots" founded a coalition to battle the government. Several (at least formerly) democratic groups, most notably the RKhDD and the KD/PNS, swung toward nationalism and associated themselves loosely with this "left-right" (or "red-brown") alliance. In the meantime, parties such as the SDPR, the RPR, and the People's Party, which did not form alliances with former enemies, turn to virulent nationalism, or abandon liberal principles, founded the coalition "New Russia."[19]

Such coalitions represented temporary marriages of convenience rather than a stable realignment of political forces. The Civic Union, for example, was united by little more than its leaders' common antipathy to Gaidar and desire to muscle their way to the top of a post-

Gaidar government. But the unions of apparently bizarre bedfellows do illuminate several realities about post-Soviet Russian politics. For one, they demonstrate that many of those who led the democratic movement before the coup attempt are scarcely immune from crass opportunism or tightly constrained by liberal principle. As disappointing as it might be to see Nikolai Travkin pull his party into alliance with resurgent forces of the old regime, or other precoup democratic luminaries such as the RKhDD's Viktor Aksiuchits join forces with ultra-nationalists, such behavior is probably inevitable as ambitious political entrepreneurs search for constituencies and jockey for position atop the ruins of the Soviet regime.[20] The persistence of much of the old apparat and the modest presence of Gorbachev-era democratic oppositionists in the postcoup government creates powerful incentives for democratic politicians who seek access to power to compromise with former enemies.[21]

Such developments also reveal the persistence, in fact intensification, of the crisis of identity that was observed among movement organizations during the Gorbachev period. As shown in chapter 4, the struggle to create collective political identities figured prominently in the internal lives of organizations and relations among groups. This struggle lay at the root of groups' ostensibly gross overexpenditure of time and energy on minor questions and helped explain the difficulties that often plagued efforts to achieve union among like-minded organizations. Still, within and among groups, activists were united by the foremost goal of destroying the Communist Party state and regime. "Democratic" identity itself—quite naturally, given the crucible in which it was forged—was defined almost completely in oppositional terms. The overriding cleavage issue in Russian politics was "the system" itself. "Democrats" by definition—and by the time of the coup attempt, most of society as a whole—stood on the "against" side of the divide, for the prosecution. There was no real "center" in Russian politics. Given the intransigence and rigidity of the Communist Party and the Union government and the intentions of the opposition, there could not be. Indeed, during the last several years of the Soviet regime, there was no political spectrum in the sense that this term is normally understood, with its socialists, liberals, nationalists, and so on. As the political vernacular of the time captured, there were only "communists" (those who supported perpetuation of the regime) and "democrats" (those who advocated change of regime, which of course included some members and former members of the Communist Party).

The battle that the protagonists under examination in this book waged was, after all, supremely *political*. It was not based primarily on economic or "class" interests. Unlike the 1917 revolution, the Polish revolution of 1989, or many rebellions leading to regime change in the developing world, it was not made primarily by or in the name of the "working class." Contrary to the mistaken notions found in Western sovietological thinking, it was not a middle-class revolution; there was no bourgeoisie to make it. Nor, in contrast with many recent rebellions in East Europe or other Soviet republics, was it predicated even partially on ethnic or national aspirations. To be sure, all groups included economic proposals and prescriptions in their platforms and plans. Almost all favored "transition to a market economy." But, from the militant strike committees of the Kuzbass to the SDPR's aficionados of scholastic debate, all were well aware that far-reaching economic change was impossible within the constraints that the political regime imposed.

Similarly, all had something to say on "national" questions and on Russia's role in the world. Yet, after the spring 1990 elections created a republican parliament that was more progressive than its Union counterpart, and after the former, under El'tsin's chairmanship, became a stronghold of resistance to Gorbachev and the Union government, most oppositionists realized that the surest way to destroy the Communist Party regime was to undermine the Soviet *Union* itself. Thus, even oppositionists who harbored nationalist sentiments and deep reservations about Russia's loss of empire, who considered "Russia" a far more extensive entity than the RSFSR, were compelled to support "full republican sovereignty" as a means of weakening the regime. In practice, this meant disintegration of the Soviet Union. One could hardly support full sovereignty for the Russian Republic while advocating perpetuation of Union hegemony over other republics. Some oppositionists did adduce well-worn myths concerning other republics' parasitical relationship with Russia. But the democrats' fight for republican autonomy did not stem primarily from economic, ethnic or national concerns. Rather, it arose logically and inexorably from their central political aim. Economic, national, and indeed all other matters were subordinated, in the context of the political struggle, to the single overriding objective of bringing down the Communist Party regime.

Nor could the custodians of the Soviet system—the antagonists of full regime change—possibly address effectively any issue other than the political struggle. They were consumed with trying to save, or "renew," the regime. By the second half of the Gorbachev period, the Union government and the Communist Party simply had no economic policy or plan of any type, as was shown by the unrelenting, almost farcical official exhortations on behalf of "transition to a market economy" coupled with rejection of any formulas for actually initiating such a transition, such as the Iavlinskii and Shatalin plans. To say that officialdom bungled every economic problem that came to it after 1988 would be an understatement. Yet its performance was hardly surprising. Real reform required substantial withdrawal of the state from the economy, which in turn meant radical reduction of the state's control over society. The latter could lead only to further pressures on the regime itself—a consequence that a decaying state system, struggling for its life against growing opposition from an increasingly restive society, could not tolerate. On "national" questions, the position of the regime's guardians, be they xenophobic Russian nationalists or true believers in proletarian internationalism, was and had to be dominated by the imperative of saving the Union—indeed, for the same reasons that oppositionists had to support "full republican sovereignty."

The political situation on the eve of the August coup attempt therefore differed strongly from that of many other countries in the throes of regime change. The nature of the struggle and the character of its protagonists only faintly resembled those found in, say, Chile in 1988. There, the campaign for a "no" vote in the referendum on the Pinochet government gave rise to an alliance of political parties, trade unions, and other organizations united by a common desire to resurrect a form of government under which the country had earlier lived. The effort to oust the dictator dominated groups' activities on the eve of the plebiscite. But most organizations also had their own agendas; they knew who they were and they constituted a real political spectrum; they had known other struggles. In Russia, by contrast, the identities of the actors who composed the opposition had been formed exclusively in the course of a relatively short-lived, unidimensional conflict with the only regime they had ever known. Here was no campaign for redemocratization; here was an effort to create democracy from scratch.

The collapse of the Communist Party and the dissolution of the Soviet Union transformed politics in two closely interrelated ways. First, since the democrats defined "we" in purely oppositional terms, the collapse and disappearance of "them"—or at least "their" breakdown into a number of smaller and less identifiable pieces—robbed the democrats of both their raison d'être and their overriding source of unity, both within and among organizations. The second consequence was the sudden disappearance of the dominant cleavage issue that structured the entire universe of political competition and struggle for as long as there had been open competition: the fate of the Communist Party system of rule. As the collapse of the economy and the break-up of the Soviet Union thrust economic and national problems to the top of the political agenda and the forefront of public consciousness, it is little wonder that the organizations that led the opposition were thrown into crisis. Groups' identities, programs, and operations, in contrast with those of analogous organizations in many other cases of rebellion leading to regime change, had never been based on these matters. All had advocated "transition to a market economy." But this goal had been more of a dream than a demand, and few had actually considered how it achieve it. Now, with both the old regime and the economy in ruins, and even the first steps toward genuine economic transformation still not taken, the path toward "the market" seemed, ironically, far more treacherous and uncertain than it had when it had been foreclosed entirely. And with the Union gone and the new country's borders confined to those of the RSFSR, nationhood and nationality suddenly acquired new and urgent meaning. The aim of "full republican sovereignty," which for reasons of revolutionary expediency had dominated oppositionists' approach to national issues before the putsch, assumed a different and less lustrous appearance once it suddenly was achieved.

How does a moribund command economy move toward capitalism? How must a "democrat"—or for that matter a "conservative"—respond to rapidly declining industrial production and hyperinflation? What is a "democratic" policy position on the disenfranchisement of the Russian-speaking population in Estonia? No one in Russia really addressed such questions before August 1991. It is therefore unsurprising that the search for answers has blurred and even obliterated old identities and engendered alliances, unions, and policy positions that, even by the standards of early "postrevolutionary" politics in other cases, appear curious and even incomprehensible.

The Persistence of the Movement Society

As discussed in previous chapters, all of the autonomous political associations that emerged during the Gorbachev period—alternative parties, strike committees and independent trade unions, informal groups, voters' clubs, and umbrella groups such as Democratic Russia—assumed the form of *movement organizations*. Their principal purpose—and singular, defining, momentous accomplishment—was expression of broad, pandemic demands for the demise of the existing system of rule. These groups established substantial infrastructure for the expression of antiregime aspirations. But they did not create stable and durable bases for interest representation. Neither did they—nor recently emergent groups—do so during the early postcoup period. Indeed, the collapse of the old regime eliminated the dominant source of identity and cohesion within and among organizations, destroyed old coalitions, and gave rise to fluid, unstable, and ostensibly improbable new ones. Over one year after the abortive putsch, the membership and followings of political parties remained extremely limited. Parties had not yet established a framework for ordering the behavior of officials in legislatures nor for organizing and articulating mass opinion.[22]

Labor organizations similarly had failed to create solid foundations for the representation of interests. The year following the coup attempt witnessed the formation of a number of workers' organizations that occasionally won concessions from authorities on wage issues. Such groups, however, were highly localized and regionalized; in no sectors or industries did unions organize successfully on a national basis or realize even the level of integration and influence that coal miners achieved during the second half of the Gorbachev period. The miners themselves, after receiving prodigious wage increases following the August events as reward for their militant opposition in the precoup period, splintered and became politically quiescent, though one may assume that their political muscle remains formidable and potentially reviviscent. Furthermore, whatever the claims of some politicians, particularly those from neo-Communist organizations, workers' groups, such as they were, remained largely estranged from parties and other organized political forces.[23]

In the absence of strong intermediary institutions, the power vacuum that the demise of the Communist Party created is rapidly being occupied by the state bureaucracy, "mafias," and groups such as Obnovlenie. Whatever their pretensions to represent broader societal interests, groups such as Obnovlenie are actually less intermediary institutions than semiofficial bureaucratic alliances, tied so closely to the state as virtually to form a part of it. That Obnovlenie enjoys no mass following but rather comprises officials from the old nomenklatura of course does not rule out the possibility that it may strongly influence government policy. Nor does it necessarily prevent it from forming alliances with more broadly based constituencies, as shown by its alliance with the DPR.

Social movements typically abate appreciably immediately following transition to a new regime. The subsidence of movement activity in Russia and the general, palpable decline of public interest in politics were probably inevitable consequences of the success that the August events brought to opposition forces. But the Russian case differs substantially from many others. In some Latin American and East and South European cases, the crucial moment that induced regime change and a subsequent decline in social movement activity was the "founding election."[24] In most transitions, such elections have produced parliaments with majorities that were clearly committed to some form of democratization. Furthermore, while the division of power between executives and legislatures (in systems where power is so divided) often has remained partially unsettled even after elections, negotiations leading to transition and elections themselves have usually established rules and norms that reduce the magnitude of contested terrain. Russia, however, has held no general elections since the coup; and the Supreme Soviet, not to mention soviets on the oblast' level, have become strongholds of resistance to both democratization and economic transition. Given the conditions under which they were held, the 1990 elections, while more "democratic" than the single-candidate-ballot charades convoked previously, in few respects qualified as genuine "founding elections." The division of power and authority between the executive and the legislatures has remained murky and utterly contested. Little progress toward enactment of a constitution resolving this problem has been made.[25]

Additionally, in many other transitions, the ebb of social movements has left behind a hard institutional residue of organizations capable of channeling some popular demands and furnishing a framework for interest representation in the postauthoritarian period. But, as argued above, the ability of Russia's autonomous societal organizations to perform such functions remains in doubt. Indeed, Russian political society remains a *movement society*—and a far more listless one than was evident during the last two years of the Soviet regime. It still does not fulfill the requirements for status as a civil society outlined in chapter 3. It demonstrated impressive capabilities for bringing pressure to bear on the old regime; but whether it provides the foundations for the consolidation of democracy remains in question. The erosion of governmental authority and the regionalization and localization of official power in post-Soviet Russia, moreover, may actually retard the growth of the institutions of civil society. As discussed in chapter 4, the decay of state power during the second half of the Gorbachev period, while creating some space for the emergence of independent societal power, may paradoxically have slowed the development of autonomous political organizations. A state that lacks effective administrative capacities and the authority to enforce universalization of the law— and the Russian state currently lacks both—may actually inhibit the growth and maturation of civil society.

In sum, if the problem of who will rule has not yet been resolved in Russia, that of who will represent whose interests—who will speak for whom—is even more uncertain. Without strong intermediary organizations capable of representing and "delivering" members and followers, the question will remain unanswered.[26] The new regime will, at best, persist as a democracy by default. Particularly given the enormous popular sacrifices involved in the transition to capitalism, the dearth of institutions capable of channeling popular demands from bottom to top and enforcing collective agreements on memberships will subject society to the danger of frequent, uncoordinated, and perhaps violent mass action. The state will remain highly vulnerable to recurrent crises of governance and legitimacy. The functions of social control intermediary organizations perform in stable democracies will revert by default to the state, creating pressures for authoritarian reversion. The prospects for overcoming the crisis of interest intermediation, and to a large extent the future of democracy, now depend on several requisites that will be discussed in the following section. These factors derive from and parallel the main independent variables that were employed in previous chapters to explain autonomous political organization during the Gorbachev period.

Democracy and Interest Representation in the New Russia

The Requisites of Democratization

The first factor is elections, and in particular when they are held, under what system of rules, and with what degree of regularity. El'tsin's failure to dissolve the soviets elected in 1990 and call new elections in the fall or winter of 1991–92 squandered a fine opportunity to capitalize on the disgrace that the failed putsch inflicted on the forces of the old order. Fresh elections would not have swept all conservatives from the soviets, particularly if they were held under the same rules that obtained in 1990. But they would have changed the political complexion of the legislatures considerably. The old guard had finally shown its stripes and been, at least apparently, defeated; political repression and fear thereof had fallen off dramatically; and El'tsin and the old regime's opponents in general enjoyed great popular esteem. The passage of time and the coup itself, moreover, had alleviated the information problems evident in the 1990 elections and discussed in chapter 5. On all levels, political reputations had been established. The difficulties that progressive voters' associations had earlier experienced in deciding which candidates to endorse would have been less acute in late 1991; the question of "who was who" was clearer than it had been earlier. Fresh elections therefore probably would have loosened the grip that conservatives held on most oblast' and many city soviets. They also would have reduced the numbers and influence of reform's adversaries in the Supreme Soviet. By leaving in place bodies that were elected earlier, El'tsin insured that most legislatures would become obstacles to rather than partners in radical reform. Were the composition of the soviets more liberal, El'tsin could afford to share a significant measure of authority for policymaking—and blame for the enormous hardships involved in economic transition—with them. Instead, to carry out his program he must circumvent the legislatures and attempt to rule by decree and through his personal plenipotentiaries.

Comprehending the causes of El'tsin's nonaction poses a difficult task. Although the legal basis for his right to call elections was unclear, he almost certainly could have gotten away with it in the aftermath of the coup. Simple oversight could have been a cause. The economic crisis, rather than political reform, dictated the new government's agenda in the early months after the coup. But calling new elections for the soviets, unlike attempting large-scale replacement of the apparat, would not have risked economic paralysis or required an army of "democratic" specialists competent in myriad administrative tasks. Nor would it have carried the danger of conservative reaction and sabotage that a wholesale purge of the apparat would have. It could have been done. In fact, it was probably the one reasonably low-cost action on behalf of democratization that the president could have taken in the early post-putsch period.

Fear of the electoral potential of reactionary and demagogic tendencies, such as those represented by Vladimir Zhirinovskii and Viktor Alksnis and their followers, may have also given the new government pause. But if fear of such forces affected the government's policy, it was probably exaggerated. These tendencies enjoyed only modest public following in the preputsch period, and there is little evidence that the August events enhanced their appeal. At any rate, the democrats' stock had never been higher. Nor, given the inevitable hardships to come, could it have been expected ever to be as high again.

The third and most likely possible cause for forgoing a fresh ballot stemmed from an intention to weaken the legislatures in order to establish presidential dominance over the new regime. As discussed in the previous chapter, the conservative cast of most oblast' and city soviets, along with the chaos and deadlock that prevailed in soviets that did include a substantial "democratic" fraction, enhanced neither the public reputations nor the institutional efficacy of the legislatures, though many deputies in the RSFSR Supreme Soviet did for a time play the role of opposition to the Communist Party and the Union government. El'tsin may have believed, not without reason, that ineffective and/or unpopular soviets would be easier to handle than reinvigorated ones. The old soviets, if left in place, would continue to "discredit themselves," thus facilitating the expansion of executive authority. Even if new elections could have been expected to produce more progressive bodies, a weak enemy can be far less bothersome than a strong and independent ally. As many democrats' responses to El'tsin's economic program showed, the president could scarcely be certain that even more progressive legislatures would prove to be pliant and reliable.

El'tsin's decision to forgo new elections was a grave mistake. By mid-1992 the national legislature had become a major hindrance to reform, and among its deputies the government's opponents clearly outweighed its supporters in both numbers and influence.

Whatever El'tsin's reasons for leaving the old soviets in place, the current growth in executive power, however necessary for implementing the initial phases of economic transition, may augur poorly for the growth of political parties and for democratization in general. The emasculation of legislatures and the absence of a fresh plan for elections and electoral reform raise the threat of drift toward *dictablanda*, or "liberal autocracy."[27] Such a form of government might include considerable respect for civic freedoms but not rules and procedures needed to guarantee the primacy of accountable, elected bodies over unelected state agencies. Until elections are scheduled, moreover, power holders, aspirants, and holders of private wealth will have only limited interest in investing substantial time, energy, and money in political parties.[28]

But if elections are to stimulate the emergence of a vigorous multiparty system, they must be held under different rules and conditions than those that obtained in 1990. Even if parties enjoy full legal protection and operate without harassment, the absence of repression may not be enough. If "work collectives" in enterprises and other nonparty groups retain substantial sway over nominations, elections may stay largely "party-free" affairs. One way to animate parties would be a system of proportional representation (PR) that grants parties broad control over authority to nominate candidates for office. Rules providing for PR would furnish political entrepreneurs of every stripe with a fillip to undertake party-building, and both voters and holders of private wealth with incentives to join or associate themselves with party organizations. If electoral rules are to engender programmatic parties and interparty competition rather than personalism and intraparty competition such as prevail in, say, Brazil, parties should enjoy the authority to fix lists of candidates. The intraparty preference vote that affords voters the freedom to rearrange the ordering of candidates on party lists should be avoided.[29] No form of PR—and of course there are many—would ensure a smooth democratic transition. Indeed, the experiences of some Latin American countries suggest that a strong presidency combined with PR elections for legislatures may not always promote governmental efficacy and political stability.[30] But PR might help generate cohesive programmatic parties—a crucial institutional link between state and society—and perhaps even create some organizational basis for overcoming the chaos and hyperindividualism that have enervated soviets on all levels.

Whatever the advisability of particular electoral arrangements, the challenge of promoting accountability through elections and electoral reform deserves far more attention than Russia's leaders and Western analysts gave it during the first year of the postcoup period. Expressing frustration with the conservative intransigence of many local and provincial officials, El'tsin stated in September 1992: "If regional authorities prefer to live on an island of 'developed socialism,' planning prices and rationing food, it is up to them to do so. But they are ultimately responsible for the results of these policies before their voters."[31] But in the absence of arrangements ensuring elected officials' control over unelected agencies, it is difficult to see how the threat of popular wrath can enforce accountability—or, for that matter, control corruption—among power holders. The longer elections and electoral reform are deferred, moreover, the greater will be the temptation—indeed, the necessity—for El'tsin to concentrate power in the executive and at the center and efface the legislatures altogether. The longer a vote is put off, the less confident progressive forces can be in achieving friendly majorities once elections are convened, particularly given the adversity that reform has already begun to impose on broad segments of the population.

The second determinant of democratization in Russia concerns the agencies of state security. As demonstrated in chapters 4 and 5, official repression and control exerted strong and manifold effects on independent political life during the Gorbachev period. The agency at the center of the state's efforts to weaken the opposition was the KGB. Many democrats therefore have regarded destroying this agency or redefining and severely curtailing its operations as a crucial requisite of democratization.[32]

The KGB on Russian territory was renamed (it became the Ministry of Security of the Russian Federation) and partially reorganized after August 1991. But it was not dismantled, subjected to sweeping personnel reductions, stripped of its technological capabilities, or fully subordinated to civilian authority. After a brief interregnum under the directorship of Vadim Bakatin, who expressed a desire radically to reduce the size of the agency and the scope of its operations, leadership in post-Soviet Russia returned to long-time veterans of the security establishment who have resisted thoroughgoing reform. Despite some progressive deputies' efforts, the Ministry of Security remains virtually free from parliamentary oversight. At the urging of leaders of the security apparat, Supreme Soviet Chairman Khasbulatov even thwarted efforts to investigate and publicize the identities of security agency employees working in parliament. Perhaps most ominously, there exists evidence that infiltration and monitoring of independent political organizations continues. The KGB directorate responsible for political repression was initially abolished but was subsequently reborn in the form of a new department of the Ministry of Security. Its representatives have made clear their intention to maintain formidable networks of informers.[33]

Faced with the option of attempting to eradicate the secret police or leaving it largely intact and bringing it under his own authority, El'tsin chose the latter. Given the abundance of his enemies and the treacherousness of present-day Russian politics, his decision may not be surprising. Yet even if he does both exercise strict control and hold a firm commitment to eliminating the political functions of the security organs—neither of which is certain—there exist no safeguards against his successor redeploying these agencies for other purposes. Political persecution of all types has declined steeply since the collapse of the Communist Party and the Soviet Union. But the institutional endurance of an immense and only partially reconstructed internal state security apparat continues to threaten the advancement to a free society and the consolidation of democracy.

The third major influence on democracy and interest representation is privatization and the transformation of property rights and relations. Privatization has received a great deal of notice and has been the source of much controversy. Most debate, however, has focused on the economic rather than the political consequences of changes in property ownership.

Privatization promises to affect political life in three interrelated ways. First, via its influence on socioeconomic structure, it will transform the interest basis of politics. The crucial question from a political standpoint is whether privatization will be—or can be—carried out in a manner that eventually gives rise to a sizable middle class of small property holders. The large-scale scheme that the State Privatization Committee drew up in the summer and fall of 1992 contains a number of progressive provisions, including a voucher system designed to "popularize" property ownership.[34] The plan is based on liberal principles and demonstrates the government's interest in departing from "nomenklatura privatization." The ability of the voucher system to disperse wealth widely, however, remains in doubt. Given the legacy of the Soviet system, moreover, no privatization scheme or other economic reform can be expected immediately to foster the emergence of a genuine middle class in Russia. Such profound social-structural change can occur only gradually, even under the most propitious set of governmental policies and programs.[35]

Even relatively moderate plans such as the voucher program quickly collided with powerful interests that stand to lose from the deconcentration of wealth. Enterprise directors and managers, for example, advanced alternative plans that would convert their de facto control over enterprise assets into formal ownership. By establishing closed corporations and distributing stock in advance of the introduction of the voucher system, setting up interlocking directorates among newly formed corporations to restrict capital movement and by-pass antimonopoly provisions, and lobbying successfully for exempting from privatization those sectors whose productive units are too large to be owned and managed by a small circle of directors, industrialists scored major victories in 1992. Due in part to the enormous dislocations induced by demilitarization, the explosion of interenterprise arrears, and the breakdown of old networks of material supply and credit provision, arguments that privatization must be weighted heavily in favor of those who "know how to make things work" found growing acceptance among many government officials in 1992.[36]

The actors in the struggle over privatization are of course not unitary. Considerable differences of interest may exist within as well as between social and occupational groups. Among enterprise directors, interests may vary depending on their firms' profitability and their personal relations with employees and local state officials. Nor can "labor," white-collar employees, or new entrepreneurs yet be safely regarded as holders of discrete and identifiable group interests. Mass privatization is still in its early stages, and the outcome of the battle over who gets what is scarcely clear at the present time. Much privatization is occurring "spontaneously" and under inscrutable and legally dubious circumstances. Privatization's precise effects on social structure will not be evident for at least a decade.

If privatization does engender some basis for popular capitalism in Russia, it may foster political parties, trade unions, and interest associations based on class, profession, and sector. If, on the other hand, it concentrates the lion's share of wealth in a thin stratum of state officials and enterprise directors, it may beget patterns of interest representation based on communal, patron-client, familial, and personalist relations. The changes in social structure that privatization will induce will not determine fully the character of intermediary institutions, but they will powerfully reshape the interest bases of politics.

The second way in which privatization will influence politics is closely related to the first and regards the resource-mobilization potentials of intermediary organizations. Most autonomous associations struggled in poverty during the Gorbachev period. Few enjoyed highly gainful ties with independent sources of wealth. Privatization has already begun to carve out space for the growth of loci of independent economic power—potential founts of financial support for intermediary organizations. Privatization's effect on organizations' resource-mobilization potentials, like its influence on socioeconomic structure, depends on how it distributes resources among social groups. The strongest and best-endowed political organizations that formed in the early post-Soviet period were those that claimed to speak for Russia's emerging business class, such as Obnovlenie and the Economic Freedom Party. Precisely how broad a stratum such groups will represent, and whether or not powerful parties, unions, and interest groups representing other strata emerge, rest to some degree on how rapidly and equitably privatization is carried out.

In addition to its effects on social stratification and resource mobilization, privatization may alter fundamentally the relationship between state and citizen in Russia. As discussed in chapter 5, the dependence of the overwhelming majority on the state for both employment and access to scarce goods supplied through the workplace checked the growth of organized political opposition during the Gorbachev period. As long as the majority remains directly dependent on the state for the means of subsistence, as it still does today, the separation of *grazhdanin* from *rabotnik*—of citizen from employee—will be incomplete. A crucial link in what Ferenc Fehér, Agnes Heller, and György Markus called the "dictatorship over needs" will endure. The organizational rights and political freedoms of most individuals will remain tenuous and subject to fluctuations in the political climate. Thus, in order for privatization to liberate society from dependence on the state, it must be carried through on a very large scale—above all in the huge production units that constitute the mainstay of the national economy and employ a large proportion of the country's work force.[37]

In conclusion, the extent of change during the first year of the post-Soviet period in the variables that shaped and restricted the formation of autonomous political organizations during the Gorbachev years has been limited, though certainly not insignificant. The absence of new elections means that the birth defect that previous elections left in the party system has remained untreated, with serious consequences for the government's reform program as well as party formation and democratization in general. State interference in autonomous political life has declined dramatically. Still, the lack of progress toward radical reform of the organs of state security leaves the sword of arbitrary state power dangling over the new polity. Mass privatization promises to begin dissolving the cement that fused state and economy for seven decades. But whether it will disperse property widely and give rise to a sizable class of independent property holders, merely convert old patterns of control into formal ownership, or produce some other outcome remains in question.

Where Is Russia's Transition Leading?

Precise understanding of the current transition, not to speak of prediction of its eventual outcome, is of course impossible at such an early stage. Brief consideration of several alternative outcomes, ranging from "best" to "worst" cases, however, may provide a framework for thinking about Russia's political future.

The first possible outcome would be full, "consolidated" democracy.[38] It could assume a variety of forms but would require some stable and legally defined division of competence between the executive and the legislature on the national level. On lower levels, it might include establishment of directly elected executive offices, with *gubernatory* for oblasts and *mepy* for cities. The soviets might be preserved in the oblasts but replaced by city councils and other smaller bodies at the city and lower levels. During the Gorbachev period, many oppositionists considered such arrangements, which are based largely on the American model, highly desirable and even inevitable components of democratization. In mid-1991 some cities and oblasts drew up plans for the creation of governorships and mayoralties and direct elections for these offices. After the coup attempt, El'tsin postponed such elections indefinitely and sent his own appointees to fill executive positions in the oblasts and cities.

Democracy would not require adoption of such a model. Both executive and legislative functions could be invested in the soviets, without creating executive offices. The abolition or reconstitution of executive committees in soviets in either case would be desirable. Periodic, open, competitive elections for legislative and executive offices on all levels would in any event be necessary. The size and scope of operations of the organs of state security would have to be curtailed. Provisions for civilian control, including close presidential supervision, some legislative oversight, and independent media scrutiny, would have to be established.

Interests might be intermediated through a variety of means and could be weighted toward "electoralist" or "societal corporatist"

arrangements.[39] In any case, the consolidation of democracy would necessitate political parties capable of structuring the vote during elections and ordering behavior in legislatures after elections. It would
also require trade unions and employers', professional, and other associations that enjoy some capacity to engage in and enforce the terms
of collective bargaining. Some Russian and Western analysts have
spoken of the possibility that Russia may achieve democracy without
the political parties, unions, and interest associations normally found
in democracies in the West and/or the developing world. But the experiences of many countries counsel skepticism on this question. If the
Russian polity is capable of generating uniquely Russian forms and
institutions of interest representation, it has not yet demonstrated this
capability.

Full democracy would probably include a significant measure of
self-government for ethnic minorities. Given the overwhelming preponderance of ethnic Russians within the Russian Federation, the
smallness and linguistic Russification of many of the non-Russian peoples, and the peripheral geographical location of most non-Russian-
majority areas, arrangements probably need not be as sophisticated
and finely calibrated as those in democracies that feature large measures of "consociationalism" such as Switzerland, Belgium, or even
Spain or pre-1970s Lebanon. In Russia, some rather rough mechanisms
that provide for a reasonable degree of federalism without threatening
the integrity of the Russian state might suffice.

The chances that consolidated democracy lies in Russia's near future
are remote. Democratization does not occupy a place of prominence
on power holders' agendas; the economic crisis dominates both high
politics and broader public attention; the democratic movement, such
as it was, has broken apart and some of its constituent parts have abandoned democratic goals and moved into alliances with reorganized
remnants of the old regime; and the mobilization potentials of autonomous political organizations that do seek full democracy have, if anything, declined since the coup attempt. The organizations of independent society are by no means strong and effective enough to secure the
consolidation of democracy.

The second, and more likely possible future is democracy by default,
or perpetual "unconsolidated" democracy. It would include some elements of democracy, such as elections and considerable civil and cultural freedoms, but not durable and stable rules and institutions that
enjoy wide popular and official recognition and acceptance. On the national level, the division of functions and authority between the executive and the legislature might remain highly contested. Alternatively,
the government might become a type of plebiscitary democracy, with

most power invested in the chief executive and his or her agencies, and popular control over the state limited mainly to occasional mass participation in presidential elections. The organs of state security might retain some independence. But they would to a considerable degree fall under civilian control and refrain from extensive interference in political and social life. The legislature would enact laws and the president decree them; but laws would retain a relative and contested character, with substantial variation evident in implementation and observation across regions.

Interest intermediation might be carried out through an amalgam of mechanisms and institutions, with independent unions capable of collective bargaining operating in some sectors and more "traditional" (i.e., clientelist, personalist, and familial) relations predominating in others; and genuine political parties or at least organizations that resemble parties operating in some regions but not others. Such institutions might be supplemented by the occasional rise and fall of ad hoc social movement organizations formed to express a particular social demand or set of demands. Unlike full democracy, democracy by default could be maintained even in the absence of a well-developed civil society. But it would require that society be adequately strong and capable of self-organization to protect itself by a variety of means against state power, and that no one organized force or coalition of forces acquire both the strength and the will to assume full control of the state and impose dictatorship.

In many respects, present-day Russia falls into this category of regime types. Whether it will stay there or slide toward some form of "soft" or "moderate" authoritarianism, the third possible form of government, is an open question. Such a system would place more restrictions on associational and expressive freedoms than would an unconsolidated democracy. But it would not involve a full reversion to total state control over communicative, associational, intellectual and cultural life such as prevailed until the last few years of the Soviet period. Authoritarianism in Russia would probably entail overweening executive power, feeble, largely decorative legislatures, and a substantial political role for the agencies of coercion. Unlike in full democracy, interest intermediation would not be ordered by stable representative institutions created largely by society itself; nor, unlike in unconsolidated democracy, would it be left mainly to chance and fulfilled by diverse, fluid, and often ad hoc arrangements. Rather, it would be managed in large part by official and semiofficial organizations created and dominated by state agencies. As in all "state corporatist" systems, interest intermediation would include some means for channeling demands from the bottom to the top, but the dominant current would run the other way. A combination of economic decline and chaos, persistent weakness of large-scale societal organizations, and the outbreak of spontaneous, uncoordinated strikes in vital sectors might create pressures for movement toward this type of system.

Capture of the state by the captains of industry would almost certainly place the country on the road to some form of authoritarianism. The interests of enterprise directors, at least of those who oversee the military-industrial complex and loss-making industries that dominate production, would be best served by preservation of some elements of the command economy. These include some measure of economic isolationism, a reversal of economic demilitarization, selective preservation of producers' monopolies, state provision of massive subsidies and low-interest credit, and so on. Under present circumstances, such policies would lead inexorably to hyperinflation; which in turn could be combated only by strong repression of wage demands and imposition of price controls; which would spark strikes and raise the danger of mass unrest; which, finally, would generate strong pressures for movement toward some type of state-led corporatism. To many enterprise administrators and state officials, most of whose careers have revolved around the twin goals of fulfilling state orders and enforcing labor quiescence, such arrangements, whatever specific forms they took, would have a comfortable feeling of familiarity.

Many in Russia now speak admiringly of a modernizing, "progressive" form of authoritarianism. But a post-Communist authoritarian system in Russia might differ substantially from some of the bureaucratic-authoritarian regimes of Latin America and East Asia. In most cases of bureaucratic authoritarianism, armies have been the makers or at least the ultimate guarantors of the regime. The corporate identity and mission of the Russian/Soviet Army, however, have normally been defined in terms of national security and external threat (or opportunity), not control over the state and/or repression of popular demands. Enforcement of the regime, and to some extent control over the state, has fallen to the organs of state security. In a future authoritarian regime, these agencies would very likely assume a prominent part. The army would probably play only a tacit supporting role. Furthermore, the ethos and structure of a future authoritarian regime in Russia might be more feudal, parasitic, corrupt, and extractive than national, modernizing, and developmental. Whatever their professed admiration for a South Korean, Taiwanese, or Chilean model, few industrialists or political leaders who advocate postponing democratization have articulated a plan for economic development that reaches beyond enriching themselves with public funds, propping up inefficient industries with massive state subsidies, and printing money with abandon.[40] This state of affairs, combined with problems such as the country's primitive banking system and shortage of highly qualified technocratic specialists, reduces the possibility for Russia quickly to establish an "effective," modern bureaucratic-authoritarian regime.

The fourth and final possible outcome would be reversion to totalitarian or extremely harsh authoritarian dictatorship. Such a regime could assume the form of revived communism or fascism/national socialism. It would entail full or nearly full re-étatization of associational, cultural, and intellectual life, closing of borders, and abolition of even limited political pluralism.

Only the most inauspicious and unlikely combination of events could force such a reversion. Full economic collapse combined with the outbreak of civil war would create pressures for regression to such a form of government. Still, however dire the economic crisis at the present time, Russia has survived worse. Furthermore, the overwhelming preponderance of ethnic Russians, while scarcely precluding the outbreak of interethnic conflict on the territory of the Russian Federation, reduces the chances of a civil conflagration of the type seen in Yugoslavia, Georgia, Moldova, or Tadzhikistan. In the absence of economic and civil catastrophes, it is difficult to see how a full reversion to the old system or a new type of totalitarianism or harsh authoritarianism could succeed. Even conservatives who feel great nostalgia for the pre-Gorbachev Soviet regime would very likely balk at erasure of the civic, cultural, and travel freedoms achieved during the past several years.

In sum, both democratic consolidation and full reversion are highly unlikely. Either democracy by default or moderate authoritarianism is the most likely outcome over the next half-decade. During the early phase of the postcoup period, Russia has been closer to the former than the latter. But the absence of fresh elections in the immediate postcoup period, the limited extent of change in the agencies of state security, and the dubious, opaque, and largely inequitable way in which changes in property rights and ownership have been carried out thus far produce some grounds for pessimism. The impressive political consolidation and reemergence of parts of the old nomenklatura, the enduring economic crisis, the breakup and subsidence of the democratic movement, and the general weakness and exhaustion of society add to the danger of backward drift.

While the future cannot be known with certainty, the critical nature of the current juncture is clear. The courses of reform in the electoral system, the agencies of state security, and property relations that Russia's leaders choose in the near future will influence profoundly the formation and development of intermediary societal organizations. The magnitude, diversity, and effectiveness of these organizations will, in turn, powerfully affect whether the new polity can bridge the vast gap that has long separated power holders from society in Russia and realize some form of democracy even while enduring the trial of economic transition. The progress of intermediary institutions will not only shape the process of democratization, but perhaps even affect the prospects for preserving the territorial integrity of the country itself. Strong parties, trade unions, and interest associations organized on a national basis could help counteract the centrifugal forces that the vastness and territorial diversity of the country, the erosion of central power, and the rapid growth of localist and regionalist pressures have created. Whatever specific forms intermediary institutions take, the state alone will not be able to structure interest representation and guide the country through the onerous and uncertain transition to capitalism—at least not without reverting to some form of authoritarianism and deferring the question of democracy indefinitely.

Epilogue _____

SINCE the final chapter of this book was written in late 1992, the new Russian polity has experienced a year of turbulence and tumult. The term "crisis," normally used to describe a temporary period of disruption between equilibria, appears to have established itself as a permanent feature of Russian political life.

The events between the time of Gaidar's ouster in late 1992 and the December 1993 parliamentary elections and constitutional referendum largely represented a denouement of the currents and conflicts that shaped the first twelve to fifteen months of the postcoup period. El'tsin attempted to preserve and expand his decree powers but was stymied by increasingly obstinate and conservative legislatures, and especially the Supreme Soviet. The referendum of April 1993, which handed El'tsin and his program a spectacular public endorsement, raised hopes that the increasingly rancorous conflict between the government and the parliament could be resolved in a manner that was both peaceful and propitious for radical reform. The parliament's staying power and contempt for the results of the referendum, deepening fissures within the government itself over the pace of economic reform, El'tsin's indecision and inability to convert the moral victory of the referendum into political capital, and the bloody confrontation of late September–early October 1993 revealed such hopes to be unfounded. Relations between the president and prodemocratic organizations, moreover, continued to deteriorate, though most progressives supported El'tsin in the referendum and continued to prefer him to his increasingly vocal and bellicose enemies.

As of the beginning of 1994, ample grounds exist for pessimism regarding Russia's political future. Although the violent confrontation between El'tsin and his Communist and nationalist opponents ended (given the alternative) in a manner propitious for the continuation of reform, the conflict itself raised serious questions regarding the viability of Russia's transition. The government ultimately commanded the force necessary to put down its opponents. But its initial confusion and helplessness in the face of marauding bands and its eleventh-hour response called into question its capacity for self-defense and the extent of its control over the agencies of coercion. Furthermore, the ferocity of the confrontation—the opposition's resort to massive violence, and El'tsin's equally violent, if belated, response—highlighted the tenuousness of Russia's transition and established a grim precedent for the resolution of future political conflicts.

The uprising in Moscow also demonstrated the radicalization and growing boldness of forces that explicitly reject democracy. And the strong showing of nationalist and Communist candidates in the December 1993 parliamentary elections revealed that the defeat of liberalism's antagonists in the streets of Moscow in early October by no means extinguished them as political forces.

Indeed, the events of 1993 provide further evidence of the extraordinary tortuousness of the path that lies between Soviet-style socialism and democracy. And yet the very conspicuousness of the conditions and trends that point toward the failure of democracy now urge the analyst to adopt a strategy of "possiblism," to undertake a search for circumstances that might push the transition forward and favor its success.[1] Such propitious conditions are less obvious than are unfavorable ones. Yet from the standpoint of democratization, the events of the past year do not compose a uniformly bleak picture. They reveal not only the enduring potency of the legacy of the Soviet period, but also the rapidity with which change propitious for democratic transition may occur once the old regime is—at least partially—swept away.

Russia has, at long last, held elections. The elections were grossly belated; El'tsin's failure to call them immediately after the April referendum, in which an overwhelming majority called for a fresh ballot for parliament, represented an extension of his blunder in not convoking them in the aftermath of the August 1991 putsch. The extreme tardiness of the elections, along with the chaotic way in which they were organized, contributed powerfully to the likelihood of a strong showing by antiliberal forces. Still, the elections themselves, however disappointing their outcome in the eyes of progressives, have had a number of beneficial effects. Above all, they stimulated party formation. As early as the spring of 1993, the promise of an early vote, and the possibility that at least some seats would be filled according to party lists (in the end, half of all mandates for the lower of the two houses were apportioned in such a manner), prompted many celebrated progressives who earlier had shown no interest in working outside government to undertake party-building. The decisions of leaders such as Egor Gaidar, Sergei Shakhrai, and Grigorii Iavlinskii to launch and lead new parties indicated that the free-lance political entrepreneurship so evident in the Gorbachev and immediate post-Soviet periods had lost its luster and viability.[2] The mediocre showing of the new progressive parties in the recent elections does not cancel the advantages of their entrance onto the political scene. Furthermore, the fact that only one of the parties that participated in the democratic movement during the Gorbachev period—the DPR—gained the support necessary to field a list of candidates in the recent elections in no way diminishes the past accomplishments of the other parties that earlier spearheaded the democratic movement. As argued in this study, such groups were not, at any rate, genuine political parties, but rather movement organizations. Their main purpose and single, defining achievement was the expression of antiregime demands and the mobilization of public support for those demands. Whether and how the new parliamentary parties—democratic, neo-Communist, and nationalist—will now structure political competition in the new legislature remains to be seen. But their presence there does raise the possibility that the new parliament will be less amorphous, chaotic, and unaccountable than its predecessor. Whether it will prove to be substantially more "progressive" is, of course, another question.

Russia entered 1994 with a new constitution as well as a new legislature. The content of the constitution, like the composition of the new parliament, has raised a host of concerns within and outside Russia. The document concentrates formidable powers in the presidency and contains some ambiguities regarding relations between the center and provincial authorities. The constitution cannot be expected, in any event, to resolve all issues of federalism, decentralization, and statehood. Such problems will be worked out only over years of conflict, bargaining, negotiation, and institution-building. But the document does furnish Russia with a far clearer, more coherent, and more democratic fundamental law than it enjoyed in the past.

A vigorous free media has established itself as a conspicuous and powerful element of Russian political life. The media has helped to overcome some of the informational and organizational problems posed by the weakness of formal intermediary institutions. The media in Russia is now diverse, and much of it is fully autonomous. To be sure, most of the electronic media tilts toward the liberals, but the extent of El'tsin's control has been exaggerated. Like their counterparts everywhere, Russian journalists tend to be less well-disposed toward those politicians who would establish rigorous control over their operations than toward those who would grant them a longer leash. It is therefore unsurprising that the media in Russia appears to conservatives to display a "liberal bias." As in the West, such a bias is more apparent than real, and to the extent that it exists it reflects more an antiauthoritarian proclivity than a particular ideological bent. Russia's current leading newspapers, such as Segodnia, Nezavisimaia Gazeta, Kommersant, and Moskovskii Komsomolets, exhibit little affection for conservatives and nationalists. But they also show the El'tsin government no mercy, and they scrupulously guard their independence.

Recent economic changes might also enhance democracy's prospects. The agonies of Russia's economic transition are obvious. Severe capital shortage and flight, high inflation, huge governmental budget deficits, and incompetence and corruption in agencies responsible for economic reform evidence the depth of crisis. Yet such phenomena tell only part of the story. In some respects, Russia made meaningful strides toward a market economy in 1993. Privatization quickened considerably. By the middle of the year, over half of all trade outlets and restaurants had fallen into private hands. As in other postsocialist countries, the privatization of large-scale enterprises has proceeded more slowly. But even here there has been significant progress. By August, one-fifth of Russia's industrial workers were employed by privatized firms.[3] Indeed, the rate of privatization in Russia has kept pace with—in some cases, outstripped—that of many East European countries.

Privatization has acquired a momentum of its own; its opponents have largely lost the power to reverse it. During the summer of 1993 the Supreme Soviet waged a major offensive against the government's program, adopting measures designed to undermine the value of privatization vouchers and drastically retard the de-étatization of enterprises. But the actions were ineffectual. The voucher's value suffered only a minor and temporary setback; and in most regions, the scale and frequency of privatization auctions were scarcely affected.[4]

It is difficult to determine in the abstract the threshold at which privatization becomes irreversible. But if the process has not yet reached such a stage in Russia, it is almost certainly on the verge of reaching it. Even a future government that did not share the current one's commitment to economic de-étatization would almost certainly have to make peace with a sizable nonstate sector.

The way in which privatization is distributing wealth across the population is still exceedingly difficult to ascertain. It is clear that those who held power and enjoyed control over use of resources to begin with have continued to benefit disproportionately. Yet it is equally obvious that the ranks of privatization's beneficiaries are no longer restricted to members of the old nomenklatura. Privatization and liberalization in general have also released a torrent of entrepreneurial energy among less advantaged segments of the population, especially the young. The privatization of dwellings, which has proceeded on a large scale in many cities, holds the potential to expand the scope of small-scale property ownership.[5] Finally, the pluralization of property relations has also created a spate of new resource mobilization opportunities for political parties, unions, and other nonstate associations. Such intermediary organizations are in many respects still weak. But those that have survived from the Gorbachev period or that formed after the August 1991 putsch are now far better endowed than the organizations of the preputsch period. As of early 1994, the days when political groups were forced to rely for material support on collections taken at public demonstrations seem long past. Many parties and other organizations now enjoy profitable connections with well-endowed private sponsors.[6]

Economic reform does not, of course, insure the success of political transition. Even if privatization does unglue polity and economy, create sources of independent economic power in society, promote interest group formation, and stimulate the rise of a substantial middle class, stable democracy will not follow inexorably. These economic transformations are not sufficient conditions for the consolidation of democracy. But they are necessary conditions; and the outlines of these requisites are now discernible.

Notes

Chapter I
Western Scholarship and the New Russian Revolution

1. Carl J. Friedrich and Zbigniew K. Brzezinski, *Totalitarian Dictatorship and Autocracy*; Zbigniew K. Brzezinski, *Ideology and Power in Soviet Politics*.

2. Hannah Arendt, *The Origins of Totalitarianism*.

3. Barrington Moore Jr., *Terror and Progress in the USSR*.

4. Kenneth Jowitt, *The Leninist Response to National Dependency*; Kenneth Jowitt, "Inclusion and Mobilization in European Leninist Regimes," *World Politics* 28, 1 (October 1975): 69–96; Kenneth Jowitt, "Soviet Neo-Traditionalism: The Political Corruption of a Leninist Regime," *Soviet Studies* 35, 3 (1983): 275–97.

5. James Scanlan, "Reforms and Civil Society in the USSR," *Problems of Communism* (March–April 1988): 41–46.

6. Andranik M. Migranian, "Dolgii put' k evropeiskomu domu," *Novyi mir*, no. 7 (July 1989): 166–84.

7. Mihaly Vajda, "East-Central European Perspectives," in John Keane, ed., *Civil Society and the State*, p. 348; see also Mihaly Vajda, *The State and Socialism*, pp. 95, 115–19.

8. "Z" (Martin Malia), "To the Stalin Mausoleum," *Daedalus* 119, 1 (Winter 1990): 295–344, esp. 328–29.

9. See Alexander Dallin, "Bias and Blunders in American Studies on the USSR," *Slavic Review* 32, 3 (September 1973): 560–76.

10. Susan Solomon, ed., *Pluralism in the Soviet Union*; Jerry Hough, "The Soviet System: Petrification or Pluralism?," *Problems of Communism* (March–April 1972): 25–45; H. Gordon Skilling and Franklin Griffiths, eds., *Interest Groups in Soviet Politics*.

11. Stephen F. Cohen, *Bukharin and the Russian Revolution*; Stephen F. Cohen, "The Friends and Foes of Change: Reformism and Conservatism in the Soviet Union," in Stephen F. Cohen, Alexander Rabinowitch, and Robert Sharlet, eds., *The Soviet Union since Stalin*, pp. 11–31.

12. Andrew Janos, "Interest Groups and the Structure of Power: Critique and Comparisons," *Studies in Comparative Communism* 12, 1 (Spring 1979): 6–20; William Odom, "A Dissenting View on the Group Approach to Soviet Politics," *World Politics* 28, 4 (July 1976): 542–67.

13. Ronald J. Hill and Peter Frank, *The Soviet Communist Party*, pp. 14, 139–40.

14. Peter Vanneman, *The Supreme Soviet: Politics and the Legislative Process in the Soviet Political System*, pp. 3, 25–26.

15. Stephen White, *Political Culture and Soviet Politics*, p. 87.

16. George W. Breslauer, "Evaluating Gorbachev as Leader," *Soviet Economy* 5, 4 (1989): 321–22; Stephen White, *Gorbachev in Power*, pp. 38–40, 51–52; Se-

weryn Bialer, "The Changing Soviet Political System: The Nineteenth Party Conference and After," in Seweryn Bialer, ed., *Politics, Society, and Nationality: Inside Gorbachev's Russia*, p. 194.

17. Stephen White, "'Democratization' in the USSR," *Soviet Studies* 42, 1 (1990): 16.

18. Dusko Doder and Louise Branson, *Gorbachev*, pp. 401–2; Ronald Hill, "Profile: The Twenty-Eighth CPSU Congress," *The Journal of Communist Studies* 7, 1 (1991): 97.

19. Jerry Hough, *Russia and the West: Gorbachev and the Politics of Reform*, pp. 178–79; Stephen F. Cohen, "Gorbachev the Great," *The New York Times*, March 11, 1991.

20. Breslauer, "Evaluating Gorbachev as Leader," pp. 317–27; Seweryn Bialer, "Gorbachev's Move," in Ferenc Fehér and Andrew Arato, eds., *Gorbachev: The Debate*, pp. 38–60.

21. George W. Breslauer, "On the Adaptability of Soviet Welfare State Authoritarianism," in Karl W. Ryavec, ed., *Soviet Society and the Communist Party*, pp. 3–25; Victor Zaslavsky, *The Neo-Stalinist State: Class, Ethnicity, and Consensus in Soviet Society*.

22. Alex Inkeles, *Social Change in Soviet Russia*; David Lane and Felicity Ann O'Dell, *The Soviet Industrial Worker: Social Class, Education and Control*; Gail W. Lapidus, *Women in Soviet Society: Equality, Development, and Social Change*.

23. Victor Zaslavsky and Robert J. Brym, "Structures of Power and the Functions of Soviet Local Elections," in Everett M. Jacobs, ed., *Soviet Local Politics and Government*, pp. 69–77.

24. Zaslavsky, *The Neo-Stalinist State*, pp. ix–x, 130–64.

25. Peter Hauslohner, "Gorbachev's Social Contract," *Soviet Economy* 3, 1 (1987): 54–89 (cited passages appear on pp. 55–56, 58).

26. S. Frederick Starr, "Soviet Union: A Civil Society," *Foreign Policy*, no. 70 (Spring 1988): 26–41; Gail W. Lapidus, "State and Society: Toward the Emergence of Civil Society in the Soviet Union," in Bialer, ed., *Politics, Society, and Nationality*, pp. 121–45; Moshe Lewin, *The Gorbachev Phenomenon*, pp. 46–50, 54–57.

27. S. Frederick Starr, "Foreword," in Vera Tolz, *The USSR's Emerging Multiparty System*, p. viii.

28. Emile Durkheim, *The Division of Labor in Society*, pp. 39–46, 70–173, 275–82, 353–61; Andrew C. Janos, *Politics and Paradigms: Changing Theories of Change in Social Science*, pp. 23–24.

29. Blair A. Ruble, "The Social Dimensions of Perestroyka," *Soviet Economy* 3, 2 (1987): 171–83.

30. See Antony Black, *Guilds and Civil Society in European Political Thought from the Twelfth Century to the Present*, pp. ix–xi, 32–43, 153–57.

31. A related point is found in Durkheim, *The Division of Labor in Society*, pp. 258–62.

32. Neil J. Smelser, *Social Change in the Industrial Revolution*, pp. 1–6, 225–341. Smelser's argument is summarized in Janos, *Politics and Paradigms*, p. 46.

33. Ferenc Fehér, Agnes Heller, and György Markus, *Dictatorship over Needs*.

34. Ibid., pp. 54–69, 112–24; György Konrad and Ivan Szelenyi, *The Intellectuals on the Road to Class Power*.

35. Fehér, Heller, and Markus, *Dictatorship over Needs*, pp. 159–65. See also Zygmunt Bauman, "On the Maturation of Socialism," *Telos*, no. 47 (Spring 1981): 48–54; Jan Pakulski, "Legitimacy and Mass Compliance: Reflections on Max Weber in Soviet-Type Systems," *British Journal of Political Science* 16, 1 (January 1986): 35–56.

36. Fehér, Heller, and Markus, *Dictatorship over Needs*, p. 196; Jacques Rupnik, "Totalitarianism Revisited," in Keane, ed., *Civil Society and the State*, pp. 268–71; Leszek Kolakowski, "Ideology in Eastern Europe," in Milorad M. Drachkovitch, ed., *East-Central Europe: Yesterday, Today, and Tomorrow*, pp. 46–48.

37. Kolakowski, "Ideology in Eastern Europe," p. 46.

38. Vaclav Havel, "The Power of the Powerless," in Vaclav Havel et al., *The Power of the Powerless: Citizens against the State in Central-Eastern Europe*, ed. John Keane, pp. 28–31.

39. Fehér, Heller, and Markus, *Dictatorship over Needs*, pp. 245–61.

40. Ibid., pp. 132–43.

41. Ibid., pp. 180–82; Jeno Szucs, "Three Historical Regions of Europe," in Keane, ed., *Civil Society and the State*, pp. 291–332, esp. pp. 321–22.

42. György Konrad, *Anti-Politics*.

43. Zagorka Golubovic, "Why 'Dictatorship over Needs' Is Not Socialism?," *Praxis International* 4, 3 (1984): 322–35.

44. See "Glossary," in David Collier, ed., *The New Authoritarianism in Latin America*, pp. 402–3.

45. Giovanni Sartori, *Parties and Party Systems: A Framework for Analysis*, 1:131–33.

46. Sidney Tarrow, "Aiming at a Moving Target: Social Science and the Recent Rebellions in Eastern Europe," *PS: Political Science and Politics* (March 1991): 12–20.

Chapter II
The Transformation of Politics: A Historical Overview

1. Karl Marx, "On the Jewish Question," in Robert C. Tucker, ed., *The Marx-Engels Reader*, pp. 35, 42–44; Karl Marx and Friedrich Engels, "The German Ideology," in Marx and Engels, *Collected Works*, 5:50, 414–17; Karl Marx, "Economic and Philosophic Manuscripts of 1844," in Marx and Engels, *Collected Works*, 3:317.

2. John Keane, *Democracy and Civil Society*, pp. 52–56.

3. Eduard Bernstein, *Evolutionary Socialism*, pp. 109–87.

4. N. I. Bukharin, *Selected Writings on the State and the Transition to Socialism*, pp. 269–70.

5. See Fehér, Heller, and Markus, *Dictatorship over Needs*, pp. 162–66; Bauman, "On the Maturation of Socialism," pp. 48–54; "Garantii dlia 'neformalov'," *Literaturnaia Gazeta*, September 13, 1989.

6. Discussion here focuses on *organized independent* politics, which was largely erased during the pre-Gorbachev period. Small informal circles of relatively progressive, often young officials *within* the party apparat existed since the early 1960s. See David Remnick, "The Pioneers of Perestroika: Back to the Intellectual Roots of Soviet Reforms," *The Washington Post National Weekly Edition*, March 19–25, 1990.

7. "Garantiia uspekha—nashi sobstvennye deistviia," *Izvestiia*, April 21, 1987.

8. O. Golenkina, V. Zolotarev, and M. Globachev, "Konstitutsionno-Demokraticheskoe dvizhenie: Sentiabr' 1987-Mai 1990," in V. Zolotarev, ed., *Kadety: Sbornik dokumentov*, p. 16.

9. O. G. Rumiantsev, *O samodeiatel'nom dvizhenii obshchestvennykh initsiativ, neformal'nye ob"edineniia i ikh rol' v perestroike obshchestvennoi zhizni v SSSR*, pp. 9–11.

10. On the emergence of informal groups in Moscow, see Boris Kagarlitsky, *Farewell to Perestroika: A Soviet Chronicle.*

11. Vera Tolz, *The USSR in 1989: A Record of Events*, pp. 52–53.

12. TASS, May 10, 1988, in *Foreign Broadcast Information Service, The Soviet Union*, May 11, 1988 (hereafter cited as *FBIS*); Moscow World Service, June 10, 1988, in *FBIS*, June 13, 1988; Moscow World Service, August 23, 1988, in *FBIS*, August 24, 1988; Iu. N. Prokhorov, "Nesanktsionirovannye vystupleniia neformal'nykh grupp i ob"edinenii kak sotsial'no-pravovoe iavlenie," in *Sbornik, Voprosy teorii i praktiki ugolovnogo prava, kriminalogii i kriminalistiki*, pp. 113–20.

13. Cited in Rumiantsev, *O samodeiatel'nom dvizhenii obshchestvennykh initsiativ*, p. 4.

14. "Uchenyi idet k 'neformalam'," *Komsomol'skaia Pravda*, December 11, 1987; "Samozvantsy i 'samodel'shchiki'," *Komsomol'skaia Pravda*, January 31, 1988; "Obratnyi khod," *Izvestiia*, September 9, 1988; I. Sundiev, "Nashestvie Marsian?" in S. N. Iushenkov, ed., *Neformaly: sotsial'nye initsiativy*, p. 4.

15. "Ne mogu postupat'sia printsipami," *Sovetskaia Rossiia*, March 13, 1988.

16. "Informatsionnoe soobshchenie o khode XIX vsesoiuznoi konferentsii KPSS," and "Dvorets s"ezdov, den' tretii," *Izvestiia*, July 1, 1988.

17. "Posle dolgogo zapreta," *Izvestiia*, May 17, 1988.

18. Information on the development of the democratic movement during the election campaign was gleaned largely from numerous personal conversations with activists who were involved in organizational efforts. I am particularly indebted to V. O. Bokser (interview, January 30, 1991, Moscow) and V. F. Kriger (interview, June 17, 1991, Moscow). Both were leading figures in the Moscow Union of Voters and, later, Democratic Russia.

19. *Novosti Narodnogo Fronta, Informatsionnyi biulleten' Moskovskogo Narodnogo Fronta*, no. 1 (1989).

20. Bokser interview, January 30, 1991.

21. Coverage of the proceedings of the Congress is found in *Izvestiia*, May 25–June 2, 1989.

22. "U radikal'noi perestroiki net al'ternativy," *Informatsionnyi biulleten' mezhregional'noi gruppy narodnykh deputatov SSSR*, September 15, 1989.

23. Interview with V. Kardail'skii (Social Democratic Party of Russia), May

11, 1990, Moscow; Bokser interview, January 30, 1991; Zolotarev, ed., *Kadety*, pp. 17–21.

24. "Khronika perestroiki," *Pozitsiia*, no. 3 (November 1989); Moscow World Service, October 25, 1989, in *FBIS*, October 27, 1989; Paris AFP, September 18, 1989, in *FBIS*, September 19, 1989.

25. "Muchenikam zemli sovetskoi," *Demokraticheskaia Rossiia*, no. 5 (November 1990).

26. TASS, February 24, 1989, in *FBIS*, March 9, 1989; TASS, July 12, 1989, in *FBIS*, July 28, 1989; "Kooperativy i tseny," *Trud*, June 29, 1989.

27. *Spravochnik Periodicheskogo Samizdata*, pp. 2–6.

28. "Konflikta moglo i ne byt'," *Izvestiia*, March 10, 1989; "Na piatye sutki," *Pravda*, April 13, 1989.

29. "Shakhtery vozvrashchaiutsia v zaboi," *Izvestiia*, July 26, 1989; "Protivostoianie," *Pozitsiia*, no. 5 (December 1989); *IV Konferentsiia soiuza trudiashchikhsia Kuzbassa*, November 18–19, 1989 (Novokuznetsk).

30. "Protivostoianie," *Kuzbasskie Vedomosti*, no. 2 (1989).

31. *Pervyi (uchreditel'nyi) s"ezd Ob"edinennogo Fronta Trudiashchikhsia SSSR: Dokumenty i materialy*, July 15–16, 1989 (Leningrad, 1989); *Pervyi (uchreditel'nyi) s"ezd Ob"edinennogo Fronta Trudiashchikhsia Rossii: Dokumenty i materialy*, September 9, 1989 (Sverdlovsk, 1989); "Iaroslavskii rabochii klub ob ob"edinennom fronte trudiashchikhsia," *Vestnik Rabochego Dvizheniia*, no. 1 (October 1989) (Iaroslavl'); "Novye pravila dlia staroi igry?," *Sotsialisticheskaia Industriia*, July 11, 1989.

32. "Zachem nam nuzhen soiuz iuristov," *Komsomol'skaia Pravda*, June 20, 1989.

33. "Kooperatory ob"ediniaiutsaia," *Izvestiia*, August 4, 1989.

34. "Zakon SSSR o pechati i drugikh sredstvakh massovoi informatsii," *Izvestiia*, December 4, 1989.

35. Tolz, *The USSR in 1989*, p. 701.

36. *Le Quotidien de Paris*, July 4, 1989, in *FBIS*, July 28, 1989.

37. "Otbleski v Petrograde," *Esdek*, no. 5 (February 1990).

38. The speech, delivered at the Academy of Sciences Institute of Physics, was printed for the first time over a year and a half later in the leading publication of the democratic movement as a posthumous tribute to Sakharov's foresightedness. "Politicheskaia zabastovka," *Demokraticheskaia Rossiia*, no. 6(12) (April 26, 1991).

39. "Problema radikalizma vchera i zavtra," *Panorama*, no. 10 (September 1990).

40. *Volzhskaia vstrecha: Sbornik dokumentov*; "Ob"edinimsia!," *Obnovlenie: Gazeta kommunistov-reformatorov*, no. 3 (January 1–15, 1990).

41. "Est' takaia partiia?" *Demokraticheskaia Platforma*, no. 2 (April 1990).

42. "Vozmozhen eshche i litovskii variant . . . ," ibid.

43. "Obshchepoliticheskaia rezoliutsiia," *Pozitsiia*, no. 13, 1990; "Dogovorit'sia o printsipakh" and "'Demokraty' pred"iavliaiut trebovaniia," *Izvestiia*, June 18, 1990.

44. "O RPRF," *Respublika*, no. 1 (1991); "K kommunistam," *Press-biulleten'*— *Pozitsiia*, no. 4 (1990); "Mimikriia totalitarizma," *Doverie*, no. 10 (August 1990).

45. TASS, April 1, 1990, in *FBIS*, April 2, 1990.

46. "Declarations of the State Sovereignty of the Russian and Ukrainian Republics," in Alexander Dallin and Gail W. Lapidus, eds., *The Soviet System in Crisis*, pp. 478–84.

47. This conclusion is based largely on extensive personal observation of street meetings and mass demonstrations in Moscow during 1989–91. Discussion of the demonstrations appears in "Fevral'skii veter," *Demokraticheskaia Platforma*, no. 2 (April 1990).

48. "Manifest," *Al'ternativa*, no. 1 (May 30–June 12, 1990); "Manifest o sozdanii Partii KD," *Grazhdanskoe Dostoinstvo*, no. 21(57) (June 1990); "Informatsionnoe soobshchenie," *Vestnik Khristianskoi Demokratii*, no. 13 (June 1990); "Multiparty System in Russia," *Moscow News*, May 28—June 4, 1990; "Informatsionnoe soobshchenie ob Uchreditel'nom s"ezde Respublikanskoi partii Rossiiskoi Federatsii," *Materialy uchreditel'nogo s"ezda Respublikanskoi Partii Rossiiskoi Federatsii, Sbornik N. 1.*

49. "Ne Zhdali? 'DemPlatforma' sozdaet novuiu partiiu," *Moskovskii Komsomolets*, July 13, 1990; interview with V. N. Shostakovskii (Republican Party of Russia), May 23, 1991, Moscow; interview with T. E. Alaiba (Republican Party of Russia), July 4, 1991, Sverdlovsk.

50. "Itogi uchreditel'nogo s"ezda dvizheniia 'Demokraticheskaia Rossiia'," *Demokraticheskaia Rossiia*, no. 5 (November 1990); "Spravka," *Dvizhenie "Demokraticheskaia Rossiia", Informatsionnyi biulleten'*, no. 4 (February 1991); "Dvizhenie 'Demokraticheskaia Rossiia' sozdano," *Doverie* no. 13 (November 1990).

51. "Fevral'skoe izbienie," *Grazhdanskoe Dostoinstvo*, no. 11(46) (March 1990).

52. "Saratov," *Al'ternativa*, no. 1 (May 30–June 12, 1990).

53. "Demplatforma v blokade," *Volzhskie Novosti* (August 1990).

54. "Svoboda udusheniia pechati," *Al'ternativa*, no. 4 (October 1990).

55. "Kogo spasaet 'Kommitet natsional'nogo spaseniia'," *Novaia Zhizn'*, no. 3–4 (1991).

56. Eduard Shevardnadze, "Speech to the Congress of People's Deputies, December 20, 1990," in Dallin and Lapidus, eds., *The Soviet System in Crisis*, pp. 698–99.

57. Vladimir Kriuchkov, "Speech to the Congress of People's Deputies, December 22, 1990," in ibid., pp. 700–702.

58. For example, *Vystuplenie na 4-om s"ezde narodnykh deputatov SSSR, Narodnogo Deputata V. Lopatina*, December 26, 1990 (mimeo).

59. "Prikaz Iazova i Pugo," *Kommersant*, January 21–28, 1991; "Rezhim delaet stavku na rumynskii variant zashchity," *Dvizhenie "Demokratecheskaia Rossiia", Informatsionnyi biulleten'* (hereafter cited as *DDRIB*), no. 4 (February 1991).

60. "Rezoliutsiia Koordinatsionnogo Soveta Dvizheniia 'Demokraticheskaia Rossiia', 'K itogam 4-go S"ezda narodnykh deputatov SSSR'," *DDRIB*, no. 1 (January 1991).

61. "Novaia strategiia gosteleradio," *Kommersant*, January 7–14, 1991; "Zaiavlenie KS 'Demokraticheskaia Rossiia' o podavlenii glasnosti v sred-

stvakh massovoi informatsii," *DDRIB*, no. 3 (February 1991); "Nasha gazeta uzhe ochen' ne ponravilas' komande Gorbacheva," *Grazhdanskoe Dostoinstvo*, no. 2(64) (May 15–22, 1991).

62. "Segodnia—Litva, zavtra—Rossiia," and "Pogibshie v noch' na 13 ianvaria v g. Vil'niuse," *DDRIB*, no. 2 (January 1991).

63. "Zaiavlenie KS Dvizheniia 'Demokraticheskaia Rossiia'," *DDRIB*, no. 4 (February 1991).

64. "Obrashchenie chrezvychainoi konferentsii soiuza trudovykh kollektivov edinogo regiona Moskvy i Moskovskoi Oblasti k trudovym kollektivam," and "Protsess poliarizatsii zavershen," *DDRIB*, no. 3 (February 1991).

65. "Rubikon nozadi," *DDRIB*, no. 6 (March 1991).

66. "Tsentr: (17 marta 1991 goda), 'Nad vsei derzhavoi bezoblachnoe nebo!,'" ibid.; "Sessiia obsuzhdaet pervye itogi referenduma," *Izvestiia*, March 19, 1991.

67. "4 Marta . . . ," *Nasha Gazeta*, no. 18(73) (March 1, 1991); "Khronika zabastovki," *Nasha Gazeta*, no. 23(78) (March 19, 1991); "Iz shakhterskikh regionov," *Demokraticheskaia Rossiia*, no. 4(10) (April 12, 1991).

68. "U vykhoda iz zala," *Demokraticheskaia Rossiia*, no. 4(10) (April 12, 1991).

69. "Aleksandr Rutskoi: My uchli oshibki demplatformy v KPSS," *Gospodin Narod*, no. 5 (1991).

70. "My idem zakonmym putem," *Gospodin Narod*, no. 4 (1991).

71. "Fond 'Demokraticheskaia Rossiia'—ekonomicheskaia baza demokratii," *DDRIB*, no. 3 (February 1991); interview with L. A. Bogdanov (Democratic Russia), June 17, 1991, Moscow.

72. "Eshche odna partiia obizhennykh kommunistov," *Novaia Zhizn'*, no. 14(48) (1991); "Bulyzhnik ili bumazhnik?" *Kapital*, no. 1 (May 1991).

73. "Politicheskoe liderstvo pereshlo k rabochim," *Demokraticheskaia Rossiia*, no. 10(16) (May 31, 1991).

74. "Krov'—kto za nee otvet," *Demokraticheskaia Rossiia*, no. 12(18) (June 14, 1991); "Demdvizhenie: otkuda i kuda," *Demokraticheskaia Rossiia*, no. 17(23) (July 19–26, 1991).

75. "Deklaratsiia konstruktivno-demokraticheskogo bloka 'Narodnoe Soglasie,'" *Demokraticheskaia Gazeta*, no. 5(8) (1991).

76. "Boris El'tsin: 'Prishla pora sozdavat' moshchnuiu partiiu!'" *Demokraticheskaia Rossiia*, no. 1(7) (March 22, 1991); "Sobranie demokratii vsei Rossii," *Al'ternativa i Reporter* (joint issue) (May 15–June 15, 1991).

77. "Lichnye ambitsii ili problema politicheskogo vybora?" *Gospodin Narod*, no. 5 (1991); "Stavki tol'ko na favorita," *Novaia Zhizn'*, no. 13(47) (1991); "O raskole kotoryi nam prorochat," *Demokraticheskaia Gazeta*, no. 5(8) (1991); "Kak Garri Kimovich possorilsia s Nikolaiem Il'ichem i zachem," *Demokraticheskaia Gazeta*, no. 6(9) (1991).

78. "Demokraty—vlast' i oppozitsiia," *Demokraticheskaia Rossiia*, no. 14(20) (June 28, 1991).

79. "Anatolii Ivanovich beretsia za karandash," *Demokraticheskaia Rossiia*, no. 5(11) (April 19, 1991).

80. "Sovershenno nepoliticheskoe ubiistvo," *Novaia Zhizn'*, no. 14(48) (1991).

244

81. "Razgrom shtab kvartiry sotsial-demokratov," *Novaia Zhizn'*, no. 15(49) (1991).

82. "Eshche ne zagovor, no uzhe sgovor," *Demokraticheskaia Rossiia*, no. 14(20) (June 28, 1991).

Chapter III
Investigating the Phenomenon: A Framework for Analysis

1. Reinhard Bendix, John Bendix, and Norman Furniss, "Reflections on Modern Western States and Civil Societies," in Richard G. Braungart, ed., *Research in Political Sociology*, 3:1–38; Andrew Arato and Jean Cohen, "Social Movements, Civil Society, and the Problem of Sovereignty," *Praxis International* 4, 3 (1984): 266–83; Christopher Pierson, "New Theories of Civil Society: Recent Developments in Post-Marxist Analysis of the State," *Sociology* 18, 4 (November 1984): 563–71.

2. Lewin, *The Gorbachev Phenomenon*, p. 80. Conceptual confusion is similarly evident in the work of Frederick Starr, who adduces the fact that Soviet courts during the first half of 1987 "sent back more cases for investigation, handed down more acquittals, and threw out more suits than in any previous six-month period of history" as convincing demonstration of "an understanding of civil society at the highest levels of the Kremlin." Starr, "Soviet Union," p. 37.

3. John Keane, *Democracy and Civil Society*, p. 14.

4. Salvador Giner, "The Withering Away of Civil Society?" *Praxis International* 5, 3 (1985): 254.

5. Some theorists have drawn a distinction between "political" and "civil" society. Alfred Stepan, for example, locates political parties within the realm of "political society" and certain types of trade unions and interest groups within "civil society." Alfred Stepan, *Rethinking Military Politics: Brazil and the Southern Cone*, pp. 3–6. Given the diverse functions of organizations of various types, such a distinction may be rather artificial, and at any rate it is not useful for investigating the emergence of nonstate organizations in Russia. In the present analysis, groups that labeled themselves political parties are included within the realm of "civil society."

6. Claus Offe, "Corporatism as Macro-Structuring," *Telos*, no. 65 (Fall 1985): 102–3.

7. Mancur Olson, *The Logic of Collective Action*, pp. 51, 60–64, 133–34.

8. Andrew Arato, "Civil Society against the State: Poland 1980–81," *Telos*, no. 47 (Spring 1981): 23–47; Kazimierz Wojicicki, "The Reconstruction of Society," *Telos*, no. 47 (Spring 1981): 98–104; David Ost, *Solidarity and the Politics of Anti-Politics: Opposition and Reform in Poland since 1968*, pp. 1–17, 100–111.

9. "Politicheskaia Programma Partii Konstitutsionnykh Demokratov," *Grazhdanskoe Dostoinstvo* (June 1990); "Programma DPR," *Demokraticheskaia Gazeta*, no. 6(9) (1991); *Put' progressa i sotsial'noi demokratii: Osnova Programmy SDPR*; "Deklaratsiia Respublikanskoi Partii Rossiiskoi Federatsii," *Gospodin Narod*, no. 1 (1990).

10. "Rossiiskie sotsial-demokraty: Kapitaliziruem sotsializm?," *Kommersant*, May 14, 1990.

11. L. Byzov, "Sovetskie Sotsial-demokraty: Kto oni?" (paper distributed at the Third Plenum of the Social Democratic Party of Russia, December 22–23, 1990); interview with K. Iankov (Social Democratic Party of Russia), January 22, 1991, Moscow; interview with T. E. Alaiba (Republican Party of Russia), July 4, 1991, Sverdlovsk.

12. Interview with N. I. Travkin (Democratic Party of Russia), January 31, 1991, Moscow.

13. *I s"ezd nezavisimykh rabochykh dvizhenii i organizatsii, Deklaratsiia osnovnykh printsipov konfederatsii truda.*

14. "Demokraty—ob"edinenie i razmezhevaniia," *Panorama* (December 1990); "S"ezd 'Demokraticheskoi Rossii,'" *Svoboda i Zhizn'*, no. 6 (1990).

15. "Vsia vlast' uchreditel'nomu sobraniiu," *Novaia Zhizn'*, no. 23 (1990); "Voina profsoiuzov neizbezhna," *Kommersant* (December 31–January 7, 1991).

16. Philippe C. Schmitter, "Democratic Theory and Neo-Corporatist Practice," *Social Research* 50, 4 (Winter 1983): 899.

17. Eduard Bernstein, *Evolutionary Socialism*, p. 158.

18. Alexis de Tocqueville, *Democracy in America*, ed. Richard Heffner, pp. 198–209.

19. "On Parliamentary Lobbyism," *Moscow News*, March 18–25, 1990.

20. Paris AFP, September 14, 1989, in *FBIS*, September 14, 1989.

21. "Tak kuda zhe poidut shakhteri?" *Rossiia*, March 23–29, 1991; TASS, September 20, 1991, in *FBIS*, September 25, 1991.

22. "Conservatism Retires," *Moscow News*, March 11–18, 1990.

23. "Mnogopartiinost' v SSSR: nikto ne khochet vykhodit' iz podpol'ia," *Kommersant*, December 31–January 7, 1991; "Registriruisia, kto mozhet!" *Rossiia*, March 23–29, 1991; interview with V. L. Sekrieru (Social Democratic Party of Russia), February 7, 1991, Apatity (Murmansk Oblast').

24. "Miting v Moskve," *Svobodnoe Slovo*, March 6, 1990.

25. "Osnovnye politicheskie printsipy" and "Nash put' k svobode i demokratii," *Sbornik dokumentov Grazhdanskogo Komiteta "Novyi Forum."*

26. Charles Tilly, "Models and Realities of Popular Collective Action," *Social Research* 52, 4 (Winter 1985): 735–36.

27. Marc Rakovski, *Towards an East European Marxism*, pp. 99–102.

28. "Demokratiia kak tsel' vospitaniia," *Demokraticheskaia Rossiia*, no. 2(8) (1991); "Vyigraet strana," *Otkrytaia Zona*, no. 1 (1990); "Deklaratsiia," *Dokumenty, 2-i s"ezd partii, "Demokraticheskii Soiuz"*; *I s"ezd nezavisimykh rabochykh dvizhenii i organizatsii, Deklaratsiia osnovnykh printsipov konfederatsii truda*; "Ot kommunisticheskoi imperii k novomu gosudarstvu" (Declaration of the Duma of the Russian Christian Democratic Movement), January 17, 1991.

29. Claus Offe, "New Social Movements: Challenging the Boundaries of Institutional Politics," *Social Research* 52, 4 (Winter 1985): 821–38; Alberto Melucci, "Social Movements and the Democratization of Everyday Life," in John Keane, ed., *Civil Society and the State*, pp. 245–46.

30. "Opasnyi vakkum," *Sovetskaia Rossiia*, May 17, 1990.

31. "Rabochee dvizhenie: izderzhki i priobreteniia," *Pravda*, January 18, 1990; "Doroga k zdravomu smyslu," *Izvestiia*, April 9, 1990.

32. "'Socialism' Awry," *Moscow News*, June 3–10, 1990.

33. Terrence Emmons, *The Formation of Political Parties and the First National Elections in Russia*, pp. 89, 128–34, 170; Christopher Rice, *Russian Workers and the Socialist-Revolutionary Party through the Revolution of 1905–07*, p. 155.

34. Feliks Gross, *The Revolutionary Party: Essays in the Sociology of Politics*, p. 50.

35. "Political Parties in Eastern Europe," *Radio Free Europe Research Report* (February 1990), pp. 6, 12–15, 37.

36. The Hungarian elections of the spring of 1990, for example, differed substantially from their Russian counterparts. The former were hastily arranged, and parties were criticized for immature campaign strategies. But parties played a prominent role in the elections and produced a coalition government not dissimilar to many of those found in Western Europe. See Zoltan D. Barany and Louisa Vinton, "Breakthrough to Democracy: Elections in Poland and Hungary," *Studies in Comparative Communism* 23, 2 (Summer 1990): 191–212, esp. 201–8. See also Janina Frentzel-Zagorska, "Civil Society in Poland and Hungary," *Soviet Studies* 4, 4 (1990): 159–77.

37. Klaus von Beyme, *Political Parties in Western Democracies*, pp. 6, 166–72. See also Alan Ware, *The Logic of Party Democracy*, pp. 39–40.

38. See Guillermo O'Donnell, "On the Fruitful Convergences of Hirschman's *Exit, Voice, and Loyalty* and *Shifting Involvements*: Reflections from the Recent Argentine Experience," in Alejandro Foxley, Michael S. McPherson, and Guillermo O'Donnell, eds., *Development, Democracy, and the Art of Trespassing: Essays in Honor of Albert O. Hirschman*, pp. 249–68, esp. pp. 258–59.

39. Gross, *The Revolutionary Party*, p. 21; Austin Ranney, *Curing the Mischiefs of Faction: Party Reform in America*, pp. 22–33.

40. This point is based on my observation of strike committee activities in Donetsk in the spring of 1991. Also see Peter Rutland, "Labor Unrest and Social Movements in 1989 and 1990," *Soviet Economy* 6, 4 (1990): 345–84.

41. Interview with S. Khramov (Sotsprof), January 8, 1991, Moscow; interview with G. I. Temkin (Sotsprof), January 20, 1991, Moscow; interview with N. V. Solov'ev (Sotsprof), March 5, 1991, Moscow.

42. Sartori, *Parties and Party Systems*, 1:96.

43. Richard S. Katz, *A Theory of Parties and Electoral Systems*, p. 116.

44. Herbert Kitschelt, *The Logics of Party Formation: Ecological Politics in Belgium and West Germany*, p. 274.

45. Maurice Duverger, *Political Parties*, pp. 61–132; Kenneth Janda, *A Conceptual Framework for the Comparative Analysis of Political Parties*, pp. 87, 104.

46. Kay Lawson, *The Comparative Study of Political Parties*, pp. 71–80; Gross, *The Revolutionary Party*, pp. 41–57.

47. von Beyme, *Political Parties in Western Democracies*, p. 141; Ware, *The Logic of Party Democracy*, pp. 37–38; Larry Sabato, *The Party's Just Begun*, pp. 15–20, 111–29; Peter H. Merkl, "The Sociology of European Parties: Members, Voters, and Social Groups," in Peter H. Merkl, ed., *West European Party Systems: Trends and Prospects*, pp. 614–67.

48. *Kommiunike 3-go plenuma pravleniia SDPR*, December 22–23, 1990; interview with V. N. Shostakovskii (Republican Party of Russia), May 23, 1991, Moscow.

49. John D. McCarthy and Mayer N. Zald, "Resource Mobilization and Social Movements: A Partial Theory," in Mayer N. Zald and John D. McCarthy, eds., *Social Movements in an Organizational Society: Collected Essays*, pp. 15–42; Jean Cohen, "Strategy or Identity: New Theoretical Paradigms and Contemporary Social Movements," *Social Research* 52, 4 (Winter 1985): 674–90.

50. Katz, *A Theory of Parties*, p. 15; Alexander L. George, "Case Studies and Theory Development," ms., Stanford University.

51. Leon D. Epstein, *Political Parties in Western Democracies*, p. 77.

52. See Michael Urban, *More Power to the Soviets: The Democratic Revolution in the USSR*, pp. 37–43, 71–72, 90–100.

53. Charles Tilly, "Social Movements and National Politics," in Charles Bright and Susan Harding, eds., *Statemaking and Social Movements: Essays in History and Theory*, pp. 311–14.

54. Guillermo O'Donnell and Philippe C. Schmitter, *Transitions from Authoritarian Rule: Tentative Conclusions about Uncertain Democracies*, pp. 15–17, 24–25.

55. The major institutional exception to the official policy of crackdown was the Supreme Soviet of the RSFSR, a substantial minority of whose deputies opposed the Union government and the CPSU. As outlined in chapter 1, though soviets are in some formal sense state institutions, they do not stand fully within the "pact of domination" as it is conceptualized here.

56. Schmitter, "Democratic Theory and Neo-Corporatist Practice," p. 899.

57. Laura Boella, "Eastern European Societies," *Telos*, no. 41 (Fall 1979): 65.

58. "Kooperativnoe dvizhenie v opasnosti," *Literaturnaia Gazeta*, January 31, 1990; "The State, Cooperatives, and Bureaucratic Capital," *Moscow News*, March 11–18, 1990; "Pravitel'stvo vnosit predlozheniia," *Sovetskaia Rossiia*, April 8, 1990; "Deceit that Kills," *Moscow News*, June 24–July 1, 1990; "Reforma tsen—ekonomicheskii Afganistan," *Demokraticheskaia Rossiia*, no. 2(8) (1991).

59. McCarthy and Zald, "Resource Mobilization," pp. 15–42; and "Appendix" by same authors in same volume, pp. 371–78.

60. Otto Kirchheimer, "Confining Conditions and Revolutionary Breakthroughs," in Frederic S. Burin and Kurt L. Shell, eds., *Politics, Law, and Social Change: Selected Essays of Otto Kirchheimer*, pp. 389–90.

61. The distinction between political development of society and political development of the polity is raised in Sartori, *Parties and Party Systems*, pp. 41, 57–58.

62. Giuseppe Di Palma, "Party Government and Democratic Reproducibility: The Dilemma of New Democracies," in Francis G. Castles and Rudolf Wildenmann, eds., *The Future of Party Government*, vol. 1: *Visions and Realities of Party Government*, p. 181.

63. Philippe C. Schmitter, "The Consolidation of Political Democracy in Southern Europe and Latin America," ms., October 1985, p. 28.

64. Sartori, *Parties and Party Systems*, p. 41.

65. Katz, *A Theory of Parties*, pp. 1–2.

66. Alan Ware, *Citizens, Parties, and the State: A Reappraisal*, pp. 157–58; von

Beyme, *Political Parties in Western Democracies*, p. 159; Epstein, *Political Parties in Western Democracies*, pp. 165–67.

67. Ware, *The Logic of Party Democracy*, p. 33.

68. Schmitter, "The Consolidation of Political Democracy in Southern Europe and Latin America," pp. 17, 22.

69. Adam Przeworski, "Some Problems in the Study of the Transition to Democracy," in Guillermo O'Donnell, Philippe C. Schmitter, and Laurence Whitehead, eds., *Transitions from Authoritarian Rule: Comparative Perspectives*, pp. 58–61.

70. Dankwart A. Rustow, "Transitions to Democracy: Toward a Dynamic Model," *Comparative Politics* 2, 3 (April 1970): 356–57. See also Terry Lynn Karl, "Dilemmas of Democratization in Latin America," *Comparative Politics* 23, 1 (October 1990): 5.

71. See John Keane, "Despotism and Democracy," in Keane, ed., *Civil Society and the State*, pp. 44–62; Larry Diamond, Seymour Martin Lipset, and Juan Linz, "Developing and Sustaining Democratic Government in the Third World" (paper prepared for the Annual Meeting of the American Political Science Association, August 1986, Washington, D.C.), pp. 77–81.

72. Sidney Tarrow, "Economic Development and the Transformation of the Italian Party System," in Giuseppe Di Palma, ed., *Mass Politics in Industrial Societies*, pp. 226–53; Maria Maguire, "Is There Still Persistence?" in Hans Daalder and Peter Mair, eds., *Western European Party Systems: Continuity and Change*, pp. 83–84.

Chapter IV
Building Independent Political Society

1. Janda, *A Conceptual Framework*, p. 83.

2. Fred Riggs, "Comparative Politics and Political Parties," in William J. Crotty, ed., *Approaches to the Study of Party Organization*, p. 51.

3. V. O. Key, *Public Opinion and American Democracy*, p. 432.

4. Lawson, *The Comparative Study of Political Parties*, pp. 1–2.

5. Ware, *Citizens, Parties, and the State*, p. 16.

6. Such a situation was not, of course, unprecedented. Political parties existed at a number of historical junctures in continental Europe even in the absence of representative government. They functioned as protest groups opposing autocratic or monarchical rule. See Gross, *The Revolutionary Party*, pp. 32–34.

7. Douglas W. Rae, *The Political Consequences of Electoral Laws*, p. 47.

8. See, for example, Alberto Melucci, *Nomads of the Present*.

9. "Mysli posle s"ezda," *Esdek*, no. 6 (April–May 1990).

10. "Politicheskii doklad chlena Prezidiuma pravleniia SDPR P. M. Kudiukina," *Novosti Sotsial-Demokratii*, no. 4 (November 1990) (hereafter cited as *NSD*).

11. Byzov, "Sovetskie sotsial-demokraty: Kto oni?"

12. See, for example, "V plenum pravleniia, 23–24 Marta, 1991," *NSD*, no. 15 (April 1991).

13. Indeed, roughly half of the over 150 activists interviewed in Moscow and eight other cities raised problems of national character and psychology in their discussions of their groups' activities. I took pains not to offer provisional answers; subjects freely adduced such explanations unprompted. Herein lies part of the appeal to Western analysts of cultural and psychological explanations for contemporary Russian politics. Participants themselves, to a greater degree than in the West or even in East Europe, habitually—and often with dark humor and weary resignation—attribute their country's political travails to national exceptionalism, to unique "defects" in the "national character," or to the country's "level of civilization."

Other Western analysts who have observed Russia's democratic organizations firsthand have also noted some of the phenomena under discussion. James Billington has remarked on oppositionists' "tendency to wallow at great length in denouncing past errors with a mixture of self-pity and self-righteousness, omitting any realistic discussion of remedies." According to Billington, this tendency evaporated during the defense of the White House on August 19–21, 1991. James H. Billington, *Russia Transformed: Breakthrough to Hope*, p. 68.

The few analysts who have addressed possible causes for such behavior have done so cursorily and have usually fallen back on political-cultural explanations or attributed groups' difficulties to "personality conflicts" and "personal ambitions," without explaining why these would be stronger and more divisive in Russia than in other countries. See, for example, Geoffrey Hosking, *The Awakening of the Soviet Union*, p. 179; Kagarlitsky, *Farewell to Perestroika*, pp. 35–38.

14. In their work on transitions from authoritarianism, Guillermo O'Donnell and Philippe Schmitter have distinguished between cases in which former political identities may easily be revived and those in which they have been long submerged and are less readily available to actors during the transition. In the latter instance: "The institutional context has had to be invented and learned almost *ex novo*. . . . Regime opponents, having been given virtually no role within the authoritarian scheme of governance and, in some cases, having returned from exile to act in societies which have undergone substantial changes, often have had to rely on precarious past identities, outmoded slogans, and unimaginative combinations." O'Donnell and Schmitter, *Transitions from Authoritarian Rule*, p. 23. If such conditions held in countries such as Chile and Portugal, they obtained even more strongly in Russia, where past identities were not precarious, but rather nonexistent. They therefore had to be created and learned completely—not merely "almost"—*ex novo*.

For more recent writings on the distinction between redemocratization and democratization "for the first time" in Latin American transitions, see J. Samuel Valenzuela, "Democratic Consolidation in Post-Transitional Settings: Notion, Process, and Facilitating Conditions," in Scott Mainwaring, Guillermo O'Donnell and J. Samuel Valenzuela, eds., *Issues in Democratic Consolidation: The New South American Democracies in Comparative Perspective*, pp. 57–104, esp. pp. 78–81; and Guillermo O'Donnell, "Transitions, Continuities, and Paradoxes," same volume, pp. 17–56.

15. Indeed, although Hungary suffered a period of Stalinization, society

was never totalized there to the extent that it was in Russia. In the former, moreover, the 1970s and 1980s witnessed the evolution of what Elemer Hankiss calls "relative autonomies" in society. Hankiss concludes that "In spite of massive mobilizational and demobilizational strategies on the part of the elite, Hungarian society has never been completely dominated or paralyzed, not even in the late 1940s and early 1950s." Elemer Hankiss, "Demobilization, Self-Mobilization and Quasi-Mobilization in Hungary, 1948–1987," *Eastern European Politics and Societies* 3, 1 (Winter 1989): 105–51 (cited passage, p. 145). In some East European countries, autonomous spaces for societal activity were largely wiped out after the installation of Soviet-type regimes and did not reopen in the 1970s and 1980s. Romania serves as perhaps the clearest example. See Vladimir Tismaneanu, "The Tragicomedy of Romanian Communism," *Eastern European Politics and Societies* 3, 2 (Spring 1989): 329–76.

16. Vaclav Havel, "Politics and Conscience," in Vaclav Havel, *Open Letters: Selected Writings, 1965–90*, pp. 269–71. See also Konrad, *Antipolitics*; Vladimir Tismaneanu, *Reinventing Politics: Eastern Europe from Stalin to Havel* (New York: Free Press, 1992), pp. 113–52.

17. See Mary McAuley, *Soviet Politics, 1917–91*, pp. 67–69.

18. As the SDPR's Kudiukin pointed out, questions that would "never even arise in Europe" were central to political debate within the democratic movement in Russia. According to Kudiukin, in Europe "everyone knows what distinguishes a social democrat from a liberal from a Christian democrat and so on." "Sotsial-demokraty v Rossii," *Demokraticheskaia Rossiia*, no. 4(10) (April 12, 1991).

19. "Ustav RPR," *Materialy uchreditel'nogo s"ezda Respublikanskoi Partii Rossiiskoi Federatsii, Sbornik N. 1* (Moscow, 1990).

20. "O RPRF," *Respublika*, no. 1 (1991); "Novie men'sheviki," *Nevskii Kur'er*, no. 18 (1990).

21. "O RPRF," *Respkublika*, no. 1 (1991).

22. "Tonutsii korabl' Demplatformy" (mimeo by V. Pribylovskii, July 1990, Moscow); "Nuzhno peredat' imushchestvo KPSS narody. Po ero resheniiu," *Gospodin Narod*, no. 5 (1991); interview with T. E. Alaiba (Republican Party of Russia), July 4, 1991, Sverdlovsk.

23. Alaiba interview, July 4, 1991.

24. "Resheniia, protokol," *NSD*, no. 5 (December 1990); "Kratkii otchet o 3'om plenume pravleniia SDPR," *NSD*, no. 6 (January 1991); "Deklaratsiia ob"edinennoi konferentsii RPR-SDPR Moskovskogo regiona," *Moskovskii Men'shevik*, no. 1 (January 1991).

25. "Informatsionnoe soobshchenie," *NSD*, no. 12 (March 1991); "Kuda idem?" *Respublika*, no. 1 (1991); "V Moskovskoi oblastnoi organizatsii," *Moskovskii Sotsial-Demokrat*, no. 2 (1991); "Kratkii otchet . . ." *NSD*, no. 6 (January 1991).

26. "Vroz' nam skuchno, vmeste tesno," *Al'ternativa*, no. 7 (April 1991).

27. "Drugie partii ishchut struktury, a respublikantsy ikh imeiut," *Gospodin Narod*, no. 3 (1991).

28. Author's minutes, Third Plenum of the SDPR, December 22–23, 1990; "Zachem nam ob"ediniat'siia?" *NSD*, no. 5 (December 1990).

29. "RPR, vzgliad iz segodnia," *Gospodin Narod*, no. 3 (1991); "Nezhdannyi povorot," *Epokha*, no. 9 (February 1991).

30. Author's minutes, Third Plenum of the SDPR, December 22–23, 1990.

31. "Mysli posle s"ezda," *Esdek*, no. 6 (April–May 1990).

32. "Sravnitel'nyi analiz programmnykh dokumentov Sotsial-demokraticheskoi i Respublikanskoi partii Rossiiskoi Federatsii," *Ob"edinenie dvukh partii: Problemy i perspektivy, Diskussionnyi listok*.

33. "Rezoliutsiia uchreditel'noi konferentsii Moskovskoi oblastnoi organizatsii," *NSD*, no. 4 (November 1990).

34. Author's minutes, Third Plenum of the SDPR, December 22–23, 1990.

35. "Kuda idem?" *Respublika*, no. 1 (1991).

36. Interview with A. M. Obolenskii (Social Democratic Party of Russia), February 7, 1991, Apatity (Murmansk Oblast').

37. Interview with V. V. Lunin (Republican Party of Russia), April 15, 1991, Moscow.

38. Samuel J. Eldersveld, *Political Parties: A Behavioral Analysis*, pp. 277–92; M. Margaret Conway and Frank B. Feigert, "Motivation, Incentives Systems, and the Political Party Organization," in David W. Abbott and Edward T. Rogowsky, eds., *Political Parties: Leadership, Organization, Linkage*, pp. 116–38.

39. "Odin den' iz zhizni SDPR i RPR," *NSD*, no. 5 (December 1991).

40. Obolenskii interview, February 7, 1991.

41. Interview with A. I. Tretiakov (Republican Party of Russia), May 8, 1991, Orel.

42. Lunin interview, April 15, 1991.

43. "Stavki tol'ko na favorita," *Novaia Zhizn*, no. 13(47) (1991). Members' beliefs in this regard were based largely on myth. The RPR did bring together a diverse and impressive assortment of professionals and intellectuals. But the SDPR and other democratic opposition groups did as well. Yet Republicans genuinely believed that merging their group with another would dilute its "intellectual potential" and thus subvert a part of its identity.

44. "Tonutsii korabl' Demplatformy" (mimeo by V. Pribylovskii), July 1990, Moscow. See also "Nuzhno peredat' imushchestvo KPSS narody . . . ," *Gospodin Narod*, no. 5 (1991).

45. "O RPRF," *Respublika*, No. 1, 1991.

46. "Predlozhenie orgkomiteta 'o nazvanii budushchei partii'" (mimeo), Moscow, 1990.

47. Kitschelt, *The Logics of Party Formation*, pp. 124–29, 143–46, 274. Kitschelt's study helps reveal the inadequacy of political-cultural and political-psychological explanations for the behavior of Russian activists. Most of the actors Kitschelt observed, though they manifested many of the same habits and traits as Russia's democratic activists, were not, after all, quarrelsome and suspicious Eastern Slavs, but rather orderly and disciplined Teutons.

48. Kirchheimer, "Confining Conditions and Revolutionary Breakthroughs," pp. 389–90.

49. Seweryn Bialer holds that Soviet society is socially "dominated by a large new middle class," while Jerry Hough refers to the Soviet Union as a "middle-class society." Seweryn Bialer, "Gorbachev's Program of Change:

Sources, Significance, Prospects," in Seweryn Bialer and Michael Mandel-baum, eds., *Gorbachev's Russia and American Foreign Policy*, p. 236; Hough, *Russia and the West*, p. 255. See also Aleksandr Meerovich, "The Emergence of Russian Multiparty Politics," *Report on the USSR* 2, 34 (August 24, 1990): 8–16.

50. See, for example, Ruble, "The Social Dimensions of Perestroyka," pp. 171–83.

51. For analyses and arguments consistent with those presented here, see Nikolai Shmelev, "Avansy i dolgi," *Novyi mir*, no. 6 (1987): 142–58; A. N. Kochetov, "Novye tendentsii v sovershenstvovanii sotsial'noi struktury sovetskogo obshchestva (1980-e gody)," *Istoriia SSSR*, no. 6 (November–December 1988): 3–16; Juan J. Linz and Alfred Stepan, "Political Identities and Electoral Sequences: Spain, the Soviet Union, and Yugoslavia," *Daedalus* 121, 2 (Spring 1992): 123–39, esp. p. 132 and n. 18.

52. Thomas Remington, "A Socialist Pluralism of Opinions: *Glasnost'* and Policymaking under Gorbachev," *Russian Review* 48, 3 (July 1989): 290.

53. "O programme SDPR," *Epokha*, no. 9 (February 1991). See also "O sotsial'no-politicheskoi situatsii v strane i zadachakh SDPR," *NSD*, no. 1 (September 1990).

54. Author's minutes, meeting of Social Democratic Forum, March 11, 1991, Moscow.

55. Obolenskii interview, February 7, 1991.

56. "Sotsial-demokratiia v sisteme lzhi sotsializma," *Esdek*, no. 6 (April–May 1990); "Sila v edinstve," *NSD*, no. 12 (March 1991); interview with K. Iankov (Social Democratic Party of Russia), January 22, 1991, Moscow.

57. Author's minutes, Third Plenum of the SDPR, December 22–23, 1990.

58. Interview with G. Ia. Rakitskaia (Social Democratic Party of Russia), March 26, 1991, Moscow.

59. Author's minutes, meeting of Social Democratic Forum, March 11, 1991, Moscow.

60. "O RPRF," *Respublika*, no. 1 (1991). See also "Deklaratsiia Moskovskoi regional'noi konferentsii Demokraticheskoi Platformy" (mimeo), Moscow, October 13–14, 1990; "Demokraticheskaia Platforma, organizatsionnyi komitet uchreditel'nogo s"ezda," September 8–9, 1990, Moscow (mimeo of public statement by V. N. Shostakovskii).

61. "Programma deistvii RPR," *Materialy uchreditel'nogo s"ezda*.

62. Interview with V. N. Shostakovskii (Republican Party of Russia), May 23, 1991, Moscow.

63. "Andranik Migranian v kadetov ne verit," *Grazhdanskoe Dostoinstvo*, no. 26(62) (December 1990).

64. "Pochemu ia ne mogy vstupit' v partiiu kotoruiu sama sozdavala," *Golos Izbiratelia*, no. 12 (18) (1990); interview with V. F. Kriger (Democratic Russia), June 17, 1991, Moscow; interview with L. A. Bogdanov (Democratic Russia), June 17, 1991, Moscow.

65. "O raskole, kotoryi nam prorochat," *Demokraticheskaia Gazeta*, no. 5(8) (1991).

66. "Pervyi predsedatel'," *Demokraticheskaia Rossiia*, no. 1 (July 1990); "Ot-

dadut li bol'sheviki vlast' sovetam?" *Demokraticheskaia Rossiia*, no. 2 (August 1990).

67. Interview with N. I. Travkin (Democratic Party of Russia), January 31, 1991, Moscow.

68. Interview with S. V. Vvedinskii (Democratic Party of Russia), February 24, 1991; Rutland, "Labor Unrest and Movements in 1989 and 1990," pp. 345–84, esp. pp. 369–70.

69. Interview with M. N. Tolstoi (Democratic Party of Russia), June 21, 1991, Moscow.

70. Interview with A. B. Terekhov (Democratic Party of Russia), May 4, 1991, Moscow.

71. Tolstoi interview, June 21, 1991.

72. Travkin interview, January 31, 1991.

73. "Programma DPR," *Demokraticheskaia Gazeta*, no. 6(9) (1991).

74. Travkin interview, January 31, 1991.

75. As one activist from the SDPR stated during a discussion of his party's program: "Of course socialism is in crisis and we seek to change the system. But we shouldn't use terms like the 'crisis of socialism'; its sounds too much like the way the Communists have always talked. And at any rate, that's Travkin's language, not ours." Author's minutes, meeting of Social Democratic Forum, March 11, 1991, Moscow.

76. "Interv'iu na temy antikommunizm," *Demokraticheskaia Rossiia*, no. 1 (July 1990).

77. Travkin interview, January 31, 1991.

78. Author's notes from meeting of DPR youth organization, February 2, 1991, Moscow; author's notes from Second Congress of the DPR, April 28, 1991, Moscow. Also "Novie men'sheviki," *Nevskii Kur'er*, no. 18 (1990); "1990," *Put'*, no. 1(4) (January 1991).

79. "KhDS: Zhit' ne po zlu," *Dialog*, no. 10 (July 1990); "The Truth Will Make You Free," *Khristianskaia Demokratiia* (in English), no. 13 (May–June 1991); interview with A. V. Zheludkov (Russian Christian Democratic Movement), March 6, 1991, Moscow; "S"ezd KhDS Rossii," *Ekspress Khronika*, no. 38(111) (September 17, 1989).

80. "Natsional'noe i ideologichekoe," and "1990," *Put'*, no. 1(4) (January 1991); "Mify kommunisticheskogo rezhima," *Put'*, no. 4(7) (1991); *RKhDD: Sbornik materialov* (Moscow, 1990); "'Zapadniki' i 'pochvenniki' segodnia," *Russkaia Mysl'* (Paris), November 10, 1989.

81. Author's minutes, meeting of the Orel organization of the Russian Christian Democratic Movement, May 9, 1991, Orel.

82. Interview with V. V. Aksiuchits (Russian Christian Democratic Movement), May 6, 1991, Moscow.

83. "Pochemy vy nazyvaete sebia partiei?" *Svobodnoe Slovo*, no. 21 (September 19, 1989); *DS: Biulleten' soveta partii*, no. 1 (February 1990); "Dem sily o perspektivakh demokraticheskogo dvizheniia," *Demokraticheskaia Rossiia*, no. 4 (October 1990); interview with Eduard Molchanov (Democratic Union), January 23, 1991, Moscow.

84. The DU frequently ridiculed other groups for requesting the permission of local authorities to hold demonstrations. It often held its own separate demonstrations and usually did not participate in the larger ones organized by Democratic Russia and other groups. "Sto bumazhnykh tsetov i sto sovetskikh spetsshkol," *Novaia Zhizn'*, no. 10(19) (May 1990); "Kratkii analiz politicheskoi situatsii v Rossii," *Al'ternativa* (Democratic Union), no. 2 (September 1989).

85. Molchanov interview, January 23, 1991.

86. "Deklaratsiia," *DS: Dokumenty 2-go s"ezda, 1989*; "Grazhdanskii put' . . . ," *Svobodnoe Slovo*, no. 5(35) (March 6, 1990); "Grazhdanskii put' i sovety," *Svobodnoe Slovo*, no. 14(44) (May 8, 1990).

87. Molchanov interview, January 23, 1991; interview with Valerii Efimov (Democratic Union), April 28, 1990, Moscow; "Kratkii analiz politicheskoi situatsii v Rossii," *Al'ternativa*, no. 2 (September 1989).

88. "Soobshchenie N. 1 organnizatsionnogo komiteta po sozdaniiu dvizheniia 'DR,'" *Golos Izbiratelia*, no. 12(18) (1990).

89. "Ustav Dvizheniia 'Demokratichekaia Rossiia'" (mimeo), Moscow, 1990.

90. "Itogi uchreditel'nogo s"ezda dvizheniia 'DR'," *Demokraticheskaia Rossiia*, no. 5 (November 1990).

91. "Konsolidatsiia: mif i real'nost'," *Demokraticheskaia Gazeta*, no. 1 (November 10, 1990); Tolstoi interview, June 21, 1991.

92. Author's minutes, meeting of the coordinating soviet of Democratic Russia, January 31, 1991, Moscow.

93. "Boris El'tsin: 'Prishla pora sozdavat' moshchnuiu partiiu!'" *Demokratichekaia Rossiia*, no. 1(7) (March 22, 1991); Lunin interview, April 15, 1991.

94. *RKhDD: Sbornik materialov*; "Programma DPR," *Demokraticheskaia Gazeta*, no. 6(9) (1991); "O programme SDPR," *Epokha*, no. 9 (February 1991); *Biulleten' partiino-politicheskoi informatsii (SDPR)*, no. 2 (January 1991); "Programma deistvii RPR," *Materialy uchreditel'nogo s"ezda Respublikanskoi Partii Rossiiskoi Federatsii*; "Proekt programmy partii Demokraticheskii Soiuz," *Demokraticheskii Soiuz: Biulleten' soveta partii*, no. 1 (February 1990).

95. "Sotsial-demokraty v Rossii," *Demokraticheskaia Rossiia*, no. 4(12) (April 12, 1991).

96. Interview with L. A. Arutiunian (Active Position), February 2, 1991, Apatity (Murmansk Oblast').

97. Interview with V. O. Bokser (Moscow Association of Voters and Democratic Russia), January 30, 1991, Moscow.

98. Interview with V. V. Gubarev (Social Democratic Party of Russia), April 1, 1991, Tula.

99. Interview with M. G. Astaf'ev (Constitutional Democrats/Party of Popular Freedom), May 6, 1991, Moscow.

100. Author's minutes, Plenum of Democratic Russia, February 22, 1991, Moscow.

101. "Ustav RPR," *Materialy uchreditel'nogo s"ezda Respublikansoi Partii Rossiiskoi Federatsii*.

102. Molchanov interview, January 23, 1991.

103. Samuel J. Eldersveld, "The Party 'Stratarchy,'" in Abbott and Rogowsky, eds., *Political Parties*, p. 102.

104. Similar, if not identical, arrangements prevailed in groups besides the two mentioned here, although the DPR was in some respects exceptional. Lunin interview, April 15, 1991; Bokser interview, January 30, 1991; interview with V. A. Rosanov (Republican Party of Russia), June 14, 1991, Moscow; interview with A. V. Romash (Russian Christian Democratic Movement), June 17, 1991, Moscow; Molchanov interview, January 23, 1991.

105. "RPR, vzgliad iz segodnia," *Gospodin Narod*, no. 3 (1991); "Lichnye ambitsii ili problema politicheskogo vybora?," *Gospodin Narod*, no. 5 (1991).

106. See, for example, "Zapros," *NSD*, no. 5 (December 1990).

107. Tolstoi interview, June 21, 1991. Also see "Otdadut li bol'sheviki vlast' sovetam?" *Demokraticheskaia Rossiia*, no. 2 (August 1990).

108. "Vystuplenie Nikolaia Travkina v Tsentral'nom Dome kinematografistov 9 marta 1991 goda," *Demokraticheskaia Gazeta*, no. 3 (March 17, 1991).

109. Author's minutes, Second Congress of the Democratic Party of Russia, April 28, 1991.

110. Melucci, *Nomads of the Present*, pp. 38–80.

111. Rumiantsev, *O samodeiatel'nom dvizhenii obshchestennykh initsiativ*, pp. 11–12, 29.

112. "'Tolpa' glazami uchenykh muzhei," and "Vozmozhen eshche i litovskii variant," *Demokraticheskaia Platforma*, no. 2 (April 1990).

113. Lunin interview, April 15, 1991.

114. Molchanov interview, January 23, 1991.

115. Shostakovskii interview, May 23, 1991.

116. Aksiuchits interview, May 6, 1991.

117. "Kratkii otchet . . . ," *NSD*, no. 6 (January 1991).

118. "KGB sredi nas," *Novaia Zhizn'*, no. 14(48) (1991).

119. "Sovershenno nepoliticheskoe ubiistvo," *Novaia Zhizn'*, no. 14(48) (1991); "Razgrom shtab-kvartiry sotsial-demokratov," *Novaia Zhizn'*, no. 15(49); "Pod opekoi KGB," *Al'ternativa*, no. 1 (May 30–June 12, 1990; "Iz stenogrammy 4-go plenuma pravleniia SDPR zasedanie 2-2-91," *NSD*, no. 8 (February 1991).

120. Author's minutes, Leadership Plenum of the Social Democratic Party of Russia, December 22, 1990, Moscow.

121. Shostakovskii interview, May 23, 1991.

122. "Stavki tol'ko na favorita," *Novaia Zhizn'*, no. 13(47) (1991).

123. Aksiuchits interview, May 6, 1991.

124. Tolstoi interview, June 21, 1991.

125. Vladimir Kriuchkov, "Speech to the Congress of People's Deputies, December 22, 1990," in Alexander Dallin and Gail W. Lapidus, eds. *The Soviet System in Crisis*.

126. Sidney Tarrow, *Struggle, Politics, and Reform: Collective Action, Social Movements, and Cycles of Protest*, pp. 32–38.

127. "Sozdana liberal'no-demokraticheskaia partiia," *Pravda*, April 1, 1990.

128. "Deistviia s mnimymi velichinami," *Demokraticheskaia Rossiia*, no. 1(6)

(1991); "Chto takoe 'tsentristskii blok' i nado li s nim borot'sia," *Gospodin Narod*, no. 3 (1991).

129. For the perspective of the miners and the democratic movement on the strikes and the official reaction, see "4 Marta . . . ," *Nasha Gazeta*, no. 18(73) (March 1, 1991); "Khronika zabastovki," *Nasha Gazeta*, no. 23(78) (March 19, 1991); "III s"ezd. Kommunisty Rossii: Za chto borolis'?" *Nasha Gazeta*, no. 29(84) (April 9, 1991); "Zapomnim etot den'," *Demokraticheskaia Rossiia*, no. 3(9) (April 5, 1991); "Iz shakhterskikh regionov," *Demokraticheskaia Rossiia*, no. 4(10) (April 12, 1991); "Tak kuda zhe poidut shakhtery?" *Rossiia*, March 23–29, 1991.

130. Interview with S. E. Morgunov, March 14, 1991, Moscow.

131. Obolenskii interview, February 7, 1991.

132. Arato and Cohen, "Social Movements, Civil Society, and the Problem of Sovereignty," pp. 274–75.

133. Keane, *Democracy and Civil Society*, p. 61.

134. An interesting examination of how various "sectors of civil society" drew on each other for support during transitions in Latin America appears in Alfred Stepan, "State Power and the Strength of Civil Society in the Southern Cone of Latin America," in Peter B. Evans, Dietrich Rueschemeyer, and Theda Skocpol, eds., *Bringing the State Back In*, pp. 317–45. The degree of development of institutional networks and sources of support available to independent societal actors in Latin American cases stood in stark—and favorable—contrast to those enjoyed by such actors in Russia.

135. "Demokraticheskaia Rossiia," *Novaia Zhizn'*, no. 23(32) (1990).

136. Bogdanov interview, June 17, 1991, Moscow.

137. Ibid.

138. Travkin interview, January 31, 1991.

139. "Obshchepoliticheskaia rezoliutsiia," *Pozitsiia*, no. 13 (1990); See also "Spasat' strany ili KPSS," in same issue.

140. "Zaiavlenie pervogo plenuma soveta predstavitelei dvizheniia 'Demokraticheskaia Rossiia'"; "Rezoliutsiia pervogo plenuma soveta predstavitelei dvizheniia 'Demokraticheskaia Rossiia'"; "Rezoliutsiia koordinatsionnogo soveta dvizheniia 'Demokraticheskaia Rossia' k itogam 4-go S"ezda narodnykh deputatov SSSR," *Dvizhenie "Demokraticheskaia Rossiia", Informatsionnyi biulleten'*, no. 1 (January 1991).

141. Author's minutes, meeting of the coordinating soviet of Democratic Russia, January 31, 1991, Moscow.

142. On the miners' strategy and thinking, see "Rekomendovano: C Ianaevym ne vstrechat'siia," *Nasha Gazeta*, no. 12(67) (February 8, 1991); and articles in same newpaper as cited in note 129 above.

143. "Leningrad," *NSD*, no. 1 (September 1990). See also "Novosibirsk" in same issue.

144. On public opinion ratings of alternative parties as of the beginning of 1991, see "'Pravyi povorot' glazami izbiratelei," *Gospodin Narod*, no. 3(1991).

145. Kriger interview, June 17, 1991.

146. See "Bor'ba za pressu v fokuse bor'by za vlast'," and "Ostorozhno: TASS!" *Demokraticheskaia Rossiia*, no. 5 (November 1990); "I belyi El'tsin v boi nas pobedet," *Demokraticheskaia Gazeta*, no. 3 (March 17, 1991).

147. "Vozglavit li El'tsin novuiu partiiu?" *Gospodin Narod*, no. 3 (1991). In the early 1970s, Samuel Barnes argued that political parties served as the crucial component of the "multiple autonomous communication channels" that served as "the strategic factor in democracy." As Geoffrey Pridham has recently written, the growing diversity and sophistication of the media has diminished the function of parties as providers of information and channels of communication in many democracies in recent decades. In Russia during the Gorbachev period, however, the persistence of state control over much of the media meant that autonomous political organizations to some degree played a role—or attempted to play a role—similar to that fulfilled by their counterparts in the West in earlier decades. Samuel H. Barnes, "Democracy and the Organization of Political Parties: Some Speculations," in William E. Wright, ed., *A Comparative Study of Party Organization*, pp. 86–87; Geoffrey Pridham, "Southern European Democracies on the Road to Consolidation: A Comparative Assessment of the Role of Political Parties," in Geoffrey Pridham, ed., *Securing Democracy: Political Parties and Democratic Consolidation in Southern Europe*, p. 37.

148. "Predlozheniia po proryvu informatsionnoi blokady," *NSD*, no. 12 (March 1991).

149. "Kak sozdat' organizatsiiu 'Demokraticheskoi Rossii' po mesty raboty," *Dvizhenie "Demokraticheskaia Rossiia," Informatsionnyi biulleten'*, no. 6 (March 1991).

150. Kriger interview, June 17, 1991.

151. Membership and work in the soviets conferred a certain personal prestige as well. Each deputy in soviets on all levels was given a *znachok*, a small badge that signified status as an elected official. The size and luster of the badges varied according to the level of the soviet in which an individual served, with larger, more handsome badges signifying deputyship in the USSR or republican legislatures, and smaller, simpler ones denoting membership in soviets on lower levels. Most deputies, regardless of political orientation, would not be seen outside the home without the *znachok* affixed to the shirt or the lapel of the jacket. Indeed, after encounters with several hundred deputies from soviets at all levels in cities throughout Russia over a three-year period, I can recall only a handful of instances in which a deputy was seen in public without his or her *znachok*.

152. See the commentary and analysis of Il'ia Zaslavskii, the progressive chairman of Moscow's October District Soviet, in "Khvatit boltat'—davaite rabotat'!" *Demokraticheskaia Rossiia*, no. 4 (October 1990).

153. See William E. Odom, "Alternative Perspectives on the August Coup," *Problems of Communism* (November–December 1991): 15–16.

154. Author's minutes, Plenum of Democratic Russia, February 22, 1991, Moscow.

155. See Iurii Afanas'ev's perceptive remarks on this problem in "Politicheskoe liderstvo pereshlo k rabochim," *Demokraticheskaia Rossiia*, no. 10(16) (May 31, 1991).

156. Scott Mainwaring has written of a similar problem in the Brazilian case, arguing that "no other democracy grants politicians so much autonomy vis-à-

vis their parties." He describes how undisciplined parties and personalist politics have undermined representation of popular interests and robbed legislatures of the structure needed for effective operation. Yet unlike in the Russian case, parties in Brazil at least do enjoy a functional monopoly over the authority to nominate candidates for office and have achieved some capacity for structuring political competition. See Scott Mainwaring, "Politicians, Parties, and Electoral Systems: Brazil in Comparative Perspective," *Comparative Politics* 24, 1 (October 1991): 21–43.

157. Interview with G. A. Anishenko (Russian Christian Democratic Movement), March 6, 1991, Moscow.

158. "Politika ne terpit improvizatsii," *Demokraticheskaia Rossiia,* no. 2(8) (March 29, 1991).

159. Michael E. Urban, "Boris El'tsin, Democratic Russia, and the Campaign for the Russian Presidency," *Soviet Studies* 44, 2 (1992): 187–207, esp. 194. See also Sheinis's remarks on El'tsin and the democratic movement in "Politika ne terpit improvizatsii."

Chapter V
The Struggle in the Provinces: A Tale of Four Cities

1. The name of each city matches that of the oblast' (province) in which it is located. Thus, the city of Tula is located in Tula Oblast', and so on.

2. Precise determination of the percentage of total production devoted to military requirements in Russia as a whole, or in any one city, is impossible. Figures provided by the Soviet government or the U.S. CIA are absolutely unreliable. The figures presented here are based on estimates given by local officials and activists in interviews with the author. While no precise figures are available, I did find rough agreement on percentages among local inhabitants in each of the four cities.

3. For example, writing in the SDPR's national internal bulletin, the Magnitogorsk chapter of the party reported that its organization had "sixty-one members, forty-one of whom fully confirm their membership." "Sobranie Magnitogorskoi organizatsii SDPR," *Novosti Sotsial-Demokratii,* no. 4 (November 1990).

4. "Gorodskaia 'Diskussionnaia Tribuna': Proekt" (mimeo), May 23, 1988, Sverdlovsk; "Ot redaktsii," *Slovo Urala* (September 1988); interview with M. O. Borisov (Democratic Party of Russia, cochair, Movement for Democratic Reform, and deputy, Sverdlovsk Oblast' Soviet), July 4, 1991, Sverdlovsk.

5. A. Verkhovskii, "Sverdlovskii Fenomen" (mimeo), 1988, Sverdlovsk; *Ekspress Khronika* (December 13, 1987).

6. Interview with A. N. Goncharenko (Iskra and deputy, Sverdlovsk City Soviet), July 5, 1991, Sverdlovsk.

7. Interview with A. Gniadek (Democratic Union), July 4, 1991, Sverdlovsk; Goncherenko interview, July 5, 1991.

8. "Samizdat na Urale," *Duma* (Nizhnii Tagil), no. 6 (1991).

9. Interview with V. Pestov (Vozrozhdenie), July 5, 1991, Sverdlovsk.

10. "Khvatit li sil i posledova—tel'nosti? Zavisit ot nas," *Ural-Vesti*, no. 1 (1990) (Sverdlovsk).

11. "Khronika," *Duma*, no. 5 (1991); "Informatsiia, kommentarii," *Slovo Urala*, no. 3(36) (March 1991).

12. "Ne dozhiv do trekhletnego vozrasta . . . ," *Na Smenu!* (Sverdlovsk), June 13, 1991; Gniadek interview, July 4, 1991; Pestov interview, July 5, 1991.

13. Interview with V. V. Andriianov (Republican Party of Russia), March 29, 1991, Tula.

14. Ibid.

15. Interview with V. V. Zaivyn (deputy chair, Tula City Soviet), S. A. Gavrilov (deputy, Tula City Soviet), and N. I. Travin (deputy, Tula City Soviet), March 29, 1991, Tula; interview with A. Glagalev (Democratic Party of Russia), March 30, 1991, Tula; Andriianov interview, March 29, 1991; interview with V. V. Gubarev (Social Democratic Party of Russia), April 1, 1991, Tula; interview with I. E. Riabov (Russian Christian Democratic Movement), March 30, 1991, Tula; "Sotsial-demokraty: tol'ko pravo samomu rasporiazhat'sia svoei sud'boi delaet cheloveka istinno svobodnym," *Molodoi Kommunar*, August 23, 1990.

16. Interview with I. D. Liubimov (correspondent, *Molodoi Kommunar*), April 1, 1991, Tula.

17. "Den'gi dlia NPG," *KAS-KOR* (Moscow), March 16, 1991; "Moi papa—zabastovshchik," *Molodoi Kommunar*, March 21, 1991; interview with V. I. Kruginin, S. P. Itokhin, and B. B. Kntsev (miners and strike committee organizers from Mosbass mining region), March 30, 1991, Tula.

18. "Miting vozle dach," *Molodoi Kommunar*, March 30, 1991; "O mitinge," *Tula*, April 3, 1991.

19. Interview with V. K. Sosipatrov (Volgograd City Voters' Committee and Deputy, Volgograd City Soviet), June 4, 1991, Volgograd.

20. "Pretendent: v kom ishchet svoego voploshcheniia mechta o 'krepkoi ruke'?" *Ogonek*, no. 1 (January 1990).

21. Sosipatrov interview, June 4, 1991; interview with I. L. Lukashev (Social Democratic Party of Russia and deputy, Volgograd Oblast' Soviet), June 4, 1991, Volgograd; interview with V. I. Zenin (Democratic Party of Russia), June 5, 1991, Volgograd; "Otstavka 'Pretendenta,'" *Ogonek*, no. 7 (February 1990); *Izvestiia*, January 31, 1990.

22. "Volgograd," *Novosti Sotsial-Demokratii*, no. 1 (September 1990); *Ekspress Khronika*, March 6, 1990; Zenin interview, June 5, 1991; Lukashev interview, June 4, 1991; Sosipatrov interview, June 4, 1991.

23. Interview with E. G. Botvinik (cofounder and correspondent, *MIG*), June 6, 1991, Volgograd.

24. "Neformal'nyi Orel," *Pokolenie* (Orel), July 28, 1990; interview with A. V. Romash (Russian Christian Democratic Movement and Miloserdie), June 17, 1991, Moscow; interview with I. S. Mendeleevich (Memorial and correspondent, *Ekspress Khronika*), May 8, 1991, Orel.

25. Romash interview, June 17, 1991; interview with N. M. Perovskii (Democratic Party of Russia), May 9, 1991, Orel.

26. *Ekspress Khronika*, August 13, 1989, February 27, 1990, March 20, 1990, and May 29, 1990; "Neformal'nyi Orel," *Pokolenie*, July 28, 1990; "Vragam na zlo," *KAS-KOR*, March 16, 1991; Romash interview, June 17, 1991.

27. Such publications included *Golos Demokrata*, put out by the Glasnost' Society, and *Slovo*, issued by the local RKhDD. See *Ekspress Khronika*, November 26, 1989, and December 10, 1989.

28. Interview with V. V. Ostroushko (correspondent, *Pokolenie*), Orel, May 9, 1991.

29. Interview with A. I. Tretiakov (Republican Party of Russia), May 8, 1991, Orel; interview with V. A. Ziabkin (Democratic Party of Russia), May 10, 1991, Orel; Romash interview, June 17, 1991; "Bol'shoi demokraticheskii sbor," *Pokolenie*, May 13, 1991; author's minutes, Second Conference of the Orel Oblast' organization of Democratic Russia, May 11, 1991, Orel.

30. Statements that express the positions of the ultra-radical current in Sverdlovsk appear in "Ne mozhet byt' svobodnyi narod," *Slovo Urala*, no. 5 (August 1988); "Net referendumu 17 marta," *Ekspress Khronika*, February 12, 1991.

31. During nominations in Sverdlovsk of candidates for the USSR Congress of People's Deputies, El'tsin swamped Sergei Kuznetsov, the celebrated radical activist from the Sverdlovsk Democratic Union who spent most of 1989 in jail for "anti-Soviet agitation." In nominations held in one district in Sverdlovsk, El'tsin received 1,200 votes to 37 for Kusnetsov. *Ekspress Khronika*, January 29, 1989.

32. The persistence of tension between the two currents is evident in, for example, " 'Radikal'noe' sumasshestvie," *Slovo Urala*, no. 3(36) (March 1991).

33. Personalism and El'tsin-worship were hardly unique to Sverdlovsk, but they were particularly strong there. A critique of the personalism of the local movement from a "maximalist" point of view is offered in "Takogo eshche ne bylo," in ibid.

34. "Informatsiia, kommentarii," *Slovo Urala*, no. 1(34) (January 1991); "Reshenie," *Slovo Urala*, no. 3(36) (March 1991).

35. Interview with A. I. Tanachova (El'tsin Club), July 4, 1991, Sverdlovsk.

36. Andriianov interview, March 29, 1991; Gubarev interview, April 1, 1991.

37. The official, speaking in an idiom familiar to analysts of preglasnost' Soviet political discourse, stated: "The democrats got a late start here, much later than in some other locations in Russia. But this meant that by the time movements got off the ground here, the working class and the intelligentsia were more receptive to groups with softer slogans. The first phase in Russia was characterized by a sharper approach. At that stage, groups like the Democratic Union and Pamiat [an organization of Russian chauvinists and neo-Stalinists] were especially active. But we didn't see much of them here, nor have we had much violence here at all." Interview with N. P. Polishuk, March 29, 1991, Tula.

38. Lukashev interview, June 4, 1991; Sosipatrov interview, June 4, 1991.

39. Ostroushko interview, May 9, 1991. E. A. Chernov was founder of the Glasnost' Society in Orel and the publisher of *Golos Demokrata*. Iu. V. Karpeev was the head of Fakel (Flame), a tiny local independent trade union. V. D.

Tokar was organizer of the Orel RPR. I found support for Ostroushko's assessment in documents produced by Chernov and Karpeev, conversation with Karpeev and other activists, and observation of local democrats' behavior at the Second Conference of the Democratic Russia organization of Orel Oblast'. Interview with Iu. V. Karpeev, May 9, 1991, Orel; author's minutes from above-mentioned conference; May 11, 1991, Orel; "Vse na vybory!" and "Vse na povtornye vybory!" (statements of the Workers' Democratic Union "Fakel") (mimeo), March 1990, Orel; "Dorogie Orlovtsy!" *Golos Demokrata*, "Probnaia," 1991.

Samarin's overwhelming electoral victory—he received 70 percent of the vote in a three-way race, with one of his opponents strongly supported by the local apparat—showed that popular skepticism toward many local democrats may have been due more to the modest quality of progressive leadership and organization than to popular support for conservative positions.

40. The conference of Democratic Russia mentioned above, for example, degenerated at times into chaos, shouting matches, and walkouts. According to some local activists, such behavior was not unusual and reflected the poor quality of relations among groups. Author's minutes.

41. Romash interview, June 17, 1991.

42. Ibid.

43. A thorough analysis from an opposition standpoint of the policies and general orientation of local organs of power appears in "Vechno vcherashnie ili slovo i dela sverdlovskoi partokratii," *Ural Vesti*, no. 1 (September 1990).

44. Information on changes in the provincial party organization appears in "Pervyi ukhodit v otstavku," *Izvestiia*, February 6, 1990; "Sostoialis' konferentsii," *Pravda*, June 3, 1990.

45. For example, "I u nas poiavilic' bezrabotnye," *Vechernii Sverdlovsk*, July 3, 1991. A trenchant assessment of the effects of official information blockade on the democratic movement, written from a radical democratic perspective, appears in "Novosti Demdvizheniia," *Slovo Urala* (January 1991).

46. "Informatsiia, kommentarii," *Slovo Urala* (July 1988); "Informatsiia, kommentarii," *Slovo Urala* (August 1988); *Izvestiia*, December 16, 1988; *Ekspress Khronika*, January 29, February 12, July 9, September 17, and December 3, 1989; "Zaiavlenie MDG . . . ," *Duma* (January 1991).

47. *Ekspress Khronika*, February 13, 1990.

48. Gniadek interview, July 4, 1991.

49. "Koe-chto o rabote 'kompetentnykh organov' ili interv'iu s byvshim agentom KGB," *Duma* (January 1991); Pestov interview, July 5, 1991.

50. Borisov interview, July 4, 1991; interview with Iu. M. Davydov (Democratic Party of Russia, cochair, DDV, and deputy, Sverdlovsk City Soviet), July 4, 1991, Sverdlovsk.

51. "Otkaz ot sovmeshcheniia postov," *Izvestiia*, August 26, 1990.

52. For instance, the deputy chair of the oblast' soviet, a self-proclaimed conservative Communist who spent years working in the party-state apparat, expressed to me her desire that "all forces of every type work together on the common task of improving life for our citizens." While the possibility that her remarks were tailored to the interview situation cannot be excluded, she ex-

pressed none of the contempt for "the democrats" that I often heard from other conservative officials. Furthermore, many Communist Party officials in Tula joined the local Committee in Support of El'tsin in the spring of 1991. Most democratic activists and journalists whom the author interviewed expressed extreme skepticism regarding the sincerity and intentions of such officials. But the former as a rule did acknowledge that local officialdom's desire to create an appearance of toleration set certain limits on the harshness of repression. Interview with N. N. Skachkova (CPSU and deputy chair, Tula Oblast' Soviet), March 29, 1991, Tula; Gubarev interview, April 1, 1991; Andriianov interview, March 29; "Provereno: demokratov net," *Molodoi Kommunar*, March 26, 1991.

53. Liubimov interview, April 1, 1991. Several other journalists with whom the author spoke informally corroborated Liubimov's statements. The origin of the threatening telephone calls cannot be known with certainty, but Liubimov, unsurprisingly, expressed confidence that the calls came from local KGB headquarters.

54. As in many other places, repression in smaller cities and towns in the oblast' was considerably more severe than in the provincial capital. In the nearby town of Novomoskovsk, for example, the first manifestation of opposition did not occur until March 1991, when several activists who had formed a chapter of the DPR launched a signature-gathering campaign in support of striking miners. The activists were arrested on charges of "disturbing the social peace." Interview with Kruginin, Itokhin, and Kntsev, March 30, 1991; "Pervyi politicheskii miting v Novomoskovske," *Molodoi Kommunar*, March 23, 1991; "Otpustili za otsustviem sostava prestupleniia," *Tula*, April 3, 1991; "Shantazh na apparatnom urovne," *Molodoi Kommunar*, March 26, 1991.

55. "Nashemu pokoleniiu predstoit dokazat' . . . ," *Komsomol'skaia Pravda*, May 19, 1990.

56. "Pretendent," *Ogonek*, no. 1 (January 1990).

57. One of the organizers of the association, V. K. Sosipatrov, related that even one of the group's cochairs, of which there were four at the time of founding, had been a KGB agent. Sosipatrov recounted that after he and several other group members became convinced of this fact and began investigating the suspected agent's origins, the latter left the group and departed the city. Sosipatrov interview, June 4, 1991.

58. Zenin interview, June 5, 1991.

59. Interview with D. D. Nesterov (Russian Christian Democratic Movement and deputy, Volgograd Oblast' Soviet), June 6, 1991, Volgograd. The "Constitutional Department" of the KGB was the agency responsible for combating "anticonstitutional activities." In non-Russian republics, it was dedicated largely to subverting national movements; in Russia, it monitored alternative parties and other independent political associations.

60. On privatization and the difficulties the cooperatives faced during the Gorbachev period, see Darrell Slider, "Embattled Entrepreneurs: Soviet Cooperatives in an Unreformed Society," *Soviet Studies* 43, 5 (1991): 797–821; Donald Filtzer, "The Contradictions of the Marketless Market: Self-Financing in Soviet Industrial Enterprises, 1986–90," *Soviet Studies* 43, 6 (1991): 989–1009. In the Soviet press, see "The State, Cooperatives, and Bureaucratic Capital,"

Moscow News, March 11–18, 1990; "Kooperativnoe dvizhenie v opasnosti," *Literaturnaia Gazeta*, January 31, 1990. Sverdlovsk's DDV offered its own highly critical assessment of "privatization Soviet style," which it referred to as "more plundering of the country than transition to the market," in "Privatizatsiia: apparat i zdes' nas naduvaet!" *Ural-Vesti*, no. 2 (1990); and "Konferentsiia DDV o privatizatsii" (mimeo statement of conference of DDV), January 5–6, 1991, Sverdlovsk.

61. Equivalent to about $200,000 at the black market rate prevailing at the time.

62. Interview with M. S. Tsagoianov (Social Democratic Party of Russia and director, Garant), June 5, 1991, Volgograd. The word *vlast'*, which is normally translated as "power" or "rule," connotes "the powers that be," or "the authorities." In its usage in contemporary Russian, the word corresponds roughly to what was defined in chapter 1 as the "pact of domination."

63. Romash interview, June 17, 1991; Ziabkin interview, May 10, 1991; Mendeleevich interview, May 8, 1991. Cited passages appear in "Zaiavlenie ONF" and "Femida v Orle," *Golos Demokrata* (June 1990).

64. Though Communist Party authorities forbade the managers of all typographical facilities in the oblast' to print *Golos Demokrata*, the paper's eccentric and irrepressible publisher, E. A. Chernov, did manage occasionally to gain access to publishing facilities outside the oblast'. Like other independent publications issued in Orel, such as *Slovo*, the newsletter of the RKhDD, *Golos Demokrata* never grew beyond a few printed pages and tiny runs. "Obkom protiv 'Golos Demokrata,'" *Ekspress Khronika*, November 27, 1990.

65. *Ekspress Khronika*, February 27, 1990, March 20, 1990, and May 29, 1990; Mendeleevich interview, May 8, 1991; Romash interview, June 17, 1991; Ziabkin interview, May 10, 1991.

66. For example, "Dokazatel'stvo ot protivnogo," *Orlovskaia Pravda*, January 31, 1991. Democratic commentary on the official press appears in "Rezoliutsiia soveshchaniia" (mimeo statement of the Orel Organization of Democratic Russia), February 7, 1991, Orel.

67. Interview with V. K. Kiselev (second secretary of the Orel City Communist Party Committee), May 11, 1991, Orel. In an unpublished evaluation of independent organizations drawn up in early 1991, the oblast' party committee divided groups into categories of "constructive," and "extremist and destructive." The party rated only the neo-Stalinist, "national-patriotic" organizations Edinstvo (Unity), Otechestvo (Fatherland), and OFT (United Workers' Front) as "constructive," and all remaining groups as "extremist and destructive." The assessment, which took the form of an internal party report, was obtained by local democratic activists, who showed it to the author.

68. Ziabkin interview, May 10, 1991.

69. See Zaslavsky, *The Neo-Stalinist State*, pp. 44–65. The best work on the political role and effects of state control over enterprises under socialism is Andrew Walder, *Communist Neo-Traditionalism: Work and Authority in Chinese Industry*.

70. Interview with N. A. Matveev (Social Democratic Party of Russia and Deputy, Tula Oblast' Soviet), March 30, 1991, Tula.

71. Such an image of the restless and independent enterprise director is found in Jeffery D. Sachs, "Spontaneous Privatization: A Comment," *Soviet Economy* 7, 4 (1991): 317–21.

72. See, for example, "Kak shlo vydvizhenie," *Demokraticheskaia Rossiia*, no. 10(16) (1991).

73. *Ekspress Khronika*, February 27, 1990.

74. Romash interview, June 17, 1991; Perovskii interview, May 9, 1991.

75. Tretiakov interview, May 8, 1991.

76. *Initsiativnaia Gruppa "Miting-87." Informatsionaia Biulleten'*, no. 2 (April 1988) (Sverdlovsk); "Otecheskaia zabota prokurora," *Slovo Urala* (September 1988).

77. Interview with T. E. Alaiba (Republican Party of Russia), July 4, 1991, Sverdlovsk.

78. Zaivyn from interview with Zaivyn, Gavrilov, and Travin, March 29, 1991.

79. The Tula Oblast' Soviet included 25 blue-collar workers in its membership of 223 deputies. Matveev's assertions were corroborated by a number of other democratic activists in Tula, as well as by a journalist who worked for *Tul'skaia Izvestiia*, the newspaper of the oblast' soviet. Matveev interview, March 30, 1991; interview with B. N. Dul'nev (correspondent, *Tul'skaia Izvestiia*), March 30, 1991, Tula; Riabov interview, March 30, 1991; "Shantazh na apparatnom urovne," *Molodoi Kommunar*, March 28, 1991; "Pomoch' shakhteram," *Molodoi Kommunar*, April 4, 1991.

80. O'Donnell and Schmitter, *Transitions from Authoritarian Rule*, p. 49.

81. Pre-1985 Russia was not, of course, without dissidents. Yet, due to the pervasiveness of repression, organized dissidence had been all but eliminated before 1985. Most dissident activity, such as distribution of underground leaflets, was carried out by single individuals acting alone or in loose coordination with persons in other cities. For example, the NTS, the main underground resistance group in the pre-1985 Soviet Union, comprised individuals who for the most part did not even know each other, and who communicated only occasionally and through elaborate channels designed to obscure and protect identities. Few cities were home to more than a handful of such persons. Even "pockets" of organized dissent, composed of several tens of individuals who knew each other personally and communicated on a regular basis, were exceedingly rare. For firsthand information on the NTS, I am particularly indebted to I. V. Likhunov of Sverdlovsk.

82. In his study of the sources of Congressional behavior in the United States, David Mayhew uses the term "saint" to refer to members who place matters of principle over the requirements of reelection. As Mayhew points out, such individuals may be conspicuous, but they are very few in number. David R. Mayhew, *Congress: The Electoral Connection*, pp. 15–16.

83. Interview with A. G. Kisliakov (chair, Orel City Soviet), May 11, 1991, Orel. Given the conservatism of the apparat and its enduring monopoly on material supply and distribution, it is unsurprising that Kisliakov did not regard association with the democratic movement as consistent with his responsibilities as chairman of the city soviet. As one local journalist who covered the

city soviet and knew its chairman remarked in an interview: "The party apparat, which of course controls supply of our city, is rather vengeful here. Kisliakov is perfectly well aware that if he makes progressive decisions, and if the city soviet tries to challenge the authority of the party, the city will likely soon find itself without meat or milk." Ostroushko interview, May 9, 1991.

84. Romash interview, June 17, 1991. Romash himself, who had a long personal history of organizing charitable societies and secret bible study meetings, largely fit the profile of the saint.

85. Ziabkin interview, May 10, 1991.

86. McCarthy and Zald, "Resource Mobilization and Social Movements," pp. 34–35; Mayer N. Zald and Roberta Ash Garner, "Social Movement Organizations: Growth, Decay, and Change," in Mayer N. Zald and John D. McCarthy, eds., *Social Movements in an Organizational Society: Collected Essays*, pp. 124–27.

87. For example, in the summer of 1991, a Christian college in Texas, intent on aiding the spread of the gospel in Russia, donated a fax machine to the RKhDD. The gift, along with a rousing sermon, was delivered to the party's leaders by a representative of the American institution, a Baptist minister. The speech, which included warnings on the need for vigilance in the face of imminent invasion by Mormons, Jehovah's Witnesses, and others intent on converting Russians to dubious creeds, seemed to perplex the RKhDD's leaders. They were nevertheless grateful for the donation. Author's minutes, meeting of the Duma of the RKhDD, Moscow, June 16, 1991.

88. Interview with L. A. Bogdanov (Democratic Russia), June 17, 1991, Moscow.

89. Andriianov interview, March 29, 1991.

90. Borisov interview, July 4, 1991.

91. Explaining how his local Democratic Russia organization raised funds at demonstrations, the normally restrained Andriianov exclaimed: "The *people* finance us! These three thousand rubles we just received show that we really are a people's movement!" Andriianov interview, March 29, 1991.

92. "Bol'shoi demokraticheskii sbor," *Pokolenie*, May 13, 1991.

93. Interview with V. N. Chupriianov (Sverdlovsk Union of Cooperatives), July 5, 1991, Sverdlovsk.

94. "Predprinimateli Tuly ob"edinilis'," *Molodoi Kommunar*, April 4, 1991.

95. Chupriianov interview, July 5, 1991.

96. Interview with E. G. Kostitsyn (Democratic Party of Russia), July 4, 1991, Sverdlovsk; Borisov interview, July 4, 1991; Alaiba interview, July 4, 1991.

97. Chupriianov interview, July 5, 1991.

98. Andriianov interview, March 29, 1991.

99. "Konkurenty raz"ediniaiutsia," *Volzhskie Novosti*, no. 21(39), June 1991; author's minutes, founding conference of the Volgograd Union of Entrepreneurs, June 6, 1991, Volgograd.

100. Tsagoianov interview, June 5, 1991.

101. Nesterov interview, June 6, 1991.

102. In personal conversations with the author, some activists in Orel expressed fear and skepticism regarding the "reliability" of fellow democrats. In

Volgograd, by contrast, groups held together famously. *Every* democratic leader interviewed reported good relations with all other democratic organizations—claims for which I found support during days spent at the local headquarters of Democratic Russia. For evidence of mistrust among democrats in Orel, see *Ekspress Khronika*, February 12, 1991; "Konferentsiia MOI," *Slovo*, no. 2 (August 1990).

103. The Second Conference of the Orel Oblast' Democratic Russia, held in May 1991 and attended by the author, was a tumultuous and rancorous affair, filled with accusations and counteraccusations. As discussed in chapter 4, meetings of democratic activists were rarely orderly and well-run events, even under the best of circumstances. Yet the conference in Orel was the most contentious and unproductive of the several dozen meetings I attended in ten Russian cities during 1989–91. Author's minutes, Democratic Russia conference, May 11, 1991, Orel.

104. Author's minutes, meeting of the coordinating soviet of Democratic Russia of Tula, Tula, March 29, 1991.

105. "DDV: a za okoshkom bylo . . . ," *Ural Vesti*, no. 5 (1991); Davydov interview, July 4, 1991.

106. Gross, *The Revolutionary Party*, pp. 41–57; Lawson, *The Comparative Study of Political Parties*, pp. 71–80.

107. See, for example, "'KGB reshil ostanovit' Gorbacheva': Rol' KGB v glasnosti i perestroike glazami vysokopostavlennogo perebezhchika," *Gospodin Narod*, no. 5 (1991).

108. See G. Davidenko, "Dve sessii," *Duma*, no. 6 (1991).

109. Comment of V. Beliaev, "Vlast' prikhodit i ukhodit . . . ," *Ural-Vesti*, no. 3 (1990).

110. "Khvatit li sil . . . ," *Ural-Vesti*, no. 1 (1990).

111. Interview with Zaivyn, Gavrilov, and Travin, March 29, 1991 (quoted passage by Gavrilov); Polishuk interview, March 29, 1991.

112. Gavrilov from interview with Zaivyn, Gavrilov, and Travin, March 29, 1991.

113. Articles that deal with the subject include "Vlast' goroda: deklaratsii i real'nost'," *Slovo Urala* (January 1991); "Peizazh posle bitvy," *Demokraticheskaia Rossiia*, no. 3(9) (1991).

114. Information on the composition, orientation, and activities of soviets is drawn from interviews with local deputies and published sources. From Tula: interviews with Skachkova, Zaivyn, Gavrilov, and Travin, Matveev; and with S. I. Kireev (deputy, Tula City Soviet), March 29, 1991, Tula; also "Aleksandr Kostikov v novom amplue," *Molodoi Kommunar*, March 23, 1991; "Chtoby vraz i vse vmeste," *Molodoi Kommunar*, March 28, 1991. From Sverdlovsk: interviews with Goncharenko, Davydov, Borisov; and with N. M. Kalinkin (deputy, Sverdlovsk Oblast' Soviet), July 5, 1991, Sverdlovsk; also "Novosti demokraticheskogo dvizheniia," *Slovo Urala* (January 1991); "Vlast' prikhodit i ukhodit," *Ural-Vesti*, no. 3 (1990); "Khvatit li sil . . ." and "Vechno vcherashnie . . . ," *Ural-Vesti*, No. 1, 1990; "Svoevremennye mysli," *Duma*, no. 4 (1991); "Fraktsiia DPR v Sverdlovskom gorsovete," *Ural-Vesti*, no. 2 (1990). From Orel:

interviews with Kisliakov, Kiselev, and Ostroushko; also "V gorsovete krizis vlasti?" *Pokolenie*, May 13, 1991. From Volgograd: interviews with Lukashev, Sosipatrov, Nesterov, and Botvinik; also "DPR idet v step'," *Volzhskie Novosti*, no. 10 (October 1990).

115. Such a conclusion is found, for example, in Jeffrey Hahn's study of local politics in Iaroslavl'. While Hahn concedes that "nomenklatura-appointed collective farm chairmen were in a better position to offer rewards for political support than their opponents," he attributes the strength of conservative candidates in nonurban areas largely to "a division of political opinion among Russians—between those from the relatively more liberal cities and their more conservative country cousins." Such an urban-rural cleavage, according to Hahn, "is reminiscent of divisions found in parts of the United States, say, between Chicago and downstate Illinois." Hahn does add that "while it may be tempting to conclude that a conservative 'silent majority' exists in rural Russia, it is not clear whether the reasons for it are comparable" to those found in Illinois. The analysis offered in the present chapter suggests strongly that "the reasons for it" are in fact disparate. Jeffrey W. Hahn, "Local Politics and Political Power in Russia: The Case of Yaroslavl'," *Soviet Economy* 7, 4 (1991): 327–28. See also Gregory J. Embree, "RSFSR Election Results and Roll Call Votes," *Soviet Studies* 43, 6 (1991), pp. 1065–84.

116. Other aspects of the nominating process, including provisions requiring the validation of candidacies by local electoral committees, also reduced democrats' prospects. These committees, which Michael Urban refers to as "filters," caused trouble for democrats in major cities as well as less urban areas. But conservative control of such committees and of the nominating process as a whole was usually more pronounced outside large cities. Urban, *More Power to the Soviets*, pp. 37–43, 71–72, 90–100. Information on the electoral process in cities covered in this chapter appears in *Ekspress-Khronika*, September 24, 1989, February 13, 1990, and March 13, 1990; "Narodovlastie po-bol'shevistskii," *Slovo Urala* (June 1989).

117. I am indebted to many interviewees for insights into how this system operated in Russia, but especially to B. N. Dul'nev and N. A. Matveev of Tula.

118. Davydov interview, July 4, 1991. The DDV, like other organizations that functioned as voters' clubs, was involved in campaigns for raion (district) soviets as well as for soviets on higher levels. District soviets, which are not discussed in this chapter, tended to be more conservative than city soviets. Democrats focused their efforts on the levels of cities and oblasts, often leaving districts largely in the hands of minor Communist Party functionaries and enterprise directors. Thus, city soviets that contained significant numbers of democrats tended, in Russian parlance, to "orient themselves" toward the RSFSR Supreme Soviet; the more conservative district soviets oriented themselves toward oblast' soviets, which in turn oriented themselves toward the USSR Supreme Soviet. In the competition within this bewildering hierarchy of legislatures (one may think of the whole complex as a Big Mac, with more conservative bodies as the bread and more liberal ones as the meat patties) lay the institutional source of what became known as the "war of laws" in Russia

during 1990–91. There were, or course, notable exceptions to the conservatism of the district soviets. The October Raion Soviet in Moscow, for example, was a site of radical activity and reform.

119. Goncharenko interview, July 5, 1991.

120. Ibid.; Davydov interview, July 4, 1991; Borisov interview, July 4, 1991; Kalinkin interview, July 5, 1991; interview with N. N. Bragin (Memorial), July 5, 1991, Sverdlovsk; "Vlast' goroda: deklaratsii i real'nost'," *Slovo Urala*, January 1991; and "Khvatit li sil . . . ," *Ural-Vesti*, no. 1 (1990).

121. For example, "Nachalo vsekh nachal," *Tula*, January 23, 1991.

122. Lukashev interview, June 4, 1991; interview with V. I. Mironenko (Democratic Russia and deputy, Volgograd City Soviet), June 4, 1991, Volgograd; Sosipatrov interview, June 4, 1991; Botvinik interview, June 6, 1991.

Across cities and oblasts, progressive deputies as a rule attended soviet sessions with greater regularity than conservative deputies. Many of the latter were enterprise directors or Communist Party officials who desired membership in a soviet but who had little interest in attending sessions. In most soviets, such as those of Sverdlovsk, Tula, and Orel oblasts, or of the city of Orel, conservatives enjoyed such numerical predominance and control over procedure that the absence of even a substantial portion of their own adherents at sessions did not threaten conservative control. In soviets such as those of Sverdlovsk city and Volgograd city and oblast', however, where neither progressive nor conservative deputies enjoyed overwhelming majorities, attendance mattered. In Sverdlovsk, where discipline among democrats left much to be desired, democrats often missed sessions at rates equivalent to those of their conservative rivals, thus squandering opportunities for effective action. In Volgograd, however, where democrats manifested better discipline and attendance, they sometimes won. Comparison across cases illustrates the analytical pitfalls involved in relying on "fraction democratic" in local soviets as a measure of the strength of democratic forces in a given city or oblast', even in the soviets themselves.

123. Kireev interview, March 29, 1991, Tula. Similar assessments by progressive deputies and activists appear in "Dve sessii," *Duma*, no. 6 (1991); "Vlast' prikhodit i ukhodit," *Ural-Vesti*, no. 3 (1990); "V gorsovete krizis vlasti?" *Pokolenie*, May 13, 1991.

Chapter VI
Democracy from Scratch

1. "Beg po zamknutomy krugu," *Izvestiia*, December 28, 1991; "Partiinye boitsy dokazali boitsovskie kachestva i v nashe vremiia," *Izvestiia*, March 27, 1992.

2. "Boris El'tsin: okrik na pressu nedopustim," *Kuranty*, July 18, 1992.

3. Popular fronts based on ethnicity, of course, cannot be regarded as unmixed blessings; nor should the absence of a strong ethnic popular front in Russia be seen in a wholly negative light. Such groups may serve as sources of unity, identity, and organization during struggles against authoritarian rule. But they sometimes degenerate into chauvinism and become sources of divi-

sion and conflict after the old regime's collapse. Indeed, ethnic popular fronts in, for example, Ukraine, Azerbaijan, and the Baltic states have not necessarily facilitated democratic transitions since the dissolution of the Soviet Union.

4. The consequences of this situation were evident in the events that followed the putsch and that forged the initial basis for the post-Soviet transition. As Timothy Colton correctly noted in a recent article, "the Soviet Union's end was crafted, not by representatives of the state in concert with a political opposition and private groups, but by public officials alone, working for the most part behind closed doors. The compact reached was one *among governments*, meaning by this time the cooperating republic governments. Nongovernmental players were not welcome at the table and were informed of what had been decided only after the fact." Timothy Colton, "Politics," in Timothy J. Colton and Robert Legvold, eds., *After the Soviet Union: From Empire to Nations*, pp. 20–21.

5. Vladimir Bukovsky, "Tumbling Back to the Future," *The New York Times Magazine*, January 12, 1992.

6. On El'tsin's extraordinary personal role and popularity in the early post-coup period, see "Nad vsei Rossiei bezoblachnoe nebo," *Rossiia*, October 16–22, 1991; "Boris El'tsin: 100 dnei posle pobedy," *Rossiia*, October 23–29, 1991.

7. "My podderzhivaem El'tsina uslovno," *Izvestiia*, October 7, 1991; "U radikalov i resheniia radikal'nye," *Rossiiskaia Gazeta*, March 26, 1992.

8. "Gaidar-Khasbulatovu: kak ia vyzhil, budem znat' tol'ko my s toboi," *Kommersant*, April 6–13, 1992; "N. Travkin: 'Ia—chelovek rezkikh suzhdenii,'" *Argumenty i Fakty* 32 (August 1992); "Semero s lozhkoi, odin s ploshkoi. S pustoi," *Kommersant*, March 23–30, 1992; "El'tsin: s glazy na glaz s partiiami," *Nezavisimiia Gazeta*, March 26, 1992.

9. "Vsevyshnii ... parlament," *Moskovskii Komsomolets*, July 21, 1992; "Spiker-solntse: Parlament—eto ia!'" *Kommersant*, August 24–31, 1992; "Hopes for a Constitution Die Hard," and "Khasbulatov Prepares for a New Parliamentary Season," *Moscow News*, September 13–20, 1992.

10. "Posle referenduma El'tsin okazhetsiia litsom k litsu s oppozitsiei," *Rossiiskaia Gazeta*, June 9, 1992; "El'tsin pogovoril s kazakami," *Nezavisimaia Gazeta*, July 23, 1992; "Direktor oblasti, ili kak razgryzt' kisel'," *Rossiiskaia Gazeta*, July 23, 1992.

11. "Za 'makroekonomiku' poluchi po 'makrobashke'!" *Kuranty*, July 18, 1992; "Pridet i spaset?" *Argumenty i Fakty* 34 (September 1992); "Tovaroproizvoditeli reshili proizvesti. Smenu pravitel'stva," *Kommersant*, August 10–17, 1992; "Naznachenie zampredov TsB: novye—eto khorosho zabytye starye," *Kommersant*, August 17–24, 1992; "Ekho bankovskoi voiny: pobeditelei vozglavili pobezhdennye," *Kommersant*, July 13–20, 1992.

12. See "Nomenklatura na 'skhodke vechevoi,'" *Nezavisimaia Gazeta*, April 2, 1992; "'Nam grozit nomenklaturnyi revansh!'" *Izvestiia*, April 3, 1992; "Nomenklaturnyi revansh?" *Rossiia*, March 11–17 and May 20–26, 1992.

13. "El'tsin i VS: 'etichiskie soobrazheniia' byli, da splyli," *Kommersant*, July 27–August 3, 1992.

14. "El'tsin—'Demrossii': moi laskovyi manezhnyi zver'," *Kommersant*, April 20–27, 1992.

15. "Kadety protiv superpartii," *Moskovskaia Pravda*, January 23, 1992; "Poslednii raskol demrossii?" *Moskovskie Novosti*, August 2, 1992.

16. "Irina Khakamada: Professor-Turned-Politician," *Commersant*, July 28, 1992; "A. Rutskoi: 'Ia—shovinist'," *Russkii Vestnik*, March 18–25, 1992; "Partiia Ekonomicheskoi Svobody vykhodit na tsenu," *Izvestiia*, June 15, 1992.

17. "Demokraty pereshli v oppozitsiiu," *Izvestiia*, May 31, 1992.

18. On the localization and regionalization of power and political activity, see "Zashchitit' sil'nogo," *Rossiia*, June 10–16, 1992; "Formiruetsia sibirskaia oppozitsiia," *Izvestiia*, March 26, 1992; "Sibir' trebuet dekolonizatsii," *Izvestiia*, March 30, 1992.

19. "Poslednii raskol demrossi?"; "Narod dolzhen kak mozhno men'she interesovat'sia politikoi," *Moskovskii Komsomolets*, June 18, 1992; "Grazhdanskii Soiuz: oppozitsiia, no konstruktivnaia," *Izvestiia*, June 22, 1992; "Rossiiskie vlasti: ikh ostavalos' tol'ko troe," *Kommersant*, August 3–10, 1992; "Bei zhidov, spasai Rossiiu, sleites' v radosti odnoi," *Kommersant*, August 24–31, 1992.

20. Unsurprisingly, such erratic and unprincipled behavior by leaders has created serious divisions within groups. For example, Gleb Iakunin quit the RKhDD over Aksiuchits's growingly vitriolic nationalism. For the same reasons, Aleksandr Romash, head of the Central Russian organization of the RKhDD, withdrew from the party in the fall of 1992. He took a number of city organizations with him and launched a new Christian Democratic group outside the RKhDD. Interview with Aleksandr Romash, October 6, 1992, Moscow.

21. For insights on how the widespread persistence in positions of authority of state officials from the pretransition period may encourage "silence and complicity" on the part of democratic opponents of the old order, see Guillermo O'Donnell, "Transitions, Continuities, Paradoxes," p. 40.

22. "Ni ogna uz politicheskikh sil ne imeet reshaiushchego perevesa," *Izvestiia*, August 24, 1992.

23. "Government Undaunted by Strikes?" and "Labour Disputes to Heighten," *Moscow News*, September 13–20, 1992.

24. O'Donnell and Schmitter, *Transitions from Authoritarian Rule*, pp. 57–64.

25. See "Hopes for a Constitution Die Hard," *Moscow News*, September 13–20, 1992.

26. Problems arising from the weakness of intermediary associations in the transition and posttransition periods are not, of course, unique to Russia. They are found, in varying degrees of intensity, in all postsocialist countries. For analysis of this issue with regard to a case that in some ways resembles that of Russia, see Gail Kligman, "Reclaiming the Public: A Reflection on Creating Civil Society in Romania," *East European Politics and Societies* 4, 3 (Fall 1990): 393–438. For a brief, preliminary comparison of transitions from socialist and nonsocialist authoritarian regimes, with reference to problems of interest intermediation, see Michael Burton, Richard Gunther, and John Higley, "Elites and Democratic Consolidation in Latin America and Southern Europe: An Overview," in John Higley and Richard Gunther, eds., *Elites and Democratic Consolidation in Latin America and Southern Europe*, pp. 345–46.

27. On the concept of *dictablanda*, see O'Donnell and Schmitter, *Transitions from Authoritarian Rule*, p. 9.

28. On the crucial link between elections and development of the party system, see Sergei Stankevich's article, "Chto takoe partiinaia zhizn' segodnia," *Izvestiia*, April 20, 1992.

29. See Mainwaring, "Politicians, Parties, and Electoral Systems," pp. 21–42.

30. Juan Linz, "The Perils of Presidentialism," *Journal of Democracy* 1, 1 (Winter 1990): 51–69; Juan Linz, Seymour Martin Lipset, and Donald Horowitz, "Debate—Presidents vs. Parliaments," *Journal of Democracy* 1, 4 (Fall 1990): 73–91.

31. El'tsin quoted in "Yeltsin Warns Regions Not to Resist Future," *The Moscow Times*, September 15, 1992.

32. Ample evidence has come to light since the coup that supports the assumptions made in this study regarding the pervasiveness of KGB activities against the opposition during the 1985–91 period. Fresh evidence also demonstrates that Gorbachev and other top party officials endorsed and directed these operations. "El'tsin byl pod kolpakom u Kriuchkova . . . A Gorbachev—u Boldina?" *Rabochaia Tribuna*, January 7, 1992; "Protsess krepchal," *Moskovskii Komsomolets*, July 28, 1992.

33. "El'tsin byl pod kolpakom . . . ," *Rabochaia Tribuna*, January 7, 1992; Alexander Rahr, "The KGB Survives under Yeltsin's Wing," *RFE/RL Research Report* 1, 13 (March 27, 1992); "Subjects of the KGB," *Moscow News*, April 1, 1992; J. Michael Waller, "When Will Democrats Control the Former KGB?" *Demokratizatsiya: The Journal of Post-Soviet Democratization* 1, 1 (Summer 1992): 27–39.

34. "Goskomimushchestvo: predprinimateli i babushki budut dovol'ny," *Kommersant*, July 27–August 3, 1992; "Ukaz o privatizatsionnykh chekakh: pochem vaucher dlia naroda?" *Kommersant*, August 17–24, 1992.

35. In a fine recent article on Poland, a country that began its transition to capitalism and democracy several years before Russia and that never experienced the degree of economic étatization that Russia did, Krzysztof Jasiewicz notes: "There is an abundance of entrepreneurs in Poland, but they operate as loose cannons, free riders, hit-and-run businessmen; there is no cohesive middle class." Krzysztof Jasiewicz, "From Solidarity to Fragmentation," *Journal of Democracy* 3, 2 (April 1992): 67–68.

36. "What Will Be the Price of 'Vouchers'?" *Moscow News*, September 13–20, 1992; "State Committee Objects to Ministry Plan," *Commersant*, September 15, 1992.

37. Rapid decentralization of power, combined with privatization that is skewed sharply in favor of enterprise directors, may actually preserve some elements of the "dictatorship over needs," albeit in somewhat altered form. For a perceptive and wide-ranging analysis that addresses this problem, see Richard E. Ericson, "Economics," in Colton and Legvold, eds., *After the Soviet Union*, pp. 49–83, esp. p. 58.

38. The idea and process of democratic "consolidation" deserve more extensive treatment than they receive here. A sophisticated conceptual discussion appears in Valenzuela, "Democratic Consolidation in Post-Transitional Settings," pp. 57–104.

39. On the distinction between "state" and "societal" corporatism, see Phi-

lippe C. Schmitter, "Still the Century of Corporatism?" *Review of Politics* 36, 1 (1974): 85–131.

40. The question posed here touches on the possible nature of capitalism itself in post-Soviet Russia. In comparing Brazilian with other forms of capitalism in Latin America, Guillermo O'Donnell remarks that "Brazilian capitalism is quite dynamic. . . what comes to mind is the more bourgeois nature of this capitalism: it is more productive, less speculative, and more oriented toward the accumulation of capital in its own market than most countries of Spanish America." O'Donnell, "Transitions, Continuities, Paradoxes," p. 40. My own guess is that Russian capitalism, particularly if it develops under an authoritarian political system, will be rather more Spanish-American than Brazilian; more Philippine than South Korean or Taiwanese.

Epilogue

1. On the concept of "possiblism," see Albert O. Hirschman, *A Bias for Hope: Essays on Development in Latin America*, pp. 28–29, 35–37.

2. See "Perevarot imeni Gaidara," *Moskovskii Komsomolets*, July 10, 1993; "Poschitali—proslezilic'," *Moskovskii Komsomolets*, August 19, 1993; "Sergei Shakhrai: my stroim svoiu partiiu tak, kak khoteli by postroit' novoe rossiiskoe gosudarstvo," *Izvestiia*, August 19, 1993.

3. "Investment Crisis Stalls, Privatization Picks up Steam" and "Far East Leads the Way in Privatization," *Commersant*, April 28, 1993; Maxim Boycko, Andrei Shleifer, and Robert W. Vishny, "Privatizating Russia" (paper prepared for the Brookings Panel on Economic Activity, September 9–10, 1993), p. 1.

4. "Vaucher protiv skeptikov," *Kuranty*, July 20, 1991; "Vaucherofobiia," *Moskovskii Komsomolets*, July 24, 1993; "Share Prices in Moscow Go Through the Roof" and "Privatization Auctions Now a Daily Occurrence," *Commersant*, June 16, 1993.

5. A fine treatment of the issue is found in Blair A. Ruble, "The Politics of Property in Iaroslavl'" (paper prepared for the annual meeting of the American Association for the Advancement of Slavic Studies, Honolulu, Hawaii, November 19, 1993).

6. "Parlamentu nuzhny umnye a ne kriklivye deputaty," *Kuranty*, July 3, 1993; "Eshche odin referendum obeshchaiut nam liberaly," *Moskovskii Komsomolets*, May 22, 1993.

Bibliography

Materials Issued by Independent Russian/Soviet Sources

(Publishers and sites of publication are listed in parentheses. Where no publisher is cited, the publication was not affiliated with a particular political organization; where no site of publication is listed, publication was based in Moscow.)

Al'ternativa (Democratic Union)
Al'ternativa (Social Democratic Party of Russia)
Al'ternativa i Reporter
Biulleten' partiino-politicheskoi informatsii (Social Democratic Party of Russia)
"Deklaratsiia Moskovskoi regional'noi konferentsii Demokraticheskoi Platformy," (Democratic Platform of the CPSU, mimeo, October 13–14, 1990)
Demokraticheskaia Gazeta (Democratic Party of Russia)
Demokraticheskaia Platforma (Democratic Platform of the CPSU)
"Demokraticheskaia Platforma, organizatsionnyi komitet uchreditel'nogo s"ezda" (Democratic Platform of the CPSU, mimeo by V. N. Shostakovskii, September 8–9, 1990)
Demokraticheskaia Rossiia (Democratic Russia)
Dokumenty, 2-i s"ezd partii, "Demokraticheskii Soiuz" (Democratic Union)
Doverie
DS: Biulleten' soveta partii (Democratic Union)
DS: Dokumenty 2-go s"ezda, 1989 (Democratic Union)
Duma ("Vozrozhdenie," Nizhnii Tagil)
Dvizhenie "Demokraticheskaia Rossiia," Informatsionnyi biulleten' (Democratic Russia)
Ekspress Khronika
Epokha
Esdek (Social Democratic Party of Russia, Leningrad)
Golos Demokrata ("Glasnost' Society," Orel)
Golos Izbratelia
"Gorodskaia 'Diskussionnaia Tribuna': Proekt" (mimeo, May 23, 1988, Sverdlovsk)
Gospodin Narod (Republican Party of Russia)
Grazhdanskoe Dostoinstvo (Party of Constitutional Democrats)
Informatsionnyi biulleten' mezhregional'noi gruppy narodnykh deputatov SSSR (Interregional Deputies Group of the USSR Congress of People's Deputies)
Initsiativnaia Gruppa "Miting-87." Informatsionnyi Biulleten' (Sverdlovsk)
Kadety: Sbornik dokumentov, 1990 (Party of Constitutional Democrats)
Kapital (Party of Free Labor)
KAS-KOR (Informational Bulletin of the Workers' and Syndicalists' Movement)

Kommersant/Commersant

Kommiunike 3'go plenuma pravleniia SDPR, December 22–23, 1990 (Social Democratic Party of Russia)

"Konferentsiia DDV o privatizatsii" (Movement for Democratic Choice, mimeo, January 5–6, 1991, Sverdlovsk)

Kuzbasskie Vedomosti (United Workers of the Kuzbass, Novokuznetsk)

Materialy uchreditel'nogo s"ezda Respublikanskoi Partii Rossiiskoi Federatsii, Sbornik N. 1 (Republican Party of Russia, 1990)

Molodezhnaia Informatsionnaia Gazeta [MIG] (Volgograd)

Moskovskii Men'shevik (Social Democratic Party of Russia)

Moskovskii Sotsial-Demokrat (Social Democratic Party of Russia)

Nash Vybor (Moscow Popular Front)

Nasha Gazeta (United Workers of the Kuzbass, Kemerovo)

Nevskie Zapiski (Leningrad)

Nevskii Kur'er (Leningrad Popular Front, Leningrad)

Nezavisimaia Gazeta

Novaia Zhizn' (Social Democratic Party of Russia)

Novosti Narodnogo Fronta, Informatsionnyi biulleten' Moskovskogo Narodnogo Fronta (Moscow Popular Front)

Novosti Sotsial-Demokratii (Social Democratic Party of Russia)

Obnovlenie: Gazeta kommunistov-reformatorov (Democratic Platform of the CPSU, Leningrad)

"Ot kommunisticheskoi imperii k novomy gosudarstvu" (Declaration of the Duma of the Russian Christian Democratic Movement, January 17, 1991)

Otkrytaia Zona (Social Democratic Association)

Panorama

Pervyi (uchreditel'nyi) s"ezd Ob"edinennogo Fronta Trudiashchikhsia Rossii: Dokumenty i materialy (United Workers' Front of Russia, Sverdlovsk, 1989)

Pervyi (uchreditel'nyi) s"ezd Ob"edinennogo Fronta Trudiashchikhsia SSSR: Dokumenty i materialy (United Workers' Front of the USSR, Leningrad, 1989)

Pozitsiia and *Press-biulleten'—Pozitsiia*

"Predlozhenie orgkomiteta 'o nazvanii budushchei partii'," (Republican Party of Russia, mimeo, 1990)

Put' (Russian Christian Democratic Movement)

Put' progressa i sotsial'noi demokratii: Osnova Programmy SDPR (Social Democratic Party of Russia, Moscow-Sverdlovsk, 1990)

Respublika (Republican Party of Russia)

"Rezoliutsiia soveshchaniia" (Orel Organization of Democratic Russia, mimeo, February 7, 1991)

RKhDD: Sbornik materialov (Russian Christian Democratic Movement, 1990)

Russkaia Mysl' (Paris)

Sbornik dokumentov Grazhdanskogo Komiteta "Novyi Forum" (New Forum)

Slovo (Russian Christian Democratic Movement, Orel)

Slovo Urala (Sverdlovsk)

Spravochnik Periodicheskogo Samizdata, 1990.

"Sravnitel'nyi analiz programmnykh dokumentov Sotsial-demokraticheskoi i

Respublikanskoi partii Rossiiskoi Federatsii," *Ob"edinenie dvukh partii: Problemy i perspektivy, Diskussionnyi listok, 1990* (Social Democratic Party of Russia and Republican Party of Russia)

"Sverdlovskii Fenomen" (A. Verkhovskii, mimeo, Sverdlovsk)

Svoboda i Zhizn'

Svobodnoe Slovo (Democratic Union)

"Tonutsii korabl' Demplatformy" (V. Pribylovskii, mimeo, Democratic Platform of the CPSU, July 1990)

Ural-Vesti (Sverdlovsk)

"Ustav Dvizheniia 'Demokraticheskaia Rossiia'" (Democratic Russia, mimeo, 1990)

Vestnik Khristianskoi Demokratii (Christian Democratic Union)

Vestnik rabochego dvizheniia (Iaroslavl')

Volzhskaia vstrecha: Sbornik dokumentov (Volgograd, 1989)

Volzhskie Novosti (Volzhskii)

"Vse na vybory!" and "Vse na povtornye vybory!" (Workers' Democratic Union "Fakel," mimeo, Orel, 1990)

Vystuplenie na 4-om s"ezde narodnykh deputatov SSSR, Narodnogo Deputata V. Lopatina (Social Democratic Party of Russia, mimeo, 1990)

I s"ezd nezavisimykh rabochykh dvizhenii i organizatsii, Deklaratsiia osnovnykh printsipov konfederatsii truda (Confederation of Labor, Novokuznetsk, 1990)

IV Konferentsiia soiuza trudiashchikhsia Kuzbassa (United Workers of the Kuzbass, November 18–19, 1989, Novokuznetsk)

Official Russian/Soviet Newspapers and Periodicals

Argumenty i Fakty

Izvestiia

Komsomol'skaia Pravda

Kuranty (Moscow City Soviet)

Literaturnaia Gazeta

Molodoi Kommunar (Tula)

Molodoi Leninets (Volgograd)

Moskovskaia Pravda

Moskovskie Novosti/Moscow News

Moskovskii Komsomolets

Na Smenu! (Sverdlovsk)

Ogonek

Orlovskaia Pravda (Orel)

Pokolenie (Orel)

Pravda

Rabochaia Tribuna

Rossiia (Supreme Soviet of the RSFSR/Russian Republic)

Rossiiskaia Gazeta (Supreme Soviet of the Russian Republic)

Sotsialisticheskaia Industriia

Sovetskaia Rossiia

Trud
Tula (Tula City Soviet)
Vechernii Sverdlovsk (Sverdlovsk)

Soviet Sources in Translation

Foreign Broadcast Information Service, The Soviet Union

Interviews

(Many individuals were associated with more than one organization. Their primary organizational affiliation, if any, is listed in parentheses.)

V. V. Aksiuchits (Russian Christian Democratic Movement), May 6, 1991, Moscow
T. E. Alaiba (Republican Party of Russia), July 4, 1991, Sverdlovsk
V. V. Andriianov (Republican Party of Russia), March 29, 1991, Tula
G. A. Anishenko (Russian Christian Democratic Movement), March 6, 1991, Moscow
L. A. Arutiunian (Active Postion), February 2, 1991, Apatity (Murmansk Oblast')
M. G. Astaf'ev (Constitutional Democrats/Party of Popular Freedom), May 6, 1991, Moscow
L. A. Bogdanov (Democratic Russia), June 17, 1991, Moscow
V. O. Bokser (Democratic Russia), January 30, 1991, Moscow
M. O. Borisov (Democratic Party of Russia), July 4, 1991, Sverdlovsk
E. G. Botvinik (*MIG*), June 6, 1991, Volgograd
N. N. Bragin (Memorial), July 5, 1991, Sverdlovsk
V. N. Chupriianov (Sverdlovsk Union of Cooperatives), July 5, 1991, Sverdlovsk
Iu. M. Davydov (Democratic Party of Russia), July 4, 1991, Sverdlovsk
B. N. Dul'nev (*Tul'skaia Izvestiia*), March 30, 1991, Tula
V. Efimov (Democratic Union), April 28, 1990, Moscow
S. A. Gavrilov, March 29, 1991, Tula
A. Glagalev (Democratic Party of Russia), March 30, 1991, Tula
A. Gniadek (Democratic Union), July 4, 1991, Sverdlovsk
A. N. Goncharenko (Iskra), July 5, 1991, Sverdlovsk
V. V. Gubarev (Social Democratic Party of Russia), April 1, 1991, Tula
K. Iankov (Social Democratic Party of Russia), January 22, 1991, Moscow
S. P. Itokhin (Mosbass Miners Strike Committee), March 30, 1991, Tula
N. M. Kalinkin, July 5, 1991, Sverdlovsk
A. Kallinin (Social Democratic Party of Russia), June 14, 1991, Moscow
V. Kardail'skii (Social Democratic Party of Russia), May 11, 1990, Moscow
Iu. V. Karpeev (Workers' Democratic Union "Fakel"), May 9, 1991, Orel
S. Khramov (Sotsprof), January 8, 1991, Moscow
S. I. Kireev, March 29, 1991, Tula
V. K. Kiselev (Communist Party of the Soviet Union), May 11, 1991, Orel
A. G. Kisliakov (Communist Party of the Soviet Union), May 11, 1991, Orel

B. B. Kntsev (Mosbass Miners Strike Committee), March 30, 1991, Tula

E. G. Kostitsyn (Democratic Party of Russia), July 4, 1991, Sverdlovsk

V. F. Kriger (Democratic Russia), June 17, 1991, Moscow

V. I. Kruginin (Mosbass Miners Strike Committee), March 30, 1990, Tula

I. V. Likhunov (Narodno-Trudovoi Soiuz [NTS]), July 4, 1991, Sverdlovsk

I. D. Liubimov (*Molodoi Kommunar*), April 1, 1991, Tula

I. L. Lukashev (Social Democratic Party of Russia), June 4, 1991, Volgograd

V. V. Lunin (Republican Party of Russia), April 15, 1991, Moscow

N. A. Matveev (Social Democratic Party of Russia), March 30, 1991, Tula

I. S. Mendeleevich (Memorial), May 8, 1991, Orel

V. I. Mironenko (Democratic Russia), June 4, 1991, Volgograd

E. D. Molchanov (Democratic Union), January 23, 1991, Moscow

S. E. Morgunov (Communist Party of the Soviet Union), March 14, 1991, Moscow

D. D. Nesterov (Russian Christian Democratic Movement), June 6, 1991, Volgograd

A. M. Obolenskii (Social Democratic Party of Russia), February 7, 1991, Apatity (Murmansk Oblast')

V. V. Ostroushko (*Pokolenie*), May 9, 1991, Orel

N. M. Perovskii (Democratic Party of Russia), May 9, 1991, Orel

V. Pestov (Vozrozhdenie), July 5, 1991, Sverdlovsk

N. P. Polishuk, March 29, 1991, Tula

G. Ia. Rakitskaia (Social Democratic Party of Russia), March 26, 1991, Moscow

I. E. Riabov (Russian Christian Democratic Movement), March 30, 1991, Tula

A. V. Romash (Russian Christian Democratic Movement), June 17, 1991, and October 6, 1992, Moscow

V. A. Rosanov (Republican Party of Russia), June 14, 1991, Moscow

V. L. Sekrieru (Social Democratic Party of Russia), February 7, 1991, Apatity (Murmansk Oblast')

V. N. Shostakovskii (Republican Party of Russia), May 23, 1991, Moscow

N. N. Skachkova (Communist Party of the Soviet Union), March 29, 1991, Tula

N. V. Solov'ev (Sotsprof), March 5, 1991, Moscow

V. K. Sosipatrov (Volgograd City Voters' Committee), June 4, 1991, Volgograd

A. I. Tanachova (El'tsin Club), July 4, 1991, Sverdlovsk

G. I. Temkin (Sotsprof), January 20, 1991, Moscow

A. B. Terekhov (Democratic Party of Russia), May 4, 1991, Moscow

M. N. Tolstoi (Democratic Party of Russia), June 21, 1991, Moscow

N. I. Travin, March 29, 1991, Tula

N. I. Travkin (Democratic Party of Russia), January 31, 1991, Moscow

A. I. Tretiakov (Republican Party of Russia), May 8, 1991, Orel

M. S. Tsagoianov (Social Democratic Party of Russia), June 5, 1991, Volgograd

S. V. Vvedinskii (Democratic Party of Russia), February 24, 1991, Moscow

V. V. Zaivyn, March 29, 1991, Tula

V. A. Ziabkin (Democratic Party of Russia), May 10, 1991, Orel

V. I. Zenin (Democratic Party of Russia), June 5, 1991, Volgograd

A. V. Zheludkov (Russian Christian Democratic Movement), March 6, 1991, Moscow

Books and Articles

Amelin, Vladimir. "Neformaly, intelligentsiia, partaktiv: politicheskie orientatsii." *Obshchestvennye Nauki*, no. 4, 1987.

Arato, Andrew. "Civil Society against the State: Poland 1980–81." *Telos*, no. 47 (Spring 1981).

Arato, Andrew, and Jean Cohen. "Social Movements, Civil Society, and the Problem of Sovereignty." *Praxis International* 4, 3 (1984).

Arendt, Hannah. *The Origins of Totalitarianism*. New York: Harcourt-Brace, 1968.

Barany, Zoltan D., and Louisa Vinton. "Breakthrough to Democracy: Elections in Poland and Hungary." *Studies in Comparative Communism* 23, 2 (Summer 1990).

Barnes, Samuel H. "Democracy and the Organization of Political Parties: Some Speculations." In William E. Wright (ed.), *A Comparative Study of Party Organization*. Columbus: Charles E. Merrill, 1971.

Bauman, Zygmunt. "On the Maturation of Socialism." *Telos*, no. 47 (Spring 1981).

Bendix, Reinhard, John Bendix, and Norman Furniss. "Reflections on Modern Western States and Civil Societies." *Research in Political Sociology*, vol. 3 (1987). Greenwich, Conn.: JAI, 1987.

Bernstein, Eduard. *Evolutionary Socialism*. New York: Huebsch, 1909.

Bialer, Seweryn. "The Changing Soviet Political System: The Nineteenth Party Conference and After." In Seweryn Bialer (ed.), *Politics, Society, and Nationality: Inside Gorbachev's Russia*. Boulder: Westview, 1989.

———. "Gorbachev's Move." In Ferenc Fehér and Andrew Arato (eds.), *Gorbachev: The Debate*. Cambridge: Polity, 1989.

———. "Gorbachev's Program of Change: Sources, Significance, Prospects." In Seweryn Bialer and Michael Mandelbaum (eds.), *Gorbachev's Russia and American Foreign Policy*. Boulder: Westview, 1988.

Billington, James H. *Russia Transformed: Breakthrough to Hope*. New York: Free Press, 1992.

Black, Antony. *Guilds and Civil Society in European Political Thought from the Twelfth Century to the Present*. London: Methuen, 1984.

Boella, Laura. "Eastern European Societies." *Telos*, no. 41 (Fall 1979).

Bonnell, Victoria E. "Voluntary Associations in Gorbachev's Reform Program." In George W. Breslauer (ed.), *Can Gorbachev's Reforms Succeed?* Berkeley: University of California Center for Slavic and East European Studies, 1990.

Boycko, Maxim, Andrei Shleifer, and Robert W. Vishny. "Privatizing Russia." Paper prepared for the Brookings Panel on Economic Activity, September 9–10, 1993.

Breslauer, George W. "Evaluating Gorbachev as Leader." *Soviet Economy* 5, 4 (1989).

———. "On the Adaptability of Soviet Welfare State Authoritarianism." In Karl W. Ryavec (ed.), *Soviet Society and the Communist Party*. Amherst: University of Massachusetts Press, 1978.

Brovkin, Vladimir. "Revolution from Below: Informal Political Associations in Russia, 1988–89." *Soviet Studies* 42, 2 (1990).

Brzezinski, Zbigniew K. *Ideology and Power in Soviet Politics.* New York: Praeger, 1962.

Bukharin, N. I. *Selected Writings on the State and the Transition to Socialism.* Armonk, N.Y.: M. E. Sharpe, 1982.

Bukovsky, Vladimir. "Tumbling Back to the Future." *The New York Times Magazine,* January 12, 1992.

Bunce, Valerie. "The Struggle for Democracy in Eastern Europe." *World Policy Journal* 7, 3 (Summer 1990).

Burton, Michael, Richard Gunther, and John Higley. "Elites and Democratic Consolidation in Latin America and Southern Europe: An Overview." In John Higley and Richard Gunther (eds.), *Elites and Democratic Consolidation in Latin America and Southern Europe.* Cambridge: Cambridge University Press, 1992.

Byzov, L. "Sovetskie Sotsial-demokraty: Kto oni?" Paper distributed at the Third Plenum of the Social Democratic Party of Russia, December 22–23, 1990.

Cohen, Jean. *Class and Civil Society: The Limits of Marxian Critical Theory.* Amherst: University of Massachusetts Press, 1983.

––––––. "Strategy or Identity: New Theoretical Paradigms and Contemporary Social Movements." *Social Research* 52, 4 (Winter 1985).

Cohen, Stephen F. *Bukharin and the Russian Revolution.* Oxford: Oxford University Press, 1980.

––––––. "The Friends and Foes of Change: Reformism and Conservatism in the Soviet Union." In Stephen F. Cohen, Alexander Rabinowitch, and Robert Sharlet (eds.), *The Soviet Union since Stalin.* Bloomington: Indiana University Press, 1980.

––––––. "Gorbachev the Great." *The New York Times,* March 11, 1991.

Collier, David (ed.). *The New Authoritarianism in Latin America.* Princeton: Princeton University Press, 1979.

Colton, Timothy J. "Politics." In Timothy J. Colton and Robert Legvold (eds.), *After the Soviet Union: From Empire to Nations.* New York: Norton, 1992.

Conway, M. Margaret, and Frank B. Feigart. "Motivation, Incentives Systems, and the Political Party Organization." In David Abbott and Edward T. Rogowsky (eds.), *Political Parties: Leadership, Organization, Linkage.* Chicago: Rand McNally, 1971.

Dallin, Alexander. "The Emergence of a Multi-Party System: Propitious and Constraining Circumstances." Paper prepared for conference on "Transitions to Democracy," Moscow, May 15, 1991.

––––––. "Bias and Blunders in American Studies on the USSR." *Slavic Review* 32, 3 (September 1973).

Dallin, Alexander, and Gail W. Lapidus (eds.). *The Soviet System in Crisis.* Boulder: Westview, 1991.

Diamond, Larry, Seymour Martin Lipset, and Juan J. Linz. "Developing and Sustaining Democratic Government in the Third World." Paper prepared for the Annual Meeting of the American Political Science Association, August 1986, Washington, D.C.

Di Palma, Giuseppe. "Party Government and Democratic Reproducibility: The Dilemma of New Democracies." In Francis G. Castles and Rudolf Wildenmann (eds.), *The Future of Party Government.* Vol. 1: *Visions and Realities of Party Government.* New York: Walter de Gruyter, 1986.

―――. *To Craft Democracies: An Essay on Democratic Transitions.* Berkeley: University of California Press, 1990.

Doder, Dusko, and Louis Branson. *Gorbachev.* New York: Viking, 1990.

Durkheim, Emile. *The Division of Labor in Society.* Glencoe, Ill.: Free Press, 1960.

Duverger, Maurice. *Political Parties.* New York: Wiley, 1963.

Eldersveld, Samuel J. "The Party 'Stratarchy.'" In David Abbott and Edward T. Rogowsky (eds.), *Political Parties: Leadership, Organization, Linkage.* Chicago: Rand McNally, 1971.

―――. *Political Parties: A Behavioral Analysis.* Chicago: Rand McNally, 1964.

Embree, Gregory J. "RSFSR Election Results and Roll Call Votes." *Soviet Studies* 43, 6 (1991).

Emmons, Terrence. *The Formation of Political Parties and the First National Elections in Russia.* Cambridge: Harvard University Press, 1983.

Epstein, Leon D. *Political Parties in Western Democracies.* New Brunswick: Transaction Books, 1980.

Ericson, Richard E. "Economics." In Timothy J. Colton and Robert Legvold (eds.), *After the Soviet Union: From Empire to Nations.* New York: Norton, 1992.

Fehér, Ferenc, Agnes Heller, and György Markus. *Dictatorship over Needs.* London: Basil Blackwell, 1983.

Filtzer, Donald. "The Contradictions of the Marketless Market: Self-Financing in Soviet Industrial Enterprises, 1986–90." *Soviet Studies* 43, 6 (1991).

Fish, Steven. "The Emergence of Independent Associations and the Transformation of Russian Political Society." *The Journal of Communist Studies* 7, 3 (September 1991).

Frentzel-Zagorska, Janina. "Civil Society in Poland and Hungary." *Soviet Studies* 4, 4 (1990).

Friedrich, Carl J., and Zbigniew K. Brzezinski. *Totalitarian Dictatorship and Autocracy.* Cambridge: Harvard University Press, 1956.

George, Alexander L. "Case Studies and Theory Development." Mss., Stanford University.

Geremek, Bronislaw. "Civil Society Then and Now." *Journal of Democracy* 3, 2 (April 1992).

Giner, Salvador. "The Withering Away of Civil Society?" *Praxis International* 5, 3 (1985).

Golubovic, Zagorka. "Why 'Dictatorship over Needs' Is Not Socialism?" *Praxis International* 4, 3 (1984).

Gooding, John. "Gorbachev and Democracy." *Soviet Studies* 42, 2 (1990).

Gross, Feliks. *The Revolutionary Party: Essays in the Sociology of Politics.* Westport, Conn.: Greenwood, 1974.

Gunther, Richard, Giacomo Sani, and Goldie Shabad. *Spain after Franco: The Making of a Competitive Party System.* Berkeley: University of California Press, 1988.

Hahn, Jeffrey W. "Local Politics and Political Power in Russia: The Case of Yaroslavl'." *Soviet Economy* 7, 4 (1991).

Hankiss, Elemer. "Demobilization, Self-Mobilization and Quasi-Mobilization in Hungary, 1948–1987." *Eastern European Politics and Societies* 3, 1 (Winter 1989).

Hauslohner, Peter. "Gorbachev's Social Contract." *Soviet Economy* 3, 1 (1987).

Havel, Vaclav. "Politics and Conscience." In Vaclav Havel, *Open Letters: Selected Writings, 1965–90.* New York: Alfred A. Knopf, 1991.

———. "The Power of the Powerless." In Vaclav Havel et al., *The Power of the Powerless: Citizens against the State in Central-Eastern Europe,* ed. John Keane. Armonk, N.Y.: M. E. Sharpe, 1985.

Heller, Agnes. *The Theory of Need in Marx.* New York: St. Martin's, 1976.

Hill, Ronald. "Profile: The Twenty-Eighth CPSU Congress." *The Journal of Communist Studies* 7, 1 (1991).

Hill, Ronald J., and Peter Frank. *The Soviet Communist Party.* London: George Allen and Unwin, 1981.

Hirschman, Albert O. *A Bias for Hope: Essays on Development in Latin America.* New Haven: Yale University Press, 1971.

Hosking, Geoffrey. *The Awakening of the Soviet Union.* Cambridge: Harvard University Press, 1991.

Hough, Jerry. *Russia and the West: Gorbachev and the Politics of Reform.* New York: Simon and Schuster, 1990.

———. "The Soviet System: Petrification or Pluralism?" *Problems of Communism,* March–April 1972.

Inkeles, Alex. *Social Change in Soviet Russia.* Cambridge: Harvard University Press, 1968.

Janda, Kenneth. *A Conceptual Framework for the Analysis of Political Parties.* Beverly Hills: Sage, 1970.

Janos, Andrew. "Interest Groups and the Structure of Power: Critique and Comparisons." *Studies in Comparative Communism* 12, 1 (Spring 1979).

———. *Politics and Paradigms: Changing Theories of Change in Social Science.* Stanford: Stanford University Press, 1986.

Jasiewicz, Krzysztof. "From Solidarity to Fragmentation." *Journal of Democracy* 3, 2 (April 1992).

Jowitt, Kenneth. "Inclusion and Mobilization in European Leninist Regimes." *World Politics* 28, 1 (October 1975).

———. *The Leninist Response to National Dependency.* Berkeley: Institute for International Studies, 1978.

———. "Soviet Neo-Traditionalism: The Political Corruption of a Leninist Regime." *Soviet Studies* 35, 3 (1983).

Kagarlitsky, Boris. *Farewell to Perestroika: A Soviet Chronicle.* London: Verso, 1990.

Karl, Terry L. "Dilemmas of Democratization in Latin America." *Comparative Politics* 23, 1 (October 1990).

Katz, Richard S. *A Theory of Parties and Electoral Systems.* Baltimore: Johns Hopkins University Press, 1980.

Keane, John. *Democracy and Civil Society.* New York: Verso, 1988.

———. "Despotism and Democracy." In John Keane (ed.), *Civil Society and the State.* London: Verso, 1988.

Key, V. O. *Public Opinion and American Democracy.* New York: Alfred A. Knopf, 1961.

"KhDS: Zhit' ne po zlu," *Dialog,* no. 10 (July 1990).

Kirchheimer, Otto. "Confining Conditions and Revolutionary Breakthroughs." In Frederic S. Burin and Kurt L. Shell (eds.), *Politics, Law, and Social Change: Selected Essays of Otto Kirchheimer.* New York: Columbia University Press, 1969.

Kitschelt, Herbert P. *The Logics of Party Formation: Ecological Politics in Belgium and West Germany.* Ithaca: Cornell University Press, 1989.

Kligman, Gail. "Reclaiming the Public: A Reflection on Creating Civil Society in Romania." *East European Politics and Societies* 4, 3 (Fall 1990).

Kochetov, A. N. "Novye tendentsii v sovershenstvovanii sotsial'noi struktury sovetskogo obshchestva (1980-e gody)." *Istoriia SSSR,* no. 6 (November–December 1988).

Kolakowski, Leszek. "Ideology in Eastern Europe." In Milorad M. Drachkovitch (ed.), *East-Central Europe: Yesterday, Today, and Tomorrow.* Stanford: Stanford University Press, 1982.

———. "The Intelligentsia." In Abraham Brumberg (ed.), *Poland: The Genesis of a Revolution.* New York: Random House, 1983.

Konrad, György. *Anti-Politics.* San Diego: Harcourt, Brace, Jovanovich, 1984.

Konrad, György, and Ivan Szelenyi. *The Intellectuals on the Road to Class Power.* Brighton: Harvester, 1974.

Laba, Roman. *The Roots of Solidarity.* Princeton: Princeton University Press, 1991.

Lane, David, and Felicity Ann O'Dell. *The Soviet Industrial Worker: Social Class, Education and Control.* London: Martin Robertson, 1978.

Lapidus, Gail W. "State and Society: Toward the Emergence of Civil Society in the Soviet Union." In Seweryn Bialer (ed.), *Politics, Society, and Nationality: Inside Gorbachev's Russia.* Boulder: Westview, 1989.

———. *Women in Soviet Society: Equality, Development, and Social Change.* Berkeley: University of California Press, 1978.

Lawson, Kay. *The Comparative Study of Political Parties.* New York: St. Martin's, 1976.

Lewin, Moshe. *The Gorbachev Phenomenon.* Berkeley: University of California Press, 1990.

Linz, Juan J. "The Perils of Presidentialism." *Journal of Democracy* 1, 1 (Winter 1990).

Linz, Juan J., and Alfred Stepan. "Political Identities and Electoral Sequences: Spain, the Soviet Union, and Yugoslavia." *Daedalus* 121, 2 (Spring 1992).

Linz, Juan J., Seymour Martin Lipset, and David Horowitz. "Debate—Presidents vs. Parliaments." *Journal of Democracy* 1, 4 (Fall 1990).

McAuley, Mary. *Soviet Politics, 1917–91*. Oxford: Oxford University Press, 1992.

McCarthy, John D., and Mayer N. Zald. "Resource Mobilization and Social Movements: A Partial Theory." In Mayer N. Zald and John D. McCarthy (eds.), *Social Movements in an Organizational Society: Collected Essays*. New Brunswick: Transaction Books, 1987.

McFaul, Michael. "Russia's Emerging Political Parties." *Journal of Democracy* 3, 1 (January 1992).

Maguire, Maria. "Is There Still Persistence?" In Hans Daalder and Peter Mair (eds.), *Western European Party Systems: Continuity and Change*. Beverly Hills: Sage, 1983.

Mainwaring, Scott. "Politicians, Parties, and Electoral Systems: Brazil in Comparative Perspective." *Comparative Politics* 24, 1 (October 1991).

Mair, Peter. "Adaptation and Control: Towards an Understanding of Party and Party System Change." In Hans Daalder and Peter Mair (eds.), *Western European Party Systems: Continuity and Change*. Beverly Hills: Sage, 1983.

Malia, Martin ("Z"). "To the Stalin Mausoleum." *Daedalus* 119, 1 (Winter 1990).

Marx, Karl. "Economic and Philosophic Manuscripts of 1844." In Karl Marx and Friedrich Engels, *Collected Works*, vol. 3. London: Lawrence and Wishart, 1975.

———. "On the Jewish Question." In Robert C. Tucker (ed.), *The Marx-Engels Reader*. New York: Norton, 1978.

Marx, Karl, and Friedrich Engels. "The German Ideology." In Karl Marx and Friedrich Engels, *Collected Works*, vol. 5. London: Lawrence and Wishart, 1976.

Mayhew, David R. *Congress: The Electoral Connection*. New Haven: Yale University Press, 1974.

Meerovich, Aleksandr. "The Emergence of Russian Multiparty Politics." *Report on the USSR* 2, 34 (August 24, 1990).

Melucci, Alberto. *Nomads of the Present*. London: Hutchinson, 1989.

———. "Social Movements and the Democratization of Everyday Life." In John Keane (ed.), *Civil Society and the State*. New York: Verso, 1988.

Merkl, Peter H. "The Sociology of European Parties: Members, Voters, and Social Groups." In Peter H. Merkl (ed.), *West European Party Systems: Trends and Prospects*. New York: Free Press, 1980.

Migranian, Andranik M. "Dolgii put' k evropeiskomu domu." *Novyi mir*, no. 7, July 1989.

Moore, Barrington, Jr.. *Terror and Progress in the USSR*. Cambridge: Harvard University Press, 1954.

Moses, Joel C. "Democratic Reform in the Gorbachev Era: Dimensions of Reform in the Soviet Union, 1986–89." *Russian Review* 48, 3 (July 1989).

Odom, William E. "Alternative Perspectives on the August Coup." *Problems of Communism*, November–December 1991.

———. "A Dissenting View on the Group Approach to Soviet Politics." *World Politics* 28, 4 (July 1976).

O'Donnell, Guillermo. "On the Fruitful Convergences of Hirschman's *Exit*,

Voice, and Loyalty and *Shifting Involvements*: Reflections from the Recent Argentine Experience." In Alejandro Foxley, Michael S. McPherson, and Guillermo O'Donnell (eds.), *Development, Democracy, and the Art of Trespassing: Essays in Honor of Albert O. Hirschman*. Notre Dame: University of Notre Dame Press, 1986.

————. "Transitions, Continuities, and Paradoxes." In Scott Mainwaring, Guillermo O'Donnell, and J. Samuel Valenzuela (eds.), *Issues in Democratic Consolidation: The New South American Democracies in Comparative Perspective*. Notre Dame: University of Notre Dame Press, 1992.

O'Donnell, Guillermo, and Philippe C. Schmitter. *Transitions from Authoritarian Rule: Tentative Conclusions about Uncertain Democracies*. Baltimore: Johns Hopkins University Press, 1986.

Offe, Claus. "Corporatism as Macro-Structuring." *Telos*, no. 65 (Fall 1985).

————. "New Social Movements: Challenging the Boundaries of Institutional Politics." *Social Research* 52, 4 (Winter 1985).

Olson, Mancur. *The Logic of Collective Action*. Cambridge: Harvard University Press, 1971.

Ost, David. *Solidarity and the Politics of Anti-Politics: Opposition and Reform in Poland since 1968*. Philadelphia: Temple University Press, 1990.

Pakulski, Jan. "Legitimacy and Mass Compliance: Reflections on Max Weber in Soviet-Type Systems." *British Journal of Political Science* 16, 1 (January 1986).

Pempel, T. J. *Uncommon Democracies: The One Party-Dominant Regimes*. Ithaca: Cornell University Press, 1990.

Pierson, Christopher. "New Theories of Civil Society: Recent Developments in Post-Marxist Analysis of the State." *Sociology*, Vol. 18, No. 4 (November 1984).

"Political Parties in Eastern Europe." *Radio Free Europe Research Report*, February 1990.

Pridham, Geoffrey. "Southern European Democracies on the Road to Consolidation: A Comparative Assessment of the Role of Political Parties." In Geoffrey Pridham (ed.), *Securing Democracy: Political Parties and Democratic Consolidation in Southern Europe*. New York: Routledge, 1990.

Prokhorov, Iu. N. "Nesanktsionirovannye vystupleniia neformal'nykh grupp i ob"edinenii kak sotsial'no-pravovoe iavlenie." In *Sbornik, Voprosy teorii i praktiki ugolovnogo prava, kriminalogii i kriminalistiki*. Voronezh, 1989.

Przeworski, Adam. "Some Problems in the Study of the Transition to Democracy." In Guillermo O'Donnell, Philippe C. Schmitter, and Laurence Whitehead (eds.), *Transitions from Authoritarian Rule: Comparative Perspectives*. Baltimore: Johns Hopkins University Press, 1986.

Rae, Douglas W. *The Political Consequences of Electoral Laws*. New Haven: Yale University Press, 1967.

Rahr, Alexander. "The KGB Survives under Yeltsin's Wing." *RFE/RL Research Report* 1, 13 (March 27, 1992).

Rakovski, Marc. *Towards an East European Marxism*. New York: St. Martin's, 1978.

Ranney, Austin. *Curing the Mischiefs of Faction: Party Reform in America*. Berkeley: University of California Press, 1975.

Reddaway, Peter. "The Quality of Gorbachev's Leadership." *Soviet Economy* 6, 2 (1990).

Remington, Thomas. "A Socialist Pluralism of Opinions: *Glasnost'* and Policymaking under Gorbachev." *Russian Review* 48, 3 (July 1989).

Remnick, David. "The Pioneers of Perestroika: Back to the Intellectual Roots of Soviet Reforms." *The Washington Post National Weekly Edition*, March 19–25, 1990.

Rice, Christopher. *Russian Workers and the Socialist-Revolutionary Party through the Revolution of 1905–07*. Houndmills, Basingstoke, Hampshire: Macmillan, 1988.

Riggs, Fred. "Comparative Politics and Political Parties." In William J. Crotty (ed.), *Approaches to the Study of Party Organization*. Boston: Allyn and Bacon, 1968.

Ruble, Blair A. "The Politics of Property in Iaroslavl'." Paper prepared for the Annual Meeting of the American Association for the Advancement of Slavic Studies, Honolulu, Hawaii, November 19, 1993.

―――. "The Social Dimensions of Perestroyka." *Soviet Economy* 3, 2 (1987).

Rumiantsev, O. G. *O samodeiatel'nom dvizhenii obshchestvennykh initsiativ, neformal'nye ob"edineniia i ikh rol' v perestroike obshchestvennoi zhizni v SSSR*. Moscow: USSR Academy of Sciences Institute of the Economy of the World Socialist System, 1988.

Rupnik, Jacques. "Totalitarianism Revisited." In John Keane (ed.), *Civil Society and the State*. New York: Verso, 1988.

Rustow, Dankwart A. "Transitions to Democracy: Toward a Dynamic Model." *Comparative Politics* 2, 3 (April 1970).

Rutland, Peter. "Labor Unrest and Social Movements in 1989 and 1990." *Soviet Economy* 6, 4 (1990).

Sabato, Larry. *The Party's Just Begun*. Glenview, Ill.: Scott, Foresman, 1987.

Sachs, Jeffery D. "Spontaneous Privatization: A Comment." *Soviet Economy* 7, 4 (1991).

Sartori, Giovanni. *Parties and Party Systems: A Framework for Analysis*, vol. 1. Cambridge: Cambridge University Press, 1976.

Scanlan, James. "Reforms and Civil Society in the USSR." *Problems of Communism*, March–April 1988.

Schmitter, Philippe C. "The Consolidation of Political Democracy in Southern Europe and Latin America." Ms., October 1985.

―――. "Democratic Theory and Neo-Corporatist Practice." *Social Research* 50, 4 (Winter 1983).

―――. "Still the Century of Corporatism?" *Review of Politics* 36, 1 (1974).

Sedaitis, Judith B., and Jim Butterfield (eds.). *Perestroika from Below: Social Movements in the Soviet Union*. Boulder: Westview, 1991.

Shmelev, Nikolai. "Avansy i dolgi." *Novyi mir*, no. 6, 1987.

Skilling, H. Gordon, and Franklin Griffiths (eds.). *Interest Groups in Soviet Politics*. Princeton: Princeton University Press, 1971.

Slider, Darrell. "Embattled Entrepreneurs: Soviet Cooperatives in an Unreformed Society." *Soviet Studies* 43, 5 (1991).

Smelser, Neil J. *Social Change in the Industrial Revolution.* Chicago: University of Chicago Press, 1959.

Solomon, Susan (ed.). *Pluralism in the Soviet Union.* New York: St. Martin's, 1983.

Starr, S. Frederick. "Soviet Union: A Civil Society." *Foreign Policy*, no. 70 (Spring 1988).

Stepan, Alfred. *Rethinking Military Politics: Brazil and the Southern Cone.* Princeton: Princeton University Press, 1988.

―――. "State Power and the Strength of Civil Society in the Southern Cone of Latin America." In Peter B. Evans, Dietrich Rueschemeyer, and Theda Skocpol (eds.), *Bringing the State Back In.* Cambridge: Cambridge University Press, 1985.

Sundiev, I. "Nashestvie Marsian?" In S. N. Iushenkov (ed.), *Neformaly: sotsial'nye initsiativy.* Moscow: Moskovskii rabochii, 1990.

Szucs, Jeno. "Three Historical Regions of Eastern Europe." In John Keane (ed.), *Civil Society and the State.* New York: Verso, 1988.

Tarrow, Sidney. "Aiming at a Moving Target: Social Science and the Recent Rebellions in Eastern Europe." *PS: Political Science and Politics*, March 1991.

―――. "Economic Development and the Transformation of the Italian Party System." In Giuseppe Di Palma (ed.), *Mass Politics in Industrial Societies.* Chicago: Markham, 1972.

―――. *Struggle, Politics, and Reform: Collective Action, Social Movements, and Cycles of Protest.* Western Societies Program Occasional Paper no. 21, Center for International Studies, Cornell University, 1991.

Tilly, Charles. "Models and Realities of Popular Collective Action." *Social Research* 52, 4 (Winter 1985).

―――. "Social Movements and National Politics." In Charles Bright and Susan Harding (eds.), *Statemaking and Social Movements: Essays in History and Theory.* Ann Arbor: University of Michigan Press, 1984.

Tismaneanu, Vladimir. *Reinventing Politics: Eastern Europe from Stalin to Havel.* New York: Free Press, 1992.

―――. "The Tragicomedy of Romanian Communism." *Eastern European Politics and Societies* 3, 2 (Spring 1989).

Tocqueville, Alexis de. *Democracy in America*, ed. Richard Heffner. New York: Mentor, 1956.

Tolz, Vera. *The USSR in 1989: A Record of Events.* Boulder: Westview, 1989.

―――. *The USSR's Emerging Multiparty System.* New York: Praeger, 1990.

Touraine, Alain. "An Introduction to the Study of Social Movements." *Social Research* 52, 4 (Winter 1985).

Touraine, Alain, et al. *Solidarity: The Analysis of a Social Movement, Poland 1980–81.* Cambridge: Cambridge University Press, 1983.

"The Truth Will Make You Free," *Khristianskaia Demokratiia* (in English), no. 13 (May–June 1991).

Urban, Michael E. "Boris El'tsin, Democratic Russia, and the Campaign for the Russian Presidency." *Soviet Studies* 44, 2 (1992).

———. "Conceptualizing Political Power in the USSR: Patterns of Binding and Bonding." *Studies in Comparative Communism* 18, 4 (Winter 1985).

———. *More Power to the Soviets: The Democratic Revolution in the USSR.* Aldershot, Hampshire: Edward Elgar, 1990.

Vajda, Mihaly. "East-Central European Perspectives." In John Keane (ed.), *Civil Society and the State.* New York: Verso, 1988.

———. *The State and Socialism.* New York: St. Martin's, 1981.

Valenzuela, J. Samuel. "Democratic Consolidation in Post-Transitional Settings: Notion, Process, and Facilitating Conditions." In Scott Mainwaring, Guillermo O'Donnell, and J. Samuel Valenzuela (eds.), *Issues in Democratic Consolidation: The New South American Democracies in Comparative Perspective.* Notre Dame: University of Notre Dame Press, 1992.

Vanneman, Peter. *The Supreme Soviet: Politics and the Legislative Process in the Soviet Political System.* Durham: Duke University Press, 1977.

von Beyme, Klaus. *Political Parties in Western Democracies.* Aldershot, Hampshire: Gower, 1985.

Walder, Andrew. *Communist Neo-Traditionalism: Work and Authority in Chinese Industry.* Berkeley: University of California Press, 1986.

Waller, J. Michael. "When Will Democrats Control the Former KGB?" *Demokratizatsiya: The Journal of Post-Soviet Democratization* 1, 1 (Summer 1992).

Ware, Alan. *Citizens, Parties, and the State: A Reappraisal.* Cambridge: Polity, 1987.

———. *The Logic of Party Democracy.* London: Macmillan, 1979.

White, Stephen. "'Democratization' in the USSR." *Soviet Studies* 42, 1 (1990).

———. *Gorbachev in Power.* Cambridge: Cambridge University Press, 1990.

———. *Political Culture and Soviet Politics.* London: Macmillan, 1979.

Winiecki, Jan. *Resistance to Change in the Soviet Economic System: A Property Rights Approach.* London: Routledge, 1991.

Wojicicki, Kazimierz. "The Reconstruction of Society." *Telos*, no. 47 (Spring 1981).

"Yeltsin Warns Regions Not to Resist Future," *The Moscow Times*, September 15, 1992.

Zald, Mayer N., and Roberta Ash Garner. "Social Movement Organizations: Growth, Decay, and Change." In Mayer N. Zald and John D. McCarthy (eds.), *Social Movements in an Organizational Society: Collected Essays.* New Brunswick: Transaction Books, 1987.

Zaslavsky, Victor. *The Neo-Stalinist State: Class, Ethnicity, and Consensus in Soviet Society.* Armonk, N.Y.: M. E. Sharpe, 1982.

Zaslavsky, Victor, and Robert J. Brym. "Structures of Power and the Functions of Soviet Local Elections." In Everett M. Jacobs (ed.), *Soviet Local Politics and Government.* London: George Allen and Unwin, 1983.

Index

civil disobedience, 108
civil rights, 62, 63
civil society: access in, 54, 57–59; autonomy in, 54, 59–60; control in, 54, 57–59; defined, 52–53, 60–61; indicators for, 53–54, 60–61; institutions in, 53–55; interest aggregation in, 53–54, 55–56; interest articulation in, 54, 57–58; interest representation in, 54, 56–57; movement society compared, 61–62, 217; political society compared, 244n.5; social changes and, 18; state's role in, 7–8, 26, 52–53, 125, 244n.2. *See also* society
class structure. *See* economic system; socioeconomic structure
Cohen, Jean, 125
Cohen, Stephen, 10
collective bargaining, 226
"collective dictatorship," 8
Colton, Timothy, 269n.4
Committee of National Salvation, 46
communication, political, 34–35, 85–86, 93, 249–50n.15, 250n.18
Communist Party of the Soviet Union. *See* CPSU
Communists for Democracy, 48
"compromisers": described, 172, 173, 174; examples of, 173, 175
"consolidated" democracy, 225–26, 271n.38
Constitutional Democrats/Party of Popular Freedom. *See* KD/PNS
constitution (Russian), 233
constitution (Soviet): Article 6 of, 38, 43, 46, 73, 82; extra-state political activity and, 31
contract theories: domination compared, 22; post-1985, 16–17; pre-1985, 15, 16
cooperatives: effects of, 76; goals of, 62; movement organizations and, 180–81, 182; under Lenin, 31
coup attempt of August 1991, 50, 113; disgrace of old regime in, 218; Moscow and, 137; nature of, 200, 201
CPSU (Communist Party of the Soviet Union): Central Committee of, 40; as central issue of struggle, 212–14; collapse of, 201, 214; Democratic Platform in, 42, 43, 44; destruction of, as movement goal, 50; election influence of, 73, 195, 267n.118; enterprise managers and, 163–64; membership by demo-

crats, 168, 172, 175, 264–65n.83; Memorial and, 33; Nineteenth Conference of, 35; in Orel, 162; as political party, 11; reform movement within, 41–42; RPR and, 43, 44; soviets and, 191–92, 193–94; speeches against, 43; splits in leadership of, 27, 35. *See also* state
culture. *See* political psychology
Czech Agricultural Party, 64
Czechoslovakia, 55, 64, 85, 171

Davydov, Iurii, 196
DDV (Movement for Democratic Choice), 141–42, 143; elections and, 196, 267n.118; internal conflict in, 143, 150; repression of, 158, 159; soviets and, 197; in Sverdlovsk, 186
defense production. *See* military production
democracy: "by default," 217–18, 226–27; "consolidated," 225–26, 271n.38; as goal of movement organizations, 43, 55, 111, 112, 212; started from scratch, 171–72, 214; "unconsolidated," 226–27; within movement organizations, 56–57, 74, 113–17
"democratic" associations, 28. *See also* movement organizations
"democratic centralism," 187
democratic movement: exposure of existing system by, 51; goals of, 50, 55; polarization with state, 47. *See also* democratization; movement organizations
Democratic Party of Russia. *See* DPR
Democratic Perestroika, 33, 38, 148
Democratic Platform, 80; coverage by press, 45; founding of, 42, 44, 86–87, 118; founding of RPR and, 43, 86–87; stance of, 127
Democratic Russia, 80; cells established by, 130; conflicts within, 110–11; decline of, 49–50, 210, 211;economic liberalization and, 207; El'tsin and, 50, 111, 210; financial support for, 126; founding of, 44–45, 109; functions of, 65, 70; identity formation in, 110–11; infiltration and sabotage of, 119; internal structure of, 114, 115, 184–85; membership of, 109–10; in Orel, 147, 162, 186, 261n.40; as a political force, 49, 56, 81; resource mobilization in, 179; in RSFSR Congress of People's Deputies, 43, 44;